ISRAEL
A BIBLICAL TOUR OF THE HOLY LAND

D1470525

ISRAEL
A BIBLICAL TOUR OF THE HOLY LAND

NEAL W. MAY

ALBURY PUBLISHING
Tulsa, Oklahoma

All scripture quotations, unless otherwise indicated, are taken from the *New King James Version.* Copyright © 1979, 1980, 1982, 1994 by Thomas Nelson, Inc. Used by permission. All rights reserved.

Scripture quotations marked KJV are taken from the *King James Version* of the Bible.

Scripture quotations marked NIV are taken from the *Holy Bible, New International Version.*® NIV®. Copyright © 1973, 1978, 1984, by International Bible Society. Used by permission of Zondervan Publishing House. All rights reserved.

Scripture quotations marked RSV are taken from *The Revised Standard Version* of the Bible. Copyright © 1946, Old Testament section copyright © 1952 by the Division of Christian Education of the Churches of Christ in the United States of America and is used by permission.

Israel: A Biblical Tour of the Holy Land
ISBN 1-57778-153-8
Copyright © 2000 by Neal W. May
10277 Valley View Road
Macedonia, Ohio 44056

Published by ALBURY PUBLISHING
P. O. Box 470406
Tulsa, Oklahoma 74147-0406

The photographs on pages 66, 81, 232, and 253 were used with permission from the Biblical Illustrators Archives. All rights reserved.

Printed in the United States of America. All rights reserved under International Copyright Law. Contents and/or cover may not be reproduced in whole or in part in any form without the express written consent of the Publisher.

DEDICATION ■

I dedicate this travel guide to my mother, Cleta D. May,

who went on to be with our Lord, October 1998.

Just prior to her passing, we had the wonderful privilege

of touring the Holy Land together.

I will cherish those memories forever.

Contents ■

Acknowledgments ■

I am deeply indebted to the many individuals who played such a special part in this unique project. The very nature of a guidebook to Israel required specific people from varying backgrounds. I am very appreciative of those who willingly gave their precious time to reflect, comment, direct, and support. I hereby acknowledge the patience of my wife, Amy, who has graciously understood the pursuit of my passion.

To my advisor, Dr. Kenneth Walther, I say thank you for your guidance, but much more for your modeling. You set before me an example, one which I emulate and also follow. Your stirring archaeological presentations proved to be a catalyst. May God bless you!

To my friend and consultant, Benji Shavit in Israel, I am grateful for your cooperative willingness to answer my questions and point me in the right direction. You were indispensable to my investigation of the Holy Land. Your stateside company, Jerusalem Tours, not only provided me with an excellent pilgrimage and quality guides, but you extended yourself both personally and professionally. In addition, I want to thank Sarah Chay for her energy and joy that she contributed to each and every tour.

To my Messianic colleague, Dr. David Friedman, your advice and insight were instrumental in shaping the document. May the Lord return unto you all that you have sown and more. I pray for the peace of Jerusalem!

Last, but certainly not least, are a host of special friends: Vern Kassouf, Reverend Kathie Kuhn, Dr. John Marino, Bruce Cummings, and Gerri Rezac. I could not have done it without you. Your encouragement and prayers made all the difference. I would especially like to point out my secretary, Reverend Ginger Martin, who patiently and untiringly typed draft after draft, addition after addition. You are a gift from God! Furthermore, I offer special thanks to Bonnie Dubay, Angie Toncar, Julie Ganim, and Scott Stephen for their editorial comments. I want to also commend Terance Oliver and Jenny and Gary Newyear for their graphic and illustrative work and Bill Werner, Kathie Kuhn, and Daniel Chase for the photographic images they have so cordially provided.

Welcome ■

I have had the wonderful opportunity of traveling to the land of Israel numerous times. For some, a tour to the Holy Land is considered just one of several vacation options, but nothing could be farther from the truth. If the right kind of preparation is undertaken, a tour can be a spiritual pilgrimage into biblical enlightenment and a trip you will never forget. Following your visit, your experience of the Holy Land will come back again and again every time you read the Bible. St. Jerome once wrote that those who see the land of Israel with their own eyes will comprehend the Scriptures with a clearer understanding. I have certainly found that to be true. After exploring historical Palestine, the words of Scripture no longer instruct me in two-dimensional black and white. The dynamics have shifted! Now I read Scripture with a colorful, living, three-dimensional panorama of the land God has visited.

The land in Israel has been colloquially termed "The Fifth Gospel." Now that I've been there, I have a tremendous sense of participating in the Bible's original events. This is why I was inspired to develop a Christian guide to the Holy Land. The interaction between the land and Scripture is so enriching that I was compelled to share it. Not only that, but after several guided visits to the biblical sites, I found that my own retention of the historicity was limited. In response, this guidebook has been prepared as a historic road map as well as a practical point of reference for tourists, tour guides, and Bible students.

As a pastoral overseas tour leader, I desire my participants to harvest as much from the trip to the Holy Land as possible. Personally, I have found that my knowledge of the land brings a clarity and understanding to my biblical studies and preaching that would not have been possible without my visits. So everyone benefits from such a trip. No student of Scripture can fully understand the Bible without at least knowing something about the many geographical and historical references. Knowing the conditions that surrounded the recipients of the original message in Scripture provides further insight into how they most likely understood the message. So unless we have had the opportunity to visit the places mentioned in the Bible, we lack a vital perspective necessary to fully understand certain events.

A tour of the Holy Land has the ability to acquaint the modern traveler with the biblical world of antiquity. Hebrew is still the language of Israel, though most Israelis speak some English and several other languages as well. The Hebrew spoken today is an updated version of the language used in Israel 2,500 years ago. In Jesus' day the people in Israel spoke Aramaic— a Semitic language used throughout the Middle East that was brought back to Israel from their exile in Babylonia. Back then, Hebrew was reserved for study and for specific official uses such as the writing of laws, census forms, and prayer.

Today, Hebrew is again the national language of choice. Its linguistic and cultural restoration was enacted a century ago by Liezer Ben Yehuda, which translates in Hebrew to Eliezer "son of Judah." You will find a street named in his honor in most Israeli towns. It took Ben Yehuda and his successors decades to update the ancient, holy tongue. It proved to be especially difficult when trying to describe contemporary concepts such as electricity and computers with the original Hebrew language's archaic words. But the task was accomplished well, and it is believed that Jesus would have no trouble understanding the Hebrew used in modern Israel today.

Most Christians are already familiar with certain Hebrew words from their Bible reading and worship experiences, although they may not realize it. There are several phrases that may prove to be beneficial and helpful when you visit Israel, so I offer them in opening to help you get around.

Not only will these words assist you in communicating, but they will also allow you to participate in the culture.

Hebrew words are pronounced with the stress on the last syllable. So emphasize the boldfaced syllable, and don't forget to smile!

Hello	sha**lom**
Good morning	**bo**ker tov
Good afternoon	sha**lom**
Good night	**lay**la tov
Excuse me	sli**ha**
My name is	**shmi**
Do you speak English?	a**ta** meda**ber** ang**lit**
Where are the toilets?	ey**fo** hasher**utim**
When/What/How	ma**tay**/ma/**eykh**
I don't understand	ey**ne**ni me**vin**
How much is this?	ma hame**hir**
What time is it?	ma hash**aa**
What does this mean?	ma per**ush** hada**var** ha**ze**
How are you?	ma Shom**cha**
Please	bevak**sha**
Waiter, please	mel**tzar**
Thank you	to**da**
You're welcome	al**lo** da**vaar**
Yes	**ken**
No	**lo**
Coca Cola	Coca Cola

If you pronounced these words correctly, you now can speak some Hebrew. Hebrew is not Yiddish. "Yiddish" was the language used by European Jews for the six hundred years that spanned the fourteenth century through the World War II Holocaust. Nearly half of the world's Jews lived in Eastern Europe during this period. And though Hebrew has replaced the language in common use today, there is a devout sect of

ISRAELI SCHOOL CHILDREN IN TRADITIONAL GARB.

Judaism that still speaks it. They are called the Hasidim (*Hasid* means devout or faithful). The Hasidic movement, a mystical and joyous form of Jewish expression, was developed in Poland in the eighteenth century. Many still wear the traditional dress adopted over 250 years ago. The costume of the Polish nobility was a black caftan, black knee britches, white stockings, and a broad-brimmed hat that was sometimes trimmed with fur. It is not uncommon to still see individuals of the Hasidim in many places in Israel. You will know a Hasidic man if you see one today because of their distinct facial hair. Men do not shave their beards or sideburns, but roll their sideburns so that they are not a hindrance. Hasidic women dress very modestly with long sleeves, high necklines, and heavy stockings. It is forbidden for any man other than her husband to see her hair. Women will often wear a head scarf or a becoming wig.

Your trip to the Holy Land will be an encounter with both something old and something new—the historical past—and the modern present. So be prepared. The sites are quite often very different from what a first-time visitor imagined. This is often the case because of popular depictions

Christian art has provided down through the centuries. Today many of the holy places have been enclosed with religious shrines. Just remember that even though they may appear a bit ornamental, the actual location has been preserved for your historical appreciation and pleasure. So enjoy the moment and the sheer wonder of walking in the footsteps of Jesus as you travel from site to site.

For your quick reference while reading each chapter, I have included icons beside the text to highlight key facts, stories, and events which will enrich your visit to each of these locations. Here are examples of each icon and what they represent:

∎ **Where Jesus Walked:** This denotes a place where Jesus taught, a site He referred to in a parable or teaching, or a place where He performed a miracle.

∎ **Old Testament:** This refers to key events from the Old Testament that happened in or near a certain place, or what the place symbolized to the Jews of that time.

∎ **Early Kings:** This was the location of an event that happened while Israel was a United Kingdom under Saul, David, or Solomon.

∎ **Greek/Roman:** These events happened while Israel was under Greek or Roman dominion, whether under Alexander the Great or one of the Roman prefects or emperors.

∎ **Between the Testaments:** This refers to events during the Hasmonean Dynasty, the brief period before Jesus' birth and between the testaments when Israel was again its own nation. The stories of this period come mainly from the Apocryphal books of First and Second Maccabees.

∎ **Byzantine:** This symbol identifies events that happened or buildings that were constructed during the Byzantine period, which began roughly with the reign of Constantine I and extended into the Middle Ages.

∎ **Crusaders:** This icon identifies structures and historical events that occurred in Israel while under the control of the European Crusaders.

∎ **The Acts of the Apostles:** This icon refers to places where the apostles lived, taught, wrote, or performed a miracle.

■ **Site of Interest:** This symbol indicates a place you might like to visit while touring this city or area.

There is nothing like personally viewing what the Israeli Ministry of Tourism calls, "The Land Where Heaven and Earth Meet," and I am thrilled that you have allowed me to be a part of it. For easy reference every town and site has been listed alphabetically in this guide. But before we begin your preliminary tour studies in Israel with the beautiful Judean town of Bethany, I would like to give you a brief history of Israel for your edification.

FROM MAP INSIDE THE FRONT COVER: 5-10, A-I.

CHAPTER ONE

A Brief History of Jerusalem and the Nation of Israel

Pray for the peace of Jerusalem:
"May they prosper who love you.
Peace be within your walls,
prosperity within your palaces."
For the sake of my brethren and companions,
I will now say, "Peace be within you."
Because of the house of the LORD our God
I will seek your good.

PSALM 122:6-9

It is impossible to fully comprehend the illustrious saga and sites of Israel without an all-around, broad-based understanding of the nation's holy city and capital, Jerusalem. So this chapter has been dedicated to providing you with a comprehensive overview of this city, which in many ways encompasses the history of Israel as a whole. When you have completed this chapter in full, your visit to Jerusalem and the Promised Land will be richer because of your historic awareness and insight.

The Development of the City of David

Jerusalem ranks among the cities of the world that have the longest records of continuous habitation. The mention of this city occurs in Egyptian Execration Texts of the eighteenth and nineteenth centuries B.C. It appears in the form, probably transliterated, *Rushalimum*.[1] Other Semitic spellings, such as by Sennacherib the Assyrian (seventh century B.C.), have it written as *Ursalimmu*: *uru* (city) and *salim* (a divine name) having a hyphenated composite meaning "the city (of the god) Salim."[2] It is biblically considered a holy city (Isa. 52:1). The Hebrew phrase is *ha-qodesh* or *haq-qodes* and literally means "the city of holiness."[3] The chief city of ancient Palestine, Jerusalem currently hosts the world's three great monotheistic religions and is sacred to Jews, Muslims, and Christians.[4] The present division of the old city into four quarters still reflects the intense religious interest of the site: Muslim (northeast), Christian (northwest), Jewish (southeast), and Armenian (southwest). The Armenians were the first nation to officially accept Christianity. So Jerusalem is a city unlike any other with a special, distinct, and unique importance to God. "The Lord loves the gates of Zion more than all the dwellings of Jacob" (Ps. 87:2).

The Bible states Jerusalem is a city that is "compact together" (Ps. 122:3). Its ancient walls enclosed an area of about 215 acres, about the size of Central Park in New York City. Yet, there is more of human history recorded in this two-square-mile locality than anywhere else on the face of the earth. Jerusalem rests some 14 miles west of the northern end of the Dead Sea and approximately 33 miles east of the Mediterranean Coast.

In the Hebrew Old Testament, "Jerusalem" is written *Yerushalayim*. It is rendered *Yerushalem* in Aramaic portions and contains two elements: 1) *yeru,* which can be seen in the form *yeruel,* meaning "founded by God" (2 Chron. 20:16; Job 38:6), and 2) *shalem* meaning "peace."[5] An abbreviated citation of Jerusalem appears in Genesis 14:18. It is here, 14 quick chapters into the Bible, that the first scriptural reference to the city is

OLD
TESTAMENT

The first mention of the city of Jerusalem in the Bible is when Abraham meets Melchizedek, king of Salem.

> *Over the centuries Jerusalem has become one of the most embattled cities in the world.*

found, with an introduction to its ruler, Melchizedek, king of Salem and priest of God. His name yields the meaning "the foundation of (the god) Shalem." "Foundation" reflects the idea of a permanent home in contrast to an impermanent tent (cf. Heb. 11:10).[6] *Salem* or *Shalem,* which came to mean "peace" (from the Hebrew *Shalom),* was possibly an early reference to the Canaanite god of dusk or twilight.[7] Benjamin Mazer says that *Shalem* is known from a Ugaritic mythological text as one of the two beautiful and gracious Canaanite gods.[8] Apparently, the Hebrews adopted a word from their heathen surroundings and declared that their city was founded on Jehovah, the God of peace. Ironically, over the centuries Jerusalem has become one of the most embattled cities in the world. The name *Salem* is used in the Psalms as a shortened poetic form of Jerusalem. The Psalmist declared:

> **In Salem also is His tabernacle, and His dwelling place in Zion.**
> Psalm 76:2

The city also had a pre-Davidic name, *Jebus.* It denoted the Jebusite people living in Jerusalem during the Exodus and the ensuing settlement of Canaan by the Israelites (Josh. 9:1). Josephus classified the Jebusites as Canaanites (*Antiq.* 7.3.1).[9] They were actually related to the Hittites who had taken possession of the city (see Judg. 19:10-12). The husband of Bathsheba, Uriah, was called a Hittite (2 Sam. 11). Previous to the city's Hebrew conquering, the Amorites had controlled the area (Josh. 10:3-5; cf. Ezek. 16:3).[10] Jerusalem was not a Jewish city originally. The locale was

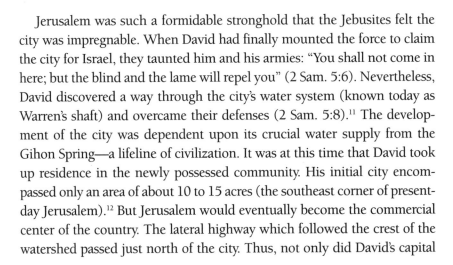

The Jebusites taunted David and his armies: "You shall not come in here; but the blind and the lame will repel you."

assigned to the tribe of Benjamin (Josh. 18:20) during the conquest of the Promised Land under the leadership of Joshua. But they were unable to capture and inhabit the city due to its fortified positions and strategic design. (It was set on a series of five hills and bordered on all sides by deep ravines except one relatively flat plain to the north.) So the Jebusites maintained control for nearly four hundred years.

> But the children of Benjamin did not drive out the Jebusites who inhabited Jerusalem; so the Jebusites dwell with the children of Benjamin in Jerusalem to this day.
>
> JUDGES 1:21

EARLY KINGS

JERUSALEM DID NOT BECOME AN ISRAELI CITY UNTIL DAVID CONQUERED IT.

Jerusalem was such a formidable stronghold that the Jebusites felt the city was impregnable. When David had finally mounted the force to claim the city for Israel, they taunted him and his armies: "You shall not come in here; but the blind and the lame will repel you" (2 Sam. 5:6). Nevertheless, David discovered a way through the city's water system (known today as Warren's shaft) and overcame their defenses (2 Sam. 5:8).[11] The development of the city was dependent upon its crucial water supply from the Gihon Spring—a lifeline of civilization. It was at this time that David took up residence in the newly possessed community. His initial city encompassed only an area of about 10 to 15 acres (the southeast corner of present-day Jerusalem).[12] But Jerusalem would eventually become the commercial center of the country. The lateral highway which followed the crest of the watershed passed just north of the city. Thus, not only did David's capital have political and religious significance, but it possessed tremendous commercial significance as well.[13]

EARLY
KINGS

One of the first establishing acts David performed after taking the city was to bring the Ark of the Covenant to Jerusalem from Shiloh implying that Jehovah would reside there (2 Sam. 6:1-15). So it was David, for the first time in the history of Israel, who merged its political and religious capitals. Since Jerusalem was a town outside the control of any one of the twelve tribes, it avoided the argument of why one of their own cities was not chosen. Every tribe accepted the declaration of Jerusalem as the capital. And before long, Jerusalem took upon itself the unique character of a holy and a royal city, keeping a balanced continuity between the Mosaic tradition and the Davidic dynasty.[14] Jerusalem would be called the "City of David" (2 Sam. 5:7) as well as the "city of God" (Ps. 46:4). David wished "God's house" to be as grand as his own (2 Sam. 7:2). Although he would not be permitted to undertake the construction of the Temple (2 Sam. 7:5-7; 1 Chron. 22:9-10). Even so, David prepared for it through the planning, collecting, and dedicating of materials (1 Chron. 22:1-19; 28:1-21; 2 Chron. 5:1) and even arranged its liturgical service (1 Chron. 23:1-26:19). By providing large quantities of iron, bronze, and cedar logs, as well as vast amounts of gold and silver, he made possible the future development of Jerusalem.[15] From this point on, Jews would make their annual pilgrimages to this hallowed place to take part in feasts and offerings. Solomon's temple would provide the sacrificial requirements prescribed by Law. During the time of Jesus and Herod the Great, the normal population could swell from 55,000 inhabitants to 180,000 who had come to Jerusalem to participate in the celebration of Passover.[16]

WHEN DAVID BROUGHT THE ARK OF THE COVENANT FROM SHILOH TO JERUSALEM, THE CITY BECAME BOTH THE POLITICAL AND RELIGIOUS CAPITAL OF ISRAEL.

Solomon erected the First Temple which took seven years to construct on what is called Temple Hill (1 Kings 6:1-38) or Mount Moriah. David was to build an altar to the Lord on this site after God stopped the plague (2 Sam. 24:17-25). Initially, David purchased the area, a threshing floor, from Araunah the Jebusite (2 Chron. 3:1). Threshing floors were often located on hilltops. The elevated position of barren bedrock, where soil could not mix with the grain, provided necessary exposure to the wind for winnowing. A threshing floor on Mount Moriah took advantage of the western winds coming off of the Mediterranean. Eventually, Solomon inherited the site and developed it. He had the furniture of the tabernacle, including the Ark, moved from Zion to the newly erected Temple for the Feast of Tabernacles that celebrated the coming of the presence of God (2 Chron. 5; 1 Kings 8:10). The tabernacle had been the previous center of worship for the Hebrews and was a simple, temporary structure brought to Palestine through their desert wanderings. The Temple was noted not so much for its size, but for its lavish and beautiful details. Its inner courts were only accessible by the priests. Lay Israelites could come to it, but could not enter. It consisted of three sections: 1) the porch, through which the Temple was entered; 2) the Holy Place, which was lighted by clerestory windows (1 Kings 6:4); and 3) the Holy of Holies (2 Chron. 3:8-13). The Temple was dedicated in 950 B.C. with an elaborate ceremony.

> Indeed it came to pass, when the trumpeters and singers were as one, to make one sound to be heard in praising and thanking the LORD, and when they lifted up their voice with the trumpets and cymbals and instruments of music, and praised the LORD, saying: "For He is good, for His mercy endures forever," that the house, the house of the LORD, was filled with a cloud, so that the priests could not continue ministering because of the cloud; for the glory of the LORD filled the house of God.
>
> 2 CHRONICLES 5:13-14

Located at the heart of the Temple was an especially restricted area of sacred space called the Holy of Holies. It was a cubed room measuring 30 feet long x 30 feet wide x 30 feet high guarded by a huge, olive wood double door that was carved with winged creatures, palm trees, and flowers. Everything was overlaid with gold including the floors, walls, and ceilings (1 Kings 6:20-31).[17] From the biblical record it is estimated that Solomon used 23 tons of gold to cover the inside of the Holy Place and possibly even more for the rest of the Temple and other buildings (2 Chron. 3:8).[18] Scripture records that the Temple was constructed without the sound of any iron tools such as hammers and chisels (1 Kings 6:7).

W. Harold Mare suggests that, since many parts of the Temple were made of wood, possibly a "pallet prefabrication system" may have been used.[19] It would have been something manufactured outside of the sacred area and later assembled silently on the Temple Mount, probably by the priests. The mandated quiet in the Temple's construction may be as theological as it is practical. The significance of the imposed silence could symbolize the honor given to the presence of God (Ex. 25:22). As remarkable as the Temple structure was, it comprised only a small section of the complex that Solomon erected on Mount Moriah (2 Chron. 3-4). Mare notes Solomon's own palace buildings were considerably larger than the Temple, that they were made of timbers from the forest of Lebanon, and of high-grade stones (cf. 1 Kings 6:2; 1 Kings 7:2; 1 Kings 7:9).[20]

OLD TESTAMENT

ISRAEL BECAME TWO NATIONS AFTER SOLOMON'S DEATH.

The Rise and Fall of the Two Kingdoms

It was the royal ideology that gave the Davidic dynasty its strength. But the united kingdom David had worked so hard to create soon collapsed after Solomon's death. The succession to the throne was not so much a matter of contention in David's capital city of Jerusalem, but it certainly was in the north. The next Davidic leader, Rehoboam, traveled from Jerusalem to Shechem to be crowned king and hoped to maintain the unity of the nation (1 Kings 12:1). But the tribes of the north rejected him as David's successor and offered the kingship to the well-known leader of an anti-Solomonic faction, Jeroboam.[1] The dispute surrounded the fact that Solomon had initiated a system of forced labor and an oppressive tax

Neither Israel . . . nor Judah . . . could withstand the eventual takeover by the rival powers on their borders. In fact, it was actually made easier because the divided kingdoms were now smaller and weaker.

system to support his building programs. As a result, the Twelve Tribes divided and reverted to the allotment lines of separation drawn in previous territorial boundaries: ten tribes formed the northern kingdom (Israel); and two tribes formed the southern kingdom (Judah).

The northern kingdom became politically independent and governed a larger population with greater military capability than the southern kingdom of Judah. It also possessed more natural resources.[2] The new northern king, Jeroboam, took immediate steps to secure religious independence from Judah. He proposed northern shrines as alternatives to the Jerusalem Temple and even went as far as to change the dates of the pilgrimage festivals. He also removed levitical administrators whom he assumed were loyal to the lineage of David (1 Kings 12:26-32). Jeroboam's new northern state established its initial capital at Shechem, on the slopes of Mount Gerizim (1 Kings 12:25). But the capital was difficult to defend against Judean attack and was eventually moved to Samaria.

The two tribes that made up the southern kingdom of Judah were more traditional and conservative. This now separate, southern kingdom was ruled by the Davidic dynasty whom the people believed was divinely appointed.[3] King Josiah of Judah (640-609 B.C.) later destroyed the places of northern worship (2 Kings 23:19-20). Nevertheless, neither Israel in the north nor Judah in the south could withstand the eventual takeover by the rival powers on their borders. In fact, it was actually made easier because the divided kingdoms were now smaller and weaker because of their separation.

The northern kingdom was the first to fall. Israel was invaded by the Assyrians in 721 B.C. and the city of Samaria was utterly destroyed. Samaria had been the northern kingdom's capital city from the time of its construction by king Omri in the early ninth century B.C. (1 Kings 16:23-24). It was the practice of the Assyrians to name a province after its capital city. So after the desolation, the name "Samaria" came to designate the district in which the capital city was located. The northern kingdom ceased to exist as an independent nation. What was left of their army was absorbed into the Assyrian army, the ruling aristocracy of Israel was deported, and people from Mesopotamia were imported to live in the region (2 Kings 17:24). The Assyrians took over 25,000 inhabitants captive (721 B.C.). The deportation was so thorough that the northern territory lost its Israeli character.

It has been estimated that through the years,
the Temple has been destroyed
and rebuilt 84 times.

The new foreign importees, combined with the descendants of Israel, constituted a mixed race.[4] The mingling of these two groups produced a people known later as the Samaritans. The immigrants eventually accepted the Jewish faith and Yahweh as their God, but they were always looked upon with suspicion, especially by the exiles who returned to Jerusalem later (2 Kings 17:26 ff.). The Samaritans came to be despised "as racial and religious half-breeds by the people of Judah," as noted by F.F. Bruce.[5] This new mixed group was regarded by the Jews as neither fully Gentile nor fully Jewish, so "Samaritan" became a term of contempt (John 8:48). The Mishna labeled the Samaritans as "Cuthites," essentially identifying them as of non-Jewish origin (cf. 2 Kings 17:7-24).[6]

The Assyrians marched on the southern kingdom two decades later in 701 B.C. taking most of the cities of Judah. However, Jerusalem and King Hezekiah were miraculously spared, by both human cunning (Hezekiah's water tunnel) and divine intervention (2 Kings 19:35). The deliverance of the city, coupled with the covenant belief regarding the house of David, led many to believe that Jerusalem could not be destroyed (Jer. 7:1-15).[7] But that didn't stop the prophets Micah and Jeremiah from continuing to prophesy the eventual destruction of the city (Jer. 7:14; Mic. 3:12).

The Rebuilding of the Temple

Jerusalem is where Israeli nationalism began—and where it will end (Isa. 19:23-25; 45:11-12). I have attempted to cover as much as possible to give you the necessary perspective if you are to truly understand this unique land chosen by God. In this section, I want you to grasp the importance of

*It was in Babylon that the Judeans
learned Aramaic, the common language
after the Exile.*

Temple worship in the life of the people, and how the situations surrounding the destruction and reconstruction of their center of worship influenced Jewish culture, as well as the city that is visited today.

The history of Israel's capital city vacillates from great prosperity and power to captivity and desolation—from the righteous rule of kings and priests to the Babylonian captivity and the ruin of the Temple. It has been estimated that through the years, the Temple has been destroyed and rebuilt 84 times. In the seventh century a new power arose, Babylonia, that threatened Assyrian domination. In 587 B.C. the southern kingdom of Judah fell to the Babylonians and Jerusalem was taken. The last king of Judah, Zedekiah, had his eyes put out, but not before seeing his sons put to death (2 Kings 25:6-7). The Judean aristocracy was carried away, the Temple of Solomon was razed, and the Ark of the Covenant disappeared.[1] Nebuchadnezzar's Babylonian army left Judea in a shambles. The towns were destroyed and weren't rebuilt for many years (Lam. 2:2,5). It was only the strength of the walls of Jerusalem that prolonged Babylon's siege for some 18 months. When they finally broke through, the Temple was burned to the ground as well as anything else that could be set on fire (2 Kings 25:8-12). Nonetheless, the site was still considered holy even though only a shell of the burned Temple remained.

As relative peace returned, refugees drifted back (Jer. 40:11-12) and offered sacrifices on the charred ruins (Jer. 41:5).[2] Many had fled from the Babylonians into Moab, Edom, and Ammon (Jer. 40:1), as well as to many other parts of the world. The dispersion of the Jews during and after the Babylonian exile is called the *Diaspora*. Thousands of Judah's leading families and those with higher education were taken into Babylonian captivity which deeply affected the Jewish people (2 Kings 25:11).[3]

> By the rivers of Babylon, there we sat down, yea, we wept when we remembered Zion. We hung our harps upon the willows in the midst of it. For there those who carried us away captive asked of us a song, and those who plundered us requested mirth, saying, "Sing us one of the songs of Zion!" How shall we sing the LORD's song in a foreign land? If I forget you, O Jerusalem, let my right hand forget its skill! If I do not remember you, let my tongue cling to the roof of my mouth— if I do not exalt Jerusalem above my chief joy. Remember, O LORD, against the sons of Edom the day of Jerusalem, who said, "Raze it, raze it, to its very foundation!"

PSALM 137:1-7

Actually, three deportations took place: the first in 597 B.C., the second in 587 B.C., and a third in 582 B.C. According to the account of Jeremiah, the deportations totaled 4,600 adult males of Israel's political, ecclesiastical, and intellectual elite. In addition, it appears that tradesmen and farmers were also transported (2 Kings 24:14; Ezek. 17:5), along with many women and children equaling, by some estimates, 10,000 in number. Only the poorest of people were left to work the fields.

In Babylon, the exiles were not treated as mere slaves, but were able to enjoy some measure of self rule and religious freedom. The most famous Babylonian captive, Daniel, demonstrated that some Jews even prospered during the Exile. While in captivity, the Jews continued to observe circumcision and the Sabbath. It was from these acts of communal identity that the synagogue, common in the New Testament's day, developed. *Synagogue* means "coming together."[4] The question facing the Judeans was how to worship without a sanctuary or a holy place. Scholars assume that Ezekiel was instrumental in establishing local houses of worship (Ezek. 11:16).[5] These exiles, though relatively few in some respects, would influence the future of Israel.[6] It was in Babylon that the Judeans learned Aramaic, the common language after the Exile. This new Aramaic language would shape the printed style of the former, slanted Hebrew alphabet. The Aramaic influence created the more square, block-type letter with which we are familiar today. The Judeans, in addition, would no longer be considered Hebrews. Because of the captivity, they started considering themselves Jews—for their longing to return to their homeland of Judah. Expectations remained high as the prophets Isaiah, Jeremiah, and Ezekiel all spoke of a coming restoration.

OLD
TESTAMENT

IT WAS DURING THE EXILE THAT MUCH OF WHAT WAS TO BECOME THE OLD TESTAMENT WAS COLLECTED TOGETHER.

It was also during this time that the exiled Judeans under the leadership of Jehozadak collected and edited their sacred writings (Hag. 1:1). The effort culminated in 560 B.C. and resulted in the publication of the "Primary History," consisting of Genesis through 2 Kings.[7] There was also a simultaneous emphasis put upon the preaching of the Law at that time, making it the center and soul of the Jewish religion. Even after the Exile, when the old hierarchic structure was re-established with the high priest maintaining supreme authority, the Law did not cease to be the soul of the nation. It was Ezra, the first scribe and alleged father of hermeneutics, who made the principle of following the Torah the difference between the Jews and non-Jews.[8] Upon their arrival to rebuild Jerusalem, the people gathered to hear Ezra read the Law at the Water Gate which was on the east wall leading to the Gihon Spring (Neh. 3:26).

> Now all the people gathered together as one man in the open square that was in front of the Water Gate; and they told Ezra the scribe to bring the Book of the Law of Moses, which the LORD had commanded Israel. So Ezra the priest brought the Law before the assembly of men and women and all who could hear with understanding on the first day of the seventh month. Then he read from it in the open square that was in front of the Water Gate from morning until midday, before the men and women and those who could understand; and the ears of all the people were attentive to the Book of the Law. So Ezra the scribe stood on a platform of wood which they had made for the purpose; and beside him, at his right hand, stood Mattithiah, Shema, Anaiah, Urijah, Hilkiah, and Maaseiah; and at his left hand Pedaiah, Mishael,

Malchijah, Hashum, Hashbadana, Zechariah, and Meshullam. And Ezra opened the book in the sight of all the people, for he was standing above all the people; and when he opened it, all the people stood up. And Ezra blessed the LORD, the great God. Then all the people answered, "Amen, Amen!" while lifting up their hands. And they bowed their heads and worshiped the Lord with their faces to the ground. Also Jeshua, Bani, Sherebiah, Jamin, Akkub, Shabbethai, Hodijah, Maaseiah, Kelita, Azariah, Jozabad, Hanan, Pelaiah, and the Levites, helped the people to understand the Law; and the people stood in their place. So they read distinctly from the book, in the Law of God; and they gave the sense, and helped them to understand the reading.

NEHEMIAH 8:1-8

> *When the exiles returned to rebuild Jerusalem and reconstruct the Temple, the Samaritans in the north offered to help. However, their gesture was not welcomed by the Judeans.*

It was the strict adherence to the Torah that guaranteed the life of Judaism (Ezra 7:25-26). Inevitably, Judaism became a religion of the Book. Since the destruction of Jerusalem and the loss of the Temple, there was little else to mark them specifically as Jews. Notwithstanding, the foundation was laid for the later development of the strict religious group often mentioned in the gospel accounts, the Pharisees.

After the invasion of Babylon by Cyrus, king of Persia (539 B.C.), the entire Babylonian Empire was brought under Persian control. In the first year of his reign the Persian king, Cyrus (538 B.C.), issued his famous proclamation that granted the Jews permission to rebuild Jerusalem

OLD
TESTAMENT

AROUND 538 B.C., CYRUS ISSUED THE PROCLAMATION THAT EVENTUALLY LED TO THE RECONSTRUCTION OF JERUSALEM AND THE TEMPLE.

(2 Chron. 36:22-23; Ezra 1:1-4; 6:3; cf. Isa. 44:28; 45:1). The resettlement of the city was gradual. First, Zerubbabel, the governor, returned with many of the exiles somewhere between 538 and 522 B.C. Then he and Joshua the high priest initiated a rebuilding program after Solomon's Temple had laid in ruins for 50 years (Ezra 3:8-13). Jerusalem had obviously ceased to be significant politically, so the new emphasis shifted to maintaining religious prominence.[9] Full-scale work was undertaken by the prompting of Haggai and Zechariah in 520 B.C. (Ezra 5:1). These two prophets proclaimed that "Yahweh, jealous for Jerusalem, would shortly return triumphantly to His house," and be victorious over those who resisted His people (Zech. 1:7-17; 8:1 ff.).

When the exiles returned to rebuild Jerusalem and reconstruct the Temple (538 B.C.), the Samaritans in the north offered to help. However, their gesture was not welcomed by the Judeans. Zerubbabel and Jeshua the high priest refused the Samaritans' assistance (Ezra 4:2-4; Neh. 2:20). Not only that, but Nehemiah infuriated matters even more when he expelled from the city the grandson of Eliashib, the high priest, because he was married to the daughter of Sanballat the Samaritan leader (Neh. 13:28). Jack Finegan suggests, "Eliashib's grandson was probably the Manasseh under whom the Samaritans set up their own rival priesthood and built their own temple on Mount Gerizim."[10]

Enraged by their rejection, the Samaritans called into question the Jew's loyalty to the Babylonians.[11] By sending letters of complaint to the ensuing Babylonian leaders, they delayed the rebuilding of the Temple for 16 years (Ezra 4:21). It was only when Darius came to the throne of the Babylonian Empire (522-485 B.C.) that the decree by Cyrus to rebuild the Temple was reaffirmed and enacted once again.[12] But by then, the Jews in Judah had lost interest. John Bright notes that the prophet "Haggai, in particular, attacked the lassitude and indifference that allowed God's people to establish themselves in their own houses while letting Yahweh's house lie in ruins."[13] It had been many, many years since the work on the Temple had begun, and it had not progressed beyond the foundations. The morale of the residents was dangerously low (Isa. 56-66),[14] and a great rift arose among the Jewish people. Only those who engaged in the rebuilding considered themselves true Israelites.[15] Haggai warned all that their difficult times were the result of divine punishment for their indifference (Hag. 1:1-11; 2:15-19). If Jerusalem had truly been chosen as the seat of divine rule, the completion of the Temple was a matter of utmost urgency. How else could Yahweh dwell among His people to bless them? So the effort was completed.

Now in the second month of the second year of their coming to the house of God at Jerusalem, Zerubbabel the son of Shealtiel, Jeshua the son of Jozadak, and the rest of their brethren the priests and the Levites, and all those who had come out of the captivity to Jerusalem, began work and appointed the Levites from twenty years old and above to oversee the work of the house of the Lord. Then Jeshua with his sons and brothers, Kadmiel with his sons, and the sons of Judah, arose as one to oversee those working on the house of God: the sons of Henadad with their sons and their brethren the Levites. When the builders laid the foundation of the temple of the Lord, the priests stood in their apparel with trumpets, and the Levites, the sons of Asaph, with cymbals, to praise the Lord, according to the ordinance of David king of Israel. And they sang responsively, praising and giving thanks to the Lord: "For He is good, for His mercy endures forever toward Israel." Then all the people shouted with a great shout, when they praised the Lord, because the foundation of the house of the Lord was laid.

But many of the priests and Levites and heads of the fathers' houses, old men who had seen the first temple, wept with a loud voice when the foundation of this temple was laid before their eyes. Yet many shouted aloud for joy, so that the people could not discern the noise of the shout of joy from the noise of the weeping of the people, for the people shouted with a loud shout, and the sound was heard afar off.

Ezra 3:8-13

The rebuilt Temple was dedicated in 515 B.C. during the reign of Darius (Ezra 6:15-18) who had confirmed the initial decree by Cyrus. The walls, however, would remain in ruin until restored later by Nehemiah. According to Haggai, this Temple was a smaller and more modest building than the original Solomonic one; yet, it did maintain the same basic architectural structure (Hag. 2:3). Evidently, those who remembered the glorious First Temple wept when they beheld the stages of the newly rebuilt Temple. The miserable circumstances under which the foundation was laid produced an overwhelming impression. The noise of weeping by the aged men was so mingled with the cry of joy from the multitude that neither could be distinguished from the other (Ezra 3:12). Once again the city had become the capital of Judea both politically and religiously, and the people were renewed as a worshiping community. But it was also a time of moral laxity addressed both by Malachi and later by Nehemiah. Priests offered sick and injured animals (Mal. 1:6-14); the Sabbath was given to business (Neh. 13:15-22); and the non-payment of tithes had forced the priests to abandon their religious duties and make a living for themselves (Mal. 3:7-10; Neh. 13:10 f.).[16]

Nehemiah was appointed governor (445 B.C.) and undertook the rebuilding of breaches in the city walls for security. Despite protests from many groups against the refortification of the city (the Samaritans included), the walls were restored in 52 days (Neh. 6:15), although, as Josephus notes, the overall project lasted two years and four months.[17] The book of Nehemiah graphically describes the condition:

> So I came to Jerusalem and was there three days. Then I arose in the night, I and a few men with me; I told no one on what my God had put in my heart to do at Jerusalem; nor was there any animal with me, except the one which I rode. And I went out by night through the Valley Gate to the Serpent Well and the Refuse Gate, and viewed the walls of Jerusalem which were broken down and its gates which were burned with fire. Then I went on to the Fountain Gate and to the King's Pool, but there

was no room for the animal under me to pass. So I went up in the night by the valley, and viewed the wall; then I turned back and entered by the Valley Gate, and so returned.

NEHEMIAH 2:11-15

THE POOL OF SILOAM AS IT APPEARS TODAY.

In Nehemiah's description of the city, several notable ancient landmarks are recognizable. The "Serpent Well" is a reference to the Gihon Spring, while the "King's Pool" is probably the Pool of Siloam (John 9:1-7) into which the water of Hezekiah's Tunnel flowed. The valley described by the prophet is most likely the Kidron Valley. When Nehemiah arrived in the twentieth year of the reign of Artaxerxes I (465-420 B.C.), the population of Jerusalem tallied a little under 50,000 inhabitants, many of whom came after the Temple was completed.[18] Ezra arrived in the year 420 B.C. and initiated social and religious reforms (Ezra 7:27; 8:36). The restoration of Jerusalem spoken of by the pre-exilic prophets (Jer. 29:10; 33:7-11) had taken place in part. But the glorious vision regarding the exaltation of Zion and the transfiguration of Jerusalem was not yet fulfilled (Mic. 4:1-8; Ezek. 40-42).[19] The expectation regarding the coming of the Davidic Messiah continued to be cherished.

GREEK/
ROMAN

ALEXANDER
THE GREAT'S
PEACEFUL
CONQUEST OF
ISRAEL IN 332
B.C. LED TO A
PERIOD OF
GREEK INFLU-
ENCE THAT
WOULD LAST
UNTIL 63 B.C.

The Infiltration of Hellenism

Persian rule came to an end when Jerusalem peacefully submitted to the armies of Alexander the Great (332 B.C.). It was then that the Hellenistic period began, lasting until 63 B.C.[1] Alexander was tutored by Aristotle in the literature and culture of Greece, which made him world history's catalyst of cultural Hellenism. Convinced of the superiority of Greek institutions, he spread Greek customs and language through military conquest. This widespread influence of the Greek language and its literary beauty and technical precision paved the way for the writing of the New Testament Scriptures, as well as an Old Testament translation into Greek, the Septuagint. The New Testament meaning of *Jerusalem* translates into two Greek words: 1) *Ierousalem*—Old Testament transliteration of the Aramaic form, and 2) *Hierosoluma* whose root (*hieros*) reflects the word "holy."[2]

During this time, Josephus notes, the Samaritans built their rival temple on Mount Gerizim (*Antiq.*11.8.4). This act led to the crystallization of the Samaritan community with their own distinctive religious identity and finalized the schism between the Jews and the Samaritans. The city of Shechem was also rebuilt after a lengthy period of desolation.[3] The Samaritans developed their own unique view of Jewish history. They believed that Mount Gerizim was where Abraham prepared to sacrifice Isaac (Gen. 22), not Mount Moriah in Jerusalem. Furthermore, they asserted that God had always intended Mount Gerizim to be the solely established location of sacrificial worship (Deut. 11:29-30; 12:5-14). The biblical canon of the Samaritans consisted of only the first five books of

MEDITERRANEAN SEA

Iturea

Abilene

Syria

Syria

Trachonitis

Galilee

Batanea

Decapolis

Samaria

Perea

Judea

Nabatea

Idumea

THIS MAP SHOWS HOW THE PROVINCES OF ISRAEL LOOKED IN THE TIME OF JESUS WHILE IT WAS UNDER THE ROMAN RULE.

Moses (the Pentateuch). They considered Moses to be the final prophet of God, as well as a superhuman being.[4]

The breach between the Jews and the Samaritans was never really healed (John 4:4-26). Jesus actually instructed His own followers not to go to Samaria during His earthly ministry (Matt. 10:5-6). The Jews only recognized three provinces: Galilee, Judea, and Perea. Samaria was excluded from the dignity of acknowledgement.[5] The name *Perea* is not designated in the Gospels, but is simply listed as "beyond the Jordan." The area stands as a tract of land east of the Jordan River (cf. Matt. 4:25; Mark 3:8). The Perean route was the road used by those wishing to circumvent the territory of Samaria and escape ritual defilement. Jesus took this route on His last journey to Jerusalem via Jericho (Matt. 19:1 ff.; Mark 10:1 ff.). Because Jesus came as the breach healer, the gospel of John documents well His personal ministry to Samaria in John 4. He also explicitly commanded His disciples to take the Gospel to Samaria on the day He ascended. (Acts 1:8). When persecution arose against the Hellenistic branch of the Jerusalem church (Acts 6:1 ff.), missionary work in Samaria was begun: "Philip went down to the city of Samaria and preached Christ" (Acts 8:5).[6] So we can see that the outpouring of the Spirit at Pentecost manifested its mighty power in the elimination of racial prejudice. Not only that, but the New Testament is consistently favorable to this oppressed and sacred people, the Samaritans. They are biblically portrayed as receiving the Gospel of Jesus Christ enthusiastically. Jesus even portrayed a Samaritan as the compassionate figure in His "Parable of the Good Samaritan" in Luke 10. Today, some 200 Samaritans still live near Gerizim.

Upon the death of Alexander, Jerusalem became vulnerable once again and underwent several attempts by foreign powers to gain control of the city. Alexander had made no provision for a replacement, consequently his kingdom was divided among his generals (known as *Diadochi* or "Successors"). One such general, Seleucus, gained control of the territory north of Israel. Another general, Ptolemy I Soter, gained territorial control south of Israel, and Palestine found itself caught right in the middle of it.[7] The Seleucids of Syria (north) and the Ptolemies of Egypt (south) both wanted the city, and Jerusalem was forced to endure one more of its constant struggles—against its destruction and/or for its reconstruction.[8]

HISTORY

GREEK/ ROMAN

IN 198 B.C., JERUSALEM BECAME PART OF THE SELEUCID KINGDOM AND JUDEANS WERE FORCED TO ADOPT GREEK CUSTOMS, CULTURE, AND LANGUAGE.

Finally, in 198 B.C., the city was incorporated into the Seleucid kingdom (Syria) and the process of Hellenization began to intensify, especially among the upper classes.[9] Judeans were being forced to adopt Greek customs, culture, and language. Division was mounting between the liberal progressives (who embraced Hellenistic ideology) and the conservative-traditionals (who saw Hellenization as a threat to their ancestral religion). The clash between Judaism and Hellenism escalated when Hellenistic kings, claiming divinity, merged Greek, Egyptian, and Persian philosophies regarding emperor worship. These ideas were adopted by the Romans who would eventually require divine worship of the Caesars by every subject in their empire.

In time, the Seleucids would lose several important battles to the rapidly expanding Roman Empire and were obligated to hefty financial payments. In order to alleviate the burden, the Seleucids levied an oppressive tax upon the citizens of Judea, Samaria, and Galilee. As if this was not enough to alienate the inhabitants of the country, the Seleucids plundered the Temple treasury in Jerusalem. Then they sold the office of Israel's high priest to the highest bidder.[10] Efforts of Hellenization in Judea included a gymnasium that was built in the Upper City of Jerusalem. One of the degrading effects of this strategy produced priests who were officiating in the Temple and then venturing across the valley to run naked in the arena on the same workday. In 174-168 B.C. the Seleucid king, Antiochus Epiphanies IV (whose name means "God made manifest"), erected a fortress in the Lower City of Jerusalem called—"the Akra." Josephus writes that "it was high enough to overlook the Temple, and it was for this

The Seleucids plundered the Temple treasury in Jerusalem. Then they sold the office of Israel's high priest to the highest bidder.

reason that he fortified it with high walls and towers and stationed a Macedonian garrison therein."[11] To the Jews, the Akra was an especially objectionable and hated symbol of foreign domination. But Antioch's Akra was only the beginning of Jerusalem's new troubles.

As the indoctrination of Hellenism continued, Antiochus outlawed the Jewish religion, desecrated the Temple by sacrificing a pig on the altar, confiscated royal treasures, burned the Holy Scriptures, abolished the worship of Jehovah, forbade the circumcision of children, and installed the statue of the Olympian Zeus in the Temple.[12] This was all done to further the work of Hellenism, including the replacement of Judaism with the worship of Greek gods. The Jews were forced to eat swine's flesh, and disobedience in any of the imposed sanctions carried the penalty of death. The horror by which loyal Jews viewed these proceedings can be seen clearly in the Maccabean books (1 Macc. 1:41-63; 2 Macc. 6:2-5).

Because there is such a strong similarity between the events and historical figures described in the book of Daniel and those in the Maccabean period, there has arisen an interesting controversy among Bible scholars as to when Daniel was written. The traditional view is that Daniel was a prophetic work written by the prophet ca. 605 B.C. The more liberal view is that the book of Daniel, or parts of it, may have been composed during the Maccabean persecutions. In the allegorical interpretation, King Nebuchadnezzar is said to be a symbolic reference to the Seleucid King Antiochus Epiphanies. Both views however, support that the Hellenistic desecration of the Temple is interpreted as being the "abomination of desolation" spoken of by Daniel (Dan. 9:27; 11:31; 12:11). To bring the God of the Jews, the "God of Heaven," into identification with the high god of the Grecian Pantheon, Zeus of Olympus, brought strong reaction. Even so, not all Jewish responses were uniform.[13] Some followed the new ideas of Hellenism and others did not. Consequently, many of the loyal Jews who resisted the Hellenistic reforms were either persecuted, killed, or they fled.

The Maccabean Revolt

The Temple desecration by the Seleucid kingdom had a reverse effect upon the Jewish political and religious scene. Rather than bringing about

HISTORY

submission and acceptance to the spread of the Hellenistic culture, it brought about a revolt by certain "pious individuals" known as *Hasidims* or "loyalists to the Law" (1 Mac. 7:11-17). In the liberal interpretation of Daniel as an allegory, the prophet himself is interpreted as an *Hasid*. He is portray as feeling compelled to resist the new Hellenistic policies by every means within his power. He encouraged his fellow Jews to do the same—holding fast to their Jewishness and their faith that Yahweh would intervene![1]

The actual rebellion against the Hellenistic requirements was led by a Jewish priest named Mattathias Asmoneus and his five sons (John, Simon, Judas, Eleazar, and Jonathan).[2] Charles Page records that Mattathias refused to obey the order to sacrifice a swine to Zeus in his home village of Modin (near modern day Tel Aviv).[3] A newly built town, Modin, has been built on the same ground of ancient Modin. It is situated on the old road from Lidda to Jerusalem.

BETWEEN THE
TESTAMENTS

JUDAS
MACCABEUS
LED JEWISH
FORCES TO THE
LIBERATION OF
JERUSALEM IN
164 B.C.

After murdering the imperial messenger, Mattathias and his sons were forced to flee into the mountains. There they began a campaign of guerrilla warfare against the Seleucids. Striking quickly and efficiently, they became known as the Maccabees, most likely derived from the Hebrew term *maccabi*, or "hammer."[4] Judas Maccabeus initially led the Jewish forces and liberated Jerusalem from Antiochus IV in 164 B.C. Only the despised fortress of Antiochus remained.[5] The Akra lasted another few years, even under Hasmonean siege. When it fell, Jerusalem declared a holiday forever. The Akra is understood by some to have been a sealed off section of the city rather than a fort,[6] perhaps on the site of the Davidic palace south of the Temple.

The Maccabeans laid siege to Jerusalem, forcing a truce with the Seleucid military legion stationed at the city. As part of the reparations, the Hasmoneans were permitted to occupy Temple Hill, to cleanse the Temple of pagan objects, and to reinstate sacrifices. Once again, the Temple lamps were lit in the name of Yahweh. Since that time, Jews have solemnly observed the feast of Hanukkah ("lights") in memory of this occasion. They understand *Hanukkah* as meaning "camped on the twenty-fifth day." The temple menorah, or candelabra, was lit on the twenty-fifth day of the month of Kislev. But because there was only one jar of olive oil found after repossessing the Temple that had not been desecrated, it is said there was only enough oil to burn for one day. Nevertheless, a miracle happened that caused the oil to burn for eight days until a new, pure supply came from Galilee. Still today, every Jewish home lights a nine-candle menorah for eight days in honor of the miraculous event.

The lighting of the Temple lamps began the Maccabean, or Hasmonean, Dynasty that lasted for a brief 100 years. The name *Hasmonean* does not appear in the Maccabean literature, but is noted in the Mishna (*Middoth* 1:6) and by Josephus (*Antiq.* 20.8.11; 20.10). Josephus refers to the sons of Asmoneus, to the Asmoneans, and to the Asmonean family.[7] The revolt was both religious and political and would eventually bring about the invasion of Rome.

The Hasmonean Dynasty, mainly associated with such

HANUKKAH CELEBRATES THE REDEDICATION OF THE TEMPLE AFTER JERUSALEM'S LIBERATION AND THE MIRACLE OF THE BURNING LAMP WHICH IS SYMBOLIZED BY THE MENORAH.

names as Judas Maccabeus (the third of Mattathias' five sons) and his brothers Jonathan and Simon, united the political-religious systems. Judas called Maccabees, or "the hammer," was so successful, that the entire revolt would commonly be known as the Maccabean War—a title after his nickname.[8] The armies of Jerusalem were now commanded by the high priest. For the first time in 450 years an independent Jewish government ruled in Jerusalem.[9] A new dynasty of Jewish high priests and kings would descend from the family of Mattathias, reigning from 142 to 63 B.C.[10]

39

Simon, who initially acted as an advisor, succeeded Judas and Jonathan and eventually drove the Seleucid soldiers from the Akra. It is written, "The yoke of the Gentiles was taken away from Israel. And the people began to write in their records and their contracts, 'in the first year of Simon, the great high priest, general, and leader of the Jew'" (1 Mac. 13:41-42).[11] Simon also consolidated the Hasidims, the Hellenists, and the Maccabees into a united nation,[12] and Jerusalem remained wholly Jewish until its destruction by the Roman armies. Successors included John Hycranus I, the son of Simon—the first to take the title "king," Aristobulus I (the son of John Hyranus I) and Alexander Jannaeus.

Josephus credits John Hycranus I with building a fortress called the Bira (Baris), on the northwest corner of Temple Mount (*Antiq.* 18.4.3).[13] During the time of Nehemiah, Jerusalem had a "citadel by the Temple" under the command of Hananiah (Neh. 2:8; 7:2). The garrison formed a final line of defense on the north to defend against any possible breach in the city wall. The Hasmonean fortress was probably constructed upon the former groundwork of the tower of Hananiah.[14] The same site would later be occupied by the Antonia Fortress during Herod's reconstruction of the Temple area.

All three Hasmonean successors (John Hycranus I, Aristobulus I, and Alexander Jannaeus) conquered vast territories in the name of Jehovah. Hycranus I assaulted the Samaritans in the north, captured Shechem, and destroyed the temple on Mount Gerizim (129-128 B.C.). He also seized the territory of Idumea (old Edom) in the south and forced the Idumeans to follow the ways of Judaism. But the devout Jews never regarded the Idumeans as anything but Edomites, semi-heathen.[15] This animosity and distrust would later be directed toward Herod—an Idumean himself who was born to an aristocratic family. The same negative feelings were extended to the Samaritans who had remained aloof during the Jewish struggle and resisted Maccabean influence. The reign of John Hycranus I was the peak of Hasmonean nobility and religious devotion. Afterwards, most of the leaders evolved into secular monarchs with average moral character at best.[16] In time, Jewish Messianic hopes turned from priestly leadership, which was growing increasingly corrupt, to that of the Son of Man. The Messianic expectation became a supernatural figure far removed from this world whose ways would be high above any natural Hasmonean priest or king.[17]

The next high priest and governor was Aristobulus I (104 B.C.). He was involved in repeated invasions against the Samaritans and the Idumeans. Under his leadership, the Hasmonean kingdom was extended even further northward, strengthening the nation. He also conquered the Itureans who inhabited what came to be called "Galilee of the Gentiles."[18] This would be the Galilee in which Jesus was raised. Aristobulus I "forcibly proselytized" a largely Gentile race making them accept the rite of circumcision and the beliefs and customs of the Jews. The significance of these events would influence Christianity forever. N. Turner notes:

> The family of which Mary came belonged, of course, to Judea, but it is likely that some of the apostles of Jesus, chosen by the Sea of Galilee and near to Capernaum, were of mixed Syrian and Greek descent, whose forebears were forced into Judaism by the sword of the Hasmonean kings.[19]

BETWEEN THE TESTAMENTS

IT WAS DURING THE TIME OF THE MACCABEES THAT THE MAJOR VARIETIES OF JUDAISM EMERGED. AMONG THESE SECTS WERE THE PHARISEES AND THE SADDUCEES.

It was during the intertestamental period, the time of Maccabees, that major varieties of Judaism emerged. Three major influential parties are noted: the Essenes, the Sadducees, and the Pharisees. They differed in religious doctrine as well as in political theory (Acts 23:6-8). The Sadducees ("the righteous ones") were a priestly aristocratic party who embraced Hellenization and its ideals and allied themselves with the Hasmoneans. They eventually disappeared from history after the destruction of

Rome deprived the Sanhedrin of the power to impose capital punishment; so to execute Jesus they needed a confirmatory death sentence from the local governor, Pilate. It is this biblical narrative that gives the Sanhedrin and Rome its most notable fame.

Jerusalem in A.D. 70. A division in the Jewish state evolved between the priestly caste and its adherents (the Sadducees), and the lay element in the state and their followers (the Pharisees). The break developed over the Sadducean interest in the Temple and the lay-interpreted Torah by the Pharisees. The fundamental doctrinal difference concerned the Pharisees' belief in resurrection and afterlife. The Sadducees rejected the teaching. The Pharisees (from the Hebrew *parush*—"one who is separate") also recoiled generally from Hasmonean policy and Hellenistic notions to remain true to their Hasidic roots. They believed that the monarchy conflicted with the Lordship of Yahweh.[20] A major disagreement that fueled the break involved the Hellenistic view of engaging high priests in military exploits. David himself was prevented from building the Temple because he had shed blood (1 Chron. 28:3).

Another notable group mentioned often in the New Testament, the Sanhedrin, also came into existence at this time (1 Macc. 12:6; 2 Macc. 1:10; 4:44). This council of state composed of 71 Jewish leaders and sages under the direction of the high priest became the supreme authority of civil and religious legal decisions in the capital city of Jerusalem. When Judea was made a Roman province (A.D. 6), the Sanhedrin and its president were given almost exclusive control over the internal affairs of the Jewish nation. In the New Testament, the senate was composed of mostly aristocracy (chief priests and Sadducees), who were answerable to the Roman governor (cf. Acts 4).[21] It was to this council that Jesus was brought for trial after His arrest (Matt. 26:57). Rome deprived the Sanhedrin of the power to impose capital punishment; so to execute Jesus, they needed a confirmatory death sentence from the local governor, Pilate. It is this biblical narrative that gives the Sanhedrin and Rome their most notable fame.

The Maccabean Dynasty was also a period that saw the beginning of monastic, communal brotherhoods. Qumran, the site of the discovery of the Dead Sea Scrolls, was home to such a community—the Essenes. They lived a somewhat secluded life, but their part in the preservation of ancient manuscripts was invaluable. They believed that the worship of the Temple had been corrupted and that they were the only true worshippers of God. In their biblical commentaries and scrolls there is a reference to a "Lion of Wrath," considered to be Alexander Jannaeus (104-78 B.C.), a Sadducee

BETWEEN THE TESTAMENTS

ANOTHER SECT THAT EMERGED DURING THIS PERIOD WAS THE ESSENES WHO WERE RESPONSIBLE FOR THE MANUSCRIPTS THAT BECAME THE DEAD SEA SCROLLS.

who was high priest. Evidently, a group of pious Judeans, Pharisees, and priests escaped his persecution and settled in the desert (Qumran). From the writings of the Essenes, it is alleged that Alexander Jannaeus disposed of his political enemies by crucifixion.[22] It is recorded that he crucified 800 captured rebels (possibly Pharisees who protested his kingship) and slaughtered their wives and children, all while he feasted with his concubines before the eyes of the horrified citizens.[23] It was also Alexander Jannaeus who assigned an individual known as Antipater as governor of Idumea. Antipater I was the grandfather of Herod the Great.

For the Jews in Jerusalem the Maccabean period was a glorious time that had not been witnessed since the days of Solomon. The First book of Maccabees portrays the Asmoneans as a family "divinely ordained" to save Israel (1 Macc. 5:62).[24] But after the death of Alexander Jannaeus, the last great Hasmonean king, inner turmoil and civil strife prevailed. Hycranus II and Aristobulus II (sons of Alexander Jannaeus) fought each other for the throne. In the upheaval both princes separately and simultaneously appealed to Rome for support. A third appeal also came to the Roman commander in chief, Pompey, probably from the Pharisees. The appeal recommended that Rome should favor neither prince and that Pompey should assume political government himself, abolish the monarchy, and permit the "theocratic rule of the priests."[25] Rome saw the moment as an opportunity and intervened with force. It was an act that would last for the next 600 years.[26]

THIS MAP SHOWS JERUSALEM AS IT WAS UNDER HEROD THE GREAT AT THE TIME OF THE BIRTH OF JESUS.

BETWEEN THE
TESTAMENTS

THE CRUMBLING OF THE HASMONEAN DYNASTY LED TO AN APPEAL TO ROME FOR MILITARY AID.

GREEK/ ROOM

ROME RECOG-
NIZED THE
OPPORTUNITY OF
JEWISH CIVIL
WAR AND ESTAB-
LISHED A RULE
IN THE
PROVINCE THAT
WOULD LAST
FOR THE NEXT
600 YEARS.

A Roman army under Pompey the Great (64 B.C.) captured Jerusalem after several months of difficult struggle. In the assault, priests were slain while they ministered at the altar, and 12,000 Jews were slaughtered.[27] Pompey dissolved the Maccabean government making Judea part of the Roman Empire. Aristobulus II was captured and paraded through the streets of Rome as a prisoner. John Hycranus II (the elder brother) was left as a high priest in charge of Jerusalem by Pompey. He later received the designation of "ethnarch" (Head of the Nation), but without the title "king." Hycranus II would be advised and supported by Antipater II, an Idumean, who had aligned himself with Rome during the takeover. And though Pompey himself did not harm the restored Temple of Zerubbabel (seeking to maintain its beauty and magnificence), nine years later the Roman consul Crassus plundered it of all its gold.

The Imperial Rule of the Roman Empire

After Pompey's assassination in 48 B.C., Julius Caesar ascended to the throne. The former Hasmonean advisor, Antipater II (for his own personal advantage), became Caesar's devoted friend and assisted him during his Egyptian campaign.[1] He was rewarded and served Rome as an overseer (*epitropos*) of Judea in 47 B.C. Caesar was murdered in 44 B.C. and Antipater II was poisoned shortly thereafter. However, Antipater II's political maneuvering had procured favorable positions for his two Idumean sons. Phasael was governor of Jerusalem. The other, Herod, who would eventually be called "the Great," became governor of Galilee. With the victory of Marc Antony and Octavian over Brutus and Cassius (42 B.C.), the "Idumean brothers," Phasael and Herod, gained political and governmental empowerment from Antony and were granted the title "tetrarchs of Judea."[2]

In the meantime, Mattathias Antigonus (son of Aristobulus II) aligned himself with the Parthians (Rome's chief enemy) who had broken Roman power in Syria. Then, in 40 B.C. Antigonus, with assistance from the Parthians, seized Jerusalem, was crowned king, and for a brief moment, the Hasmonean Dynasty was revived.[3] Hycranus II and Herod's brother Phasael attempted to negotiate with the Parthians, but were captured and taken as prisoners. Hycranus II had his ear mutilated, disqualifying him from the priesthood, and was carried off to Babylonia. Phasael committed suicide, and Herod somehow managed to escape. Leaving his family in the fortress at Masada, Herod traveled to Rome and appealed for assistance where he was then appointed "king of the Jews" (Matt. 2:2). Herod then returned to engage in the reconquest of Palestine with two Roman legions and was successful in repelling the Parthians in 37 B.C.[4] This began the long reign of Herod. Under Rome's authority, a new line of kings would assume local control. The first king directly subject to Rome was undoubtedly Antipater II, though most Christians are familiar with his son —Herod the Great (37 B.C.). He is known as the king who tried to kill the baby Jesus because he thought the Christ Child was a rival for his throne (Matt. 2:1-8). The fifth Roman procurator would be Pontius Pilate.

Herod the Great (37-4 B.C.) was an indefatigable builder. As a lover of Greek culture, he built several shrines for Greek gods. He also desired to restore the Jewish Temple in Jerusalem to its original beauty. It was an act designed to gain favor with the more devout Jews who resented his friendliness with the Romans. Herod had married the Jewess Mariamne—

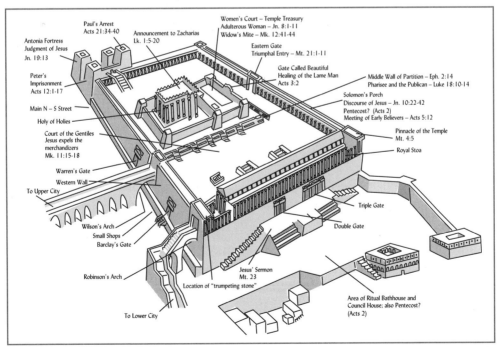

THIS RECONSTRUCTIVE DRAWING SHOWS THE PROXIMITY OF THE TOWER OF ANTONIA TO THE TEMPLE BUILT BY HEROD AS WELL AS THE SITES OF MANY OF THE EVENTS OF JESUS' MINISTRY AROUND THE TEMPLE.

GREEK/ ROMAN

HEROD THE GREAT, THE SAME MAN WHO MET THE WISE MEN AND TRIED TO KILL JESUS AS A BABY, REBUILT THE TEMPLE AROUND 20 B.C.

WHERE JESUS WALKED

JESUS WAS DEDICATED IN HEROD'S TEMPLE.

the Hasmonean princess and granddaughter of Artistobulus (through her father) and Hycranus (through her mother). Their marriage had therefore united the two branches of the Hasmonean house which were so bitterly at odds.[5] Nevertheless, Herod would eventually have her murdered.

Herod began to rebuild the Temple in 20-19 B.C. It is sometimes called the Third Temple, counting Solomon's as the First and Zerubbabel's as the Second.[6] In Jewish tradition, Herod's temple is considered *bet Lasheni*—the Second Temple. The house itself was completed in 18 months, but eight years were spent on the surrounding buildings and courts. As noted by Josephus, it was not finally finished until A.D. 66, just four years before its destruction.[7] The Jews said to Jesus that the Temple was 46 years in building, and according to these calculations, would have been completed around A.D. 28-27 (John 2:20). Herod doubled the area of the Temple Mount, which underwent its greatest and most radical changes since Solomon.[8] The walls that support the 35-acre mount area measure north 1,030 feet; south 910 feet; east 1,540 feet; and west 1,600 feet.[9] On the northwest corner of the Mount, Herod constructed the Antonia Fortress which may rest upon the previous remains of the Hasmonean citadel—the Baris. The Antonia was erected to protect and strengthen the northern defense lines. It is Herod's Temple that is so well documented in the gospel accounts of Christ and the New Testament Church, including Jesus' dedication (Luke 2:21), Jesus' visit as a 12-year-old (Luke 2:42), the casting out of the money changers (Matt. 21:12-13), the arrest of Paul (Acts 21:30), and the exploits of John and Peter as the church in Jerusalem flourished and grew.

> Now Peter and John went up together to the temple at the hour of prayer, the ninth hour. And a certain man lame from his mother's womb was carried, whom they laid daily at the gate of the temple which is called Beautiful, to ask alms from those who entered the temple; who, seeing Peter and John about to go into the temple, asked for alms. And fixing his eyes on him, with John, Peter said, "Look at us." So he gave them his attention, expecting to receive something from them. Then Peter said, "Silver and gold I do not have, but

what I do have I give you: In the name Jesus Christ of Nazareth, rise up and walk." And he took him by the right hand and lifted him up, and immediately his feet and ankle bones received strength. So he, leaping up, stood and walked and entered the temple with them—walking, leaping, and praising God.

ACTS 3:1-8

Herod was hated by the Jewish populace, so he sought to enhance his position by beginning numerous construction projects and providing work.[10] As a result, many from the city and the surrounding countryside enjoyed a prosperous period under his rulership. Jerusalem's wealth was derived from both Herod's building programs of distinctive military architecture and massive masonry as well as the half shekel tax levied on Jewish communities around the world. Notwithstanding, Jerusalem became divided economically as the poor were relegated to the Lower City, and the affluent, including the king and the high priest, resided in the Upper City.[11]

Herod's reign was marked by a paradoxical combination of ruthless cruelty and enlightened diplomacy.[12] Through his construction of a series of fortresses, the Roman-appointed king guaranteed the nation a lengthy period of peace and security that had not been previously experienced for many years. He also succeeded in providing Jerusalem with an adequate water supply and twice reduced the taxes. Despite his achievements, Josephus writes that Herod was always viewed with suspicion and was seen as a foreigner by the people, "brutish and a stranger to all humanity" (*Antiq.* 16.5.4).[13] Herod was depressed to learn that the people would be happy when he died. He was therefore determined that, upon his death, there would be mourning in the land. So he imprisoned a host of influential leaders and prominent citizens in the Hippodrome in Jericho. Herod intended to have his sister Salome carry out a mass execution.

Josephus records the instructions:

> I know well that the Jews will keep a festival upon my death; however, it is in my power to be mourned for on other accounts, and to have a splendid funeral, if you will but be subservient to my commands. Do you but take care to send soldiers to encompass

these men that are now in custody, and slay them immediately upon my death, and then all Judea, and every family of them, will weep at it whether they will or no.[14]

Nonetheless, when Herod passed away, Salome told the soldiers that Herod had rescinded the treacherous order. The prisoners were released, and throughout the territory there was great rejoicing (*War* 1.33.8).

Herod's overall accomplishments in Jerusalem were threefold. First, he transferred the seat of government to the southwestern hill where he built a lavish palace. The palace had a triad of towers named in memory of Phasael (Herod's brother), Hippicus (an unknown friend), and Mariamne (Herod's Jewish wife). Second, he transformed the old Maccabean fortress, which he renamed Antonia in honor of Marc Antony, and enlarged it with corner turrets. And, third, Herod reconstructed the Temple. Josephus said the massive plates of gold that covered Herod's temple "flashed when the first rays of the sun hit them."[15] The renovation by Herod also widened and lengthened the size of Temple Mount. The expansion doubled the size of the Temple platform and extended in three directions: north, south, and west.[16] The east wall (originally from the configuration that Solomon built) remained the same except that it needed to be lengthened on the southern end. When you visit today, a straight joint can be witnessed on the southeast wall revealing the Herodian smooth-faced addition to the original rough-bossed Solomonic structure. Many believe the wall to the right of the straight joint is probably material left from Solomon's construction and was used in the rebuilding by Zerubbabel. The union is approximately 100 feet north from the southeast corner. Due to this architectural fact, the platform area above (supported by the southeast wall) was known as Solomon's porch, another famous area mentioned in the New Testament (John 10:23; Acts 3:11; 5:12).

SITE OF
INTEREST

SOLOMON'S
COLONNADE

Around the Temple platform, Herod constructed colonnades or porticos formed by two rows of roofed columns. Jesus often expounded upon the Scriptures in the portico sometimes called Solomon's Colonnade. The general vicinity was called The Court of the Gentiles and lay outside the defined, sacred zone which was nearer to the Temple. When a rabbi desired to teach in public, he would use a question and answer format (often questions answered with questions) and would conduct his teaching session in the colonnades that surrounded the interior walls (Mark 11:27-29). There were certain religious restrictions imposed upon those who were physically handicapped from entering the inner courts, so it is interesting that Jesus worked several significant miracles along the outer galleries: "Then the blind and the lame came to Him in the temple, and He healed them" (Matt. 21:14; also see John 9:1-7). Written records reveal (*War* 5.5.2) that the double-columned colonnades were composed of single block (monolith) columns of pure white marble, each about 38 feet high with ceilings of paneled cedar.[17]

A RECONSTRUCTIVE DRAWING OF THE ROYAL STOA SHOWING THE HEIGHT, DEPTH, AND WIDTH OF THE ORIGINAL.

The aisles were 49 feet wide. The Royal Colonnade, which ran east-west along the southern edge of the Temple platform (somewhat parallel to the Kidron Valley), was called the Royal Stoa. It was an enormous structure that is described as "more noteworthy than any under the sun" (*Antiq.* 15.11.5).[18] Even the disciples of Jesus acknowledged its grandeur (Luke 21:5-6). It is to this southeast corner of the Royal Stoa that Jesus was taken in temptation, i.e., "the pinnacle of the temple" (Matt. 4:5).

The Royal Colonnade contained three aisles which were formed by four rows of columns that totaled 162 columns in all. Each pillar was 4½ feet in diameter, extending 27 feet in the air, and was adorned with Corinthian capitols and double-molded bases. The two outside aisles were 30 feet wide. The center aisle, which was 45 feet wide, had a raised, pitched roof providing the effect of a Roman basilica, as noted by Mare.[19] The area underneath the southern platform which supported the Royal Stoa still houses a series of massive structural arches: 88 pillars divide the area into 12 long-vaulted aisles.[20] The vaults were probably used as storerooms for the Temple. They were nicknamed "Solomon's stables" by the Crusaders

CRUSADERS

THE CRUSADERS NICKNAMED THE VAULTS BENEATH THE ROYAL STOA "SOLOMON'S STABLES," THOUGH IT WAS NEITHER CONSTRUCTED BY SOLOMON NOR WAS IT DESIGNED AS STABLES.

who kept their horses in the lower parts of the piers. The name has remained, even though they were not constructed by Solomon nor were they ever designed to be stables. When Jerusalem was destroyed in A.D. 70 by the Romans, some of the Zealots hid in these lower caverns. They were, nevertheless, discovered and slain. Josephus notes "upwards of two thousand dead" (*War* 6.9.4).[21]

SITE OF INTEREST

THE WAILING WALL

Surrounding the Temple Mount, massive walls of huge stones were installed to support Herod's extension. Today the original Western Wall still remains intact. It is called the "Wailing Wall" in Arabic. Some of the original stones along the valley floor are estimated to weigh between 600 and 800 tons per block and can be seen in what is now called the Western Tunnels. Josephus mentions several gates in the walls of the Temple platform. Four gates are specifically cited on the Western Wall: "The first led to the palace by a passage over the intervening ravine, two others led to the suburb, and the last led to the other part of the city from which it was separated by many steps going to the ravine and from here up again to the hill" (*Antiq.* 15.11.5).[22] Two gates provided entrance into the Temple area from the ground level north-south road that ran along the Western Wall; and two gates provided entrance to the Temple area at the platform level.

SITE OF INTEREST

WILSON'S ARCH

Philip J. King records, "The upper city, in which was located the seat of the Hasmonean government, was joined to the Temple Mount by a bridge spanning the Tyropoeon Valley."[23] Archaeologists have discovered the remains of this bridge (in the form of a supporting arch) just north of what is now called the Western Wall. It has been named Wilson's Arch, labeled after Charles Wilson who investigated it in the 1960s. The region of the Upper City, besides hosting the Hasmonean Palace, included the Xystos— a Hellenistic gymnasium that had an open-air colonnaded plaza used for public assemblies (2 Macc. 4:9). Josephus states, "The Xystos was connected to the Temple by a bridge."[24]

SITE OF INTEREST

BARCLAY'S GATE

One of the gates that led to the suburb is called Barclay's Gate (so titled by the discoverer in 1848). It is otherwise known as Coponius' Gate, after the Roman procurator (A.D. 6-9) who may have financially underwritten some of the reconstruction.[25] The lintel of the gate (25 feet long and 7 feet high) can still be seen today on the woman's side of the Wailing Wall. The rest of the gateway, which provided passageway through stone archways up to the Temple courts, is below ground.

In the southwest corner of the Temple platform was the latter gate described by Josephus as "separated by many steps going down to the ravine." Today it is called Robinson's Arch. It led from the Court of the Gentiles, through the double gate in the Western Wall of the Royal Colonnade, down to the street below, and it was the primary entrance for the poor from the Lower City.[26] Remains of this arch can still be seen today.

SITE OF INTEREST

ROBINSON'S ARCH

When the Temple complex was completed, the inner and outer perimeter near the Temple proper was segregated by a low barrier 4½ feet high with 13 gates into the smaller, sacred area. The balustrade was called *soregh* and was built of beautifully ornamented marble. This "wall of warning" literally posted a "keep out" sign to the Gentiles. Latin and Greek-inscribed stone slabs have been found which stated that no Gentile should enter the sacred space, for the action would result in the penalty of death.[27] What wonder of grace God has done in Christ!—"For he is our peace, who hath made both one, and hath broken down the middle wall of partition between us" (Eph. 2:14 KJV).

The Destruction of Jerusalem

Roman governors of Judea displayed very little respect for the Jewish religion, so turbulent times continued under their rule. Such anti-Semetic policies caused a violent insurrection against Rome in A.D. 66. The

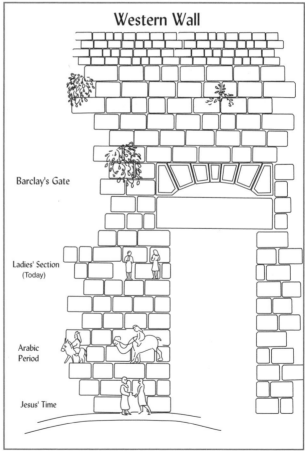

Western Wall

Barclay's Gate

Ladies' Section (Today)

Arabic Period

Jesus' Time

THIS RECONSTRUCTIVE DRAWING SHOWS THE LEVEL WHERE YOU STAND TODAY AT THE WESTERN WALL COMPARED WITH WHERE PEOPLE STOOD AT OTHER TIMES IN HISTORY.

51

THE WESTERN WALL (THE WAILING WALL) OF THE TEMPLE MOUNT AS IT APPEARS TODAY.

GREEK/
ROMAN

HEROD'S
TEMPLE WAS
DESTROYED IN
THE ROMAN
SIEGE OF
JERUSALEM IN
70 A.D.

revolt was led by Zealots, a fanatical Jewish sect. The Roman emperor Nero sent an army led by his general Vespasian to crush the revolt. But Vespasian was recalled and crowned emperor of Rome at Caesarea in the year A.D. 69 before the "fanatics" were defeated. It would be the general's son, Titus (a future emperor himself), who would finish the task. In A.D. 70 he laid siege to Jerusalem with four legions of soldiers (the Fifth, the Tenth, the Twelfth, and the Fifteenth). The Romans camped on the Mount of Olives and planned their attack from the north—the weakest line of defense topographically. A 4½-mile enclosure wall erected around the entire city, along with thirteen Roman forts, served to hasten the surrender through famine.[1]

The general urged the city to give up, sending the Jewish historian Josephus as a mediator in an attempt to convince them of their predicament, but the Jewish leaders refused. It has been recorded that the Messianic followers, at the invitation of Titus, left the city and literally passed safely through the midst of Roman armies. This phenomenal occurrence has been interpreted historically as a "rapture," a deliverance from wrath (1 Thess. 5:9) by the Christian Church. The disciples of Messiah then proceeded east across the Jordan River to Pella. Once the evacuation was complete, Titus, with his armies, entered the city, overtaking two of the three defense walls rather easily. He then not only captured Jerusalem, but in a terrible, bloody battle devastated it, throwing down its walls and leveling its buildings. Titus desired to save the Temple as a prize of victory, but his soldiers, thirsting for revenge, set it ablaze against his orders. Josephus states that the carnage and stench of the dead prior to the final destruction of the Antonia and the Temple were unbelievable (*War* 5.1.3; 5.13.7; 6.3.3).[2]

The Triumphal Arch of Titus, located in Rome, displays pictures of Roman soldiers carrying off the Temple furniture as loot. The burning of the Temple made the final break between Judaism and the Church complete (John 16:2-3). Others believe the break came later during the Second Jewish War in A.D. 130, when Messianic Jews in the Jewish Army deserted after Simon Bar Kochba was proclaimed the Messiah by Rabbi Akiva. The Christians saw these events as providential exclusion from Jewish ritual and helped establish the Church as a distinct religion separate from Israel. Following Titus' sack, Jerusalem was left in absolute ruin and would stay that way for many years. The original wall of the Temple Mount (the Wailing Wall) was left undisturbed as one of the last remaining Temple artifacts of that time. It is no wonder that it is considered holy and precious to the Jewish people today. The final fortress of the Zealots, Masada, fell to the Roman legions in A.D. 73. It continues as a monument for freedom to the Jews even to this very day. Seemingly, many of Jesus' own disciples hoped that He would lead a rebellion against their religious oppressors (Luke 24:21). Jesus continually reminded all of His hearers of the fact that His kingdom was founded on love, not hate. He also knew that a forthcoming Christ-rejecting generation would receive the Romans' A.D. 70 judgment when He prophesied the destruction of Jerusalem—40 years before its fall (Matt. 24; Luke 21).

> When Pilate saw that he could not prevail at all, but rather that a tumult was rising, he took water and washed his hands before the multitude, saying, "I am innocent of the blood of this just Person. You see to it." And all the people answered and said, "His blood be on us and on our children."
>
> MATTHEW 27:24-25

When Titus destroyed the city, he decided to leave the three towers built by Herod intact. The towers guarded the palace and the west entrance to the city. They were constructed with immense white marble blocks (30 feet long, 15 feet wide, and 7 to 8 feet thick) that were perfectly joined together. The structures at the base varied between 30 and 60 square feet and rose to varying heights of 75 to 135 feet with apartments, baths, battlements, and turrets above.[3] They were a testimony to the grandeur of Jerusalem's magnificent architectural structures that Rome had devastated.[4] The towers were described by Josephus as "for largeness, beauty, and strength beyond all that were in the habitable world" (*War* 5.4.3).[5] Structural evidence of Jerusalem's historic grandeur can be viewed today by the Jaffa Gate, though it is commonly held that the present architecture is the work of Suleiman the Magnificent from the sixteenth century. The Citadel today is popularly called "David's Tower" and stands on the site of Herod's seemingly enduring memorials on the very foundation of Phasael's campanile. The name, David's Tower, is believed to have been derived from the conversation of travelers who came to Jerusalem from the north. The tower was the first site people could see from a distance. They probably said, "There is the tower of the City of David," and the name stuck. Currently, the whole complex houses a beautiful museum of the Holy City and takes the visitor step-by-step through the history of Jerusalem.

Herod's palace adjoined the three towers and was connected to the ramparts of the city. The walls of the palace were 45 feet high. Josephus notes that its magnificence was difficult to describe. He alludes to its immense banqueting halls, bed chambers for 100 guests, and groves of various trees with canals. The facility was the residence and seat of government during the time of Jesus and is thought by many to have housed the Praetorium (administrative headquarters) of Pilate spoken of in Scripture:

> So Pilate, wanting to gratify the crowd, released Barabbas to them; and he delivered Jesus, after he had scourged Him, to be crucified.
>
> Then the soldiers led Him away into the hall called Praetorium, and they called together the whole garrison. And they clothed Him with purple; and they twisted a crown of

SITE OF
INTEREST

THE JAFFA
GATE

SITE OF
INTEREST

THE MUSEUM
OF THE HOLY
CITY

thorns, put it on His head, and began to salute Him, "Hail, King of the Jews!" Then they struck Him on the head with a reed and spat on Him; and bowing the knee, they worshiped Him. And when they had mocked Him, they took the purple off Him, put His own clothes on Him, and led Him out to crucify Him.

MARK 15:15-20

An alternative view prescribes that the Praetorium may have been located in the Antonia Fortress at the northwest corner of Temple Mount. The traditional route of the Via Dolorosa begins at the castle. Regardless, the elaborate complex and the height of the three towers (Phasael 135 feet, Hippicus 120 feet high, and Mariamne 75 feet) with the adjoining palace, created an impressive and formidable structure. When Rome occupied the city, the three towers actually formed their defenses and served as headquarters for the Tenth Roman Legion which remained until the third century A.D. Coins found in the vicinity depict the conquest and captive status of Jerusalem. Impressed on one side of a coin was the head of a Roman emperor—Vespasian, Titus, or Domitian. The opposite side was impressed with Greek words that read *Judaea Iudias* (Captive Judea) or *Judaea Devicta* (Defeated Judea).[6]

Jewish resistance to Roman occupation did not totally dissipate with the destruction of Jerusalem. Messianic expectations continued to remain at high levels. Ensuing Roman emperors, Trajan (A.D. 98-117) and Hadrian (A.D. 117-138), were forced to quench various uprisings. In order to diminish Jewish longings, Hadrian changed the name of the country from Judaea to *Palestina* (named after the Philistines) and implemented a plan to reconstruct Jerusalem that would change it into a pagan city. The Second Jewish Revolt, under the leadership of Simon Bar Kochba, occurred in A.D. 132, but victory by the Jewish populace was short-lived. Some historians believe the uprising was provoked by the suspicions that an altar to Jupiter Captolinus would be constructed on the Temple platform by Hadrian.[7] Jerome commented that there was a statue of Hadrian on horseback erected on the spot of the Holy of Holies. What is known for sure is the fact that the recurring threat of revolt led Hadrian to profane the Temple area, ban the Jews from the Holy City, and dramatically reconstruct the city's landscape.

Hadrian established his new pagan Roman city and called it *Aelia Capitolina*. The name is a composition of Hadrian's middle name (Publius Aelius Hadrianus) combined with reference to the three gods of the Roman Capitoline—Jupiter, Juno, and Minerva.[8] A badly deteriorated inscription bearing his handiwork can still be seen above the keystone on the lower eastern archway by the Damascus Gate—the main north entrance. It reads, "according to the *decurians* [the city council] of Colonia Aeilia Capitolina." The present Damascus Gate was constructed by Suleiman the Magnificent in the sixteenth century. It is considered the most elaborate gateway into the Old City today. Archaeologists have discovered the remains of Hadrian's northern entrance to Aelia Capitolina, consisting of three arched gateways flanked by two massive towers beneath the foundations of the present gate.[9] The Arabic name for the gate, *Bab el-Amud*, which means "the Gate of the Column," preserves in its language the legacy of a famous city monument. The column bore a larger-than-life statue of Hadrian and stood in the center of the courtyard just inside the triumphal archways. The fifth-century Madaba map in Jordan portrays the newly revised city in elaborate mosaic design with Hadrian's column overlooking the grand entrance opening onto the Cardo, the main street of the newly revised city. Visitors to Jerusalem today actually explore archaeological evidence from the Hadrianic reconstruction.

GREEK/ ROMAN

AFTER THE SECOND JEWISH REVOLT OF 132 A.D., HADRIAN HAD MUCH OF THE CITY OF JERUSALEM DELIBERATELY PLOWED UNDER.

Hadrian had much of the city deliberately plowed under. He also filled in any low depressions making the foundation of the city both as level and rectangular as possible. This destructive act of the emperor was interpreted by the Jews as a fulfillment of Micah's prophecy: "Zion shall be plowed like a field" (3:12). Jerusalem's streets were then redesigned by Hadrian to reflect symmetrical Roman engineering—normally oriented to the four of a compass.[10] The city had a main north-to-south street (*Cardo Maximus*) and a central east-west intersection (*Decumani Maximus*). The layout was a practical development designed to avoid a sudden gust of cold wind which could blow down any one of the several passageways. The width of an average street in Jerusalem during the Roman-Byzantine period was about 18 feet; however, the *Cardo Maximus* was 72 feet.[11] The *Cardo* was a wide avenue built in a way that made it conducive for commercial shopping. It was divided into four lanes, each 18 feet wide. There were two

This mosaic map of Jerusalem in Madaba, Jordan, dates back to the fifth century.

lanes in the center and two lanes on the outside where the merchants offered their wares. The *Cardo* has been excavated today so a visitor can walk on the very stones that paved the original thoroughfare.

Saudi Arabia became the home of Mohammed's Islamic religion in the sixth century A.D. Not long after its inception in Mecca, a Muslim army under the Caliph Omar I (successor to Mohammed), invaded Palestine and conquered Jerusalem. This occurred in A.D. 637 and secured control of the city by Arabs for the next 500 years. Islam's famed "Dome of the Rock" was built 50 years later on the Temple Mount—site of the Temples of Solomon, Zerubbabel, and Herod. The Dome is also called the "Mosque of Omar," although Mare states the title is erroneous. It was not constructed by Omar but by his successor, Umayyad Caliph of Damascus (A.D. 685-705).[12] The Mosque is built on the peak of Mount Moriah, over the rock believed to be the altar place of the Temple.

Now Solomon began to build the house of the Lord at Jerusalem on Mount Moriah, where the LORD had appeared to

THE DOME OF THE ROCK COMMEMORATES THE MUSLIM BELIEF THAT ABRAHAM WAS GOING TO SACRIFICE ISHMAEL, NOT ISAAC.

his father David, at the place that David had prepared on the threshing floor of Ornan the Jebusite.

2 CHRONICLES 3:1

The peak of the Mount has a cavern that would serve as a natural altar. This spot has long been venerated as the sacred place where Solomon's original Holy of Holies stood. It is believed by tradition to be the site where Abraham offered up his only son Isaac.

Now it came to pass after these things that God tested Abraham, and said to him, "Abraham!" And he said, "Here I am." Then He said, "Take now your son, your only son Isaac, whom you love, and go to the land of Moriah, and offer him there as a burnt offering on one of the mountains of which I shall tell you."

GENESIS 22:1-2

Muslims believe Abraham went to that site to sacrifice his son Ishmael, the father of the Arab peoples. Muslims also believe that Adam and Eve offered sacrifices to God there. More importantly, they believe that Mohammed ascended into heaven on his winged horse "El Burak" (The Lightning) from the rock in the center of the Dome located on the summit of the Mount. It is because of this belief concerning the ascension of the prophet from the rock, that Muslims hold Jerusalem to be the third most holy place in the world. The possession of the city by Muslims and the mistreatment of Christians would eventually lead to the Crusades— showing the central importance Jerusalem has always held in the Judeo-Christian faith. The Crusaders took control of Palestine by A.D. 1153, but they held the revered Holy Land only for 34 years.

CRUSADERS

THE CRUSADERS TOOK CONTROL OF PALESTINE IN A.D. 1153 AND HELD IT FOR 34 YEARS.

On July 4, 1187, the Moslem general Saladin (Salah el-Din), founder of the Ayyubid Dynasty, inflicted a stunning defeat on the combined Crusader forces. The Battle of Hattin occurred west of the Sea of Galilee. Jerusalem later surrendered peaceably. During the Ayyubid Period, Jerusalem saw the removal of the cross from the Dome of the Rock and every Christian church converted to a Mosque. One of the most celebrated of Christian sites, the Church of St. Anne, became a Muslim religious school. In response to the defeat, another Crusade by Richard the Lion-Hearted was launched (A.D. 1191), but the Crusaders only regained territory along the coast. The Moslem ruler Saladin renovated and refortified the Holy City. Even so, after his death in A.D. 1193, his empire was dismantled. In A.D. 1219 el-Malikel Mu'azzem 'Isa decided to demolish Jerusalem's walls and fortifications. His strategy in doing this was to head off the future defense of the city in the event that the Crusaders took it again. So the city remained unfortified throughout the entire 266-year Mamluk period (A.D. 1250-1516) during which Jerusalem's population declined and the city degenerated both economically and politically.[13]

The next episode of the Holy Land which resulted in a change of control took place when Palestine was easily conquered in the sixteenth century by the Turkish Ottoman Empire. The Ottoman Sultan Selim I entered Jerusalem in December of 1516. But it was the great Moslem ruler, Suleiman the Magnificent, who rebuilt the complete circuit of walls of the Holy City on their earlier foundations (1538-1541).[14] These are the walls of Jerusalem that stand around the city today. Through the centuries, Jerusalem has been possessed by 23 different armies.

The last foreign power to control the city was Britain, who took Palestine from the Turks in World War I, and subsequently agreed with the United Nations charter of Jewish repatriation in 1947.

Personal Reflections

FROM MAP INSIDE THE FRONT COVER: 8-9, F-G.

CHAPTER TWO

Bethany

Now a certain man was sick, Lazarus of Bethany,
the town of Mary and her sister Martha.

JOHN 11:1

Bethany is a village on the eastern slope of the Mount of Olives, just 1½ miles from Jerusalem. Situated on the road to Jericho, the town is thought to be the Old Testament city of Ananiah (Neh. 11:32).[1] Although the meaning of the Hebrew term *Beit-Ania* is unclear, its name is commonly held to mean, "house of dates or figs" (because of its root, *Beitan*, which denotes "a garden of fruit trees"). Bethany is near the town of Bethphage from where Jesus sent for the colt He rode during His Triumphal Entry into Jerusalem (Mark 11:1; Luke 19:29).[2] Bethphage (*Beit-Pagei*) finds its definition from the Hebrew *Pag*, "the young fruit of the fig." The significance of both towns' names do confirm the fact that the slopes of the Mount of Olives on which they are located were used to grow fruits and vegetables for the city of Jerusalem. You may recall the incident of the cursing of the fig tree in Mark 11:12-21 which occurred near Bethany.

WHERE JESUS WALKED

JESUS OFTEN
VISITED BETHANY,
WHICH COULD BE
CONSIDERED HIS
JUDEAN HOME.

WHERE JESUS WALKED

BETHANY
RECEIVED ITS
GREATEST
NOTORIETY AS
THE SITE OF THE
RAISING OF
LAZARUS.

Bethany is most widely known for the events which occurred in the New Testament. It was the home of the sisters Mary and Martha and their brother Lazarus (cf. Luke 10:38-42). Jesus often visited Bethany since it was just outside the city of Jerusalem, especially when He and the disciples attended Temple ceremonies during Passover (Luke 21:37; Mark 11:19).[3] Many pilgrims came to Jerusalem during special events. The so-called "tourists" were not allowed to stay within the city. So they camped outside its walls at night and came to the Temple during the day. Bethany could be considered Jesus' Judean home. After the jubilant "Hosanna" welcome into Jerusalem, known in more contemporary times as "Palm Sunday," Jesus returned to Bethany where He spent the evening (Matt. 21:17).

Bethany was also the home of Simon the leper, in whose house Jesus was anointed with an alabaster jar of ointment (Mark 14:3-9; Luke 7:36-50; John 12:1-8). However, the city receives its greatest notoriety from the raising of Lazarus, one of the most notable miracles in the ministry of Jesus. When He was informed of Lazarus' illness, Jesus purposely delayed His arrival for several days. More than likely it was to eliminate any suspicion that the event was prearranged with His friends. By the time of His arrival, everyone in the village knew Lazarus had died.

Ancient literature taught that the real strength of mourning did not occur until the third day because the soul returned to the grave thinking it would reenter the body. However, when it saw the color of its own face, it left. One should remember that in days of old, there were cases of people occasionally being buried alive, both accidentally as well as religiously (as with the Amorites). Burial practices among the Jews attempted to alleviate this error. Often, people went to the gravesite for a period of three days to make sure the person had not come back to life. The mention that Jesus explicitly waited four days establishes that Lazarus was truly dead beyond all doubt, for "he stinketh." According to Jewish belief, the physical corruption was now irreversible and recognition of the person rendered impossible. This also carried legal consequences. If Jesus had raised Lazarus before death was allegedly finalized, the miracle could have been contested.

So when Jesus came, He found that he had already been in the tomb four days. Now Bethany was near Jerusalem, about two miles away. And many of the Jews had joined the women around Martha and Mary, to comfort them concerning their brother. Then Martha, as soon as she heard that Jesus was coming, went and met Him, but Mary was sitting in the house. Now Martha said to Jesus, "Lord, if You had been here, my brother would not have died. But even now I know that whatever You ask of God, God will give You." Jesus said to her, "Your brother will rise again." Martha said to Him, "I know that he will rise again in the resurrection at the last day." Jesus said to her, "I am the resurrection and the life. He who believes in Me, though he may die, he shall live. And whoever lives and believes in Me shall never die. Do you believe this?" She said to Him, "Yes, Lord, I believe that You are the Christ, the Son of God, who is to come into the world."

And when she had said these things, she went her way and secretly called Mary her sister, saying, "The Teacher has come and is calling for you." As soon as she heard that, she arose quickly and came to Him. Now Jesus had not yet come into the town, but was in the place where Martha met Him. Then the Jews who were with her in the house, and comforting her, when they saw that Mary rose up quickly and went out, followed her, saying, "She is going to the tomb to weep there." Then, when Mary came where Jesus was, and saw Him, she fell down at His feet, saying to Him, "Lord, if You had been here, my brother would not have died." Therefore, when Jesus saw her weeping, and the Jews who came with her weeping, He groaned in the spirit and was troubled. And He said, "Where have you laid him?" They said to Him, "Lord, come and see." Jesus wept. Then the Jews said, "See how He loved him!" And some of them said, "Could not this Man, who opened the eyes of the blind, also have kept this man from dying?"

Then Jesus, again groaning in Himself, came to the tomb. It was a cave, and a stone lay against it. Jesus said, "Take away the stone." Martha, the sister of him who was dead, said to Him, "Lord, by this time there is a stench, for he has been dead four days." Jesus said to her, "Did I not say to you that if you would

THE TOMB OF LAZARUS IN BETHANY.

believe you would see the glory of God?" Then they took away the stone from the place where the dead man was lying. And Jesus lifted up His eyes and said, "Father, I thank You that You have heard Me. And I know that You always hear Me, but because of the people who are standing by I said this, that they may believe that You sent Me." Now when He had said these things, He cried with a loud voice, "Lazarus, come forth!" And he who had died came out bound hand and foot with graveclothes, and his face was wrapped with a cloth. Jesus said to them, "Loose him, and let him go."

Then many of the Jews who had come to Mary, and had seen the things Jesus did, believed in Him.

JOHN 11:17-45

Because of the significance of this and Jesus' historic connection with the village, Bethany was revered by early Christians. In the fourth century, a sanctuary was constructed over the cave where Jesus raised Lazarus. The famous miracle is still preserved in the name of the Arab village *El-Azariyeh* ("the place of Lazarus").[4]

According to the gospel of Luke, Bethany is also where the ascension of the Lord took place (Luke 24:50-51). Bethany is included in the area of the Mount of Olives, so the traditional site for the ascension on top of the Mount would be correct.

There is another biblical reference to a town called Bethany, sometimes referred to as "Bethany beyond the Jordan," near the city of Jerusalem.[5] But the specifics of such a locale remain unknown. The expression "beyond the Jordan" could mean either east or west of the river. Some maps show a Bethany on the east side of the Jordan River, north of the Dead Sea.[6] The *King James Version* of the Bible notes the site as "Bethabara" (John 1:28), where John was baptizing. Origen, a leading theologian in the early Greek church (A.D. 185-254), suggested that Bethabara meant "house of preparation," and that it was an appropriate location for John's ministry.[7] It was there that John was confronted by a delegation of priests and Levites from Jerusalem (John 1:19-28).[8] A few maps identify the baptismal Bethabara as "Aenan near Salim, because there was much water" (John 3:23). As a result, K.W. Clark states, "Another questionable Bethany is sometimes located west of the Jordan ca. 30 miles below the Sea of Galilee."[9] Pierson Parker notes that the Greek can mean "opposite" as well as "beyond" the Jordan. He paraphrases: "Those things took place in Bethany, which is across from the point of the Jordan where John had been baptizing" (John 1:28). Therefore, the Johannine reference is to the well-known Bethany, near Jerusalem.[10]

The Madaba map mosaic in southern Jordan locates a town named Bethabara on the west bank of the Jordan. It is near where the river flows into the Dead Sea.[11] All in all, it seems that two Bethany sites are identifiable: One on the east side of the Mount of Olives; and a second site, the district of Batanaea (Old Testament Bashan), close to where the Jordan enters the Dead Sea. It was along the Jordan River where John was engaged in ministry and Jesus was baptized.

WHERE JESUS
WALKED

LUKE'S GOSPEL
STATES THAT IT
WAS FROM
BETHANY
THAT JESUS
ASCENDED
TO HEAVEN.

BETHANY

Personal Reflections

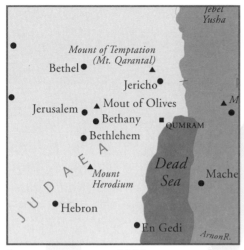

FROM MAP INSIDE THE FRONT COVER: 8-9, F-G.

CHAPTER THREE

Bethlehem

So it was, when the angels had gone away from them
into heaven, that the shepherds said to one another,
"Let us now go to Bethlehem and see this thing that has
come to pass, which the Lord has made known to us."

LUKE 2:15

"The little town of Bethlehem" is best known by Christians for its connection to the Christmas story as the birthplace of Jesus and is honored as the geographical home of the promised Messiah (Matt. 2:1-16; Luke 2:4-15; John 7:42). After the conquest of Canaan, it is referred to in the *King James Version* as Bethlehem-Judah (Judg. 17:7-9; Ruth 1:1-2; 1 Sam. 17:12) to distinguish it from another town located in Zebulun with the same name (Josh. 19:15).[1] It was the northern-most border settlement of the tribe of Judah (Josh. 19:11-12) and is situated only 5½ miles from Jerusalem on the road known as the "way of the Patriarchs" (the Beersheba-Hebron Jerusalem-Bethel road).[2] Bethlehem was also the normal starting point for

WHERE JESUS WALKED

JESUS FULFILLED THE PROPHECY THAT THE MESSIAH WOULD BE BORN IN BETHLEHEM, A TOWN "LITTLE AMONG THE THOUSANDS OF JUDAH."

BETHLEHEM

people traveling to Egypt during the period of Jeremiah the prophet (Jer. 41:17). He mentions the caravan inn of Chimham near Bethlehem, which may be similar to the one in the New Testament gospel accounts.[3]

This town, which was "little among the thousands of Judah," acquired great fame for divine purposes. It was prophesied to be the town where Messiah would be born (Mic. 5:2), but not without consequence. Herod, in his attempt to kill the King of the Jews, murdered all of its male children under two years of age.

> Then Herod, when he saw that he was deceived by the wise men, was exceedingly angry; and he sent forth and put to death all the male children who were in Bethlehem and in all its districts, from two years old and under, according to the time which he had determined from the wise men. Then was fulfilled what was spoken by Jeremiah the prophet, saying:
> "A voice was heard in Ramah,
> Lamentation, weeping, and great mourning,
> Rachel weeping for her children,
> Refusing to be comforted,
> Because they are no more."
> MATTHEW 2:16-18

According to the Scriptures, Joseph and Mary journeyed from Nazareth and returned to their home in Bethlehem for the census ordered by Caesar Augustus (Luke 2:1-5). The city was so overcrowded upon their arrival

Early accounts note that the actual events of Jesus' birth took place on the outskirts of town in a natural cave that was used as a stable.

that, according to Luke 2:7, Mary gave birth to Jesus "in a manger, because there was no room for them in the inn." Early accounts note that the actual events of Jesus' birth took place on the outskirts of town in a natural cave that was used as a stable. The early church father, Justin Martyr (A.D. 165), confirmed this fact in his writings.[4] First-century inns would often be built over caverns which served as protective quarters for the livestock. It was in these humble surroundings that Mary gave birth to her firstborn Son, wrapped Him in swaddling clothes, and placed Him in the manger.[5] Not long after, Mary and Joseph departed from Bethlehem to present their newborn and firstborn Son in the Temple at Jerusalem in accordance with Jewish custom (Luke 2:22-24).

And it came to pass in those days that a decree went out from Caesar Augustus that all the world should be registered. This census first took place while Quirinius was governing Syria. So all went to be registered, everyone to his own city. Joseph also went up from Galilee, out of the city of Nazareth, into Judea, to the city of David, which is called Bethlehem, because he was of the house and lineage of David, to be registered with Mary, his betrothed wife, who was with child. So it was, that while they were there, the days were completed for her to be delivered. And she brought forth her firstborn Son, and wrapped Him in swaddling cloths, and laid Him in a manger, because there was no room for them in the inn.

Now there were in the same country shepherds living out in the fields, keeping watch over their flock by night. And behold, an angel of the Lord stood before them, and the glory of the Lord shone around them, and they were greatly afraid. Then the angel said to them, "Do not be afraid, for behold, I bring you good tidings of great joy which will be to all people. For there is born to you this day in the city of David a Savior, who is Christ the Lord. And this will be the sign to you: You will find a Babe wrapped in swaddling cloths, lying in a manger." And suddenly there was with the angel a multitude of the heavenly host praising God and saying: "Glory to God in the highest, and on earth peace, goodwill toward men!"

So it was, when the angels had gone away from them into heaven, that the shepherds said to one another, "Let us now go to Bethlehem and see this thing that has come to pass, which the Lord has made known to us." And they came with haste and found Mary and Joseph, and the Babe lying in a manger. Now when they had seen Him, they made widely known the saying which was told them concerning this Child. And all those who heard it marveled at those things which were told them by the shepherds. But Mary kept all these things and pondered them in her heart. Then the shepherds returned, glorifying and praising God for all the things that they had heard and seen, as it was told them.

LUKE 2:1-20

OLD
TESTAMENT

THE EARLY
INHABITANTS
OF BETHLEHEM
WERE RELATED
TO THE FAMILY
OF CALEB.

The early inhabitants of Bethlehem were related to the family of Caleb, son of Hezron, son of Perez, son of Judah (1 Chron. 2:51-54; 4:4). In the biblical text, Salma of Caleb, who is among the descendants, is noted as the "father of Bethlehem" (1 Chron. 2:51).[6] The town lies, as stated, south-southwest of Jerusalem near the main north-to-south route that links Jerusalem with Hebron and Egypt. Because of this strategic location, Bethlehem received new prominence overlooking the roads that led to the newly constructed fortresses, Herodium and Masada, built by Herod.[7] Bethlehem's name means "House of Bread" and suggests the fertility of the surrounding valleys and slopes that abounded with figs, vines, almonds, and olive groves.[8]

Bethlehem supplied much of the staple commodities that sustained life in ancient times. How fitting it was that Jesus, born in Bethlehem, called Himself "the bread of life" (John 6:35). Bread was not merely a commodity of ancient life, it was also considered a utensil that is compared to our modern fork or spoon. The significance of this comparison implies that without Christ, we cannot live.

SITE OF
INTEREST

THE TOMB OF
RACHEL, JACOB'S
WIFE

The town of Bethlehem has a rich and full biblical history. In Jacob's time it was called Ephrath, meaning "fruitful."[9] The tomb of Jacob's wife Rachel (who gave birth to Jacob's two youngest sons, Joseph and

AN ENTRANCE TO THE BASILICA OF THE NATIVITY IN BETHLEHEM.

Benjamin) greets all visitors at the entrance of the village and is revered by the people of Israel as a sacred Jewish shrine.

So Rachel died and was buried on the way to Ephrath (that is, Bethlehem).
GENESIS 35:19

The details of Rachel's death and burial are recounted by Jacob to Joseph again later in Scripture (Gen. 48:7).

Bethlehem was also the setting for most of the book of Ruth (Ruth 1:1-2,19,22; 2:4; 4:11). It was here that the famous romance between Boaz and Ruth the Moabitess was enacted. The biblical account gives the student of Scripture wonderful pictures of God's grace and redemption as humankind's "Kinsman Redeemer." It is noteworthy that Ruth could see the mountains of her native land in Moab from her new home in Bethlehem.

Bethlehem's greatest Old Testament notoriety is due to its connection with Ruth's great-grandson, David.[10] It was here in David's hometown that the boy tended his flocks until the prophet Samuel called and anointed him king of Israel (1 Sam. 16:1-13; 17:12; 20:6). King David's exploits would later earn Bethlehem the title of "the city of David" (Luke 2:4,11).

OLD TESTAMENT

BETHLEHEM IS ALSO THE SETTING FOR MOST OF THE BOOK OF RUTH.

EARLY KINGS

IT WAS HERE IN BETHLEHEM THAT DAVID WAS ANOINTED KING OF ISRAEL BY SAMUEL.

73

One such exploit involved David's "three mighty men" who broke through a Philistine garrison, which was camped in Bethlehem, to bring David water from Bethlehem's well (2 Sam. 23:14; 1 Chron. 11:16-18). Since the town had no spring, water had to be collected in cisterns.[11] Bethlehem is mentioned again at the time of the reoccupation after the exile, when about 123 "sons of Bethlehem" returned from Babylon together with 56 "men of Netophah" (Neh. 7:26; Ezr. 2:22).[12] When Rome declared Jerusalem its new *Aelia Capitolina* (A.D. 135), Jewish members of the 24 priestly courses emigrated to Bethlehem.[13]

Bethlehem currently lays claim to the oldest church in all of Christendom. The town's most distinguished landmark is the Basilica of the Nativity built over the site of Jesus' birth. The Basilica, which boasts an octagonal chapel that looks much like a citadel for defense, was constructed over a series of caves by the emperor Constantine and his mother Helena in A.D. 330.

According to author Rivka Gonen, the Romans had previously attempted to eliminate the memory of this revered place by planting a grove dedicated to the pagan god Adonis (lover of Venus) in the vicinity of the cave, to establish his cult in the Grotto.[14] But when Christianity was declared the official religion of the Roman Empire, Constantine and his mother constructed churches to commemorate the holy sites and had the area cleared of any pagan references and rituals.[15]

Renowned for its mosaic floors, frescoed walls, and marble columns, Constantine's Church of the Nativity attracted visitors from all over the known world.[16] After the building was damaged, Justinian I (A.D. 527-565) erected a larger church which extensively altered the original plan of the emperor, though part of the initial structure still stands. The original mosaic floor was excavated in 1934 so that today sections of its impressive design can be witnessed through opened ground-level, protective wood doors.[17] Tradition has it, as noted by Sarah Kochav, that the original church "was spared destruction by the Persians in A.D. 614 because the three Magi portrayed on the facade were dressed in the Persian style."[18]

Despite modifications that were made in the Middle Ages, the traditional manger site that stands today remains the one designed and built by Justinian. The Crusaders found the church in ruins after hundreds of years

SITE OF
INTEREST

THE BASILICA
OF THE
NATIVITY

BYZANTINE

THE BASILICA
WAS
CONSTRUCTED
OVER A SERIES
OF CAVES BY
THE EMPEROR
CONSTANTINE
AND HIS
MOTHER
HELENA IN
A.D. 330.

CRUSADERS

BALDWIN THE
THIRD RESTORED
THE BASILICA
WHILE ISRAEL
WAS UNDER
CRUSADER RULE.

THE STAR OF BETHLEHEM WHICH MARKS THE TRADITIONAL SITE OF JESUS' BIRTH.

of Muslim rule, so another restoration was carried out by Baldwin III.[19] Much of the original rich interior had been vandalized or looted, and the shrine's marble facing had been taken for use in Muslim holy places such as the Dome of the Rock.[20]

The Church of the Nativity is built over the Grotto, honoring one of the most esteemed holy sites in Israel. St. Jerome wrote that perhaps it is "the earth's most sacred spot."[21] It is presently shared by the Greek and Armenian church but is precious to both Christians and Muslims alike. A flight of steps led down to the Grotto. One side of the cave displays a fourteen-pointed silver star that marks the proposed spot of the Savior's birth. An inscription overlaying the area reads: "Here Jesus Christ was born to Virgin Mary" (*Hie de Virgine Maria Jesus Christus natus est*).[22] On the other side of the cave is the manger site and an altar dedicated to the Magi from the East. The Grotto of the Nativity rests beneath a crypt 39 feet long, 11 feet wide, and 9 feet high—hewn out of the rock and lined with

SITE OF
INTEREST

THE GROTTO
OF THE NATIV-
ITY

SITE OF
INTEREST

THE CHURCH
OF ST.
CATHERINE

SITE OF
INTEREST

THE ARMENIAN
MONASTERY
WHERE JEROME
WROTE THE
LATIN VULGATE

CRUSADERS

THE CHURCH OF
THE NATIVITY
SERVED AS THE
CORONATION SITE
OF THE FIRST
TWO CRUSADER
KINGS OF ISRAEL.

marble.[23] It is connected with the Church of St. Catherine which is inhabited by the Franciscans who had originally built a church there in 1871.

South of the Church of the Nativity you will see an Armenian Monastery which houses a large colonnaded hall with Byzantine capitols. Jerome, secretary to Pope Damascus, arrived at Bethlehem on pilgrimage to visit Constantine's church in A.D. 386. The next thirty years of this notable scholar's life were spent in the subterranean caverns beneath the structure while he translated the Bible into Latin.[24] The Latin Vulgate (*Vulgate* meaning "common") became the accepted Bible of the Roman Catholic Church worldwide and maintains this honorable position even today. Several small tombs have been located near the room in which Jerome worked, which are believed to be the burial site of some of the children killed by Herod.

When Bethlehem was granted permission to serve as a bishopric, the Church of the Nativity was raised to the status of a cathedral by the Pope. Because of the town's notoriety, it served as the coronation site of the first two Crusader kings of Jerusalem: Baldwin I (1101) and Baldwin II (1109).[25]

THIS STAINED GLASS WINDOW CELEBRATES JEROME BEING INSPIRED TO CREATE THE LATIN VULGATE.

Personal Reflections

FROM MAP INSIDE THE FRONT COVER: 8-9, B-C.

CHAPTER FOUR

Bethsaida

Then He came to Bethsaida; and they brought
a blind man to Him, and begged Him to touch him.

MARK 8:22

Bethsaida of Galilee means "house of fishing."[1] It was a small fisher-man's settlement on the northwest side of the Sea of Galilee. And, it was located in the land of Gennesaret, a plain that stretched about three miles along the northwest shore (Matt. 14:34; Mark 6:53). The village was thought to have been very close to Capernaum and therefore a part of its fishing district next to the lake. This would help explain the textual diffi-culty between similar biblical references in the gospel of John and the gospel of Mark. Some scholars believe there were two towns of the same name: one to the east of the Jordan River and one to the west.[2]

John states that Philip, Andrew, and his brother Peter were from Bethsaida (John 1:44; 12:21). In fact, because of the proximity of Jesus' calling, the Bible infers that Bethsaida was probably home to as many as five of the twelve apostles: Peter, Andrew, Philip, John, and James.

ACTS OF THE
APOSTLES

BETHSAIDA WAS
PROBABLY THE
HOME OF AS
MANY AS FIVE OF
THE TWELVE
DISCIPLES.

And as He walked by the Sea of Galilee, He saw Simon and Andrew his brother casting a net into the sea; for they were fishermen. Then Jesus said to them, "Follow Me, and I will make you become fishers of men." They immediately left their nets and followed Him. When He had gone a little farther from there, He saw James the son of Zebedee, and John his brother, who also were in the boat mending their nets. And immediately He called them, and they left their father Zebedee in the boat with the hired servants, and went after Him.

MARK 1:16-20

One of Bethsaida's infamous claims is that it was reprimanded along with Capernaum and Chorazin for its unbelief (Matt. 11:20-23; Luke 10:13-15).[3] This contributes to the belief that the city was of some importance. The Gospels refer to Bethsaida seven times, third only to Jerusalem and Capernaum.

In addition, one other Bethsaida, i.e., *et-Tell* or Bethsaida-Julias, is mentioned in Scripture. Philip the Tetrarch raised this village to the rank of a city and called it *Julias,* in honor of Julia, the daughter of Augustus.[4] The historian Josephus declared it to be situated in the lower Gualanitis region and that the Jordan River entered Galilee just below it. Its actual location is two miles inland from the Sea of Galilee on the east side of the Jordan. Traces of an aqueduct and a Roman road join the site with lower Bethsaida, the fishing settlement.

Bethsaida-Julias, or a deserted place nearby belonging to it, is biblically notable for its stated location as the scene of the feeding of the 5,000.

SITE OF
INTEREST

TRACES OF AN
AQUEDUCT AND A
ROMAN ROAD

WHERE JESUS
WALKED

IT WAS NEAR
BETHSAIDA-JULIAS
THAT JESUS FED
THE 5,000.

And the apostles, when they had returned, told Him all that they had done. Then He took them and went aside privately into a deserted place belonging to the city called Bethsaida. But when the multitudes knew it, they followed Him; and He received them and spoke to them about the kingdom of God, and healed those who had need of healing. When the day began to wear away, the twelve came and said to Him, "Send the multitude away, that they may go into the surrounding towns and country, and lodge and get

THE ARCHEOLOGICAL SITE OF THE VILLAGE OF BETHSAIDA HAS YET TO BE EXCAVATED.

provisions; for we are in a deserted place here." But He said to them, "You give them something to eat." And they said, "We have no more than five loaves and two fish, unless we go and buy food for all these people." For there were about five thousand men. And He said to His disciples, "Make them sit down in groups of fifty." And they did so, and made them all sit down. Then He took the five loaves and the two fish, and looking up to heaven, He blessed and broke them, and gave them to the disciples to set before the multitude. So they all ate and were filled, and twelve baskets of the leftover fragments were taken up by them.

LUKE 9:10-17

After feeding the 5,000, Jesus sent His disciples by boat, toward Capernaum, unto Bethsaida (Mark 6:30-44; John 6:5-15; John 6:17; Mark 6:45). But they were blown off their course and landed in Gennesaret.

Now when evening came, His disciples went down to the sea, got into the boat, and went over the sea toward Capernaum. And it was already dark, and Jesus had not come to them. Then the sea arose because a great wind was blowing. So when they had rowed about three or four miles, they saw Jesus walking on the sea and drawing near the boat; and they were afraid. But He said to them, "It is I; do not be afraid." Then they willingly received Him into the boat, and immediately the boat was at the land where they were going.

On the following day, when the people who were standing on the other side of the sea saw that there was no other boat there, except that one which His disciples had entered, and that Jesus had not entered the boat with His disciples, but His disciples had gone away alone—however, other boats came from the Tiberias, near the place where they ate bread after the Lord had given thanks—when the people therefore saw that Jesus was not there, nor His disciples, they also got into boats and came to Capernaum, seeking Jesus.

JOHN 6:16-24

WHERE JESUS
WALKED

JESUS ALSO
HEALED A
BLIND MAN ON
HIS WAY TO
BETHSAIDA.

Jesus also healed a blind man on His way to Bethsaida from Magdala (Matt. 15:39). The gospel of Mark locates this miracle in the "district of Dalmanutha" (Mark 8:10-13).

Then He came to Bethsaida; and they brought a blind man to Him, and begged Him to touch him. So He took the blind man by the hand and led him out of the town. And when He had spit on his eyes and put His hands on him, He asked him if he saw anything. And he looked up and said, "I see men like trees, walking." Then He put His hands on his eyes again and made him look up. And he was restored and saw everyone clearly. Then He sent him away to his house, saying, "Neither go into the town, nor tell anyone in the town."

> Now Jesus and His disciples went out to the towns of Caesarea Philippi; and on the road He asked His disciples, saying to them, "Who do men say that I am?"
> Mark 8:22-27

While many of the villages in the territory of Caesarea Philippi were frequented by the ministry of Jesus and were home to a quarter of His apostles, His ministry seems to have been rejected here.

> "Woe to you, Chorazin! Woe to you, Bethsaida! For if the mighty works which were done in you had been done in Tyre and Sidon, they would have repented long ago in sackcloth and ashes."
> Matthew 11:21

SITE OF
INTEREST

BETHSAIDA IS THE ONLY SITE YOU CAN TOUR TODAY CONNECTED WITH THE LIFE OF JESUS THAT REMAINS UNCHANGED SINCE BIBLICAL TIMES.

Today, after being lost for thousands of years, Bethsaida is being excavated. Speaking at the dig site following its discovery, American theologian Elizabeth McNamer said, "From a Christian point of view, this is the most important town after Jerusalem."[5] The uniqueness of the ancient town's discovery is that it is the only area associated with the life of Jesus that remains unchanged since biblical times. Because the city was never rebuilt after its residents dispersed when the Sea of Galilee receded, archaeological finds are from the original period and display the village as it initially stood.[6] Even fishing hooks have been found among the ruins.

BETHSAIDA

BETHSAIDA

From map inside the front cover: 8-9, C-D.

Chapter Five

Beth-Shean

Then David went and took the bones of Saul, and the bones of Jonathan his son, from the men of Jabesh Gilead who had stolen them from the street of Beth Shan, where the Philistines had hung them up, after the Philistines had struck down Saul in Gilboa.

2 Samuel 21:12

The ancient city of Beth-Shean, also spelled Beth Shan, is geographically located in the Valley of Jalud (now called Nahal Harod). It was positioned strategically at the southern end of the Jezreel Valley and hosted the most important passageway through northern Palestine. The original city sat on a high impressive mound (a "tell") 15 miles south of the Sea of Galilee and four miles west of the River Jordan.[1] Situated on a promontory, it stood as a sentinel over the junction where the Jezreel and Jordan Valleys came together, guarding several trade routes. The Jordan Valley provided a major north-south corridor (The Kings Highway). The Jezreel Valley, running

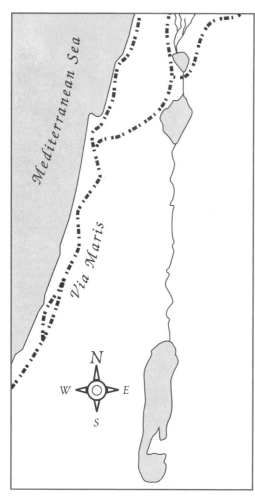

THE VIA MARIS WAS ONE OF THE MOST IMPORTANT TRADE ROUTES OF THE ANCIENT WORLD.

east to west, connected with the Esdraelon plain and provided a major artery for trade moving westward to the coastal road, the Via Maris.[2] The city therefore held an elevated position of great military importance. Its high location provided a wide view of the area and watched over the roads south along the River Jordan, north to Syria by the way of the Sea of Galilee, and west to the Mediterranean coast.[3] Its steep surrounding incline provided a natural defense system.[4] Merchants from all points in the Near East were easily monitored. The mound, the highest in Palestine, has a present height of 300 feet.

The region surrounding Beth-Shean was one of the most agriculturally productive in the land, so resources in the area were plentiful and abundant. The intense summer heat combined with the rich soil created a subtropical paradise.[5] Since the location was fed by several springs and the Jalud River, a perennial water source which emptied eastward into the Jordan, the site has been continuously settled since the ancient Neolithic and Chalcolithic periods.[6] The name in the prehistoric era was *Tell-el Husn*. Archaeological excavations reveal some 20 levels of occupation that extend from the fifth millennium B.C. to the early Arab period. A group of temples were found and are believed to have been built by the Egyptian occupiers in honor of local deities (1400-1200 B.C.). The name *Beth-Shean* is mentioned as one of the conquered cities in the Egyptian texts of Pharaoh Thutmose III (1468 B.C.).[7] After the battle of Megiddo, Beth-Shean became a major base of Egyptian military operations, and it was apparently an important center of worship. At least five or six temple complexes have been unearthed at the site including offering stands, numerous cult objects, and dedicatory inscriptions that mention various deities.[8] One interpretation of *Beth-Shean* means "house of rest" or "quiet." But more than likely it means "the temple of Shan"—the latter being a deity that some have identified with the Sumerian serpent-god Sahan.[9]

OLD TESTAMENT

The biblical references to Beth-Shean relate to the period from Joshua to the United Monarchy. During the conquest of Canaan, the town was given to the tribe of Manasseh (Josh. 17:11) even though it was located in the territory of Issachar (Gen. 49:14-15). However, due to the iron chariots of the Canaanites, Beth-Shean remained in non-Israeli control (Jos. 17:12-16; Judg. 1:27). While King Saul reigned, Israel tried to recapture the highway and break the Philistine hold on the Jezreel Valley (1 Sam. 28:4). But Saul died in the attempt. Scripture teaches that Saul and his army gathered at Mount Gilboa, on the high ground above Beth-Shean, while the Philistines camped at Shunem nearby. In the battle, Saul was wounded, and in order to avoid being taken captive, he fell on his own sword (1 Sam. 31:3-4).

THE BIBLICAL REFERENCES TO BETH-SHEAN RELATE TO THE PERIOD FROM JOSHUA TO THE UNITED MONARCHY.

EARLY KINGS

After the defeat (1006 B.C.), the Philistines decapitated the bodies of Saul and his son Jonathan, then hung them on the wall of the city where a temple of Ashtaroth was located (1 Sam. 31:9-12). Their heads were sent to the main center of Philistia as an announcement of victory (1 Sam. 31:9). Saul's head was displayed in the temple of Dagon, a Philistine deity (1 Chron. 10:8-10). But Saul had once saved Jabesh-Gilead from disaster, and some valiant men from the city daringly rescued the bodies of Saul and Jonathan to return the king's good deed. They took the fallen leader to Jabesh and later to David's men in Benjamin for a proper burial (2 Sam. 21:12-14). Archaeological excavations at Beth-Shean found two temples erected during the Philistine occupation (1700-1000 B.C.) and are thought to be those of Ashtaroth and Dagon. Saul's armour was kept in the "House of Ashtaroth," a well-known fertility goddess. She was also known in other areas of the Near East as Ashtart and Astarte, and as Ishtar to the Babylonians.[10] The temple was about 80 feet long and 62 feet wide. Inside the temple, excavators found a basalt monument which bore the figure of the goddess. She is depicted as wearing a long dress and conical crown customary of all Syrian goddesses.[11] The second temple, "the House of Dagon" was where Saul's head was placed.

IT WAS NEAR BETH-SHEAN THAT SAUL AND JONATHAN DIED DURING BATTLE.

BETH-SHEAN

EARLY KINGS

BETH-SHEAN WAS EVENTUALLY CONQUERED BY DAVID AND INHERITED BY HIS SON SOLOMON.

GREEK/ ROMAN

DURING THE HELLENISTIC PERIOD, THE CITY WAS REBUILT AND RENAMED SCYTHOLOPOLIS.

BETWEEN THE TESTAMENTS

FIRST MACCABEES STATES BETH-SHEAN'S INHABITANTS WERE SPARED MASSACRE BECAUSE OF THEIR HOSPITAL-ITY TO THE LOCAL JEWISH POPULATION.

Beth-Shean was eventually conquered by David and inherited by his son Solomon. The town appears later in Hebrew history in a list of cities included in Solomon's fifth administrative district. The area included the whole Valley of Jezreel reaching into the Transjordan and was controlled by Baana (1 Kings 4:12). Shortly thereafter Sheshonk I, the Egyptian Pharaoh, plundered the city (926 B.C.) and it was not heard from again until Hellenistic times.[12] During the Hellenistic period (in the reign of Antiochus IV, 175-164 B.C.) the city was rebuilt and renamed Scytholopolis—"City of the Scythians."[13] The change came about when the area was settled by a colony of Scythian mercenaries serving the Egyptian king Ptolemy II. At this time temples to the Greek deities Dionysus and Zeus were built. As the city grew, it expanded south from the tell to the valley. The lower city is well excavated and provides a wonderful display of historical ruins. The topography of the location did not allow the city to be constructed in the typical grid pattern of Greek and Roman cities.[14] So it developed much differently around two colonnaded avenues lined with shops, impressive public buildings, and special monuments. Excavations reveal remains of a massive temple on a piazza where the roads of the city converged. The temple may have been dedicated to either Dionysus (god of wine) or to Tyche (goddess of fortune). A Byzantine sixth century mosaic was uncovered which presents the goddess Tyche holding a horn of plenty and wearing a crenellated headdress that may depict the city walls.[15] Under the reign of the Seleucids in the second century B.C., the city acquired an additional name, *Nysa Scytholopolis*. Nysa was a Greek nymph, the nurse of Dionysus, who held a special place in the eyes of the pagan population.[16] Tradition states that Nysa was buried here.

During the Hasmonean Dynasty, Beth-Shean became an important administrative center. It was captured by John Hycranus in 107 B.C. and remained in Maccabean rule until 63 B.C.[17] It is mentioned in the apocryphal Maccabean books as the scene of several confrontations (1 Macc. 5:52; 12:40-42). First Maccabees states that Beth-Shean's inhabitants were spared massacre because of their hospitality to the local Jewish population.[18] It seems Jewish and Gentile communities peaceably co-existed, although the city was predominately Gentile (2 Macc. 12:25-31). Roman forces under Pompey later captured Beth-Shean, keeping the city free until the Arab conquest. In the Roman period, the population was made up of a mixture of pagans, Jews, and Samaritans.

As the Romans continued the expansion of the city north, east, and westward, they also furthered the architectural developments. The theater, with seating capacity near 8,000 people, was built at this time. It was the main cultural attraction of the city. Measuring 270 feet wide and 190 feet deep, the spectators entered through eight vaulted passageways around the circumference (still visible) and two main entrances at the stage level. The theater had three tiers of seating, though only two are actually noticeable.

SITE OF INTEREST

THE ROMAN AMPHITHEATER

The first tier is completely preserved and is still used for special presentations. The foundations of the second tier are still recognizable, though very deteriorated. Some ruins of pilasters behind the theater point to a third, upper-level tier. The stage that was originally paved with stone slabs has been reconstructed. Behind it was an elaborate backdrop with granite and marble columns. The orchestra pit was also paved with marble, believed to have come from Asia Minor, with special seats for dignitaries.[19]

The Romans added a hippodrome on the southern end of the city in the second century A.D. It was enclosed with a wall that supported ten to twelve rows of benches which could seat some 6,000 spectators. The facility was used for gladiatorial events but fell into

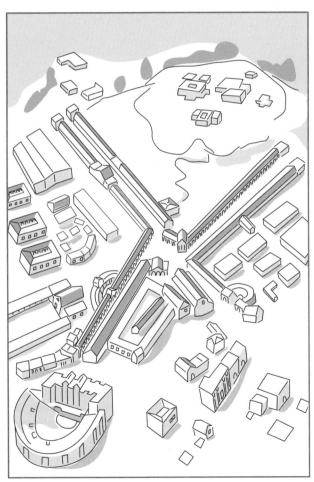

BETH-SHEAN AS IT MIGHT HAVE APPEARED DURING THE TIME OF POMPEY.

BETH-SHEAN

THE ROMAN AMPHITHEATER OF BETH-SHEAN IS STILL USED TODAY FOR SPECIAL PERFORMANCES.

SITE OF
INTEREST

THE ROMAN
HIPPODROME

BYZANTINE

DURING THE
BYZANTINE
PERIOD, SEVERAL
CHURCHES WERE
CONSTRUCTED
HERE.

disuse after the acceptance of Christianity in A.D. 326.[20] Consequently, many of the stones of the facility were taken to be used for construction in other parts of the city. Nonetheless, the general shape remains, and several rows of benches can still be seen. An aqueduct and other public buildings also date to this period. Beth-Shean became the chief city of the Decapolis in the times of the New Testament and obtained considerable prosperity (Matt. 4:25; Mark 5:20; 7:31). The Decapolis was a league of Greco-Roman cities founded by Alexander's veterans. The term is derived from *deka* "ten" and *polis* "city." Beth-Shean was the only city of the confederation that was west of the Jordan River (*Antiq.* 14.5.3). The other nine lay to the east.[21]

Near the end of the fourth century, Scythopolis became the capital of Second Palestine (*Palestina Secunda*)—a province that included the Plain of Esdraelon, Galilee, and part of the northern Transjordan.[22] Scythopolis became the home of Count Joseph, a promoter of early church construction and was visited by Epiphanius and Eusebius.[23] It was during the Byzantine period that several churches were constructed on the site. Most

BETH-SHEAN

impressive was the round church, a cathedral on the summit of the tell that is no longer visible. It had the same floor plan as the original Church of the Holy Sepulcher.[24] A sixth-century monastery was uncovered just north of the mound and the Jalud River which contained several lovely mosaic floors and many inscriptions. A Byzantine bathhouse was also discovered. The heating system was found in the floor and along the walls. The bathing rooms were built into an earlier Roman structure that was roofed with both vaults and domes. The walls were decorated with colored plaster while the floors were covered with marble mosaics.[25]

After the Islamic conquest of A.D. 640, the Greek name for the city, Scytholopolis, was replaced and its old name of Beth-Shean was restored. The conquerors described the event as the "day of Beisan."[26] The area was totally devastated by an earthquake a century later in January of A.D. 749. Then, finally, the site was utterly destroyed by the Crusaders and never regained its former prominence. In time, dust and vegetation covered what was once the most populous and flourishing city of Palestine. Teams of archaeologists have labored to restore this renowned city through the years so that tourists can get a glimpse of its former splendor. The area continues

CRUSADERS

THIS CITY WAS FINALLY DESTROYED BY THE CRUSADERS AND NEVER REGAINED ITS FORMER PROMINENCE.

BETH-SHEAN

THE HIPPODROME OF SCYTHOLOPOLIS (BETH-SHEAN'S GREEK NAME) COULD SEAT 6,000 AND HOSTED GLADIATORIAL EVENTS.

to be inhabited in modern Israel but is known by its new name of *Beisan*, which is adjacent to the old ruins and retains its ancient designation.

BETH-SHEAN

Personal Reflections

FROM MAP INSIDE THE FRONT COVER: 7-8, C-D.

CHAPTER SIX

Caesarea Maritima

And the following day they entered Caesarea.
Now Cornelius was waiting for them, and had
called together his relatives and close friends.
As Peter was coming in, Cornelius met him
and fell down at his feet and worshiped him.
But Peter lifted him up, saying,
"Stand up; I myself am also a man."
And as he talked with him, he went in
and found many who had come together.

ACTS 10:24-27

Caesarea on the Mediterranean was originally a Phoenician fortification called Strato's Tower.[1] According to the Jewish historian Josephus, the city was built by a Sidonian king (Abdashtart, or Strato, using the king's name in Greek) in the fourth century because there was no natural harbor

GREEK/
ROMAN

MARC ANTONY
MADE CAESAREA
A GIFT TO
CLEOPATRA, BUT
WHEN HE WAS
DEFEATED AT
ACTIUM, THE
CITY WAS GIVEN
TO HEROD THE
GREAT.

between Sidon and Egypt. It was later seized during the Maccabean conflict in 96 B.C. by the Hasmonean king Alexander Janneaus, who subsequently opened it as a Jewish settlement.[2] The city was eventually occupied by the Romans when it was captured by the forces of Pompey in 63 B.C. In order to weaken the Hasmonean kingdom, Pompey annexed Strato's Tower and other coastal towns to Roman Syria. Marc Antony proceeded to make Caesarea a gift to Cleopatra of Egypt, but when he was defeated at Actium, the city was given to Herod the Great by the Roman ruler Augustus.[3] The town was in a state of decay (31 B.C.) when Octavian (Caesar Augustus) restored it to the Jewish state. Rome's appointed king, Herod, ambitiously began an extensive rebuilding project that lasted nearly twelve years (25-13 B.C.).[4] He acquired only the most proficient architects and engineers available and employed the most skilled artisans of the time. In honor of his patron, Caesar Augustus, he renamed the city "Caesarea" and its seaport "Sebastos," which is Latin for "Augustus."[5] Roman coins identify it as *Pontius Agusti*.[6]

Herod believed the rebuilding of Caesarea in the style of a Roman provincial capital would be a tangible demonstration of his commitment to the traditions of Rome.[7] Robert Hohlfelder states, "In addition, Herod, a Jew who would eventually rebuild the Second Temple in Jerusalem, could show his sympathy and support for his non-Jewish subjects through the construction of a great Greco-Roman urban center, complete with pagan temples and other structures that were inimical to his Jewish constituency."[8] Caesarea was to be a counterpart to Herod's rebuilding of the Jewish Temple. The 8,000-acre site that encompassed Caesarea Maritima was situated 65 miles west of Jerusalem and 23 miles south (down the coast of Palestine) from Mount Carmel and modern Haifa. It was positioned in the beautiful Plain of Sharon adjacent to the fertile crescent.[9] Because of its location, the city provided a strategic maritime outlet for the agricultural abundance of the region. It was also conveniently stationed on the great caravan trade route, the *Via Maris* ("road along the sea"), between Tyre and Egypt, serving as a busy commercial center for inland trade.[10] Jars have been excavated with age-old grains still inside which testify to the rich fertility of the area.

GREEK/
ROMAN

CAESAREA WAS A
COUNTERPART TO
HEROD'S
REBUILDING OF
THE TEMPLE IN
JERUSALEM.

CAESAREA MARITIMA

Herod intended the city to be the capital of Judea and Samaria and to make it a prosperous international port. He spared no expense in developing its stature, confirming his place in history as a great statesman and master builder.[11] Since the coastline offers few natural harbors and experiences strong currents and battering storms, an artificial harbor was erected which offered safe anchorage for large ships. The protected harbor's construction included a breakwater about 200 feet wide and 120 feet in depth by setting large stones on top of the reefs. Its stones were 50 x 18 x 9 feet in size.[12] These mammoth stones can still be seen extending 160 yards from the shore.[13]

It was Josephus who described how Herod built the impressive harbor (a literary description that is unique in

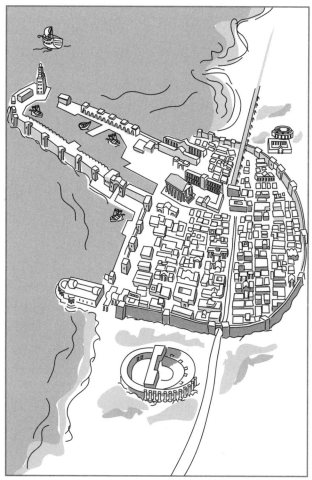

THIS RECONSTRUCTIVE DRAWING SHOWS HOW CAESAREA MARITIMA MIGHT HAVE LOOKED AFTER HEROD I REBUILT OF THE CITY.

ancient texts).[14] His description of the construction was originally considered a conscious exaggeration. But underwater excavations have proven his declarations accurate. The undertaking was an engineering marvel of the age.[15] The curved breakwater was built by pouring conglomerate hydraulic cement into wooden frameworks.[16] The concrete was a combination of earth, crushed limestone, and volcanic ash from Mount Vesuvius in Italy.[17] As the mixture absorbed the sea water, which was forced out through the wooden walls, it hardened in place. The artificial bay consisted of three parts—the inner basin, the middle basin, and the

CAESAREA'S AQUEDUCTS HAVE BEEN PRESERVED IN THE COASTAL DUNES AND ARE STILL VISIBLE TODAY.

CAESAREA MARITIMA

curved breakwater which enclosed a vast area. The middle basin, notes Sarah Kochav, was the main harbor into which "the entrance of water was regulated by a system of sluices designed to force through a current of water to wash away the sediment silting up."[18] The aesthetics of the harbor entrance included elaborate buildings with statues of Herod's family on elevated, massive platforms to guide and welcome its sailors. The harbor was also guarded by a lighthouse entitled Drusus—so named after Herod's friend.[19] The port was so immense that it could accommodate nearly 150 ships in its inner and outer harbors.[20] Merchant trade flourished in the port so tremendously that an inscription on a coin of Nero bears the name *Caesarea by Augustus' Harbor.*[21]

The rebuilt city (on the former Phoenician site) was dedicated in 10 B.C. It was renowned for hosting magnificent games and was declared the official seat and capital of Palestine.[22] The city featured Roman engineering and Hellenistic-type construction: a theater (built on the edge of the coast with a view of the sea), a hippodrome (horse racing facility) that sat 30,000 spectators, colonnaded streets, hotels for the seamen, a spa center

SITE OF
INTEREST

THE
AMPHITHEATER
BUILT BY HEROD
THE GREAT

complete with pools and hot water, harbor warehouses, underground sewers that were flushed by the action of the sea, a market place (agora), paved streets laid out on a grid plan, and an amphitheater. The amphitheater, which is still functional, displays such precise acoustics in its round construction that a whisper from the stage can be heard in the gallery. This marvel of engineering was also, very unfortunately, the site of much Roman aggression toward the Jews and was used to murder many Christians. To celebrate the birthday of his brother Domitian (A.D. 70), the Roman ruler Titus marched 2,500 Jews into the amphitheater to be eaten by wild beasts.[23] The facility, measuring 195 by 310 feet, was larger than the world-renown Coliseum built in Rome a century later.[24]

The water system of Caesarea is considered one of the best conceived in the entire country. Water was brought to the site by a system of aqueducts. Its two artificial waterways were made water-tight by a coating of plaster. The system's "high-level aqueduct" brought drinking water from the southern slopes of Mount Carmel. Its "low-level aqueduct" brought water for irrigation from the dam across the Zanga River (*Nahal Tanninim*).[25] Ruins of the bridge-like structures have been preserved in the coastal sand dunes and are still visible.

SITE OF
INTEREST

CAESAREAN
AQUEDUCTS

The focal point of Herod's city was a vast, impressive temple dedicated to the divine Caesar and Rome.[26] Inside the temple were colossal statues of Caesar Augustus and Roma (the goddess of the city of Rome). The edifice was visible from the Mediterranean Sea and exemplified the meeting point of the city and harbor.[27] It was situated on the shoreline overlooking the bay in a prominent position that provided a monumental landmark for incoming ships.

GREEK/
ROMAN

IT WAS FROM
CAESAREA
THAT ROME
ORDERED THE
CENSUS THAT
BROUGHT
JOSEPH AND
MARY TO
BETHLEHEM.

In A.D. 6, Caesarea was absorbed by the Romans into their vast empire and from that time forward was considered a part of the new Roman province of Judea. The city became the new provincial capital and administrative center of the country from where Rome ordered a census of the country (recorded in the gospel of Luke 2:1-2) to determine tax liabilities.[28] It was at this time that the city became known as *Caesarea Maritima*.[29] Since Caesarea was one of several cities of the same name, Greek and Latin sources have specified the city as Caesarea near Sebastos—the harbor, Caesarea of Straton, and (most common) Caesarea of Palestine. The

CAESAREA MARITIMA

GREEK/ ROMAN

PONTIUS
PILATE'S MAIN
RESIDENCE WAS
IN THE GOVER-
NOR'S PALACE
IN CAESAREA
WHEN HE
CONDEMNED
JESUS TO THE
CROSS.

ACTS OF THE APOSTLES

IT WAS IN
CORNELIUS'
CAESAREAN
HOME THAT
GENTILES
FIRST
RECEIVED THE
GOSPEL.

popularity of the name of *Caesarea Maritima* has been debated by histori-ans and considered by some to be relatively unknown in antiquity.[30]

The city of Caesarea has a rich biblical history. It was the official residence of both the Herodian kings and the Roman procurators.[31] The most famous of these procurators, Pontius Pilate, resided in the gover-nor's palace while he was procurator of Judea (John 19). It was during this time that he traveled to Jerusalem for the Passover and condemned Jesus to the cross.

Caesarea was also the military headquarters for Rome's forces in Judea, as well as the home of Cornelius the centurion. By his invitation, Simon Peter was summoned to Caesarea from Joppa after receiving a vision from God that declared, "What God has cleansed you must not call common" (Acts 10:9-19). It was there in Cornelius' Caesarean home that Peter first preached to the Gentiles that God shows no partiality, and "the Holy Spirit fell upon all those who heard the word" (Acts 10:44). It was an event that would change the shape of Christianity forever.

> There was a certain man in Caesarea called Cornelius, a centurion of what was called the Italian Regiment, a devout man and one who feared God with all his household, who gave alms generously to the people, and prayed to God always. About the ninth hour of the day he saw clearly in a vision an angel of God coming in and saying to him, "Cornelius!" And when he observed him, he was afraid, and said, "What is it, lord?" So he said to him, "Your prayers and your alms have come up for a memorial before God. Now send men to Joppa, and send for Simon whose surname is Peter. He is lodging with Simon, a tanner, whose house is by the sea. He will tell you what you must do." And when the angel who spoke to him had departed, Cornelius called two of his household servants and a devout soldier from among those who waited on him continu-ally. So when he had explained all these things to them, he sent them to Joppa.
>
> ACTS 10:1-8

CAESAREA MARITIMA

Caesarea was also the residence of Philip the evangelist who had four unmarried daughters who prophesied (Acts 8:40; 21:8-9). They hosted Paul and Luke on the return from their third missionary journey. And, Caesarea was home to Herod Agrippa, who departed from Jerusalem to his seaside home at the time of Peter's miraculous escape from prison.

ACTS OF THE
APOSTLES

PHILIP THE
EVANGELIST
HOSTED PAUL
AND LUKE IN
CAESAREA ON
THE RETURN OF
THEIR THIRD
MISSIONARY
JOURNEY.

> But when Herod had searched for him and not found him, he examined the guards and commanded that they should be put to death. And he went down from Judea to Caesarea, and stayed there.
>
> ACTS 12:19

It was also in Caesarea that Herod later arrayed himself in royal apparel as a god and was smitten dead by the angel of the Lord.

> Now Herod had been very angry with the people of Tyre and Sidon; but they came to him with one accord, and having made Blastus the king's personal aide their friend, they asked for peace, because their country was supplied with food by the king's country. So on a set day Herod, arrayed in royal apparel, sat on his throne and gave an oration to them. And the people kept shouting, "The voice of a god and not of a man!" Then immediately an angel of the Lord struck him, because he did not give glory to God. And he was eaten by worms and died. But the word of God grew and multiplied.
>
> ACTS 12:20-24

Caesarea has a notable position in the book of Acts as a political and religious center. After the arrest of the apostle Paul at Jerusalem and the plot was unveiled to kill him (Acts 21:15-34), he was secretly taken under guard to Caesarea to be held as a prisoner. As a result, Caesarea became Paul's "enforced" residence for two years during his appearances before Felix, Festus, the council, and Agrippa II (Acts 23:23-27:1).

ACTS OF THE
APOSTLES

CAESAREA
BECAME PAUL'S
"ENFORCED"
RESIDENCE FOR
TWO YEARS
DURING HIS
APPEARANCES
BEFORE FELIX,
FESTUS, THE
COUNCIL, AND
AGRIPPA II.

CAESAREA MARITIMA

"Therefore, King Agrippa, I was not disobedient to the heavenly vision, but declared first to those in Damascus and in Jerusalem, and throughout all the region of Judea, and then to the Gentiles, that they should repent, turn to God, and do works befitting repentance. For these reasons the Jews seized me in the temple and tried to kill me. Therefore, having obtained help from God, to this day I stand, witnessing both to small and great, saying no other things than those which the prophets and Moses said would come—that the Christ would suffer, that He would be the first to rise from the dead, and would proclaim light to the Jewish people and to the Gentiles."

Now as he thus made his defense, Festus said with a loud voice, "Paul, you are beside yourself! Much learning is driving you mad!" But he said, "I am not mad, most noble Festus, but speak the words of truth and reason. For the king, before whom I also speak freely, knows these things; for I am convinced that none of these things escapes his attention, since this thing was not done in a corner. King Agrippa, do you believe the prophets? I know that you do believe." Then Agrippa said to Paul, "You almost persuade me to become a Christian." And Paul said, "I would to God that not only you, but also all who hear me today, might become both almost and altogether such as I am, except for these chains." When he had said these things, the king stood up, as well as the governor and Bernice and those who sat with them; and when they had gone aside, they talked among themselves, saying, "This man is doing nothing deserving of death or chains." Then Agrippa said to Festus, "This man might have been set free if he had not appealed to Caesar."

ACTS 26:19-32

Paul finally set sail in chains from Caesarea on his famous voyage to Rome after being detained for many years (Acts 27:1-28:31).[32] Transported along with certain other prisoners, Caesarea served as the apostle's starting point from where he fulfilled the word of the Lord: "Be of good cheer, Paul; for as you have testified for Me in Jerusalem, so you must also bear witness at Rome"(Acts 23:11). The scripturally documented journey included very perilous and miraculous events (Acts 27:9-44; 28:1-10).

Though Caesarea was predominantly pagan, the city maintained a substantial Jewish minority. The mixed population, not unlike other New Testament Mediterranean communities, made for a volatile climate that often erupted into disputes between Jew and Gentile.[33] The Greek-Syrian population of Caesarea supported Roman policy; however, the city's large Jewish community opposed it. So clashes were inevitable.[34] One such skirmish resulted in the desecration of the synagogue Knestha d'Meredtha which precipitated the First Jewish/Roman War.[35] Josephus notes the war actually began with Caesarea's A.D. 65-66 Jewish/Gentile riots in which 20,000 Jews were slaughtered in an hour. During this time of unrest, the Tenth Roman Legion was sent from Syria to join up with other auxiliary forces which amassed an army that numbered 60,000 strong.[36] After Nero appointed Vespasian commander of the Roman forces in Judea, the Roman commander wintered at Caesarea and used it as his main support base during the Jewish revolt. To show his appreciation when Vespasian was appointed emperor, he granted the city the rank of a Roman colony making it *Colonia Prima Flavia Augusta Caesariensis*. Severus Alexander eventually gave it the title Metropolis of the province Syria Palestina.[37]

GREEK/
ROMAN

JOSEPHUS NOTES THE FIRST JEWISH/ROMAN WAR ACTUALLY BEGAN WITH CAESAREA'S RIOTS IN WHICH 20,000 JEWS WERE SLAUGHTERED IN AN HOUR.

THE CRUSADER MOAT AND WALLS THAT ONCE PROTESTED CAESAREA MARITIMA.

The Jewish rebels, who at this time had taken control of Jerusalem and other areas of the countryside, were ill-equipped, untrained, and divided among themselves.[38] So Vespasian, realizing that Jerusalem was torn by civil war, took advantage of the situation and conquered Perea, Judea, and Idumea.[39] He was about to attack Jerusalem when he received the news of Nero's death and his appointment as emperor in Rome (A.D. 69). When Vespasian departed to be crowned, he left his son Titus in charge of the military operations in Judea. So it was from historic Caesarea that the armies of Titus embarked on their campaign to besiege the city of Jerusalem in A.D. 70; and it was back to Caesarea that the Jewish prisoners were paraded in triumphal procession to be forced into the empire's theaters as food for wild beasts.[40] The Roman armies under Flavius Silva (one of Titus' generals) returned to Caesarea in A.D. 73 after conquering the fortress at Masada in eastern Judea.

Despite all the conflicts, Christianity would eventually flourish here. The scholar Origen came to Caesarea in A.D. 231 and revived the city as a Christian center. He accumulated an expansive library that attracted many students and other scholars.[41] The famous church historian Eusebius, author of the history of the early Church, compiled a book of place names in the Holy Land, the *Onomasticon* (a Greek term for "name list"), in the fourth century.[42] Eusebius also served as archbishop of Caesarea from A.D. 313-337 and was religious advisor to Constantine.[43] A Christian church would actually be built on Caesarea's old temple platform. Nonetheless, Christians would once again be massacred in this coastal metropolis; but this time, by Jews and Samaritans in A.D. 548.[44] Caesarea would ultimately pass into the control of the Muslims in A.D. 638 and was retaken by Christians only for a short time during the Crusades.[45] Visitors to the area experience the influence of European architecture from the Crusader Period, including such sights as the moat, walls, and the main gate. The ancient name in the Arabic form, *Kaiseriyeh,* remains with the site.[46]

While only partial excavations have been attempted at Caesarea, there was a very important archaeological discovery in 1959. A stone was uncovered with an inscription that bears the name of Pontius Pilate and the emperor Tiberius. It reads "Pontius Pilate, the Prefect of Judea, has dedicated to the people of Caesarea a temple in honor of Tiberius."[47] It is

CRUSADERS

CAESAREA STILL
EXHIBITS
EUROPEAN
ARCHITECTURE
BUILT BY THE
CRUSADERS.

CAESAREA MARITIMA

the first known archaeological record that lends credibility to the gospel account concerning Pilate's existence and status. In addition, an archives building was excavated on the coast and revealed several inscriptions on its mosaic floors. Included among the inscriptions were two quotations from the Greek text of the book of Romans.[48]

> For rulers are not a terror to good works, but to evil. Do you want to be unafraid of the authority? Do what is good, and you will have praise from the same.
>
> Romans 13:3

This stone was discovered in Caesarea in 1959. The inscription is translated, "Pontius Pilate, the Prefect of Judea, has dedicated to the people of Caesarea a temple in honor of Tiberius."

Personal Reflections

CAESAREA MARITIMA

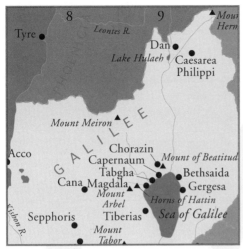

FROM MAP INSIDE THE FRONT COVER: 8-9, A-B.

CHAPTER SEVEN

Caesarea Philippi

When Jesus came into the region of
Caesarea Philippi, He asked His disciples, saying,
"Who do men say that I, the Son of Man, am?"

MATTHEW 16:13

Caesarea Philippi (*Kaisareia he Philippou*) is another strategic city mentioned in the Bible. It sat on a rocky terrace at the southwest lower slope of Mount Hermon in the extreme north of Israel.[1] Situated near the spring Nahe Baniyas (one of the three sources of the River Jordan that gushes from a cave in the bluffs), the area is one of the most beautiful and luxurious in Israel. Because it experiences water in abundance, rich groves of fruitful trees and grassy fields invited a city of considerable size that possessed a guardian position over the fertile plains of Syria and Israel.[2] It was, and still is, an inspiring setting.

The site has always maintained a religious/cultic presence and was sought as popular place of worship for Semetic deities.[3] Baal, the Canaanite deity, was worshipped here during the time of the Old

A PLACE OF WORSHIP TO THE GREEK GOD, PAN.

Testament (Josh. 11:17; 12:7; 13:5; Judg. 3:3; 1 Chron. 5:23). The Greeks later worshiped their deity, Pan, at the same location earning the locale the name of *Paneasar Panias*—"the deity of Pan" (the god of springs and shepherds of ancient Greece).[4] It was pronounced *Banias* in Arabic because there is no "p" in the Arabic alphabet.[5] A niche cut in an area rock surrounded by a decorative couch design still bears an inscription that honors the nymph Echo and the Greek god, Diopan, "lover of music."[6] The shrine already maintained religious prominence and probably was simply rededicated to the new deity. Scholar Bargil Pixner suggests that pagans may have made sacrifices to the gods and demons of the underworld at this site. A local cave was thought to be the passageway to Hades during the Hellenistic and Roman periods.[7]

GREEK/ ROMAN

THE ROMAN CITY PANIAS WAS RENAMED CAESAREA PHILIPPI UNDER PHILIP THE TETRARCH.

Before the city was renamed Caesarea Philippi, the city (then called Panias) was given to King Herod by the Roman Emperor Augustus. Josephus records that Herod constructed an elaborate palace and a temple of white marble in honor of the emperor.[8] After the death of Herod, his son, Philip the Tetrarch, became ruler of the region and made Panias his capitol. It was then that he renamed it, Caesarea Philippi, in honor of himself and Caesar Augustus. The name *Kaisereia Philippi* came to be used to distinguish it from the Caesarea on the Mediterranean coast (Acts 8:40).[9] The city later formed part of the kingdom of Agrippa II who named it Neronias,

CAESAREA PHILIPPI

in honor of Nero, but the name did not remain in the daily usage of the culture.[10] Josephus mentions the city as a stopping place for the Roman armies under Vespasian and Titus during the Jewish War of A.D. 66-70, marching "from that Caesarea which lay by the seaside and came to that which is named Caesarea Philippi."[11]

In the New Testament, Caesarea Philippi controlled the large area surrounding it, including neighboring villages (Mark 8:27). Holy Scripture also has referred to it as "the district" (Matt. 16:13 NASB).[12] It was here that Jesus questioned His disciples about His Messianic identity and began to prepare them for His approaching suffering, death, and resurrection. It is significant that Jesus addressed His disciples concerning His deity at this alleged mystical spot. He is the fulfillment of everything that humankind has ever misguidedly sought through foreign and false deities.

WHERE JESUS WALKED

IT WAS HERE THAT JESUS QUESTIONED HIS DISCIPLES ABOUT HIS MESSIANIC IDENTITY.

> Now Jesus and His disciples went out to the towns of Caesarea Philippi; and on the road He asked His disciples, saying to them, "Who do men say that I am?" So they answered, "John the Baptist; but some say, Elijah; and others, one of the prophets." He said to them, "But who do you say that I am?" Peter answered and said to Him, "You are the Christ."
> MARK 8:27-29

WHERE JESUS WALKED

THE MOUNT OF TRANS-FIGURATION IS ALSO NEAR CAESAREA PHILIPPI.

Also located near Caesarea Philippi is the Mount of Transfiguration referred to by Peter as the "holy mountain" (2 Peter 1:18). It is from the gospel narratives that one may gather that Jesus went with His disciples from Bethsaida to the neighboring Caesarea Philippi (Matt. 17:1 ff., Mark 9:2 ff., Luke 9:28 ff.). Some six or eight days later, He went up into a high mountain to pray, taking with Him Peter, James, and John. After descending the next day, He healed a demonically oppressed boy and then passed through Galilee to Capernaum.

> Now after six days Jesus took Peter, James, and John, and led them up on a high mountain apart by themselves; and He was transfigured before them. His clothes became shining, exceedingly white, like snow, such as no launderer on earth can whiten

CAESAREA PHILIPPI

them. And Elijah appeared to them with Moses, and they were talking with Jesus. Then Peter answered and said to Jesus, "Rabbi, it is good for us to be here; and let us make three tabernacles: one for You, one for Moses, and one for Elijah"— because he did not know what to say, for they were greatly afraid. And a cloud came and overshadowed them; and a voice came out of the cloud, saying, "This is My beloved Son. Hear Him!" Suddenly, when they had looked around, they saw no one anymore, but only Jesus with themselves. Now as they came down from the mountain, He commanded them that they should tell no one the things they had seen, till the Son of Man had risen from the dead. . . .

And when He came to the disciples, He saw a great multitude around them, and scribes disputing with them. Immediately, when they saw Him, all the people were greatly amazed, and running to Him, greeted Him. And He asked the scribes, "What are you discussing with them?" Then one of the crowd answered and said, "Teacher, I brought You my son, who has a mute spirit. "And wherever he seizes him, he throws him down; he foams at the mouth, gnashes his teeth, and becomes rigid. So I spoke to Your disciples, that they should cast it out, but they could not." He answered him and said, "O faithless generation, how long shall I be with you? How long shall I bear with you? Bring him to Me." Then they brought him to Him. And when he saw Him, immediately the spirit convulsed him, and he fell on the ground and wallowed, foaming at the mouth. So He asked his father, "How long has this been happening to him?" And he said, "From childhood. And often he has thrown him both into the fire and into the water to destroy him. But if You can do anything, have compassion on us and help us." Jesus said to him, "If you can believe, all things are possible to him who believes." Immediately the father of the child cried out and said with tears, "Lord, I believe; help my unbelief!" When Jesus saw that the people came running together, He rebuked the unclean spirit, saying to it: "Deaf and dumb spirit, I command you,

CAESAREA PHILIPPI

come out of him and enter him no more!" Then the spirit cried out, convulsed him greatly, and came out of him. And he became as one dead, so that many said, "He is dead." But Jesus took him by the hand and lifted him up, and he arose. And when He had come into the house, His disciples asked Him privately, "Why could we not cast him out?" So He said to them, "This kind can come out by nothing but prayer and fasting."

Then they departed from there and passed through Galilee, and He did not want anyone to know it.

MARK 9:2-9,14-30

The importance of Caesarea Philippi to Christianity in general increased with time. The Christian community suffered much initial persecution in the area. But by the fourth and fifth centuries it had been established as an episcopacy that provided two of its bishops to participate in the early church councils—the Nicene Council in A.D. 325, and the Council of Chalcedon in A.D. 451.[13]

CAESAREA PHILIPPI

Personal Reflections

FROM MAP INSIDE THE FRONT COVER: 8-9, B-C.

CHAPTER EIGHT

Cana

This beginning of signs Jesus did in Cana of Galilee, and manifested His glory; and His disciples believed in Him.

JOHN 2:11

Cana of Galilee (*Kana tes Galilaias*) is mentioned only four times in the Bible, all in the gospel of John. Cana was in the highlands of Galilee west of the lake (as one had to go "down" from there to Capernaum).[1] It was the location at which Jesus worked His first miracle, and it was the home of Nathanael—one of the twelve (John 21:2).

The Greek term *Kana*, probably transliterates from an old Hebrew form, *Qana*, "place of reeds."[2] It is an appropriate description of Cana, for it overlooks a marshy plain where reeds are still plentiful today. The full name, Cana of Galilee, was used to distinguish it from other places with the same name (Josh. 16:8; 19:28) such as Kanah located near the Phoenician city of Tyre.[3]

Jewish weddings in Jesus' time had some interesting customs. The celebration was generally open to the community, so that all were

113

WHERE JESUS
WALKED

JESUS WORKED
HIS FIRST
RECORDED
MIRACLE IN
CANA.

welcome. And it was at such a wedding in Cana that Jesus performed His first miracle of turning water into wine. The festivities continued as long as food and drink remained. This would explain in part why the host ran out of wine at the wedding Jesus attended. Another tradition was to be married on a Tuesday: "And the third day there was a marriage in Cana of Galilee" (John 2:1). This practice springs from the Creation account in the book of Genesis. On the third day of creation, Tuesday, God twice pronounced the words "It was good." So Tuesday was a day associated with double blessings. It became customary to begin a marriage or a long journey on a Tuesday. Even today, it is difficult to reserve a hall in Israel for this special occasion on a Tuesday.

On the third day there was a wedding in Cana of Galilee, and the mother of Jesus was there. Now both Jesus and His disciples were invited to the wedding. And when they ran out of wine, the mother of Jesus said to Him, "They have no wine." Jesus said to her, "Woman, what does your concern have to do with Me? My hour has not yet come." His mother said to the servants, "Whatever He says to you, do it." Now there were set there six waterpots of stone, according to the manner

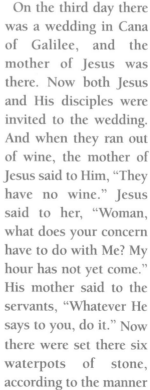

A WATER POT OF STONE SET HERE TO HONOR JESUS' TURNING WATER INTO WINE.

of purification of the Jews, containing twenty or thirty gallons apiece. Jesus said to them, "Fill the waterpots with water." And they filled them up to the brim. And He said to them, "Draw some out now, and take it to the master of the feast." And they took it. When the master of the feast had tasted the water that was made wine, and did not know where it came from (but the servants who had drawn the water knew), the master of the feast called the bridegroom. And he said to him, "Every man at the beginning sets out the good wine, and when the guests have well drunk, then the inferior. You have kept the good wine until now!" This beginning of signs Jesus did in Cana of Galilee, and manifested His glory; and His disciples believed in Him. After this He went down to Capernaum, He, His mother, His brothers, and His disciples; and they did not stay there many days.
JOHN 2:1-12

It is apparent in this passage of Scripture that Jesus worked this miracle at the behest of his mother to relieve the embarrassment caused by the shortage of marriage-feast wine. It was also in Cana of Galilee that Jesus later worked another miracle when He announced to the official from Capernaum the healing of his dying son. This miracle was received by believing "the word that Jesus spoke" even though Jesus had not directly laid His hands on the official or had any personal contact with the child in any way. The officer simply believed what Jesus had said.

So Jesus came again to Cana of Galilee where He had made the water wine. And there was a certain nobleman whose son was sick at Capernaum. When he heard that Jesus had come out of Judea into Galilee, he went to Him and implored Him to come down and heal his son, for he was at the point of death. Then Jesus said to him, "Unless you people see signs and wonders, you will by no means believe." The nobleman said to Him, "Sir, come down before my child dies!" Jesus said to him, "Go your way; your son lives." So the man believed the word that Jesus spoke to him, and he went his way. And as he was now going

down, his servants met him and told him, saying, "Your son lives!" Then he inquired of them the hour when he got better. And they said to him, "Yesterday at the seventh hour the fever left him." So the father knew that it was at the same hour in which Jesus said to him, "Your son lives." And he himself believed, and his whole household. This again is the second sign Jesus did when He had come out of Judea into Galilee.
JOHN 4:46-54

When Titus took military action to defeat the Jewish rebels in the First Jewish War of A.D. 70, Cana became the headquarters for the defense of Galilee by Josephus, who later became a famous Jewish historian.[4]

Personal Reflections

FROM MAP INSIDE THE FRONT COVER: 8-9, B-C.

CHAPTER NINE

Capernaum

A few days later, when Jesus again entered Capernaum,
the people heard that he had come home.

MARK 2:1 NIV

Capernaum was an important place in the Galilean ministry of Jesus and was considered the headquarters of His greater public ministry (Matt. 4:13). He may have moved here in response to His rejection at Nazareth. Scripture cites Capernaum as "His own city" (Matt. 9:1).[1] It is the only place in the Gospels of which it is said that Jesus was "at home" (Mark 2:1 NASB). It is here that Jesus, following the cleansing of the Temple, brought His family and His disciples to stay "for a few days" (John 2:12 NIV).[2] Though it was a small, unfortified farming and commercial fishing city, it was still the most significant city on the northern shore of the lake.

Capernaum is considered to be the original location of Tell Hum—a site inhabited continuously from the first century B.C. through the seventh century A.D.[3] Tell Hum (as called by the Arabs) was the nearest village to the Jordan River. It was also near a bountiful spring that watered the plain

119

He healed a crippled hand, cast out demons,

healed the woman with the issue of blood,

raised Jairus' daughter from the dead, healed

Peter's mother-in-law, and cured the palsied man

who had been lowered down through

the roof . . . in Capernaum.

of Gennesaret (Mark 6:53; John 6:22,59) the site of *et-Tabgha* or *Heptapegon* in Greek; i.e., "the Place of Seven Springs."[4] Josephus refers to the springs of Heptapegon as the springs of Capharnaum.[5] According to Theodosius (A.D. 530), if one traveled from Tiberias to the northwestern shores of the Sea of Galilee, the route to each site (in Roman miles) would be: Magdala (two miles), Heptapegon or Tabgha—Place of Seven Springs (two miles), Capernaum (two miles), and Bethsaida (six miles).[6]

WHERE JESUS
WALKED

CAPERNAUM WAS
CONSIDERED THE
HEADQUARTERS
OF JESUS'
GREATER PUBLIC
MINISTRY.

It was here in Jesus' chosen ministry base that many of His miracles occurred (Luke 4:23). He healed a crippled hand (Matt. 12:10-13), cast out demons (Luke 4:33-36), healed the woman with the issue of blood (Matt. 9:20-22), raised Jairus' daughter from the dead (Mark 5:22-24), healed Peter's mother-in-law (Luke 4:38-39), and cured the palsied man who had been lowered down through the roof by his friends (Luke 5:17-25). It was also in Capernaum that Jesus taught His disciples their spiritual need to "eat My flesh" and "drink My blood" (John 6:51-58). Some of His own disciples rejected Him over this so-called "hard saying" (John 6:60-66).

The populace of Capernaum was comprised mainly of poor people who were completely dependent upon God and nature. They depended on the rains for prosperous harvests and good weather for fishing success. So they were a very open-hearted people and received the ministry of Jesus with enthusiasm. The Sea of Galilee was everything for the local citizens including commerce, food, and even transportation. When a miracle occurred connected with the lake, it had a deep impact upon the villagers and caused many area residents to follow Jesus and His disciples.

Understandably, because Capernaum was Jesus' home of residence, many of His biblically recorded ministry activities took place there. A great number of Jesus' parables were taught in Capernaum: the sower (Mark 4:1-9), the tares and the wheat (Matt. 13:24-30), the grain of mustard seed (Mark 4:30-32), the leaven (Luke 13:20-21), the treasure hidden in the field (Matt. 13:44), and the parable of the fishing net (Matt. 13:47-50).[7] Three of His disciples also resided in Capernaum—Peter, Andrew, and Matthew. It seems Peter and Andrew moved from Bethsaida to this seaside village before they heard the call of the Master (John 1:44; Mark 1:29). And, it was from his Capernaum-based office that Matthew the tax collector departed to follow Jesus (Matt. 9:9-13). It was also in this lake-side village that the Pharisees challenged the beliefs and actions of Jesus (Mark 2:24-28; 7:5-13), and near where surrounding area crowds, after being fed, attempted to force Him into a political position.[8] Because of the teaching and healing ministry of Jesus, multitudes came to Capernaum to be near the Master. So one of the earliest congregations of the new religion formed in this city and played a prominent role in the beginning and development of Christianity.[9]

Capernaum (*Kapernaoum* in Greek and/or *Kaphar-Nahum*, "village of Nahum" in Hebrew) is not specified in the Old Testament. However, the city whose ruins stretch over a mile had political importance in the Gospels of the New Testament.[10] This significance is indicated by the presence of a Roman centurion and a detachment of troops, a customs station where Matthew worked, and the placement of a high officer of the king, Herod Antipas (Matt. 8:5-9; 9:9; John 4:46). Its tollhouse was in the proximity to major east-west highways and trade routes (Mark 2:14). Tax collections from passing caravans prospered the city greatly.[11] Jesus' pronouncement of doom upon Capernaum also advances the weightiness, prominence, and importance that the city occupied in ancient times.

> "And you Capernaum, who are exalted to heaven, will be brought down to Hades."
> MATTHEW 11:23

WHERE JESUS WALKED

A GREAT NUMBER OF JESUS' PARABLES WERE TAUGHT IN CAPERNAUM.

WHERE JESUS WALKED

CAPERNAUM WAS THE PLACE FROM WHICH MATTHEW WAS CALLED TO BE A DISCIPLE

An important ruin of Capernaum is a third or fourth-century synagogue considered to be the best preserved in Palestine.[12] It may be the same site mentioned in the New Testament scriptures noting the miracle of the paralyzed servant of the Roman centurion.

> Now when He concluded all His sayings in the hearing of the people, He entered Capernaum. And a certain centurion's servant, who was dear to him, was sick and ready to die. So when he heard about Jesus, he sent elders of the Jews to Him, pleading with Him to come and heal his servant. And when they came to Jesus, they begged Him earnestly, saying that the one for whom He should do this was deserving, "for he loves our nation, and has built us a synagogue." Then Jesus went with them. And when He was already not far from the house, the centurion sent friends to Him, saying to Him, "Lord, do not trouble Yourself, for I am not worthy that You should enter

THE STONE "ARK" DISPLAYED IN CAPERNAUM.

under my roof. Therefore I did not even think myself worthy to come to You. But say the word, and my servant will be healed. For I also am a man placed under authority, having soldiers under me. And I say to one, 'Go,' and he goes; and to another, 'Come,' and he comes; and to my servant, 'Do this,' and he does it." When Jesus heard these things, He marveled at him, and turned around and said to the crowd that followed Him, "I say to you, I have not found such great faith, not even in Israel!" And those who were sent, returning to the house, found the servant well who had been sick.

LUKE 7:1-10

The synagogue measures 65 feet in length, is two stories high, and is constructed of white limestone rather than the local black basalt found in abundance in the area. Beneath the ruins, traces have been found of an earlier synagogue built on the same plan as the latter one, but with thicker walls of black basalt. This earlier discovery is probably the synagogue mentioned in the New Testament.[13] The later white limestone edifice more than likely dominated the cityscape in size, elaborateness, and color—pitted against the black basalt houses. The building was a basilica with a gabled roof and galleries for women on three sides that were reached by an exterior set of stairs.[14] The "chief seats" rest along the side and at the south end of the structure (towards Jerusalem). There also remains a carved stone likeness of what looks like a small temple on wheels, which may or may not be a representation of Old Testament Israel's Ark of the Covenant. Also on display are reliefs of the seven typical, natural fruits of the land of Israel: wheat, barley, dates, pomegranates, figs, olives, and grapes. Because of the Old Testament's law against graven images, faces and human figures were not allowed (Ex. 20).

But the ornamentation in the synagogue is unusual and includes mythological and geometrical figures which are not in accord with the strict interpretation of Jewish law. It appears that sometime later these carvings were disfigured and replaced by more ornamental motifs that were more in keeping with the stricter interpretation of the commandment forbidding images.[15] An Aramaic inscription in the synagogue reads

THE REMAINS OF AN ANCIENT SYNAGOGUE IN CAPERNAUM.

"Alphaeus, son of Zebedee, son of John, made this column; on him be blessing."[16] There is also a carved manna pot by the lintel of the door that faced the pulpit and reading desk of the synagogue. Its position may have suggested the text from which Jesus preached His sermon:

> "I am the bread of life. Your fathers ate the manna in the wilderness, and are dead. This is the bread which comes down from heaven, that one may eat of it and not die. I am the living bread which came down from heaven. If anyone eats of this bread, he will live forever; and the bread that I shall give is My flesh, which I shall give for the life of the world." The Jews therefore quarreled among themselves, saying, "How can this Man give us His flesh to eat?" Then Jesus said to them, "Most assuredly, I say to you, unless you eat the flesh of the Son of Man and drink His blood, you have no life in you. Whoever eats My flesh and drinks My blood has eternal life, and I will raise

him up at the last day. For My flesh is food indeed, and My blood is drink indeed. He who eats My flesh and drinks My blood abides in Me, and I in him. As the living Father sent Me, and I live because of the Father, so he who feeds on Me will live because of Me. This is the bread which came down from heaven—not as your fathers ate the manna, and are dead. He who eats this bread will live forever." These things He said in the synagogue as He taught in Capernaum.

JOHN 6:48-59

The city of Capernaum at the time of Jesus was laid out according to the Hellenistic orthogonal, or *Hippodamian,* urban plan. The grid pattern consisted of a main north-south thoroughfare (*the Cardo Maximus* or *Via Principolis*) and numerous east-west intersecting streets (*Decumani*).[17] The synagogue was constructed on the center of this directional axis. The surrounding dwellings consisted of two types: clan dwellings and individual dwellings. Virgillio Corbo notes, "The clan dwellings were arrayed around internal courts, which numbered at times as many as three."[18] Much of the town's family life took place in these courts which contained millstones for grain, hand presses, and hearths. Steps also led out of the courtyard to roofs made of wooden beams which were covered with a layer of packed mud.[19] The Capernaum home of Simon Peter is said to have been a "clan dwelling" that had three courts, around which were arrayed the living rooms.

Jesus frequently visited Capernaum crossing the Sea of Galilee with His disciples to Gennesaret (John 6:16-24; Matt. 14:34). On one such occasion, He cured Peter's mother-in-law of a fever (Mark 1:29-31). The house of Simon Peter is mentioned several times in the Gospels and must have been a favorite spot to stop and renew acquaintances, as well as strength (Matt. 17:25; Mark 2:1; 3:19-20; 9:33). Archaeological evidence indicates that the residence was later transformed into a "house church" during the apostolic period.[20] The *Midrash* (a Jewish commentary) implies that a Judeo-Christian community existed in Capernaum at the beginning of the second century.[21] In time, Peter's house church was radically renovated when a friend of Constantine, Count Joseph of Tiberias, restructured the historical setting in the fourth century. When the nun, Egeria, came to Capernaum in A.D. 383,

ACTS OF THE APOSTLES

SIMON PETER HAD A HOME IN CAPERNAUM.

BYZANTINE

THE
BYZANTINES
BUILT A
CHURCH OVER
THE WALLS OF
SAINT PETER'S
HOUSE TO
MAINTAIN THE
SANCTITY OF
THE
DWELLING.

she stated that she was shown a church (*Domus Ecclesia*) which incorporated the walls of the house of the apostle Peter.[22] She wrote, "The house of the prince of apostles (Peter) was changed into a church; the walls however (of that house) are still standing as they were (originally)."[23] In the fifth century, an octagonal church was erected on the same spot to preserve the site.[24] To maintain the sanctity of St. Peter's house, the Byzantines built the central octagon of the church over the walls of the dwelling.[25] Today, yet another church commemorates this favored place.

Recent harbor discoveries around the Sea of Galilee have revealed that the town of Capernaum was a bustling port in Roman times. A 2,500 foot-long paved avenue lined the shore, supported by an 8-foot-wide sea wall.[26] It is just one of the many examples that have been detected under the water line. Archaeological draftsmen have shown the house of the apostle Peter to lie between the synagogue in which Jesus preached (John 6:59) and the harbor area. The ancient harbor extended from the church now owned by the Franciscans to the Greek Orthodox Church further to the east. The church is distinguished by several beautiful, reddish cast domes.

During the many visits to Capernaum by Jesus and His disciples, He delivered numerous messages, addressed the crowds, healed the sick, and fed the multitudes. But in

THIS DRAWING SHOWS CAPERNAUM'S HARBOR AS IT MIGHT HAVE APPEARED IN PETER'S TIME.

spite of Jesus' miraculous signs and striking words, the people did not repent. As previously noted, because of the city's rejection of Jesus' ministry in His final earthly days, He predicted its total ruin and devastation in Luke 10:15:

> "And you, Capernaum, who are exalted to heaven, will be brought down to Hades."

His prophecy was so completely fulfilled that the actual historical site of the village is still a matter of ongoing debate. In time, it simply disappeared.

Personal Reflections

CHAPTER TEN

Chorazin

"Woe to you, Chorazin! Woe to you, Bethsaida! For if the mighty works which were done in you had been done in Tyre and Sidon, they would have repented long ago in sackcloth and ashes."

MATTHEW 11:21

The city of Chorazin was situated about two to three Roman miles off the northern tip of the Sea of Galilee. A Roman mile was 4,860 feet (Matt. 5:41). The evidence of the location agrees with that provided by Eusebius in A.D. 174 in his *Onomasticon,* and with Jerome's A.D. 175 writings in *The Sites and Names of Hebrew Places.*[1] The Talmud mentions the town under the name Kerazim and acknowledges its fame for the quality of its wheat (*Menahoth.* 85a), which was regularly used in the Temple rituals at Jerusalem. Chorazin (*Khirbet Kerazeh*) sits high above Capernaum on the basalt hills of the Galilean region. Evidence indicates the site was inhabited as early as the later Stone Age. The town was originally of medium size.

But it experienced an influx in the second century A.D. when the population of the region expanded as a result of the Bar Kokhba Revolt.

While the city of Chorazin maintained some ancient importance due to its location along the great caravan route leading past the lake to Damascus, it had limited biblical reference. Jesus performed many miracles in this area, but due to the lack of responsiveness by the people and the absence of true repentance, the cities of Chorazin, Bethsaida, and Capernaum were censured by Him (Matt. 11:20-24; Luke 10:13-15). R.H. Mounce states, "Apparently there was a tradition that the Antichrist would come from Chorazin, and the severe words spoken to the city by Jesus may be related to this tradition."[2] The city ceased to be inhabited around the second half of the third century.

WHERE JESUS WALKED

CHORAZIN, BETHSAIDA, AND CAPERNAUM WERE SEVERELY CHASTISED BY JESUS FOR THEIR LACK OF FAITH DESPITE AN ABUNDANCE OF MIRACLES.

> Then He began to rebuke the cities in which most of His mighty works had been done, because they did not repent: "Woe to you, Chorazin! Woe to you, Bethsaida! For if the mighty works which were done in you had been done in Tyre and Sidon, they would have repented long ago in sackcloth and ashes. But I say to you, it will be more tolerable for Tyre and Sidon in the day of judgment than for you. And you, Capernaum, who are exalted to heaven, will be brought down to Hades; for if the mighty works which were done in you had been done in Sodom, it would have remained until this day. But I say to you that it shall be more tolerable for the land of Sodom in the day of judgment than for you."
>
> MATTHEW 11:20-24

SITE OF INTEREST

AN EXCAVATED SYNAGOGUE

Although only a small percentage of the 80-acre site upon which the city was founded has been excavated, what has been exposed displays some important historical discoveries. A synagogue constructed of black volcanic rock, plentiful around the Galilean countryside, dominates the cityscape. It is similar to the synagogue at Capernaum and has three monumental entrances that face south towards Jerusalem. It was first discovered in 1869, but was not excavated until 1905. Dating to the third or fourth centuries, Chorazin's synagogue was built on the foundations of

EXTERIOR OF THE SYNAGOGUE AT CHORAZIN.

the edifice in which Jesus, no doubt, would have preached. The structure is very well preserved and includes friezes (decorative bands) adorned with geometrical, floral, and anthropoid imagery. The architectural fragments make it an important site for the study of post-Temple Judaism and the architecture of synagogues.[3] Because the economy of the Jewish population was so devastated during the period of Jewish Revolts (A.D. 66-135), little evidence of synagogues before the third century remain.[4] The synagogue found at Gamla, just east of the Sea of Galilee, is the only known first-century edifice near the lake. The similarity of Gamla's bench-lined structure to the halls at Masada and Herodium strengthens its identification as a synagogue that was used by people who were among the crowds listening to Jesus.

The synagogue at Chorazin is a Galilean type and measures 70 feet by 50 feet. The interior of the building was divided by three rows of columns into a nave 20 feet wide and three aisles each 6 feet wide. Benches were erected along the walls.[5] Archaeologists dug pits both around and inside the synagogue that uncovered a plethora of coins which helped in dating the various levels of construction. Robert Smith says these coins could indicate that the city was a regular stop along the journey of early Christian pilgrims. Evidently, they came to witness the fulfillment of the reproach of Jesus and tossed the coins into the ruins.[6]

> Then Jesus spoke to the multitudes and to His disciples, saying: "The scribes and the Pharisees sit in Moses' seat."
> MATTHEW 23:1-2

Among the finds in the synagogue at Chorazin was a basalt throne decorated with a rosette on the back support. It was a stone-carved seat (*Cathedra Mosis*) with an Aramaic inscription in honor of the donor. It is probably a good example of the famous "Moses' Seat" mentioned in Matthew 23:2 which was used during the reading of the Torah. A replica of the discovery can be seen in the southeast corner of the building.

JESUS MAY HAVE TAUGHT IN THIS SYNAGOGUE.

All synagogues had one thing in common: the prayer halls faced Jerusalem. External features of the sacred edifice usually included a cistern set in a convenient place for worshippers to wash before entering to pray. Inside the building was a recess in the wall nearest Jerusalem that contained a cupboard in which the scrolls of Scripture were stored. Worshippers entered and sat on steps along the sides. It was customary for men to sit on one side and women on the other. The congregation prayed facing the Torah, and therefore Jerusalem. The central area of the hall remained empty. The men wore long, fringed prayer shawls (Matt. 23:5). Once everyone was seated, the service would begin with the cupboard removal and the placement of the Scripture scrolls on a reading desk in the center of the hall (Luke 4:16-21).

SITE OF INTEREST

ANCIENT HOUSES

Several homes containing three underground chambers have been located near the synagogue in Chorazin. Most notable was a ritual bath, a *miqvah,* that was connected by a channel to the cistern. The *miqvah* and the cistern were enclosed by a wall which formed a court and were partially roofed for greater comfort.[7]

The traveler to the Holy Land may find the site of Chorazin surprisingly more interesting than some of the other locations that have become over commercialized and developed. Being situated just off the normal path of tourist activity, the area is not subject to the usual congestion of wandering crowds.

Personal Reflections

CHORAZIN

FROM MAP INSIDE THE FRONT COVER: 8-9, G-H.

CHAPTER ELEVEN

The Dead Sea

The waters which came down from upstream stood still,
and rose in a heap very far away at Adam, the city that
is beside Zaretan. So the waters that went down into the
Sea of the Arabah, the Salt Sea, failed, and were cut off;
and the people crossed over opposite Jericho.

JOSHUA 3:16

The Dead Sea has several names in Scripture: the "sea of plain" (Deut. 3:17 KJV), the "Sea of the Arabah" (Josh. 12:3), and the most ancient biblical term the "Salt Sea" (Gen. 14:3).[1] Later prophetic passages refer to it as the "Eastern Sea" indicating the lake's position on the eastern boundary of the territory of Israel (Joel 2:20; Zech. 14:8).[2] The name "Dead Sea" was introduced into Greek and Latin usage by Justin Martyr in the second century. Though the Dead Sea is in a desert area and the soil is very salty, modern agriculture thrives along its shorelines. The main fields produce dates, but vegetables are also grown, especially during the wintertime when it is too cold in other parts of Israel.

SITE OF
INTEREST

THE DEAD SEA IS
THE LOWEST SPOT
ON THE FACE OF
THE EARTH.

The Dead Sea is the lowest spot on the face of the earth, 1290 feet below sea-level. It is located on a geological fault that extends from Syria through the Red Sea into Africa.[3] Measuring 47 x 10 miles (approximately 300 square miles), it is located at the south end of the Jordan River. The area surrounding the sea is very arid, desolate, and harsh. The evaporation rate accounts for the fact that 6.5 million tons of water enter the Dead Sea each day but none flows out. Rain in this region evaporates before it ever touches the ground! It is this high rate of evaporation over the lake that leaves behind the solids. As a result, the Dead Sea is extremely buoyant. It has a 25 percent mineralogical content (seven percent salt) in which a bather cannot sink, nor can anything live, thus earning its name of the *Dead* Sea. W. H. Morton notes, "The water is bitter and distasteful to the mouth, disconcertingly painful to the eyes, oily to the touch, and a certain and speedy reminder of all abrasions of the skin."[4] The high mineral count does have some unique healing properties (bromine, sulphur, calcium, chloride, iodine, magnesium, and potash). Though it receives from the Jordan River and other small fresh-water streams, the sea has no outlet; consequently, it maintains a high concentration of chemicals and is unable to support normal marine life.[5] The Dead Sea has recently been diminishing in size due to the upstream use of the waters of the Jordan River.

> The waters which came down from upstream stood still, and rose in a heap very far away at Adam, the city that is beside Zaretan. So the waters that went down into the Sea of the Arabah, the Salt Sea, failed, and were cut off; and the people crossed over opposite Jericho.
>
> JOSHUA 3:16

OLD
TESTAMENT

SODOM AND
GOMORRAH MAY
WELL LIE
BENEATH THE
DEAD SEA.

The Arabs call the Dead Sea, "The Sea of Lot," because the city of Sodom was built on its southern shore. At that time it was considered a well watered garden (Gen. 13:10). But after the destruction of Sodom and Gomorrah in 2067 B.C., the area became a barren wasteland (Gen. 18:20; 19:24-25; Deut. 29:23). Some scientists believe the lower portion of the lakeside was once some 30 feet higher in elevation and that it dropped into the sea when God destroyed the wicked cities. It is also believed that the

THIS CAVE IN QUMRAM IS WHERE AN ARABIC SHEPHERD BOY DISCOVERED THE DEAD SEA SCROLLS IN 1947.

concentrated chemical deposits were ignited by an earthquake and that the effects of the combustion produced a shower of fire and brimstone that fell upon the cities at the south end of the lake.[6] The Bible records how Lot's wife, stopping to look back, became a pillar of salt (Gen. 19:15-28). Some think she was overcome by the raining salt. The barrenness of the area made it an appropriate symbol of devastation—a pronouncement visited upon those who despised the principles of God.[7] Throughout the Old Testament, the Dead Sea acted as a barrier between Judah, Moab, and Edom (2 Chron. 20:1-30).[8] A wonderful vision in Ezekiel depicts a stream of fresh water issuing from the Temple in Jerusalem that flows down into the Dead Sea bringing healing life to it in the coming age (Ezek. 47:1-12). The transformation of the Dead Sea to a life-giving body will occur during the time of Messiah. It is believed that the New Testament offers a parallel reference (John 21:6-11).

On the western shore of the Dead Sea lies Qumram, site of the New Testament Essene community. The Essenes were massacred by the armies of

THE FALLS OF EN-GEDI TODAY.

Titus on their way to crush the revolt in Jerusalem (A.D. 68).[9] It was in Qumran that the Dead Sea Scrolls were found in a cave in 1947. Evidently, the Essenes had hidden away their library in the local terrain as the Roman soldiers approached. The scrolls were almost perfectly preserved copies of the Old Testament books, minus the book of Esther. The Dead Sea Scrolls predate any other ancient written materials by nearly 1,000 years. They were mostly penned in Hebrew. The one complete scroll of the book of Isaiah is essentially the same as the autograph in the Bible today. It displays how accurately the sacred texts were preserved. Another scroll, "The War Between the Children of Light and the Darkness" provides an apocalyptic interpretation of the events just before the end of the world.[10] The scrolls were recovered by an Arab shepherd tending his flocks in the hills between Jericho and the Dead Sea. He was searching for a goat when he found the sealed jars, that contained the scrolls, standing in ordered ranks along the cavern walls. The scrolls were wrapped in linen cloths that, under carbon dating, were dated around A.D. 33. They were beautifully copied on animal skins that were ruled with horizontal lines for writing and vertical lines for margins.[11] In addition,

THE DEAD SEA

there were also two copper scrolls. Altogether, the scrolls represent the most important discovery of ancient manuscripts that confirm the authenticity of the Bible, the Jewish religion, and the beginnings of Christianity.[12] Numerous other scrolls have been found in other caves since the initial discovery.

En-Gedi, which lies below or south of Qumran, means "spring of the kid" or "goat's spring."[13] It is a beautiful oasis with a fresh-water spring in the Judean desert. Located just west of the Dead Sea, its geographical position makes it possible to produce semi-tropical vegetation. En-Gedi is known for its palms, vineyards, and balsam (Song of Sol. 1:14).[14] It was originally occupied by the Amorites, but was taken by King Chedorlaomer in the attack on the five kings of the area (Gen. 14:1-12). Later, David and his men took shelter in the caves at En-Gedi. It was in one of these caves that David displayed his loyalty to Saul by merely cutting off part off his skirt and sparing his life while he slept unguarded (1 Sam. 23 & 24). It is also the place where the Ammonites, Moabites, and Meunites gathered to invade Judah during the time of Jehoshaphat (2 Chron. 20:2). They presumably hoped to gain the element of surprise by attacking one of the weak spots on the eastern flank of the Judean wilderness. But their movement was recognized and God destroyed them all without one spear, shield, or sword.

EARLY KINGS

DAVID AND HIS MEN TOOK SHELTER IN THE CAVES AT EN-GEDI.

THE DEAD SEA

> It happened after this that the people of Moab with the people of Ammon, and others with them besides the Ammonites, came to battle against Jehoshaphat. Then some came and told Jehoshaphat, saying, "A great multitude is coming against you from beyond the sea, from Syria; and they are in Hazazon Tamar" (which is En Gedi). And Jehoshaphat feared, and set himself to seek the LORD, and proclaimed a fast throughout all Judah. So Judah gathered together to ask help from the LORD; and from all the cities of Judah they came to seek the LORD. . . .
>
> And he said, "Listen, all you of Judah and you inhabitants of Jerusalem, and you, King Jehoshaphat! Thus says the LORD to you: 'Do not be afraid nor dismayed because of this great multitude, for the battle is not yours, but God's. . . . "'You will not need to fight in this battle. Position yourselves, stand still and

see the salvation of the LORD, who is with you, O Judah and Jerusalem!' Do not fear or be dismayed; tomorrow go out against them, for the LORD is with you." . . .

And when he had consulted with the people, he appointed those who should sing to the LORD, and who should praise the beauty of holiness, as they went out before the army and were saying: "Praise the LORD, for His mercy endures forever." Now when they began to sing and to praise, the LORD set ambushes against the people of Ammon, Moab, and Mount Seir, who had come against Judah; and they were defeated.

2 CHRONICLES 20:1-4,15,17,21-22

Personal Reflections

FROM MAP INSIDE THE FRONT COVER: 8-9, F-G.

Chapter Twelve

Jericho

And the LORD said to Joshua: "See! I have given Jericho into your hand, its king, and the mighty men of valor."

JOSHUA 6:2

Jericho is considered one of the world's oldest inhabited cities. There are biblical references to it in Genesis that imply it existed some 5,000 years before Abraham. The Neolithic site of the city (the latest period of the Stone Age) served as an oasis and was first settled by the Natufian people sometime between 11,000 and 8500 B.C.[1] The historical account of Jericho, memorialized in the Bible because of its supernatural destruction, is considered one of the most fascinating stories in all of Scripture. It was one of the initial cities in Palestine to be excavated.[2]

Jericho is located five miles west of the Jordan River and seven miles north of the Dead Sea just above the largest spring in all of Palestine.[3] Due to lack of rainfall, the city's oasis is dependent upon the spring of Elisha that abundantly supplies and permits the valley to grow various crops in a tropical habitat.[4] The Jordan Valley, according to the biblical record, "was well watered everywhere. . . like the garden of the Lord" (Gen. 13:10).[5] The

143

THE EXCAVATED REMAINS OF STONE WALLS AT JERICHO.

underground water level is very close to the surface, and fresh water can be found readily by merely drilling a few feet. The bountiful supply of water enables farmers to irrigate their fields. Located at the south end of the Jordan Valley along the east-west trade route, the city was the key defense position for the western section of the massive plain. It was the first city in Israel's conquest of the Promised Land. After miraculously crossing the Jordan, the army under Joshua's command (thirteenth century B.C.) proceeded across the field and began its assault on the well-fortified "double walls" of the city. The Bible states the city was surrounded by a wall (Josh. 2:15) and that it had a gate which was closed at night (Josh. 2:5). Excavations revealed that the inner wall of Jericho was 12 feet thick and the outer wall 6 feet.[6] Israel's conquest and victory at Jericho present a powerful portrait of the miraculous that can happen through faith in God.

OLD
TESTAMENT

ISRAEL
CONQUERED
JERICHO BY
FOLLOWING THE
PLAN GOD GAVE
JOSHUA.

Now Jericho was securely shut up because of the children of Israel; none went out, and none came in. And the LORD said to Joshua: "See! I have given Jericho into your hand, its king, and the mighty men of valor. You shall march around the city, all you men of war; you shall go all around the city once. This you shall do six days. And seven priests shall bear seven trumpets of rams' horns before the ark. But the seventh day you shall march around the city seven times, and the priests shall blow the trumpets. It shall come to pass, when they make a long blast with the ram's horn, and when you hear the sound of the trumpet, that all the people shall shout with a great shout; then the wall of the city will fall down flat. And the people shall go up every man straight before him."

Then Joshua the son of Nun called the priests and said to them, "Take up the ark of the covenant, and let seven priests bear seven trumpets of rams' horns before the ark of the LORD." And he said to the people, "Proceed, and march around the city, and let him who is armed advance before the ark of the LORD."

So it was, when Joshua had spoken to the people, that the seven priests bearing the seven trumpets of rams' horns before the LORD advanced and blew the trumpets, and the ark of the covenant of the LORD followed them. The armed men went before the priests who blew the trumpets, and the rear guard came after the ark, while the priests continued blowing the trumpets. Now Joshua had commanded the people, saying, "You shall not shout or make any noise with your voice, nor shall a word proceed out of your mouth, until the day I say to you, 'Shout!' Then you shall shout." So he had the ark of the LORD circle the city, going around it once. Then they came into the camp and lodged in the camp.

And Joshua rose early in the morning, and the priests took up the ark of the LORD. Then seven priests bearing seven trumpets of rams' horns before the ark of the LORD went on continually and blew with the trumpets. And the armed men went before them. But the rear guard came after the ark of the LORD, while the priests continued blowing the trumpets. And the second day they marched around the city once and returned to the camp. So they did six days.

But it came to pass on the seventh day that they rose early, about the dawning of the day, and marched around the city seven times in the same manner. On that day only they marched

around the city seven times. And the seventh time it happened, when the priests blew the trumpets, that Joshua said to the people: "Shout, for the LORD has given you the city! Now the city shall be doomed by the Lord to destruction, it and all who are in it. Only Rahab the harlot shall live, she and all who are with her in the house, because she hid the messengers that we sent."
JOSHUA 6:1-17

Archaeologists have confirmed that Jericho was once destroyed in a great conflagration that involved an earthquake.[7] According to one archaeological estimate, the ground shook like jelly in a bowl.[8] Although Joshua had cursed Jericho that it might not be rebuilt without costing the life of a firstborn (Josh. 6:26), it was distributed as part of the conquered land and awarded to the tribe of Benjamin (Josh. 18:21). The road between Jericho and Bethel later became the boundary between Benjamin and Ephraim.[9] The city remained a ruin for centuries before being rebuilt by Hiel the Bethelite (during Ahab's reign) when the death of his son literally fulfilled Joshua's curse. (1 Kings 16:34).[10]

OLD
TESTAMENT

THE FALL OF
JERICHO WAS AN
EXAMPLE OF THE
COMMUNAL FAITH
OF ISRAEL, BUT IT
ALSO SHOWS THE
POWER OF
INDIVIDUAL
FAITH.

The fall of Jericho was an example of the communal faith of Israel, but it also shows the power of individual faith. "Rahab the harlot" demonstrated her courage by hiding the two spies who had previously entered the city on the command of Joshua the son of Nun (Josh. 2). Her blemished reputation is overshadowed by her belief for which she is commended in the New Testament.

> By faith the walls of Jericho fell down after they were encircled for seven days. By faith the harlot Rahab did not perish with those who did not believe, when she had received the spies with peace.
> HEBREWS 11:30-31

Rahab's actions brought her family into the safety, security, and acceptance within the camp of Israel. She eventually married one of the two spies and, by God's grace, is mentioned in the bloodline that brought forth the Messiah.

Salmon begot Boaz by Rahab, Boaz begot Obed by Ruth, Obed begot Jesse, and Jesse begot David the king. David the king begot Solomon by her who had been the wife of Uriah.

MATTHEW 1:5-6

At the time of Elijah's translation by a whirlwind, there was a school of the prophets in Jericho (2 Kings 2:4-18). Elijah's understudy, Elisha, was waiting expectantly to receive the prophet's mantle. His first act under the "double-portion anointing" was to purify a spring at Jericho by throwing salt into it (2 Kings 2:19-22). It is known today as the "Spring of Elisha" and still provides fresh water. Ezra and Nehemiah both speak of Jericho after the exile in Babylon (Ezra 2:34; Neh. 7:36). And Nehemiah notes that the men of Jericho assisted in the rebuilding of the walls of Jerusalem (Neh. 3:2). Jericho, at this time, was evidently parallel to the Jericho of the time of the Judges and David.[11] This "City of Palms" which Eglon later captured in the time of the Judges may have been Jericho (Deut. 34:3; Judg. 3:13).[12] Certain ambassadors for King David also stayed at Jericho to let their beards grow after being insulted by the king of the Ammonites (2 Sam. 10:5).

A small Hellenistic force was stationed at Jericho during the Hellenistic Period to guard the road from the Jordan Valley to Jerusalem. Situated on the eastern flank of Judea, Jericho still maintained a position of strategic military importance (1 Macc. 9:50). Simon, one of the Maccabees, was killed at Jericho. T. A. Holland notes, "The continued settlement of the area until the present day and the existence of the modern town of Jericho testify to its endurance and its unrivaled status as being the oldest continually inhabited oasis in the world."[13]

It is believed that Herod the Great founded the city of Jericho mentioned in the New Testament Scriptures. After Herod returned to Judea with military support from Rome, he routed the Parthians in 37 B.C. delivering the fortress at Masada and capturing the regions of Idumaea, Samaria, and Galilee.[14] Herod then proceeded to execute Mattathias Antigonus (last of the Hasmonean kings) which brought an end to the Hasmonean Dynasty.[15] But not long after he became ruler of the Jordan Valley, it was given to Cleopatra by Antony. Recognizing the potential of the fertile area, the king rented it

OLD TESTAMENT

ELISHA'S FIRST ACT UNDER THE "DOUBLE-PORTION ANOINTING" WAS TO PURIFY A SPRING AT JERICHO BY THROWING SALT IN IT.

EARLY KINGS

SOME OF KING DAVID'S AMBASSADORS STAYED AT JERICHO TO LET THEIR BEARDS GROW AFTER BEING INSULTED BY THE KING OF THE AMMONITES.

BETWEEN THE TESTAMENTS

SIMON MACCABEUS WAS KILLED AT JERICHO.

JERICHO

Not long after Herod became ruler of the Jordan Valley, it was given to Cleopatra by Antony. Recognizing the potential of the fertile area, the king rented it back from Cleopatra and developed it.

back from Cleopatra and developed it.[16] His new Jericho stood about a mile south of the familiar Old Testament site.[17]

Renowned for his personal cruelty, Herod is best remembered for his architectural accomplishments. These include the extension of Temple Mount, the harbor at Caesarea, the construction of Masada, and the expansion of the winter palace at Jericho. Herod actually built three independent palaces at Jericho, but they were ultimately utilized as one. Alexander Jannaeus (103-76 B.C.) has been credited with the original construction of the winter palace complex, but Herod's extravagant refurbishment added its courtyards, special rooms, a swimming pool, a bathhouse, an installation for heating water, servants' quarters, colonnades, and both sunken and formal ornamental gardens. The palace walls were covered with frescoes and the ceilings were adorned with elaborate stucco work.[18]

GREEK/
ROMAN

HEROD'S RECONSTRUCTION OF JERICHO WAS GREATLY INFLUENCED BY HIS RELATIONSHIP WITH ROME.

Herod's reconstruction of Jericho was greatly influenced by his relationship with Rome. Many sites that appeared at Jericho also appeared at Pompeii. Howbeit, because Jericho was a much larger city than Pompeii, Herod had room to develop the kind of pools, parks, villas, and civic buildings which were typical of a Greco-Roman metropolis.[19] Ruins of a unique combined complex have been found which encompassed a horse racetrack, a chariot-racing course, a theater, and special areas for athletics. Netzer believes the superstructure may be the buildings to which Josephus refers when he notes the hippodrome, a theater, and an amphitheater at Jericho.[20]

JERICHO

148

The name *Jericho* may be derived from the Canaanite moon god, or it could be associated with the word for "smell." The name could reflect the pleasant odors and fragrances of the fruits and spices which grew in the area.[21] Beggars were also found in these rich cities, because almsgiving was highly meritorious.[22] The Synoptic Gospels (Matthew, Mark, and Luke) all depict ministry by Jesus to such beggars at Jericho, through which He passed on numerous occasions (Matt. 20:29-34; Mark 10:46-52; Luke 18:35-43).

WHERE JESUS
WALKED

JESUS HEALED
BLIND
BARTIMAEUS IN
JERICHO.

> Now they came to Jericho. As He went out of Jericho with His disciples and a great multitude, blind Bartimaeus, the son of Timaeus, sat by the road begging. And when he heard that it was Jesus of Nazareth, he began to cry out and say, "Jesus, Son of David, have mercy on me!" Then many warned him to be quiet; but he cried out all the more, "Son of David, have mercy on me!" So Jesus stood still and commanded him to be called. Then they called the blind man, saying to him, "Be of good cheer. Rise, He is calling you." And throwing aside his garment, he rose and came to Jesus. So Jesus answered and said to him, "What do you want Me to do for you?" The blind man said to Him, "Rabboni, that I may receive my sight." Then Jesus said to him, "Go your way; your faith has made you well." And immediately he received his sight and followed Jesus on the road.
>
> MARK 10:46-52

WHERE JESUS
WALKED

JESUS WAS ENTER-
TAINED IN
ZACCHAEUS'
JERICHO HOME.

Zacchaeus, who was one of the prominent tax collectors in the biblical narratives, held an office in Jericho. Because the city acted as the winter capital and was surrounded by rich plantations (balsam groves from which medicine was extracted and valuable sycamore trees), Zacchaeus' practice was highly lucrative. When Jesus was entertained by Zacchaeus (Luke 19:1-10), He was greeted in one of the finest homes in the city.[23] Jericho was a stopping place for Galilean pilgrims on their way to and from Jerusalem. They came through the territory of Perea (known in the Gospels as the land "beyond the Jordan") to avoid defilement by contact with the Samaritans (Matt. 19:1). The presence of springs of water and

JERICHO

WHERE JESUS WALKED

IN THE
PARABLE OF
THE GOOD
SAMARITAN,
THE TRAVELLER
WAS ATTACKED
AS HE WAS
GOING
"DOWN" FROM
JERUSALEM TO
JERICHO.

constant sunshine made the area a green oasis in the middle of a dry region.[24] Its climate today is in striking contrast to the "bone-chilling, damp winter of Jerusalem" as noted by J. L. Kelso.[25] In the parable of the Good Samaritan (Luke 10:29-37), the traveller was attacked as he was going "down" from Jerusalem to Jericho—a winding road that passed through the desolate Judean wilderness which was a frequent hiding place for bandits and criminals. The elevation drops over 4,000 feet in a 14- to 15-mile stretch.[26] Jericho is actually considered the lowest town on the surface of the earth. It is over 800 feet below sea level.[27] The Inn of the Good Samaritan was a midway rest area for travellers to receive refreshing.

Then Jesus answered and said: "A certain man went down from Jerusalem to Jericho, and fell among thieves, who stripped him of his clothing, wounded him, and departed, leaving him half dead. Now by chance a certain priest came down that road. And when he saw him, he passed by on the other side. Likewise a Levite, when he arrived at the place, came and looked, and passed by on the other side. But a certain Samaritan, as he journeyed, came where he was. And when he saw him, he had compassion. So he went to him and bandaged his wounds, pouring on oil and wine; and he set him on his own animal, brought him to an inn, and took care of him. On the next day, when he departed, he took out two denarii, gave them to the innkeeper, and said to him, 'Take care of him; and whatever more you spend, when I come again, I will repay you.' So which of these three do you think was neighbor to him who fell among the thieves?" And he said, "He who showed mercy on him." Then Jesus said to him, "Go and do likewise."
LUKE 10:30-37

Because of Jericho's political significance and materialistic prominence, the city may have been the locale used by the devil to symbolize all the cities of the world (Matt. 4:8). When Jesus left Jericho on the road to Jerusalem, He would pass by the same mountains that were the scene of His earlier temptations (Matt. 4:1-11). At the close of His ministry, Jesus

JERICHO

would once again pass the same setting on His way to the Holy City, which was His final testing.

Jericho also served as a Roman garrison for Vespasian's army as it prepared to attack Jerusalem in A.D. 70 and was therefore spared annihilation. On the other hand, several miles to the south, the Essene community in Qumram was destroyed.[28] After the destruction of Jerusalem, Jericho declined in status and slowly dissipated into time.

FROM INSERT IN THE MAP INSIDE THE FRONT COVER.

CHAPTER THIRTEEN

Jerusalem

*"Behold, we are going up to Jerusalem, and the
Son of Man will be betrayed to the chief priests and
to the scribes; and they will condemn Him to death,
and deliver Him to the Gentiles to mock and to scourge
and to crucify. And the third day He will rise again."*

MATTHEW 20:18-19

It is now time to look at a few of the historical, biblical sights of the
Holy City of Jerusalem. Put them on your tour agenda. Each of them that
I mention played a significant role in the life of the Jewish Messiah's
redemptive sacrifice that occurred on Jerusalem soil. A good place to start
is the Pool of Bethesda. It is just outside the perimeter of the Temple Mount
and was made known in the New Testament gospel of John.

The Pool of Bethesda

Pools in ancient Jerusalem were mainly for the sojourners, merchants,
and pilgrims. Many poor and sick gathered around these areas waiting for

WHERE JESUS WALKED

JESUS HEALED A LAME MAN AT THE POOL OF BETHESDA.

the travellers to give them money or goods. The Pool of Bethesda is a spring-fed, twin pool in northeast Jerusalem. It is located just inside St. Stephen's Gate, also known as the Lion's Gate.[1] Assorted spellings of the pool's name occur in various manuscripts that reveal differing attempts to translate the original Hebrew or Aramaic. Officially, there are three versions: Bethesda (house of mercy or house of two springs); Bethsaida (house of the fisherman); and Bethzatha (house of olive oil).[2] Some scholars use the name *Bethzatha* (RSV), while the *King James Version* and others follow the Received Text and translate the name as *Bethesda* (NASB, NIV).[3] Some Bible versions read *Bethsaida* and should not be confused with the village of Bethsaida on the northern shore of the Sea of Galilee.

The northeast corner of Jerusalem was called "the Bezetha" or "the Beth-zetha" where the pool was situated.[4] Since the pool is near the north wall and coincided with the wall of the Temple, it would have faced the hill district of Bezetha. Opposite the Antonia Fortress, and across the valley and a deep moat (purposely dug), a new district was built which carried the Greek name of New Town or Bezetha.[5] It was for this reason that the name of the pool was designated by the locality. Olive orchards were also located near the vicinity, so the name reflected this fact as well.[6] The fourth of the five hills upon which Jerusalem was built (north of the Temple Mount) is called by Josephus *Bethzetha* in Greek.[7] Also, the famous fifth-century mosaic map which can be viewed at Madaba in Jordan, positioned the Pool of Bethesda at Bezetha. So the location of the pool is most likely situated in the suburb north of the Temple as mentioned in 1 Maccabees 7:19 as *Beth-zaith*.

The pool was surrounded by five porches and literally means "house of mercy" (Aramaic) or "place of outpouring" (Hebrew).[8] The translation from the Hebrew supports the interpretation *Bethesda*—"the place of poured out water."[9] The site was originally very large and had "an elongated trapezoid shape" as noted by Rivka Gonen: 300-330 feet long, 180-240 feet wide, and 21-24 feet deep.[10] The pool was an open-air reservoir constructed during the Second Temple period to meet the demands of a growing population.[11] It lay in a small valley that ran from the area of the Damascus Gate to the northeastern corner of the Temple Mount. Further down the valley lay the Pool of Probatica (in Greek, *probatike* means

JERUSALEM

It was here that the infirm waited to be healed. According to the gospel of John the sick waited to step down into the waters which were thought to have healing properties.

"sheep") where the sacrificial lambs were washed before being taken into the Temple. Both the Pool of Bethesda and the Pool of Probatica are near the Sheep Gate—a Jerusalem gate mentioned by Nehemiah. When the walls of the city were rebuilt, the gate was constructed by the priests as an entrance to the Temple area (Neh. 3:1,32; 12:39). According to Nehemiah's description, it was located in the north by the Tower of Hananel (possible future site of the Antonia Fortress).

The Pool of Bethesda was carved out of rock into two basins and divided by an uncut rock ledge. Its four porticos, and a fifth on the ledge, came between the two pools.[12] It was here that the infirm waited to be healed. According to the gospel of John, the sick waited to step down into the waters which were thought to have healing properties. Biblical scholarship notes that the the last half of John 5:3 and 5:4 may have been added to later manuscripts to explain the reason the man needed to be first into the pool (verse 7) and what he meant by the waters being stirred. However, Tertullian (A.D. 145-220) is apparently aware of this reference and comments regarding an angel troubling the waters.[13] In John's account, Jesus healed a man waiting in one of the porches who had been sick for 38 years. Many pilgrims over the years saw this man in an infirm condition. The notoriety of this miracle more than likely spread the popularity of Jesus throughout the city and beyond.

> After this there was a feast of the Jews, and Jesus went up to Jerusalem. Now there is in Jerusalem by the Sheep Gate a pool, which is called in Hebrew, Bethesda, having five porches. In

155

these lay a great multitude of sick people, blind, lame, paralyzed, waiting for the moving of the water. For an angel went down at a certain time into the pool and stirred up the water; then whoever stepped in first, after the stirring of the water, was made well of whatever disease he had. Now a certain man was there who had an infirmity thirty-eight years. When Jesus saw him lying there, and knew that he already had been in that condition a long time, He said to him, "Do you want to be made well?" The sick man answered Him, "Sir, I have no man to put me into the pool when the water is stirred up; but while I am coming, another steps down before me." Jesus said to him, "Rise, take up your bed and walk." And immediately the man was made well, took up his bed, and walked. And that day was the Sabbath.

JOHN 5:1-9

GREEK/
ROMAN

THE RUINS OF A
TEMPLE
DEDICATED TO
AESCULAPIS, THE
GRECO-ROMAN
GOD OF HEALING,
IS NEAR THE
POOL OF
BETHESDA.

The reputation produced by the Pool of Bethesda's healing tradition continued in Jerusalem's history beyond Jesus' day.[14] Although Jerusalem was destroyed in A.D. 70, archaeological digs have proven that a belief in the curative power of the waters was embraced by the pagan citizens of the new Roman colony established upon the old ruins of the city. The ruins of a Roman temple dedicated to Aesculapis, the Greco-Roman god of healing, were found next to the pool in Hadrian's reconstructed city (A.D. 135) named *Aelia Capitolina*. In it were found marble representations of healed organs, including feet and ears, which were votive offerings to the god.[15] Allegedly, a priest of the cult would throw a snake (symbol of the pagan healing deity) into the pool of water. Then, the first person to get into the water after the snake was supposed to have been cured.[16]

If the pagan temple functioned during the time of Jesus, it would have served the Roman soldiers stationed in the Antonia Fortress nearby. The consideration of this possibility may provide insight concerning the textual difficulties associated with the Johannine passage (ca. John 5:4). Notwithstanding, it would bring greater significance to the healing by Jesus. As Lord and Christ, He fulfills all the aspirations of a seeking, yet afflicted world as the true healer of all our infirmities. However, the

THE MOUNT OF OLIVES AS SEEN FROM THE WALLS OF THE OLD CITY OF JERUSALEM.

building of this temple was more likely a pagan sacrilegious act to mar a former sacred site; an act much like the design of the pagan temple Hadrian built to Venus or Aphrodite (Greek goddess of love) over the traditional location of Golgotha—The Church of the Holy Sepulchre.

Adjacent to the Bethesda pools is St. Anne's Church, named after Mary's mother. The area is believed to be identified with the person of the Virgin Mary during her childhood. The Crusaders built the church in A.D. 1140.[17] Its rich acoustical interior is considered one of the finest in the entire world. While the church of St. Anne was being repaired in 1888, a reservoir was discovered. The reservoir is approached by a flight of steep, winding steps, and on the wall is a faded fresco which depicts an angel troubling the water. The area was initially preserved as a Christian holy site by Eudoxia, a Byzantine empress, who had a Basilica constructed over the pool in the fifth century.[18] The remains of the pool and the Byzantine church are still visible today.

SITE OF INTEREST

SAINT ANNE'S CHURCH

CRUSADERS

THE CRUSADERS BUILT ST. ANNE'S CHURCH IN A.D. 1140.

JERUSALEM

THIS CAVE AT GETHSEMANE COMMEMORATES JESUS' NIGHT OF PRAYER BEFORE HIS CRUXIFICTION. ARCHAEOLOGICAL EVIDENCE MAKES MANY BELIEVE THAT THE GETHSEMANE OF THE GOSPELS WAS A CAVE AND NOT A GARDEN.

The Garden of Gethsemane

Near the foot of the Mount of Olives, on the western slope, above the Kidron Valley, is the site of the Garden of Gethsemane.[1] *Gethsemane* comes from the Aramaic word for "oil press" and suggests a grove of olive trees (Matt. 26:36; Mark 14:32).[2] Although Matthew and Mark report the site as a "field," Luke (without giving the name) merely calls it "the place." He also portrays it as "the place" Jesus customarily visited (Luke 22:40). Luke's unique use of the Greek word for "place," *topos,* is described differently in Matthew 26:36 and in Mark 14:32. They both call it a "property or land" (*chorion*) and indicate that Gethsemane was an enclosed piece of ground. According to John they entered into (*eis*) it. Without naming it either, John states it was a "garden" (*kepos*) across the Cedron (Kidron) Valley from Jerusalem. But the Greek term for "garden" used in John 18:1, *kepos,* implies that it could have been anything from a large orchard, plantation, or a small cultivated area.[3] Nevertheless, it is from his citation that the traditional name "Garden of Gethsemane" has been derived.[4] Some believe the olive groves were privately owned and that Jesus and His disciples were granted special permission to

JERUSALEM

retreat into this area.[5] Some even suggest that this spot was owned by Mary, the mother of Mark.[6] Jesus and His disciples passed the tract regularly on their way in and out of Jerusalem and would have been very familiar with the local terrain and nearby caves as places in which to lodge.

Actually, a cave is much more feasible as the authentic biblical site of Gethsemane. The New Testament does not mention a *"Garden* of Gethsemane,*"* nor does it specifically mention a *"cave* of Gethsemane.*"* What the biblical text does provide is that Jesus "went out" (*exelthen*) of something within the garden to meet the soldiers (John 18:4). In A.D. 382, the pilgrim nun Egeria described visitors going "into Gethsemane" with candles "so that they could see." Evidently, Gethsemane was located in somewhat of a dim interior.[7]

When the term "Gethsemane" is analyzed in the Hebrew or Aramaic, it reveals literally "a press of oils" (*Gat-shemanim*). In rabbinic literature, as Joan E. Taylor acknowledges *gat* refers to a place for the preparation of oil and displays the probable name of the cave.[8] Archaeological evidence points to a cave in the Garden of Gethsemane that was once used for the pressing of olives.[9] Theodosius also mentioned Gethsemane as a large cave in the sixth century.[10] In fact, it is not until the twelfth century that the concept of a "Garden of Gethsemane" developed. A cave would be a normal place in ancient times to seek shelter from the damp evenings, especially during Passover when thousands would migrate to the city. Any available space in the city would have been offered to host the visitors. And today, a cave in the hillside can be visited that commemorates the chamber with an altar.

WHERE JESUS
WALKED

GETHSEMANE
IS BEST KNOWN
AS THE SACRED
SPOT OF JESUS'
AGONY AND
ARREST.

Gethsemane is best known as the sacred spot of Jesus' agony and arrest. Its historic location is believed to be somewhere on the side of the Mount of Olives, above the road from Jerusalem to Bethany. However, the exact place is known only by tradition. Scripturally, it is considered a stone's throw up the hill (Luke 22:41). When Constantine's mother, Helena, came to Jerusalem on her pilgrimage in 326 A.D., she fixed the site at the Church of the Tomb of the Virgin.[11] The traditional site has eight large olive trees. The Roman emperor, Titus, supposedly destroyed all the trees around Jerusalem during the siege of the city in 70 A.D., as asserted by Josephus.[12] So the eight ancient olive trees cared for by the Franciscans may or may not be as old as the time of Jesus. Armenian, Greek, and Russian churches claim other olive groves nearby as the correct site. Regardless, the vicinity and setting are definitely memorable. The agony of Jesus as He prayerfully approached his hour, His betrayal by a kiss, and the humiliation of His arrest in the Garden bring reverence to the heart of every true believer (Mark 14:43-50; John 18:1-12). It is said that Christianity's custom of kneeling in prayer has its roots in Jesus' actions in this garden as He prayerfully knelt before the Father the night before His death (Luke 22:41).[13]

> Then Jesus came with them to a place called Gethsemane, and said to the disciples, "Sit here while I go and pray over there." And He took with Him Peter and the two sons of Zebedee, and He began to be sorrowful and deeply distressed. Then He said to them, "My soul is exceedingly sorrowful, even to death. Stay here and watch with Me." He went a little farther and fell on His face, and prayed, saying, "O My Father, if it is possible, let this cup pass from Me; nevertheless, not as I will, but as You will." Then He came to the disciples and found them sleeping, and said to Peter, "What? Could you not watch with Me one hour? Watch and pray, lest you enter into temptation. The spirit indeed is willing, but the flesh is weak." Again, a second time, He went away and prayed, saying, "O My Father, if this cup cannot pass away from Me unless I drink it, Your will be done." And He came and found them asleep again, for their eyes were heavy. So He left them, went away again, and prayed the third time, saying the same words. Then He came to His disciples and said to them, "Are you still sleeping and resting? Behold, the hour is at hand, and the Son of Man is being betrayed into the hands of sinners. Rise, let us be going. See, My betrayer is at hand."
>
> MATTHEW 26:36-46

It was also in Gethsemane that Jesus healed the ear of the high priest's servant after Peter cut it off during Christ's arrest (Matt. 26:51-52). And, it

THE APSE AREA OF THE CHURCH OF ALL NATIONS.

was from here, that everyone of Jesus' disciples deserted Him after He was taken (Matt. 26:56).

There are several churches in Gethsemane's Mount of Olives area that commemorate this sacred spot. The Church of All Nations (or sometimes referred to as The Church of the Agony) is one of the most striking buildings. This monument was designed by the Italian architect Barlozzi. It was built with donations that came in from all over the world between 1919-1924, earning its name "All Nations." A gable, on the front of the basilica which faces the Jerusalem-Jericho road, reveals a spectacular mosaic depicting the Gethsemane experience. Over the head of Jesus appear the Greek letters "Alpha and Omega" as stated in the book of Revelation: "'I am the Alpha and the Omega, the Beginning and the End,' says the Lord" (Rev. 1:8). Standing on pillars are the four Evangelists: Matthew, Mark, Luke, and John. In addition, there are two deer which face the cross that depict David's verse from Psalm 42:1, "As the deer pants for the water brooks, so pants my soul for You, O God."[14] Inside the church, wrought

SITE OF INTEREST

THE CHURCH OF ALL NATIONS

JERUSALEM

161

SITE OF
INTEREST

THE CHURCH
OF THE
ASCENSION

iron resembling thorns encloses a rock which is believed to be the spot where Jesus sweat blood.

Another religious edifice, The Church of the Ascension, was built on the Mount of Olives by Helena, the mother of the emperor Constantine, in the fourth century. Then, in the twelfth century, Crusaders built a new church on the site. It is believed to surround the rock from which Jesus is said to have ascended. The church sustained deterioration in the Moslem occupation and was never rebuilt. At the very summit of the Mount of Olives stands one of the best-known landmarks of Jerusalem: The Russian church. This edifice has a bell tower that dominates the landscape in a spire that rises 214 steps above ground level. The bells for the tower were dragged all the way from the port of Joppa by women pilgrims who attended to the convent of the White Sisters of Russia. The painting on the domed ceiling depicts the Ascension of Jesus as the disciples watch, and it is believed that the bell tower is standing on the actual spot of the biblical event. A stone inside the church is believed to be the place where Mary stood and watched.

SITE OF
INTEREST

THE PATER
NOSTER
CHURCH

An additional sacred structure, the Pater Noster Church, has the Lord's Prayer in 60 languages inscribed on its walls. It is called the Church of Eleona, and it is one of the four churches Emperor Constantine ordered to be built in the Holy Land. The present-day church was constructed in 1875.[15] Inside is a shallow cave thought by tradition to be the location where Jesus taught His disciples to pray.[16] Both the Bordeaux Pilgrim (who made a pilgrimage to Jerusalem by way of Rome in A.D. 333) and Egeria (a nun from either northern Spain or southern France who also made a pilgrimage to the Holy Land in A.D. 385-382) report in their journals that they visited the cave.[17] Egeria spent several months in Palestine, including Holy Week and Easter. In her writings she provides details of worship, vestments, processions, routes, as well as descriptions of Holy Places.

WHERE JESUS
WALKED

THE TOWER OF
ANTONIA IS
MOST NOTED AS
THE LOCATION
OF THE TRIAL OF
JESUS.

The Tower of Antonia

The Antonia Fortress, or Tower ("Castle") of Antonia, receives its notoriety from the trial of Jesus, although it has a long-standing history. It is believed that Solomon may have first built this fortress near the Temple Mount,[1] and that later, when the Jewish exiles returned to Jerusalem to

JERUSALEM

Taken from the Garden of Gethsemane and condemned by the Sanhedrin . . . Jesus was led to the hall called Praetorium, the administrative headquarters which was located either at the Fortress or Pilate's residence. Here He was mocked, scourged, crowned with thorns, and sentenced to die.

rebuild the city, the fortress was erected once again (Neh. 2:8). The castle faced "outward" to guard against northern enemies and external attack. It was once again rebuilt by the Maccabean John Hycranus and was known as the *Baris* ("castle" or "tower"). Then it was destroyed again by Pompey (63 B.C.).[2] Throughout the history of the city, the fortress, as well as the Temple, suffered periodic destructions because of its northern position. The natural defenses of Jerusalem consisted of steep valleys on the east, west, and south. In addition, large stone walls ensured protection. But the city remained vulnerable on its north end from where an invading army could easily approach upon the flat plain. If an enemy was to attack, it usually was from the north because of the accessibility. This is why the prophets declared, "From the north the enemy will come." In response, the northern defenses were fortified with three walls.

When Herod the Great rebuilt the Temple and expanded the Temple Mount, he also renovated and enlarged the Maccabean castle. The military fortification was built strategically on a high rock that overlooked both Temple and city.[3] While this actual location has remained an archaeological debate, it seems the only possible location is the northwest corner. It is the only hill that rises above the Temple area.[4] The position of the fortress made it nearly impregnable. It was located on a rocky precipice 75 feet high that was faced with smooth and slippery flagstones. On the west was

JERUSALEM

163

GREEK/
ROMAN

HEROD THE
GREAT NAMED
THE TOWER OF
ANTONIA IN
HONOR OF HIS
FRIEND MARC
ANTONY.

the Tyropoeon Valley. To the north was also a deep trench with a wall and moat that separated it from the hill of Bezetha.[5] The castle was lavishly fabricated with great splendor including apartments, baths, and court-yards. Herod named it Antonia in honor of his friend Marc Antony who was instrumental in making him ruler over Judea.[6] The fortress was built in the form of a massive square with additional four-corner turrets; conversely, in Herod's reconstruction of this area, part of the Antonia was designed to face "inward," towards the city, to guard against internal revolt. Each turret was 75 feet high except in the southeast corner. This specific tower was 100 feet high and faced the Temple court. The Antonia served as the center of Roman control over the worship festivals of the Jews (exhibited by Herod's request that the vestments of the high priest be kept in the fortress).[7] The fortress also served as housing for Herod before constructing his elaborate palace on the west side of the city.

According to the Jewish historian Josephus, the Antonia Fortress also served as the official royal residence for the Roman procurators and quartered their Roman guard. It was capable of accommodating 500 to 600 men.[8] There was also an impressive open area, called the *Lithostrotos* from the Greek or *Gabbatha* in Aramaic (literally "the stone pavement"), which was used for parades, games, the training of Roman legionaries, and public speaking.[9] As mentioned earlier, Jesus may have been taken here to stand trial. Presently, two theories exist regarding where Jesus stood before Pilate. One is the palace of Herod in the western corner of the city by Jaffa Gate. It was not uncommon for an official to retreat to his palace at midday to avoid the rising temperatures. The second is the Castle Antonia.[10]

Taken from the Garden of Gethsemane and condemned by the Sanhedrin at the house of Caiphas (Matt. 26:57 ff.), Jesus was led to the hall called Praetorium, the administrative headquarters which was located either at the Fortress or at Pilate's residence (Mark 15:15-16). Here He was mocked, scourged, crowned with thorns, and sentenced to die. Before continuing, however, it should be noted that although many leaders of the Jews rejected Jesus as Messiah and condemned Him to die, many more Jews believed in Him. Moreover, the very early Church consisted primarily of Jews.

Near the alleged site of the Antonia Fortress is an etching on a Roman floor in the lower level of the Convent of the Sisters of Zion. The floor is about ten feet beneath the actual present-day street level. It is still visible today and depicts a dice game (*basilikos* or "king") that the Roman soldiers played using prisoners as "mock kings" in a life-and-death match. It is stated that the "King's Game" was a means to lift the morale of the soldiers posted in Judea—an assignment considered the worst in the Roman army. The soldiers would choose a burlesque "king" who would be mocked and abused verbally as well as physically.[11] Jesus was possibly mocked on these very pavement stones (Matt. 27:27-31; Mark 15:16-20).

THE "KING'S GAME"—ROMAN SOLDIERS WOULD CHOOSE A BURLESQUE "KING" TO MOCK AND ABUSE PHYSICALLY FOR THEIR ENTERTAINMENT.

Howbeit, archaeological calculations question the authenticity of his location and date the stones to the time of Hadrian (A.D. 135).[12] The stones of the Lithostratos are proposed to be another possible location of the forum. In the central plaza of the town stood a typical Roman triumphal arch. A piece of this arch is still visible just outside the Convent and has been called the Ecce Homo Arch ("Behold the man"). It was once thought to be the place where Pontius Pilate uttered those momentous words in John 19:5 when showing Jesus to the crowd. Archaeological exploration, however, dates both the

Arch and the pavement stones to the time when the city was turned into a Roman colony *(Colonia Aelia Capitolina)*—nearly 100 years after the earthly presence of Jesus.[13] The Arch was erected to commemorate the suppression by Hadrian of the Second Jewish Revolt (A.D. 132-135).[14] It had a large central arch with smaller lower arches on either side.

Now Jesus stood before the governor. And the governor asked Him, saying, "Are You the King of the Jews?" So Jesus said to him, "It is as you say." And while He was being accused by the chief priests and elders, He answered nothing. Then Pilate said to Him, "Do You not hear how many things they testify against You?" But He answered him not one word, so that the governor marveled greatly.

Now at the feast the governor was accustomed to releasing to the multitude one prisoner whom they wished. And at that time they had a notorious prisoner called Barabbas. Therefore, when they had gathered together, Pilate said to them, "Whom do you want me to release to you? Barabbas, or Jesus who is called Christ?" For he knew that they had handed Him over because of envy. While he was sitting on the judgment seat, his wife sent to him, saying, "Have nothing to do with that just Man, for I have suffered many things today in a dream because of Him." But the chief priests and elders persuaded the multitudes that they should ask for Barabbas and destroy Jesus. The governor answered and said to them, "Which of the two do you want me to release to you?" They said, "Barabbas!" Pilate said to them, "What then shall I do with Jesus who is called Christ?" They all said to him, "Let Him be crucified!" Then the governor said, "Why, what evil has He done?" But they cried out all the more, saying, "Let Him be crucified!" When Pilate saw that he could not prevail at all, but rather that a tumult was rising, he took water and washed his hands before the multitude, saying, "I am innocent of the blood of this just Person. You see to it." And all the people answered and said, "His blood be on us and on our children." Then he released Barabbas to them; and when he had scourged Jesus, he delivered Him to be crucified.

Then the soldiers of the governor took Jesus into the Praetorium and gathered the whole garrison around Him. And they stripped Him and put a scarlet robe on Him. When they had twisted a crown of thorns, they put it on His head, and a reed in His right hand. And they bowed the knee before Him and mocked Him, saying, "Hail, King of the Jews!" Then they spat on Him, and took the reed and struck Him on the head. And when they had mocked Him, they took the robe off Him, put His own clothes on Him, and led Him away to be crucified. MATTHEW 27:11-31

Though the Antonia is not specifically named in Scripture, it is referred to by the term "barracks" or "castle" in the book of Acts. It is also considered to be the location of Peter's imprisonment and miraculous angelic deliverance (Acts 12:5-7). Paul was granted permission to address the Jews in the Temple court and to defend himself against the Jews from the steps of this castle (Acts 21:40). J. L. Kelso notes, "Several stairs led down from the castle to the porticoes of the Temple at its north end."[15] It was also the place of Paul's scourging before declaring, "Is it lawful for you to scourge a man that is a Roman, and uncondemned?" (Acts 22:24-30). Paul was then protected inside the fortress after addressing Ananias the high priest and the council, "the chief captain fearing lest Paul should have been pulled to pieces by them" (Acts 23:1-10). He was then taken secretly, by night, to Caesarea on the coast (Acts 23:23-25).

ACTS OF THE APOSTLES

THIS TOWER IS ALSO BELIEVED TO HAVE BEEN THE SITE OF PETER'S IMPRISONMENT DESCRIBED IN ACTS 12.

When the Roman armies under Titus attacked Jerusalem, the Tower of Antonia was the central command point from where he directed his final assault on the Temple area. The exact spot on which the fortress was constructed has yet to be determined. It was destroyed during the siege of 70 A.D.[16]

GREEK/ ROMAN

TITUS DIRECTED HIS FINAL ASSAULT ON THE TEMPLE AREA FROM THE TOWER OF ANTONIA.

JERUSALEM

The Via Dolorosa

The Via Dolorosa is the traditional route Jesus traveled on the day of His death from Pilate's judgment hall (the Praetorium) to His crucifixion on

Calvary (John 19:1-22). But again, the exact placement of Pilate's headquarters is in question. Some place it near the Jaffa Gate at the Palace of Herod. Others believe it was positioned at the Antonia Fortress which is situated adjacent to the northwest corner of the Temple Mount. Since the city was destroyed so thoroughly (twice—once by the Romans in A.D. 70 and again by Rome in A.D. 135), it is hard to pinpoint an accurate location.[1] Even the ancient streets were obliterated! Traditionally, the Via Dolorosa begins at the Tower of Antonia and proceeds to the Church of the Holy Sepulchre, the legendary site of Golgotha and the tomb of Joseph of Arimathea. *Via Dolorosa* means "the sorrowful way."[2] It was Roman custom to have those who had been condemned to take a death walk through the city with their name and details of their conviction displayed.[3]

During the fourth and fifth centuries, processions honored the route from Gethsemane to Golgotha. The street was later marked by monkish tradition in the fourteenth century with fourteen stations of the cross to aid in personal devotion. The first two stations are located in the Tower of Antonia. Several others are denoted along the way by markings or pictures on houses. The last five stations are in the Church of the Holy Sepulchre. Of the fourteen stations, nine are accounted for from the biblical text and five come from Catholic tradition.[4]

1) Jesus is condemned to die in Pilate's Hall:

Then he delivered Him to them to be crucified. So they took Jesus and led Him away.
JOHN 19:16

2) Jesus receives the cross:

And He, bearing His cross, went out to a place called the Place of a Skull, which is called in Hebrew, Golgotha.
JOHN 19:17

3) Jesus falls under the weight of the cross (traditional).

4) Jesus meets His mother (traditional).

JERUSALEM

5) Jesus is assisted by Simon the Cyrene:

Now as they came out, they found a man of Cyrene, Simon by name. Him they compelled to bear His cross.
MATTHEW 27:32

6) Jesus' face is wiped by Veronica and an image is transformed onto her cloth (traditional).

The name *Veronica* may have been derived from two words, *Vera* and *ikon,* that symbolize the beautiful deed of this anonymous woman. According to tradition, Veronica wiped the "true face" *(vera ikon)* of Jesus. Through time the terms came to designate an individual rather than the compassionate act.

7) Jesus falls a second time (traditional).

8) Jesus consoles the women of Jerusalem:

A PORTICO ALONG THE VIA DOLOROSA SHOWING JESUS MEETING HIS MOTHER, MARY.

But Jesus, turning to them, said, "Daughters of Jerusalem, do not weep for Me, but weep for yourselves and for your children. For indeed the days are coming in which they will say, 'Blessed are the barren, wombs that never bore, and breasts which never nursed!' Then they will begin 'to say to the mountains, "Fall on us!" and to the hills, "Cover us!"' For if they do these things in the green wood, what will be done in the dry?"
LUKE 23:28-31

9) Jesus falls a third time (traditional).

10) Jesus is stripped of His garments:

Then the soldiers, when they had crucified Jesus, took His garments and made four parts, to each soldier a part, and also the tunic. Now the tunic was without seam, woven from the top in one piece. They said therefore among themselves, "Let us not tear it, but cast lots for it, whose it shall be," that the Scripture might be fulfilled which says: "They divided My garments among them, and for My clothing they cast lots."
JOHN 19:23-24

11) Jesus is nailed to the cross:

Then they crucified Him, and divided His garments, casting lots, that it might be fulfilled which was spoken by the prophet:
  "They divided My garments among them,
  And for My clothing they casts lots."
MATTHEW 27:35

12) Jesus dies on the cross:

So when Jesus had received the sour wine, He said, "It is finished!" And bowing His head, He gave up His spirit.
JOHN 19:30

13) Jesus' body is removed from the cross:

> After this, Joseph of Arimathea, being a disciple of Jesus, but secretly, for fear of the Jews, asked Pilate that he might take away the body of Jesus; and Pilate gave him permission. So he came and took the body of Jesus.
> JOHN 19:38

14) Jesus' body is placed in the tomb:

> Then they took the body of Jesus, and bound it in strips of linen with the spices, as the custom of the Jews is to bury. Now in the place where He was crucified there was a garden, and in the garden a new tomb in which no one had yet been laid.
> JOHN 19:40-41

The Place of Crucifixion: Golgotha

The penalty of crucifixion is believed to be the brutal innovation of the ancient Phoenicians which was instituted around the tenth century B.C. It was later adopted by the Assyrians as a method of torture known as impaling. But it would be the Romans who would perfect it as a means of execution for slaves, state criminals, and rebels. Despite the widespread mention of the practice of crucifixion in ancient literature; i.e., the Dead Sea Scrolls, the writings of Josephus, the Talmud, various Roman annals, and the New Testament, no actual archaeological evidence of a crucified victim had ever been found.[1] However, in 1968, the remains of a crucified man were discovered in an ossuary in a northern suburb of Jerusalem. An ossuary (Latin *ossus*—"bones") is a depository box, often decorative, for the bones of the dead. They could be made of stone or wood and inscribed with designs on the sides and tops and often had names inscribed on them as well. They were essentially secondary burial boxes. Bodies were initially placed in tombs for the disintegration of the flesh; then the bones were gathered and placed in an ossuary.

JERUSALEM

Jesus and the two criminals that died next to Him were crucified on the afternoon of the Feast of Passover before Sabbath at sundown. Consequently, the Jewish rulers demanded a quick execution so as not to desecrate the approaching holy day.

The first-century ossuaries were used by both Jews and early Christians. The symbol of the Cross was sometimes etched on the stone coffins and are the oldest record of Christian faith ever found. It was Jewish custom to have two burials. The first phase is actually depicted in the burial practices applied to the body of Jesus (John 19:39-42). The body was treated with spices and carefully wrapped with a separate covering for the head. It is no wonder that John believed when he saw the "handkerchief" used for the headdress lying off to the side of the empty tomb (John 20:7). Lazarus, on the other hand, needed help as he was unable to loose himself when called forth from the grave (John 11:44). The resurrection of Jesus is surely a manifestation of divine glory and power. Typically, a body lay in the tomb for one year. The bones would then have been collected and subsequently put into an ossuary commemorating a second burial. This cultural tradition may help us understand Jesus' seemingly callous response to the individual who first wanted to go and "bury his father" before fulfilling the call of discipleship.

Then another of His disciples said to Him, "Lord, let me first go and bury my father." But Jesus said to him, "Follow Me, and let the dead bury their own dead."

MATTHEW 8:21-22

Rabbinic sources convey that the act of decomposition had a purifying effect, that is, atoning spiritually for the sins of the deceased. Consummation of the spiritual process was the secondary burial a year later. However, in the theology of Jesus, only God can atone for sin. Thus, He interprets the man's request as an excuse, one that seeks to put off the call to discipleship. Jesus instructs him to "Follow Me" and let his ancestors gather the bones and place them in the ossuary. He was to go and preach the kingdom of God, telling of the true means of atonement, rather than waiting for the flesh to decompose, which cannot atone for sin.

The significance of the ossuary box found at Giv' at ha-Mirtar, just north of the Mount of Olives, is that it contained evidence of the practice of crucifixion dating to the time of Jesus. Excavations uncovered the skeleton of a Jewish man in an inscribed ossuary with the Aramaic name *Yohannan ben Ha'galgol.* Doctors from Jerusalem's Hadassah Medical School examined the bones.[2] The results showed the skeletal remains belonged to a man who had died in his late 20's or early 30's—close to the same age Jesus was at the time of His death.

WHERE JESUS
WALKED

HISTORY HAS
RECORDED THE
SUFFERING
ASSOCIATED
WITH BEING
CRUCIFIED.

Inside the ossuary was discovered an ankle bone pierced with a seven-inch-long crucifixion nail, still attached to a piece of wood from a cross. Apparently when the man was crucified, the iron nail struck a knot in the olive-wood upright post (called a *patibulum*).[3] The nail was so imbedded into the post that the victim could not be removed from the cross without retaining both the nail and the fragment from the cross. The evidence is an important archaeological witness to the crucifixion of Jesus described in the Bible. It affirms that the method of execution as portrayed in the gospel autographs is historically accurate. Jesus said, "Behold My hands and My feet" (Luke 24:39). Normally, the horizontal crosspiece was carried by the victim to the site of crucifixion where the vertical shaft was already in place. Sometimes the extremities of the victim were tied with ropes, with the arms hanging over the back of the crosspiece. If the arms were nailed, the spike passed between the bones of the arm at the wrist.[4] It is not clear from the anthropological evidence of the body in the ossuary if the arms were nailed or tied.

The posture of a crucified body on a cross has long been debated. Proposed illustrations demonstrate that crucifixion was either with legs

JERUSALEM

THE CHURCH OF THE HOLY SEPULCHRE IS THE TRADITIONAL SITE OF JESUS' CRUCIFIXION AND BURIAL.

bent and turned adjacent to the body or nailed on either side of the upright beam. Another position depicts that crucifixion was in an open position with knees apart. In any case, the weight of the body was forced upon the nails, causing terribly painful muscle spasms. Death came eventually through the excruciating process of asphyxiation. A cross might have a narrow ledge on which the victim could perch for support. So to hasten the victim's death, legs were often broken, eliminating any leverage he might have used to get air to the lungs. Unable to bear the weight of the body, the victim would hang by the arms producing a squeezing in the chest which closed the breathing passages. The leg bones found in Yohannan's ossuary revealed that his knees had been doubled up and laid sideways, and that his shin bones had been broken.[5] Jesus and the two criminals who died next to Him were crucified on the afternoon of the Feast of Passover before Sabbath at sundown. Consequently, the Jewish rulers demanded a quick execution so as not to desecrate the approaching holy day (John 19:31-32). Scripture reveals prophetic fulfillment that not a bone of Jesus would be broken (Num. 9:12; John 19:36). The discovery of Yohannan ben Ha'galgol's nail-pieced ankle bone demonstrates that a crucified victim, like Jesus, could receive a proper Jewish burial.

Other excavations have found Herodian family tombs on Mount Scopus. An inscription of one of these ossuaries identifies the contents as belonging to someone from the family of Nicanor. He is the Alexandrian who donated the copper gates for the inner court of the Temple.[6] An Aramaic inscription on another tomb bears the name Simon who is honored as "builder of the Temple." Another Jerusalem tomb discovered in 1990 contained several ossuaries inscribed with the name Caiaphas. It is thought that they were members of the priestly family which includes the high priest who presided over the late-night trial of Jesus (John 11:49-53; 18:14). Caiaphas served as leader of the Sanhedrin from A.D. 18-36. The remains were found by accident when workers were building south of the Temple Mount in Jerusalem's Peace Forest.[7] The discovery exposed a burial chamber with 12 limestone ossuaries. One such box was exquisitely decorated and testifies to the wealth of a high-ranking official. On it was carved in two places "Caiaphas" and "Joseph, son of Caiaphas." Josephus gives the full name of Caiaphas of the New Testament as "Joseph who was called Caiaphas of the high priesthood."[8]

There are several locations which lay claim to being the site of the crucifixion and burial plot of Jesus. The Bible gives five distinct clues concerning these locations.

- First of all, we are informed that the crucifixion occurred outside the city walls and/or outside one of its gates (Heb. 13:12).

- Second, we are told that Jesus bore the cross near the city, for many Jews read the inscription on the cross (John 19:20).

- Third, we are informed the event took place on a road because the account speaks of people passing by (Mark 15:29).

- Fourth, because the crucifixion could be observed from a distance, we can assume it may possibly have occured on a hill (Mark 15:40).

- And, fifth, concerning His burial site, we are told His tomb was located nearby in a garden (John 19:41).[9]

Eusebius places Golgotha, or Calvary, north of Mount Zion in the direction of the two most acclaimed sites: Church of the Holy Sepulchre

SITE OF
INTEREST

THE CHURCH
OF THE HOLY
SEPULCHRE

BYZANTINE

CONSTANTINE I
ORIGINALLY
FORMULATED
THE CHURCH
OF THE HOLY
SEPULCHRE.

(traditional) and "Gordon's Calvary" (modern). The Church of the Holy Sepulchre was originally formulated by Constantine, so this lends historical credibility. The history of the area shows that it was used as a stone quarry until the first century A.D. The Church of St. Stephen is nearby and confirms the location as a place of execution. It is believed that some execution victims were thrown off the hill into the quarry and finished off by stoning. It was also common for abandoned quarries to be used for tomb complexes.[10] The rock upon which the church was built can still be partly seen. It exhibits evidence of earthquake activity which fits the Gospel story (Matt. 27:51). The excavated area reveals that it was a rejected portion of a pre-Exilic white stone quarry.[11] By the first century B.C., the rejected quarry had gone from being a refuse drop to a burial site. Randall Price notes that Peter's citation of Psalm 118:22—"The stone which the builders rejected"—may have a double meaning (Acts 4:11; 1 Peter 2:7).[12] This quarry was located on a public road outside the city walls in the time of Jesus. So it would therefore fulfill both the Jewish and Roman requirements as a place of execution (Lev. 24:14).

Eusebius notes the Romans attempted to violate the early sacredness of this plot of

THIS STATUE SHOWS HELENA, THE MOTHER OF CONSTANTINE, HOLDING THE CROSS SHE FOUND IN THE GOLGATHA CISTERN.

JERUSALEM

ground by erecting a temple to Aphrodite—a sacrarium which Constantine later destroyed.[13] In 135 A.D., when Jerusalem became the Roman colony *Aelia Capitolina*, the emperor Hadrian issued orders to construct a temple to Zeus on Golgotha and an altar to Venus (the Roman equivalent to the Greek goddess Aphrodite) over the sepulchre. In his "Letter to Paulinuis" (A.D. 395), Jerome also verifies that the place of the resurrection of Jesus was occupied by a statue of Jupiter from the time of Hadrian to Constantine. The rock where Christ was crucified is said to have supported a marble statue of Venus.[14] Eusebius, the Bishop of Caesarea who participated in the dedication of the Church of the Holy Sepulchre in A.D. 335, confirms that Hadrian blanketed the area with dirt, covered it with a layer of stone pavement, and erected a shrine to Venus. The temple structure and pavement remained until A.D. 326 when Helena, Constantine's mother, came to Jerusalem and had them removed.[15] Helena just might be the first known archaeologist. She began a tradition of searching for relics that lasted well into the Middle Ages. In her interest to discover the site of the crucifixion and the "True Cross" of Christ, Hadrian's temple was destroyed, the former quarry was excavated, and the polluted pagan soil was removed. The exact location was revealed to her in a dream and confirmed by local inquiries. What was uncovered was a rocky precipice considered to be Golgotha. The dig also turned up three crosses in a cistern. In order to verify whether or not the "True Cross" of Christ had been found, the "Lazarus test" was applied. A recently deceased individual was laid upon each cross. Supposedly, when the body touched the third cross, it was revived and stood up to walk. So Constantine instructed the bishop of Jerusalem, Macarius, to build a structure "as a house of prayer worthy of the worship of God on this hallowed plot of ground."[16] The finished product was the Church of the Holy Sepulchre that was built to commemorate the location. Eusebius called it a basilica. It is the first time the term was used in literary reference to define a Christian church.[17]

GREEK/ ROMAN

EUSEBIUS NOTES THE ROMANS ATTEMPTED TO VIOLATE THE EARLY SACREDNESS OF THIS PLOT OF GROUND BY ERECTING A TEMPLE TO APHRODITE.

The original church of Constantine has been destroyed and reconstructed several times; nonetheless, it has fixed the site as a revered traditional landmark since its dedication in A.D. 335. It is presently in the Christian quarter of the city and is run by six Christian denominations: Catholic, Greek Orthodox, Copts, Armenians, Syrians, and Ethiopians. It is also the largest church in Jerusalem. The original church was laid out on an east-west plan.

JERUSALEM

> *The place of Jesus' crucifixion, Golgotha, is a rendering of the Hebrew word "gulgoleth" which implies a bold, round, skull-like mound.*

The tomb was covered by a great circular building, the Anastasis, that was crowned with a golden dome. In the courtyard, the rock of Golgotha lay in a large garden area.[18] The place of the crucifixion was marked by the basilica where its steps descended to the main north-south street, the *Cardo Maximus*.

> After this, Joseph of Arimathea, being a disciple of Jesus, but secretly, for fear of the Jews, asked Pilate that he might take away the body of Jesus; and Pilate gave him permission. So he came and took the body of Jesus. And Nicodemus, who at first came to Jesus by night, also came, bringing a mixture of myrrh and aloes, about a hundred pounds. Then they took the body of Jesus, and bound it in strips of linen with the spices, as the custom of the Jews is to bury. Now in the place where he was crucified there was a garden, and in the garden a new tomb in which no one had yet been laid. So there they laid Jesus, because of the Jews' Preparation Day, for the tomb was nearby.
> JOHN 19:38-42

The place of Jesus' crucifixion, Golgotha, is a rendering of the Hebrew word *gulgoleth* which implies a bold, round, skull-like mound.[19] The term translates in the Old Testament in the literal sense as the "skull" of Jezebel (2 Kings 9:35). It also is translated "skull" in modern Hebrew. The Aramaic rendering *gulgulta* means "the place of skull." Jerome (346-420 A.D.) suggested skulls lay about unburied outside the city.[20] The Greek expression *kranion topos* ("topography-skull") is thought to have derived from

THE FACE OF A SKULL IN THE ROCK AT GORDON'S CALVARY.

the cranial shape of the hill (Luke 23:33).[21] The Latin word for Calvary, *Calvaria,* used in the Vulgate also means "skull"; i.e., the place of execution where skulls are found. Three of the Gospels use the Hebrew-Aramaic term, *Golgotha* (Matt. 27:33; Mark 15:22; John 19:17) and only one uses the Greek equivalent, *Calvary* (Luke 23:33). The use of the definite article, *"the* place of the skull" indicates that the place was well-known.[22] An English version of the Bible may give the name as either Golgotha, Calvary, or Place of the Skull.

> And they brought Him to the place Golgotha, which is trans-lated, Place of a Skull. Then they gave Him wine mingled with myrrh to drink, but He did not take it. And when they crucified Him, they divided His garments, casting lots for them to deter-mine what every man should take. Now it was the third hour, and they crucified Him. And the inscription of His accusation was written above: THE KING OF THE JEWS.

JERUSALEM

With Him they also crucified two robbers, one on His right and the other on His left. So the Scripture was fulfilled which says, "And He was numbered with the transgressors." And those who passed by blasphemed Him, wagging their heads and saying, "Aha! You who destroy the temple and build it in three days, save Yourself, and come down from the cross!" Likewise the chief priests also, mocking among themselves with the scribes, said, "He saved others; Himself He cannot save. Let the Christ, the King of Israel, descend now from the cross, that we may see and believe." Even those who were crucified with Him reviled Him.

Now when the sixth hour had come, there was darkness over the whole land until the ninth hour. And at the ninth hour Jesus cried out with a loud voice, saying, "Eloi, Eloi, lama sabachthani?" which is translated, "My God, My God, why have You forsaken Me?" Some of those who stood by, when they heard that, said, "Look, He is calling for Elijah!" Then someone ran and filled a sponge full of sour wine, put it on a reed, and offered it to Him to drink, saying, "Let Him alone; let us see if Elijah will come to take Him down." And Jesus cried out with a loud voice, and breathed His last. Then the veil of the temple was torn in two from top to bottom. So when the centurion, who stood opposite Him, saw that He cried out like this and breathed His last, he said, "Truly this Man was the Son of God!" There were also women looking on from afar, among whom were Mary Magdalene, Mary the mother of James the Less and of Joses, and Salome, who also followed Him and ministered to Him when He was in Galilee, and many other women who came up with Him to Jerusalem.

Now when evening had come, because it was the Preparation Day, that is, the day before the Sabbath, Joseph of Arimathea, a prominent council member, who was himself waiting for the kingdom of God, coming and taking courage, went in to Pilate and asked for the body of Jesus. Pilate marveled that He was already dead; and summoning the centurion, he asked him if

He had been dead for some time. So when he found out from the centurion, he granted the body to Joseph. Then he bought fine linen, took Him down, and wrapped Him in the linen. And he laid Him in a tomb which had been hewn out of the rock, and rolled a stone against the door of the tomb. And Mary Magdalene and Mary the mother of Joses observed where He was laid.

MARK 15:22-47

SITE OF INTEREST

Just north of the present Damascus Gate, very close to the city walls, is the site of "Gordon's Calvary"—the proposed Protestant site of the crucifixion, death, and burial place of Jesus. A hill at this location rises about 50 feet above the local terrain in plain view of the entire area (Matt. 27:36-54). The side that faces Jerusalem bears a resemblance to an image of a human skull. It demonstrates caverns for its eyes, a protruding rock for its nose, and a long opening with a ledge that serves as the mouth and chin. In addition, there is a garden tomb very close by. General Charles Gordon confirmed this site in 1885.[23] Even though the face of the hill has endured some artificial excavation and erosion and appears different than it did in

GORDON'S CALVARY IS THE PROPOSED PROTESTANT SITE OF JESUS' CRUCIFIXION.

GORDON'S GARDEN TOMB IS ANOTHER SUPPOSED SITE OF JESUS' TEMPORARY BURIAL.

JERUSALEM

181

biblical times, the sight has found contemporary acceptance and popularity.[24] It does provide a serene setting and a sense of piety to the area. Excavations within the Church of the Holy Sepulchre (1976) uncovered a 35-foot mound of rock with two caves providing a skull-like appearance as well. During the time of Christ, the mound—claimed as genuine Calvary, would have been located outside the city wall.[25] But, neither the New Testament nor any of the early church fathers provide any evidence that the crucifixion actually occurred on a raised hill.

Gordon's Garden Tomb appears to be the type of a tomb from the First Temple period and reused in Byzantine times; i.e., a trough burial place. When the tomb was discovered, it displayed two Byzantine crosses painted in red on the east wall of the chamber. In addition, other Byzantine tombs have been located in the area.[26] The tomb described in the New Testament was "a new tomb, in which no one had yet been laid" (John 19:41-42). Upon scriptural definition, the actual tomb of Jesus would seem to have been a first-century arcosolium type rather than the oblong burial niches or loculi type (kokim) as seen at Gordon's Calvary.

AN EXAMPLE OF A ROCK USED TO SEAL ANCIENT TOMBS.

The loculi tombs are associated with the First Temple period and were cut in the rock walls for bodies. The biblical description of the angels seated at the head and feet of Jesus would only be possible in an arcosolium tomb—"a bench-like aperture with an arched ceiling hewn in the length of the wall" as stated by Rachel Itaclili.[27] The later arcosolium type of burial (which corresponds with the Temple of Herod) would have been the kind used around Jerusalem.

Now when the Sabbath was past, Mary Magdalene, Mary the mother of James, and Salome bought spices, that they might come and anoint Him. Very early in the morning, on the first day of the week, they came to the tomb when the sun had risen. And they said among themselves, "Who will roll away the stone from the door of the tomb for us?" But when they looked up, they saw that the stone had been rolled away—for it was very large. And entering the tomb, they saw a young man clothed in a long white robe sitting on the right side; and they were alarmed. But he said to them, "Do not be alarmed. You seek Jesus of Nazareth, who was crucified. He is risen! He is not here. See the place where they laid Him. But go, tell His disciples—and Peter—that He is going before you into Galilee; there you will see Him, as He said to you." So they went out quickly and fled from the tomb, for they trembled and were amazed. And they said nothing to anyone, for they were afraid.

Now when He rose early on the first day of the week, He appeared first to Mary Magdalene, out of whom He had cast seven demons. She went and told those who had been with Him, as they mourned and wept. And when they heard that He was alive and had been seen by her, they did not believe.

After that, He appeared in another form to two of them as they walked and went into the country. And they went and told it to the rest, but they did not believe them either.

Later He appeared to the eleven as they sat at the table; and He rebuked their unbelief and hardness of heart, because they did not believe those who had seen Him after He had risen. And He said to them, "Go into all the world and preach the gospel to every creature. He who believes and is baptized will be saved; but he who does not believe will be condemned. And these signs will follow those who believe: In My name they will cast out demons; they will speak with new tongues; they will take up serpents; and if they drink anything deadly, it will by no means hurt them; they will lay hands on the sick, and they will recover."

So then, after the Lord had spoken to them, He was received up into heaven, and sat down at the right hand of God. And they went out and preached everywhere, the Lord working with them and confirming the word through the accompanying signs. Amen.

MARK 16:1-20

OLD
TESTAMENT

BENEATH THE
MOUND OF
CALVARY IS
BELIEVED TO
BE THE CAVE
WHERE
JEREMIAH
WROTE THE
BOOK OF
LAMENTATIONS.

Beneath the mound of Calvary is believed to be the cave of Jeremiah. It was here that he wrote the book of Lamentations. Other traditions state this is also the burial place of the skull of the first man, Adam, and that it was this belief that gave the mound its name.[28] This was first mentioned by Origen (A.D. 185-254).[29] The general area includes two quarries.

The Upper Room

In New Testament times a room was frequently built on the roof of a house or houses. These rooftop rooms were especially popular because of the cool conditions they afforded in the summer months. It was in this kind of upper room, (Greek *anogeon,* "a room upstairs" or *hyperoon,* "upper")[1] which were common among the wealthy, that several significant events in Jerusalem took place (2 Kings 1:2; 23:12; Jer. 22:13 f.).[2]

It was in an upper room such as this that Jesus shared His last Passover meal (the Last Supper) with the disciples (Matt. 26:18; Mark 14:15; Luke 22:12). The present location, adjacent to the Benedictine Monastery, is sometimes referred to as "The Cenacle" and dates from the Medieval Period.[3] *Coenaculum* is the Latin term for a small dining room on the upper floor. Dining rooms were characteristic of middle and upper-class homes of the Roman Empire.[4] A meal would be eaten in such dining rooms at a *triclinium* table (a "U" shape that surrounded three sides) which was most often used by the wealthy.[5] It was the custom in Israel during the first century for the people to eat the Passover in a reclining position, or on one elbow (John 13:21-23). Accordingly, this meant that God had made all Jews wealthy by their deliverance from slavery during the Exodus from Egypt. Such a posture is indicated in John's account of the Last Supper who depicts a disciple as lying close to the breast of Jesus. Seats were arranged in a specific order of importance so that an observer, facing the table, would know the prominence of the individuals. The host always occupied position two. To the left was the seat of honor, while to the right the seats were arranged in a descending order. Understanding this cultural placement, it appears that John and Judas sat on either side of

AN INTERIOR VIEW OF THE TRADITIONAL UPPER ROOM.

Jesus. The last seat to the right was the place of least importance and had the responsibility of washing the feet of the guests.[6] This may have been Peter's position because of the discussion involving foot washing that took place between Jesus and Peter when Peter failed to carry out his responsibility (John 13:1-12). It is also possible that this same room is the one in which the disciples gathered after Jesus was crucified.

Epiphanius (a monk who wrote a Bible dictionary dealing with the geography of Palestine), stated that the emperor Hadrian discovered the

JERUSALEM

CRUSADERS

THE HOLY
ZION CHURCH
WAS REBUILT
BY THE
CRUSADERS IN
1099.

building, of which the Upper Room was a part, still standing when he visited Jerusalem in A.D. 135. The Bordeaux Pilgrim also mentions it in his treatise in A.D. 333.[7] The building was later distinguished in a series of lectures given in 348 A.D. by Cyril, Bishop of Jerusalem.[8] In addition, Theodosius (an unknown individual who left us the itinerary of his pilgrimage to places in the Holy Land) identifies the Holy Zion Church (Upper Room, A.D. 530) as the site of the house of St. Mark the Evangelist (cf. Acts 12:12).[9] He located it 200 paces from Golgotha. The church was rebuilt by the Crusaders in approximately 1099 and purchased in 1335 by the Franciscans. John McRay states it was they who altered the cenacle, "giving it the Gothic appearance it now possesses."[10]

Repairs to the Holy Zion Church, or the Upper Room, were done in 1951 after a mortar shell had damaged the edifice in the War of Independence. At this time, excavations by archaeologist Jacob Pinkerfield were undertaken. He found the remains of a Roman-period structure beneath the ruins of the Byzantine church which he identified as a Jewish synagogue.[11] The identification was determined by the discovery of a niche used as a repository for Torah scrolls. It resembled niches in other synagogues of the period. However, Bargil Pixner has further demonstrated that the structure was a Roman-period Judeo-Christian synagogue—the Church of the Apostles.[12] He believes the building signifies the site where the apostles prayed when they returned from the Mount of Olives after the Ascension by Jesus into heaven (Acts 1:1-13). Pixner maintains that since the niche is directed toward the Church of the Holy Sepulchre rather than towards the Temple (which was the practice of Jewish synagogues erected before A.D. 70), it signifies the location of the Last Supper and the visitation of the Holy Spirit at Pentecost.[13] So, it is possible that "The Cenacle" site is the actual room in which Jesus appeared to the eleven after His resurrection (Mark 16:14; Luke 24:33-43) even though the door was locked.

> Then, the same day at evening, being the first day of the week, when the doors were shut where the disciples were assembled, for fear of the Jews, Jesus came and stood in the midst, and said to them, "Peace be with you." When He had said this, He

JERUSALEM

showed them His hands and His side. Then the disciples were glad when they saw the Lord. So Jesus said to them again, "Peace to you! As the Father has sent Me, I also send you." And when He had said this, He breathed on them, and said to them, "Receive the Holy Spirit. If you forgive the sins of any, they are forgiven them; if you retain the sins of any, they are retained."

Now Thomas, called the Twin, one of the twelve, was not with them when Jesus came. The other disciples therefore said to him, "We have seen the Lord." So he said to them, "Unless I see in His hands the print of the nails, and put my finger into the print of the nails, and put my hand into His side, I will not believe." And after eight days His disciples were again inside, and Thomas with them. Jesus came, the doors being shut, and stood in the midst, and said, "Peace to you!" Then He said to Thomas, "Reach your finger here, and look at My hands; and reach your hand here, and put it into My side. Do not be unbelieving, but believing." And Thomas answered and said to Him, "My Lord and my God!" Jesus said to him, "Thomas, because you have seen Me, you have believed. Blessed are those who have not seen and yet have believed."

JOHN 20:19-29

Jesus ascended from Mount Olivet which is from Jerusalem a "Sabbath day's journey"—nearly three quarters of a mile or 2,000 cubits. This was the extent one could walk without breaking a sweat, thus not be considered work. The lawful distance was fixed by tradition that in the camp of the Israelites, (when coming from Egypt) no part of the camp was more than 2,000 paces from the tabernacle. As a result, this became the distance permitted to travel for worship and was the extent of the suburbs in the Levitical cities (Num. 35:5). The disciples, upon witnessing Jesus' ascent, returned to Jerusalem and went into an upper room. There they continued with one accord in prayer and supplication, with the women and the brethren (Acts 1:12-15). Matthias was selected at this time as the apostle to replace Judas. But The Upper Room is seemingly best remembered as the site of the arrival of the Holy Spirit on the Day of Pentecost.

ACTS OF THE
APOSTLES

THE UPPER
ROOM IS BEST
REMEMBERED
AS THE SITE OF
THE ARRIVAL
OF THE HOLY
SPIRIT ON THE
DAY OF
PENTECOST.

JERUSALEM

187

When the Day of Pentecost had fully come, they were all with one accord in one place. And suddenly there came a sound from heaven, as of a rushing mighty wind, and it filled the whole house where they were sitting. Then there appeared to them divided tongues, as of fire, and one sat upon each of them. And they were all filled with the Holy Spirit and began to speak with other tongues, as the Spirit gave them utterance.

ACTS 2:1-4

THE CHURCH OF THE DORMITION IS THE TRADITIONAL SPOT OF MARY'S DEATH. CONSTANTINE'S CHURCH OF MOUNT ZION STOOD ON THE SAME SPOT.

According to Leviticus 23:15-17, on the fiftieth day after the waving of the barley sheaf of firstfruits, the priest was to offer two loaves made of new, fine leavened flour from the harvest for a firstfruit wave offering of joy and gratitude unto the Lord. It was a one-day festival in which sacrifices were offered. Originally, it was a harvest festival (Ex. 23:16; 34:22; Lev. 23:15-21; Deut. 16:9-10; Num. 28:26). It is possible that the festival was associated with the giving of the Law at Sinai. Thus, the apostle Luke's Christian interpretation is that the giving of the Spirit is parallel to the giving of the Law. The feast of the harvest was called the Feast of Weeks, or *Pentecost,* which means "fiftieth,"

JERUSALEM

because of the seven weeks that had elapsed between the two wave offerings. Pentecost indicated that the period of waiting had come to an end and that the Old Testament prophecies were about to be fulfilled. The Sadducees interpreted the "Sabbath" mentioned in the book of Leviticus to be the weekly Sabbath after Passover. Hence, it caused Pentecost to occur on a Sunday, the fiftieth day.

The New Testament Scriptures do not specifically name the place where Pentecost actually occurred. Most believe the traditional understanding to be the Upper Room. Others consider two possible sites on the Temple Mount, one being the colonnades around the perimeter of the courts such as Solomon's Porch. Peter's statement that it was "the third hour of the day" (9:00 A.M.) has caused some to believe the disciples were in the Temple area for the required time of morning prayer (Acts 2:15). Moreover, the Temple is called a "house" in the book of Acts (7:47). The other location on Temple Mount may be on the southern steps. Many people would be entering and exiting the Temple from this area. Just below the steps were the ritual baths in which a crowd of 3,000 could be baptized (Acts 2:38-47). If Pentecost did take place in the Upper Room, it no doubt spilled over into the streets.

Next door to the Upper Room is the beautiful, modern, German Church of the *Dormition* ("sleeping") with beautiful mosaics that depict events of religious history. It has superb concert acoustics. It was built between 1906 and 1910 on the location where, tradition notes, Mary died, or rather "fell asleep." Constantine's Church of Mount Zion, one of the earliest churches in Jerusalem, stood on the same spot. Tradition states that the body of St. Stephen was brought to Jerusalem and laid in the edifice where the Church of the Dormition now stands. The land was eventually gifted to Kaiser Wilhelm II of Germany in 1898 by an Ottoman Sultan. The Church of the Dormition is a unique, circular building with a distinct, conical gray roof.[14] When observed with the nearby belfry, the two structures combine to make a notable landmark in the Holy City.

Just below the Upper Room is the Tomb of David. This tomb was designated as such by the Crusaders because of Peter's statement in his sermon at Pentecost: "Men and brethren, let me speak freely to you of the patriarch

SITE OF
INTEREST

THE CHURCH OF
THE DORMITION

SITE OF
INTEREST

THE TOMB OF
DAVID

JERUSALEM

David, that he is both dead and buried, and his tomb is with us to this day" (Acts 2:29 KJV). But the actual location is in question.

I hope my commentary provided in this section on Jerusalem will serve your visit to the Holy City in the way I have intended. And now that you have been exposed to its wondrous presence, you undoubtedly realize that you are beholding thousands of years of history in its ancient structures. Jerusalem is the city that time forgot! It remains today much as it did in the year the Roman calendar began. But most importantly, your awareness of the sights pertaining to the death, burial, resurrection, and ascension of Jesus, who is called Christ, has been enhanced. I pray you will continue to seek Him who is the author of life. The only fact that will ever overshadow the truth that God's Passover Lamb bore the sins of humankind in this divinely appointed city is the fact that He will one day return to this special place.

> Now it shall come to pass in the latter days that the mountain of the LORD's house shall be established on the top of the mountains, and shall be exalted above the hills; and peoples shall flow to it. Many nations shall come and say, "Come, and let us go up to the mountain of the Lord, to the house of the God of Jacob; He will teach us His ways, and we shall walk in His paths." For out of Zion the law shall go forth, and the word of the LORD from Jerusalem.
> MICAH 4:1-2

Personal Reflections

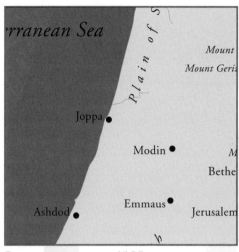

FROM MAP INSIDE THE FRONT COVER: 6-7, E-F.

CHAPTER FOURTEEN

Joppa

"Send therefore to Joppa and call Simon here, whose surname is Peter. He is lodging in the house of Simon, a tanner, by the sea. When he comes, he will speak to you."

ACTS 10:32

Joppa means "beautiful"[1] and is descriptive of its picturesque setting on the Mediterranean. This historic city was built on a rock hill over 100 feet high which projects beyond the coastline to form a small cape. It was the only natural harbor on the Mediterranean shoreline between Acco (near modern Haifa) and Egypt. The harbor was formed by a natural breakwater of rocks parallel to the coast. To the north lies the Plain of Sharon, while the Plain of Philistia lies to the south.[2] The modern city of Tel Aviv encompasses the ancient city and offers the visitor the tranquil quietness of the old and the contemporary nightlife of the new.

In the conquest of the Promised Land by Israel, the territory of Joppa was allotted to the tribe of Dan and formed their northern border.

OLD TESTAMENT

THE TERRITORY OF JOPPA WAS ALLOTTED TO THE TRIBE OF DAN.

JOPPA

Jehud, Bene Berak, Gath Rimmon, Me Jarkon, and Rakkon, with the region near Joppa. And the border of the children of Dan went beyond these, because the children of Dan went up to fight against Leshem and took it; and they struck it with the edge of the sword, took possession of it, and dwelt in it. They called Leshem, Dan, after the name of Dan their father.

JOSHUA 19:45-47

But seemingly, Joppa never fully passed into Israelite possession. The Danites were resisted by the Philistines and migrated northward (Judg. 18:1-2). So Joppa was rarely under Israelite rule. It was recaptured from the Philistines by David, then Solomon eventually developed the facilities so that Joppa became a major port serving as the Mediterranean gateway to Jerusalem 35 miles away.[3] The harbor area proved to be inadequate due to its shallowness and dangerous rock formations; consequently, most of the trade activity was accomplished by transfer boats. The Bible does record that rafts of cedar from Lebanon were floated to Joppa and then sent to Jerusalem for use in the original construction of the Temple by Solomon (2 Chron. 2:16). It was repeated once again in the later rebuilding of the Temple (Ezra 3:7) by those who returned to the Holy City by the decree of Cyrus (538 B.C.).[4]

OLD
TESTAMENT

JOPPA MAY BEST
BE REMEMBERED
AS THE CITY
FROM WHICH
JONAH FLED
FROM THE
PRESENCE OF THE
LORD.

Joppa may best be remembered from an Old Testament story as the city from which Jonah fled the presence of the Lord. At the time, Phoenicia had control:

Now the word of the Lord came to Jonah the son of Amittai, saying, "Arise, go to Nineveh, that great city, and cry out against it; for their wickedness has come up before Me." But Jonah arose to flee to Tarshish from the presence of the LORD. He went down to Joppa, and found a ship going to Tarshish; so he paid the fare, and went down into it, to go with them to Tarshish from the presence of the LORD.

But the LORD sent out a great wind on the sea, and there was a mighty tempest on the sea, so that the ship was about to be broken up. Then the mariners were afraid; and every man cried out to his god, and threw the cargo that was in the ship into the sea, to lighten the load. But Jonah had gone down into the lowest parts of the ship, had lain down, and was fast asleep. So the captain came to him, and said to him, "What do you mean, sleeper? Arise, call on your God; perhaps your God will consider us, so that we may not perish." And they said to one another, "Come, let us cast lots, that we may know for whose cause this trouble has come upon us." So they cast lots, and the lot fell on Jonah. Then they said to him, "Please tell us! For whose cause is this trouble upon us? What is your occupation? And where do you come from? What is your country? And of what people are you?" And he said to them, "I am a Hebrew; and I fear the LORD, the God of heaven, who made the sea and the dry land."

Then the men were exceedingly afraid, and said to him, "Why have you done this?" For the men knew that he fled from the presence of the LORD, because he had told them. Then they said to him, "What shall we do to you that the sea may be calm for us?"— for the sea was growing more tempestuous. And he said to them, "Pick me up and throw me into the sea; then the sea will become calm for you. For I know that this great tempest is because of me." Nevertheless the men rowed hard to return to land, but they could not, for the sea continued to grow more tempestuous against them. Therefore they cried out to the LORD and said, "We pray, O LORD, please do not let us perish for this man's life, and do not charge us with innocent blood; for You, O LORD, have done as it pleased You." So they picked up Jonah and threw him into the sea, and the sea ceased from its raging. Then the men feared the Lord exceedingly, and offered a sacrifice to the LORD and made vows.

Now the LORD had prepared a great fish to swallow Jonah. And Jonah was in the belly of the fish three days and three nights. . . .

Now the word of the LORD came to Jonah the second time, saying, "Arise, go to Nineveh, that great city, and preach to it the message that I tell you." So Jonah arose and went to Nineveh, according to the word of the LORD. Now Nineveh was an exceedingly great city, a three-day journey in extent. And Jonah began to enter the city on the first day's walk. Then he cried out and said, "Yet forty days, and Nineveh shall be overthrown!"

So the people of Nineveh believed God, proclaimed a fast, and put on sackcloth, from the greatest to the least of them.

JONAH 1:1-17; 3:1-5

GREEK/ ROMAN

WHEN ALEXANDER THE GREAT CONQUERED THE CITY, HE CHANGED THE NAME FROM THE HEBREW JAPHO (KJV) TO JOPPA.

Joppa was a city that experienced a violent and vacillating history. Its ownership had changed hands on numerous occasions among the Assyrians, the Babylonians, and the Persians.[5] The Egyptians captured the city by trickery in 1450 B.C. They sent large baskets of gifts into the walled city as a token of their friendship; however, hidden inside the baskets were soldiers who took the city by surprise.[6] Joppa is also listed as one of the cities destroyed by Sennacherib the Assyrian in 726 B.C. (2 Kings 18:13 ff.; 2 Chron. 32:1 ff.; Isa. 36:1 ff.). When Alexander the Great conquered Joppa, he changed the Old Testament name from the Hebrew *Yapho* or *Japho* (Josh. 19:46 KJV) to *Joppa* (which is *Ioppe* in Greek and *Yafa* in Arabic).[7] Antiochus IV Epiphanes landed at Joppa in 168 B.C. en route to Jerusalem to enforce his program of Hellenization. Once in the Holy City, the Syrian king sought to stamp out the Hebrew religion. It was this harsh ruler with whom we dealt thoroughly in our chapter on the history of Israel who proceeded to rob, pillage, and desecrate the Temple in Jerusalem by forcing the high priest to sacrifice swine upon the holy altar. This action precipitated the Maccabean revolt.

ACTS OF THE APOSTLES

TABITHA WAS RAISED FROM THE DEAD IN JOPPA.

Joppa continued to experience aggression and conquest through the years until Roman occupation under Pompey in 66 B.C.[8] In 47 B.C., Julius Caesar returned Joppa to the Jews for services rendered to the state; thereafter, the city was gifted by Marc Antony to Cleopatra. It was then transferred once again by Caesar back to Herod in 37 B.C.[9] An early Christian community arose in Joppa during the beginning stages of development of the Church in the book of Acts. Peter's recorded ministry there initially involved the raising of a woman named Tabitha (Dorcas) from the dead (Acts 9:36-42).

ACTS OF THE APOSTLES

JOPPA IS WHERE PETER HAD THE VISION OF "THE CLEAN AND THE COMMON."

Peter stayed in Joppa at the house of one Simon the Tanner (Acts 10:5-6). It was there that Peter had the vision of the "clean and common" and

JOPPA

simultaneously received an invitation from Cornelius the centurion to come to Caesarea (Acts 10:9-20). As a result of the vision, Peter preached the Gospel to the Gentiles up the coast in Caesarea (Acts 10:33-48), and the Gentile church was birthed.

The next day, as they went on their journey and drew near the city, Peter went up on the housetop to pray, about the sixth hour. Then he became very hungry and wanted to eat; but while they made ready, he fell into a trance and saw heaven opened and an object like a great sheet bound at the four corners, descending to him and let down to the earth. In it were all kinds of four-footed animals of the earth, wild beasts, creeping things, and birds of the air. And a voice came to him, "Rise, Peter; kill and eat." But Peter said, "Not so, Lord! For I have never eaten anything common or unclean." And a voice spoke to him again the second time, "What God has cleansed you must not call common." This was done three times. And the object was taken up into heaven again.

Now while Peter wondered within himself what this vision which he had seen meant, behold, the men who had been sent from Cornelius had made inquiry for Simon's house, and stood before the gate. And they called and asked

THIS DOOR MARKS ONE OF THE POSSIBLE SITES FOR THE HOME OF SIMON THE TANNER.

whether Simon, whose surname was Peter, was lodging there. While Peter thought about the vision, the Spirit said to him, "Behold, three men are seeking you. Arise therefore, go down and go with them, doubting nothing; for I have sent them." Then Peter went down to the men who had been sent to him from Cornelius, and said, "Yes, I am he whom you seek. For what reason have you come?" And they said, "Cornelius the centurion, a just man, one who fears God and has a good reputation among all the nation of the Jews, was divinely instructed by a holy angel to summon you to his house, and to hear words from you." Then he invited them in and lodged them. On the next day Peter went away with them, and some brethren from Joppa accompanied him.

ACTS 10:9-23

Joppa was also a principal city in the revolt against Rome. The city was inhabited by zealous Jews and suffered heavily for its Jewish loyalties. In A.D. 66, the Romans killed 8,400 of its citizens. W. Ewing notes that in response, Joppa became "a resort of the enemies of Rome, who turned pirates and preyed upon shipping vessels in the neighboring waters."[10] It was destroyed by Vespasian in A.D. 68 but was later rebuilt. Today it is known as Jaffa, a suburb of Tel Aviv.[11]

CRUSADERS

THE CRUSADERS ENTERED THE HOLY LAND THROUGH JOPPA IN A.D. 1095.

The Crusaders, who responded to a plea by Pope Urban to rescue the Holy Land from Islam (A.D. 1095), entered Palestine through the port of Jaffa.[12] The Holy Land was taken back by Saladin, Sultan of Egypt and Syria, before being lost to the Crusaders again when Richard the Lion-Hearted launched another crusade which regained limited territory. Part of the negotiations for peace gave the Crusaders the rights of pilgrimage to Jerusalem and the territory along the coast between Tyre and Jaffa.[13] This was particularly significant because most other coastal points of entry had been destroyed by the Moslems to prevent Christian pilgrimages.

SITE OF INTEREST

MODERN JAFFA OFFERS SHOPPING AMONG GALLERIES AND UNIQUE SHOPS, AN UNDER-GROUND MUSEUM, AND THE CHURCH OF ST. PETER.

Today, the city of Jaffa provides a wonderful shopping experience. Galleries and unique shops line the many scenic alleyways along the edge of the sea. There is also an underground museum at the site of the ancient mound of Jaffa. Moreover, the life of Peter is commemorated at the Church of St. Peter in this pleasant, seaside town.

Personal Reflections

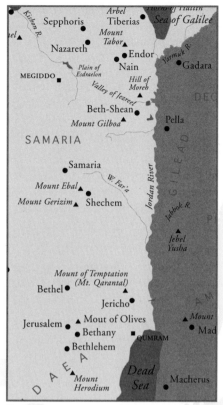

Map labels: Kishon R., Sepphoris, Arbel, Tiberias, Horns of Hattin, Sea of Galilee, Mount Tabor, Nazareth, Endor, Yarmuk R., Plain of Esdraelon, Nain, MEGIDDO, Hill of Moreh, Gadara, Valley of Jezreel, DEC, Beth-Shean, Mount Gilboa, Pella, SAMARIA, GILEAD, Samaria, W. Far'a, Jordan River, Mount Ebal, Mount Gerizim, Shechem, Jabbok R., P, Jebel Yusha, Mount of Temptation (Mt. Qarantal), Bethel, A M, Jericho, Mout of Olives, Mount, Jerusalem, Bethany, Mad, QUMRAM, Bethlehem, E A, Dead Sea, Macherus, Mount Herodium

From map inside the front cover: 8-9, C-G.

CHAPTER FIFTEEN
The Jordan River

It came to pass in those days that Jesus came from Nazareth of Galilee, and was baptized by John in the Jordan.

MARK 1:9

The Jordan River is the largest river in Palestine and is best known to Christians as the place where Jesus was baptized by John (Mark 1:9). It may very well be the most famous river on the face of the earth and plays a significant role in the history of Israel. It meanders in a north-south direction through the Jordan Valley (a series of the world's lowest depressions in the earth's crust). The Jordan begins in the snowy heights of Mount Hermon (site of the Transfiguration). Though the length of the Jordan Valley only stretches some 70 miles between the Sea of Galilee and the Dead Sea,[1] the river itself is hundreds of miles long as it twists and turns. The Great Rift, a geological fault in the area, was formerly filled by the Lisan Lake, but when it receded (affected by changing climatic conditions), it left three separate bodies of water all fed by the Jordan River.[2] It was between these three bodies of water that the narratives of the Old Testament were frequently portrayed. The river initially flows 7 miles before entering Lake Huleh, or Semachonitis as noted by Josephus.[3] It flows another 10 miles before entering into the Sea of Galilee and emerges 12-14 miles later. Then it continues on its serpentine route falling some 3000 feet to its final destination into the Dead Sea—the lowest point on earth (1296 feet below sea level). The river empties five million tons of fresh water into the Dead Sea each and every day. Nonetheless, because the Dead Sea has no outlet, the water simply stagnates.

A VIEW ALONG THE JORDAN RIVER.

Due to its descent and 27 rapids between the Sea of Galilee and the Dead Sea, the river experiences no traffic or trade. Because of the swampy conditions of the valley, the presence of wild animals, and tremendous heat, no large city was ever constructed directly on the Jordan's banks.[4] However, there are river-area cities associated with the ministry of Jesus (Matt. 4:25); i.e., the Decapolis, a federation of ten Greek cities (nine of which are on the eastern side of the Jordan). One of the cities, Pella, is thought to be the city to which the Christians fled during the time of the destruction of Jerusalem (A.D. 70).[5]

The word *Jordan* is derived from the Hebrew term *hayyarden* meaning "flowing downward," or "the descender, to descend rapidly."[6] Its name originally came from ancient Egyptian records which provide the spelling as *ya-ar-du-na,* the equivalent of the Canaanite *yardon.*[7] It is probable that the term *Jordan* is produced from *Yored Dan,* "descending Dan," and designates a river that begins in the northern territory of the city of Dan. It is one of several source streams that merge to form the Jordan as we know it. The River Jordan is very narrow in certain places, looking like little more than a creek; yet, in several episodes in Scripture, it is presented as an impassable barrier and a line of defense for those who desired to cross. In many instances it took a miracle such as the occurrence at Gilgal when Israel crossed over with Joshua (Josh. 3:15-17). The Jordan was the last obstacle that the Israelites faced before they could possess the land. Moses' final desire was to cross the river, but he was denied permission (Deut. 3:23-25). Subsequently, leadership was transferred to Joshua who was entrusted with the commission to "go over this Jordan" (Josh. 1:2).[8]

The Jordan River has frequent and important interaction in both the Old and New Testaments. It is called "the river of the wilderness" (Amos 6:14 KJV) and "the pride of the Jordan" (Zec. 11:3). The historic river is joined 20 miles below the Sea of Galilee by another river that descends through the Valley of Jezreel between Mt. Gilboa and Little Hermon. This valley provided Jews who desired to avoid ceremonial contamination by contact with the Samaritans a route from Jerusalem to Nazareth.[9] The "land beyond the Jordan" is called Perea (Matt. 19:1). The route proceeded past Bethshan, where the bodies of Saul and Jonathan were publicly exposed by the Philistines (1 Sam. 31:1-13). It continued past Shunem and Nain—the place where Jesus raised a widow's son from the dead (Luke 7:11), just six miles south of Nazareth.

OLD
TESTAMENT

The River Jordan is first mentioned in Scripture when Lot separated from Abram, chose "all the plain of Jordan," and settled near Sodom (Gen. 13:10-11). Lot was shortly thereafter taken captive by eastern kings. Abram took his servants and friends and followed the marauders back to the sources of the Jordan (in the region of Dan near Caesarea Philippi) and rescued him. S. Cohen states that Abram probably routed them in a night assault as they crossed the Jordan, attacking the "slow-moving and heavily

THE RIVER JORDAN IS FIRST MENTIONED WHEN LOT SEPARATED FROM ABRAM, CHOSE "ALL THE PLAIN OF JORDAN," AND SETTLED NEAR SODOM.

burdened" rear division.[10] The Jordan is also the place where Jacob wrestled with the Angel of the Lord (Gen. 32:22-32).

Midway between the Sea of Galilee and the Dead Sea (approximately 40 miles), the brook Jabbok intersects the Jordan. It is at this junction of the rivers that the site known as "Adam" is located. This later became the designation of the boundary separating Ammon from Gilead (Num. 21:24; Josh.12:2). J. M. Houston notes, "Between the Jabbok confluence and the Dead Sea, crossings are more difficult owing to the swift current."[11] It is here that the waters were held back when Israel crossed over in their conquest of Jericho (Josh. 3:16-17). One mile east of Jericho, on the western shore of the river, was the city of Gilgal—an important religious center (Josh. 4:19-20; 1 Sam. 7:16; 2 Kings 2). *Gilgal* means "circle" in Hebrew and may reflect Israel's memorial established to the "mighty hand of God" with the twelve stones on which the priests stood during the crossing of the Jordan.[12] Gilgal was the first place Israel encamped. And it was here that they celebrated the first Passover in the land of Canaan. The manna having ceased, they ate the fruit of the land (Josh. 4:19-5:12). The Jordan River also parted for the prophet Elijah (2 Kings 2:8); it then parted once again when his successor Elisha returned from the desert with the prophet's mantle.

> Then it happened, as they continued on and talked, that suddenly a chariot of fire appeared with horses of fire, and separated the two of them; and Elijah went up by a whirlwind into heaven.
>
> And Elisha saw it, and he cried out, "My father, my father, the chariot of Israel and its horsemen!" So he saw him no more. And he took hold of his own clothes and tore them into two pieces. He also took up the mantle of Elijah that had fallen from him, and went back and stood by the bank of the Jordan. Then he took the mantle of Elijah that had fallen from him, and struck the water, and said, "Where is the Lord God of Elijah?" And when he also had struck the water, it was divided this way and that; and Elisha crossed over. Now when the sons of the prophets who were from Jericho saw him, they said, "The spirit

of Elijah rests of Elisha." And they came to meet him, and bowed to the ground before him.
2 KINGS 2:11-15

OLD
TESTAMENT

NAAMAN THE
SYRIAN WAS
HEALED IN THE
WATERS OF THE
JORDAN WHEN
HE OBEYED THE
INSTRUCTIONS
OF ELISHA.

The well-known healing of Naaman the leper also occurred in the Jordan's waters. Naaman was the captain of the host of the king of Syria (2 Kings 5:1) and was encouraged by his Jewish servant to seek healing from Elisha the prophet of Israel. When he arrived, Elisha did not pray for the man but merely instructed him to "dip" in the Jordan seven times to receive his cure.

> Then Naaman went with his horses and chariot, and he stood at the door of Elisha's house. And Elisha sent a messenger to him, saying, "Go and wash in the Jordan seven times, and your flesh shall be restored to you, and you shall be clean." But Naaman became furious, and went away and said, "Indeed, I said to myself, 'He will surely come out to me, and stand and call on the name of the LORD his God, and wave his hand over the place, and heal the leprosy.' Are not the Abanah and the Pharpar, the rivers of Damascus, better than all the waters of Israel? Could I not wash in them and be clean?" So he turned and went away in a rage. And his servants came near and spoke to him, and said, "My father, if the prophet had told you to do something great, would you not have done it? How much more then, when he says to you, 'Wash, and be clean'?" So he went down and dipped seven times in the Jordan, according to the saying of the man of God; and his flesh was restored like the flesh of a little child, and he was clean. And he returned to the man of God, he and all his aides, and came and stood before him; and he said, "Indeed, now I know that there is no God in all the earth, except in Israel; now therefore, please take a gift from your servant."
> 2 KINGS 5:9-15

WHERE JESUS
WALKED

THE JORDAN IS
BEST KNOWN
AS THE PLACE
JESUS WAS
BAPTIZED BY
JOHN THE
BAPTIST.

Overall, the Jordan River is probably most heralded for its many strategic roles recorded in the gospel accounts. It was the location of the ministry of John the Baptist (Matt. 3:6; Mark 1:5; John 1:28; 3:26). Jesus

BAPTISMAL FACILITIES ALONG THE RIVER JORDAN.

came to John for baptism in an area of the Jordan near the city of Jericho. There are, however, only sporadic references to Jesus' ministry on the far side of the Jordan (Matt. 19:1; Mark 10:1). In the closing days of His ministry, while trying to elude those who would make Him king, Jesus "went away again beyond the Jordan to the place where John was baptizing at first, and there He stayed" (John 10:40).

> Then Jesus came from Galilee to John at the Jordan to be baptized by him. And John tried to prevent Him, saying, "I need to be baptized by You, and are You coming to me?" But Jesus answered and said to him, "Permit it to be so now, for thus it is fitting for us to fulfill all righteousness." Then he allowed Him. When He had been baptized, Jesus came up immediately from the water; and behold, the heavens were open to Him, and He saw the Spirit of God descending like a dove and alighting upon Him. And suddenly a voice came from heaven, saying, "This is My beloved Son, in whome I am well pleased."
> MATTHEW 3:13-17

SITE OF
INTEREST

BAPTISMAL
FACILITIES
ALONG THE
JORDAN RIVER.

THE JORDAN RIVER

In the past, enthusiastic tourists used to stop along the road and conduct baptismal services in the River Jordan. I had the opportunity on several occasions to participate. These were surely spirited moments, but conditions were not always conducive to safety and meaning. In response, the Israeli government created a beautiful setting on the river's edge where the Jordan departs south out of the Sea of Galilee. Greeting the baptismal candidates are special facilities that offer changing rooms, baptismal robes, guided walkways into the river, refreshments, and of course souvenir shopping. Participants are even presented with an official baptismal certificate upon completion of their immersion. Along the shoreline, several unique and inviting areas have been made out of rock that allow for worship and ministry, leaving everyone with the feeling of a true Holy Land experience. I highly recommend it. One of my most meaningful times of public devotion happened at this picturesque location.

Christianity in the first century had a deep sense of community, as contrasted to our post-modern individualistic religion of today. New converts and genuine disciples did not distinguish between salvation and the Church. As a matter of historical understanding, to be "added to the church," was the same as being "added to the Lord," and vice versa (Acts 2:47). God's grace was encountered corporately as the Church. The early Christians would not have understood someone's salvation experience which was not completed by baptism. Salvation included not only identification with Christ, but also identification with His people. Baptism brought a convert into a new kind of special relationship, initiating individuals into a new community. The distinguishing mark was that all prior personal factors that represented identity definitions were now transcended.[13] Individual identities became secondary to their common identity in Jesus. There was neither Jew nor Gentile, male nor female, bond nor free—all were one in Christ Jesus (Gal. 3:25-29).

The usual and customary perception of baptism as a mere symbol seems far from its biblical presentation. What happened that caused the true significance of this rite to drift so far from its scriptural basis? After the fifth century, when the Emperor Constantine experienced a vision of a cross in the sky, he proclaimed Christianity to be the state religion of the Roman Empire. Everyone was declared to be Christian, not by the personal invitation of Christ into one's heart, but by imperial edict. By this decree, everyone was exempted from the necessity of personal conversion. Baptism was subsequently redefined to celebrate physical birth, not spiritual birth. Constantine's proclamation reinforced "in-group" identity versus "new identity" as the community of faith.[14]

If the sacramental understanding of baptism remains merely a symbolic outward washing, there is no reason nor power to raze the walls of bias, prejudice, or racism that separate us and keep us distant one from the other. But for those baptized into Christ, He has "broken down the middle wall of separation" (Eph. 2:14). We are, thus, commissioned to walk in the light of new relationships with each other in fellowship and in community. The writers of the new gospel autographs repeatedly portray the true disciples of Jesus Christ in communal terms such as family, children, and a body. It is assumed that Christians who are a distinct community will share a common life together—wherever they are found. The Bible presents an inescapable conclusion—that we discover spirituality together. We grow in Christ by our interaction with each other.

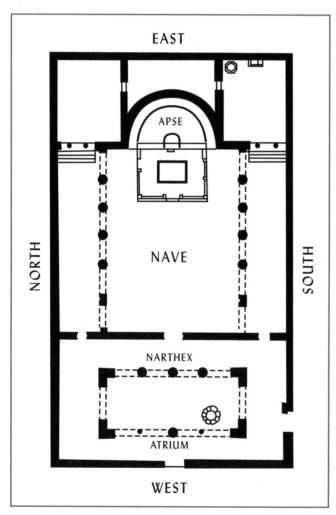

A MODEL OF THE FLOOR PLAN OF A TYPICAL EARLY CHRISTIAN CHURCH.

In early Church history, when a convert was received as a Christian (after baptism), they turned, faced west, and renounced the works of darkness. In worship, believers faced east—the direction of the ascension and return of Jesus Christ. Hence, they turned their back to the devil. It is to renounce personal secret patterns, secret habits, and secret ways. If you come to Christ, you must turn your back on the devil. Evidently, it was important enough not only to influence the posture of the new convert, but to influence the design of the church edifice as well. To many pilgrims who travel to the Holy Land, old ruins all look the same. After awhile, excavations may appear to be just a pile of displaced stones. I have provided a typical floor plan of an ancient church. The dots represent columns and demonstrate how the architecture divided the structure into distinct areas and aisles. Almost all ancient churches follow this schematic and faced east.

The apse was the focal point and was usually constructed over a sacred spot. Thus, the church commemorated some special event or miracle in the ministry of Jesus. Sometimes a wall or curtain separated the apse from the nave, not unlike the Holy of Holies. The nave was the center of the church and had two side aisles with a baptistery on the southern wall. One entered the facility from the west. The atrium was for "seekers." They were to mingle with the congregants, and if they expressed more interest, they would be permitted to the narthex. From there, the "seeker" became a "hearer." After several hearings, when they knew enough to be baptized, they could enter the nave.

Personal Reflections

FROM MAP INSIDE THE FRONT COVER: 8-9, G-H.

CHAPTER SIXTEEN

Masada

"Long ago we resolved to serve neither the Romans nor anyone other than God Himself, who alone is the true and just Lord of mankind. The time has now come that bids us prove our determination by our deeds."

EXCERPTS FROM BEN-YAIR'S ORATION

On the border between the Judean Desert and the Dead Sea Valley rises Masada, about 15 miles south of En-Gedi. Masada is Israel's finest natural fortification. It appears in Greek and Latin transcripts and may be an Aramaic form of *namesad*—"the fortress."[1] Ehud Netzer notes that Masada runs along the Afro-Syrian geological break, and stands as a rocky mountain, "separated from the cliff to form a natural fortress."[2] It is situated 1380 feet high on a plateau 1900 feet long (north-south) and 1000 feet wide (east-west) with a bird's-eye view of the Dead Sea below.[3] The top is flat and encompasses an area of approximately 20 acres, or two large city blocks.[4] The only two passageways up to Masada are the famous "snake path" (torturous and narrow) on the eastern side, and the easier approach

211

MASADA

on the western side which was eventually guarded by a tower.[5] Its unique location, high above the eastern Judean desert, is far removed from the usual trade routes and maintains a choice strategic position that overlooks highways which lead north to Jerusalem, south to the Red Sea, and west to the Mediterranean port of Jaffa. The activities of the Jewish revolt that occurred in Masada are not mentioned specifically in the Bible, but they do maintain pre-eminence in the history of Israel and the Jewish people. Today, pilgrims can take a scenic cable-car ride to the top that offers a spectacular panoramic view of the Dead Sea and surrounding landscape.

The two main sources available for the study of Masada are Josephus and the fortress' own archaeological record.[6] The first person to recognize the unique military features of Masada was a high priest named Jonathan. Josephus states that he gave it the name *Masada*, meaning "mountain stronghold" (cf. Judg. 6:2; 1 Sam. 23:14).[7] There are some scholars who consider the Hasmonean Alexander Jannaeus (103-76 B.C.) to be Jonathan on the basis of some coins found at the site. Others believe the name can be attributed to ancient kings or Jonathan Maccabeus who became high priest in 153-152 B.C.[8]

This celebrated hilltop was purposely turned into a formidable defense by Herod the Great in his stand against Rome's chief archenemy, the Parthians, in 42 B.C. The Parthians were revered for their notorious cavalry and expert bowmanship. It is believed by some that the biblical references in the book of Revelation regarding the sting of the serpent are statements inspired by the Parthian mounted archers (Rev. 9:13-19).[9] Their dreaded image, as Scripture records, portrays them with the ability to wound with both their mouths and tails. Caird suggests that this implies the tactics of the Parthian cavalry shooting a volley of arrows as they charged and another volley of arrows over the tail of the horses as they withdrew beyond the range of the weapons of their opponents.[10]

BETWEEN THE
TESTAMENTS

HEROD THE
GREAT FLED TO
MASADA WHEN
MATTATHIAS
ANTIGONIUS
TOOK CONTROL
OF JUDEA FROM
HEROD'S FATHER,
ANTIPATER II.

Mattathias Antigonus, a Hasmonean, eventually took control of Judea (with the aid of Parthian invaders) from Herod's father, the Roman procurator, Antipater.[11] So Herod fled Jerusalem during the time of unrest (40 B.C.) and sought refuge for his family in Masada while he personally requested Roman military assistance from Marc Antony and Octavius Caesar.[12] At the urging of Marc Antony, the Roman Senate declared him king of Judea. In his absence, Masada was attacked by Antigonus, and Herod's family almost died of thirst during the siege. They only survived due to a sudden rainfall that filled the cisterns on the summit. When Herod returned from Rome with a complement of eleven Roman legions (39-37 B.C.), he delivered the citadel and Judea. If Masada experienced a weakness as a natural fortress, it was the shortage of a needed water supply. So after his victory, Herod determined to solve Masada's dilemma of insufficient drinking water. Located in the desert with limited precipitation, a system of reservoirs was designed to collect the seasonal resource.[13] It has been calculated that the 12 cisterns of Masada on the northwest face of the fortress could hold up to 10½ million gallons of water.[14] Water was often laboriously carried up to

MASADA AS IT APPEARED AFTER HEROD'S FORTIFICATION. THE PULL-OUT BOX SHOWS HIS HANGING PALACE.

the two rows of parallel cisterns either by manpower or animal. Herod then embellished the fortress at Masada for use as a residence in case he was removed from his kingdom by Marc Antony. Herod feared that Antony might gift Judea to the Egyptian queen, Cleopatra.[15] In addition, Herod feared another possible Jewish revolt. Masada was to be his safe haven in case of either internal or external difficulties. Josephus notes, "For it is said that Herod furnished this fortress as a refuge for himself, suspecting a twofold danger: peril from the Jewish people lest they should depose him and restore their former dynasty to power, and the greater and more serious threat from Cleopatra, queen of Egypt."[16]

While Herod only occasionally visited Masada as a winter getaway, it is considered the best fortified bastion in the ancient world. During the years 36-30 B.C., the king enclosed the entire top of the 23-acre plateau with a great white casement wall. It was 4,590 feet long, 20 feet high, and 13 feet wide with three gates and thirty defense towers (each 75 feet high).[17] He also erected a royal palace with a throne room, living and reception quarters, luxurious baths with colored mosaic floors, and elegant apartments. In addition, on the mesa were colonnaded porticos, walkways, groves, gardens, and storerooms for provisions and military arms sufficient to supply 10,000 men for several years. Sarah Kochav records, "The interior walls of the palace were decorated with brightly colored frescoes, . . . painted with floral and geometric motifs, and designed to resemble marble."[18] Herod also constructed a three-tiered hanging palace on the northern precipice—an architectural wonder of the ancient world.

After Herod's death in 4 B.C., a Roman garrison was stationed at Masada and occupied the plateau until the Jewish revolt in A.D. 66. An extremist group called the *Sicarri*, "dagger men", displaced the Romans from Masada during the uprising and were further strengthened in their numbers when more zealous Jews fled across the Judean wilderness during Titus' A.D. 70 seige of Jerusalem.[19] It was in this impregnable fortress that the last of the Jewish patriots determined to continue their battle for freedom. And, it was in this outpost that 960 Jewish zealots eventually committed suicide rather than submit to Roman domination and reign (73 A.D.).[20]

GREEK/
ROMAN

IT WAS AT THE
OUTPOST OF
MASADA THAT
960 JEWISH
ZEALOTS
COMMITTED
SUICIDE RATHER
THAN SUBMITTING
TO ROMAN
CONQUEST.

The Roman leader, Flavius Silva, took his Tenth Legion and auxiliary troops and surrounded Masada with approximately 25,000 soldiers. He established eight fortified camps around the base of the mountain.[21] The Roman walls can still be distinguished today as one looks down from the summit above. They laid siege to the fortress for three years. It has been estimated that 850 mules brought fresh water for the troops every day from the springs of En-Gedi. After several futile attempts to scale the plateau, the Romans constructed a ramp built of dirt and stone while under fire from the small band at the top of a siege tower on Masada's western side. The Romans eventually forced thousands of their Jewish captives who had been enslaved in Jerusalem to carry out the project.[22] The Jewish resisters at the top were hesitant to fire upon their own countrymen. So within a few months, the Romans were successful in making a breach in the Jewish defenses. Overall, nearly 5,000 Roman soldiers were killed in the assault. The Romans, ascending the earthen ramp, placed iron battering rams against the walls. The small band of Jewish resisters were directed by Eleazer, leader of the Zealots. They put up another wall of wooden planks and dirt, but the Romans set fire to the fortification allowing them entrance the next day.[23] After a moving speech by Eleazer, the defenders ended their lives at their own hands rather than become slaves to Rome.

> "Brave and loyal followers! Long ago we resolved to serve neither the Romans nor anyone other than God Himself, who alone is the true and just Lord of mankind. The time has now come that bids us prove our determination by our deeds. At such a time we must not disgrace ourselves. Hitherto we have never submitted to slavery, even when it brought no danger with it. We must not

THE SIEGE RAMP BUILT BY JEWISH CAPTIVES THAT ALLOWED THE ROMANS TO REACH THE TOP OF MASADA.

choose slavery now, and with it penalties that will mean the end of everything if we fall alive into the hands of the Romans. . . . God . . . has given us this privilege, that we can die nobly and as free men. . . . In our case it is evident that the daybreak will end our resistance, but we are free to choose an honourable death with our loved ones. . . . Let our wives die unabused, our children without knowledge of slavery. After that, let us do each other an ungrudging kindness, preserving our freedom as a glorious winding-sheet. But first, let our possessions and the whole fortress go up in flames. It will be a bitter blow to the Romans, that I know, to find our persons beyond their reach and nothing left for them to loot. One thing only let us spare——our store of food: it will bear witness when we are dead to the fact that we perished, not through want but because, as we resolved at the beginning, we chose death rather than slavery. . . . Come! While our hands are free and can hold a sword, let them do a noble service! Let us die unenslaved by our enemies, and leave this world as free men in company with our wives and children."

EXCERPTS FROM BEN-YAIR'S ORATION

Before their deaths, which were carried out by certain chosen men, the Zealots burned personal belongings and anything that could be of use to the Romans. They preserved a vast store of food to display they had died willingly.[24] Josephus writes, "When the Romans reached the height the next morning, they were met with silence." Only two women and five children remained alive to tell the courageous story of Masada. The Romans could take no pleasure in the victory but could only wonder at the courage that was displayed.[25]

Masada is still a symbol of Jewish spirit today. In the words of John McRay, "In a real sense it is Israel's Alamo."[26] Fragments of fourteen scrolls including biblical, apocryphal, and community writings were discovered in a storage room on the mountain fortress. Most were written in Hebrew or Aramaic, but some very rare writings were done in Latin and Greek.[27] In total, the scrolls contained five chapters of the Psalms, a fragment of the Songs of the Sabbath Sacrifice, the book of Jubilees, and fragments of Genesis, Leviticus, and Ezekiel.[28]

Personal Reflections

FROM MAP INSIDE THE FRONT COVER: 7-8, C-D.

CHAPTER SEVENTEEN
Megiddo

(The Valley of Armageddon)

And they gathered them together to
the place called in Hebrew, Armageddon.

REVELATION 16:16

Megiddo (spelled in the KJV Megiddon) was an important Canaanite, and later Israeli, city overlooking the Valley of Jezreel on the Plain of Esdraelon. *Jezreel* is the Old Testament name for the valley which separated Samaria from Galilee. The western portion of the valley is referred to as Esdraelon and includes the Valley of Megiddo. The eastern portion is referred to as the Valley of Jezreel. It is the major corridor through the rugged hills of Palestine (the Carmel Mountain range) some 20 miles south-southeast from Haifa.[1]

The significance of *Jezreel* is twofold. First of all it means "God sows" or "May God make fruitful" and describes the fertility of the valley.[2] Its richness was recognized in biblical times as well as today. Jewish settlers have revived the land in the last century by drying up some of the swampy

219

MEGIDDO

OLD
TESTAMENT

**JEZREEL WAS THE
SCENE OF THE
BLOODY ATROCI-
TIES OF AHAB
AND JEZEBEL.**

areas. Jezreel has been called an agricultural bread basket because its harvest literally feeds the modern world.[3] The second connotation of the name of the valley recalls one of the most violent periods in the history of Israel. Jezreel was the scene of the bloody atrocities of Ahab and Jezebel who were avenged by the hand of Jehu (2 Kings 9:1-10:11; Hos. 1:4-5). Consequently, the name *Jezreel* means not only "blessing" but is also associated with violence, murder, and the wanton shedding of blood.

Archaeological excavations reveal that Megiddo, the western portion of the valley near the foot of Mount Carmel, was identified with Tell el-Mutesellin ("the mound of the commander").[4] It is difficult to find a more strategic site than Megiddo. Napoleon called it the most perfect battlefield in the world. Battles have been fought in this area that involved the Egyptians, Canaanites, Philistines, Israelites, Assyrians, Greeks, Romans, Persians, and the British in World War I.[5] From its summit can be seen the entire breadth of the Plain of Esdraelon to the hills of Galilee on the north, as well as the length of the valley itself that runs along Mount Carmel on

THE PLAIN OF MEGGIDO, WHICH IS ALSO CALLED THE VALLEY OF ARMAGEDDON.

the west, and eastward toward Mount Gilboa and Little Herman. (To the right of Little Herman rises Mount Tabor.)

There are two very important ancient trade routes that intersected the valley: 1) the road that linked Egypt with the Fertile Crescent, and 2) the road that linked central and eastern Palestine with the Phoenician coast.[6] Control of Megiddo meant lordship of the entire valley and ownership over the bountiful trade routes and plentiful commerce linking Africa, Asia, and Europe. The only alternative route meant going overland to Haifa, by sea to Joppa, and on to Jerusalem. Megiddo was positioned on the Via Maris— the ancient coastal road that connected Egypt (south) with Damascus (north).[7] The road was used for the peaceful flow of merchandise, but it was also an important route over which the armies of antiquity marched.[8] The importance of the city is reflected in a quotation by an Egyptian king who stated, "The capture of Megiddo was the capture of a thousand towns."[9] Because of its strategic location both commercially and militarily, Megiddo was the scene of many struggles. The real victory was to have possession of the city and thus the control of Palestine. It has been suggested that its name perhaps means "place of troops."[10] Megiddo has experienced at least 25 different levels of occupation that built up a deposit of debris nearly 75 feet high.[11] It has been the scene of many great battles and notable leaders spanning from Thutmose III (fifteenth century B.C., Egypt), Napoleon (1799), and General Allenby (World War I).[12]

THE VALLEY
OF
ARMAGEDDON

Most Christians are familiar with Megiddo because of its relationship with a final biblical battle between good and evil which has been dubbed, the Battle of Armageddon. According to *Strong's Concordance, Armageddon* comes from a Hebrew derivative and is a symbolic name.[13] In the Greek, *Armageddon* comes from two words: 1) *ar* or *har* meaning "mountain or range of hills," and 2) *magedon* from Megiddo or *gadad* meaning "to cut, attack, or maraud."[14] It is a variation of Jeremiah's "destroying mountain" (Jer. 51:25). Frank Gaebelein suggests taking *magedon* as deriving from the secondary sense of the Hebrew *gadad* that means "to gather in troops or bands."[15] This is equivalent to the biblical reference (Rev. 16:12-16) and alludes to the prophetic expectation of the gathering of the nations for judgment (Joel 3:2,12). Being in such a perfect, strategic position and the largest plain in Israel, it became associated with the final war.

> Then the sixth angel poured out his bowl on the great river Euphrates, and its water was dried up, so that the way of the kings from the east might be prepared. And I saw three unclean spirits like frogs coming out of the mouth of the dragon, out of the mouth of the beast, and out of the mouth of the false prophet. For they are spirits of demons, performing signs, which go out to the kings of the earth and of the whole world, to gather them to the battle of that great day of God Almighty. "Behold, I am coming as a thief. Blessed is he who watches, and keeps his garments, lest he walk naked and they see his shame." And they gathered them together to the place called in Hebrew, Armageddon.
>
> REVELATION 16:12-16

Since no "Mount" Megiddo is known to either ancient or modern geographers, scholars propose that in the book of Revelation (an apocalyptic letter that abounds with symbolic language), the term could carry a symbolic meaning. If so, the final conflict, promoted by prophecy teachers to take place on this spot, could be one of idealogies—God's truth versus Satan's error, both historical and real. Robert H. Mounce states the cryptic nature of the cited text has "defeated all attempts at a final answer."[16] He concludes, "The great conflict between God and Satan, Christ and Antichrist, good and evil, that lies behind the perplexing course of history will in the end issue in a final struggle in which God will emerge victorious and take with Him all who placed their faith in Him. This is Har-Magedon."[17] It is an "end-time" confrontation where God will meet the powers of evil in their final defeat.

SITE OF
INTEREST

THE ANCIENT
CITY OF
MEGIDDO

Megiddo was a prosperous city but enjoyed very little peace. Archaeological excavations show that the city was destroyed and rebuilt 26 times. Because it was a military stronghold, a casement wall twelve feet thick surrounded the city. One of the remaining ancient artifacts among the ruins is a unique water system. It was dug from inside the city out to a spring lying to the southwest to ensure a water supply during a siege. It consisted of a deep vertical shaft and a long, horizontal, rock-hewn tunnel leading from the shaft to a spring in a cave at the foot of the mound. Water flowed from the cave through the tunnel to the bottom of the shaft allowing the spring to remain concealed.[18] The combination of a good water supply, farmland, and a strategic, defensible location attracted generations of settlers.[19]

During the possession of the Promised Land by Israel, the king of Megiddo was killed by the Israelites (Josh. 12:21). When the spoils were dispersed, Megiddo, which was situated in the territory of Issachar, was allotted to the tribe of Manasseh (Josh. 17:11; 1 Chron. 7:29).[20] But according to the book of Judges, the children of Israel were not able to occupy Megiddo at the time.[21]

MEGIDDO WAS ALLOTTED TO THE TRIBE OF MANASSEH AFTER ITS CONQUEST BY THE ISRAELITES UNDER JOSHUA.

> However, Manasseh did not drive out the inhabitants of Beth Shean and its villages, or Taanach and its villages, or the inhabitants of Dor and its villages, or the inhabitants of Ibleam and its villages, or the inhabitants of Megiddo and its villages; for the Canaanites were determined to dwell in that land. And it came to pass, when Israel was strong, that they put the Canaanites under tribute, but did not completely drive them out.
>
> JUDGES 1:27-28

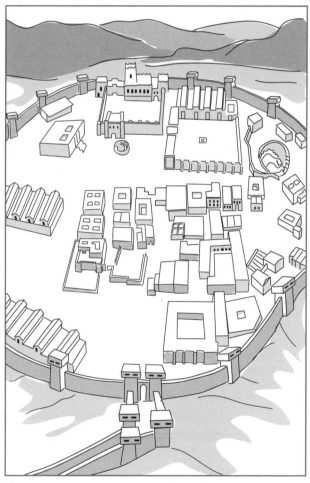

MEGIDDO AS IT MIGHT HAVE APPEARED IN THE TIMES OF SAUL AND DAVID.

Due to the strategic military position of Megiddo and the

THE RUINS OF ANCIENT MEGIDDO.

EARLY KINGS

MEGIDDO WAS AGAIN CONQUERED DURING THE REIGN OF SAUL.

Canaanite's superior weapons and iron chariots (Josh. 17:16), its overthrow by Israel was delayed. During the time of Judges, the Israelite armies under Deborah and Barak annihilated the Canaanites and their leaders in the battle "by the waters of Megiddo" (Judg. 5:19).[22]

Megiddo was again conquered by the Israelites during the reign of Saul. It was during Solomon's occupation that Megiddo was later transformed from an urban center to a fortified, royal chariot city (1 Kings 9:15). The project was undertaken by using forced labor.

> And this is the reason for the labor force which King Solomon raised: to build the house of the LORD, his own house, the Millo, the wall of Jerusalem, Hazor, Megiddo, and Gezer. . . . All the storage cities that Solomon had, cities for his chariots and cities for his cavalry, and whatever Solomon desired to build in Jerusalem, in Lebanon, and in all the land of his dominion.
> 1 KINGS 9:15,19

224

> And Solomon gathered chariots and horsemen; he had one
> thousand four hundred chariots and twelve hundred horse-
> men, whom he stationed in the chariot cities and with the king
> in Jerusalem.
>
> 2 CHRONICLES 1:14

Many of the stables built by Solomon are still visible today. Each stable contained several units, consisting of a paved central aisle flanked by two rows of stalls equipped with tie posts and mangers for a total of 450 to 480 horses. Outside was an enclosed exercise ring with a water trough in the center.[23] Megiddo reached its greatness in the Solomonic period and is listed among the cities in the charge of Baana, one of the twelve officers responsible in rotation for the monthly provisions of the king and his court (1 Kings 4:12).[24] After Solomon's death, Megiddo became part of the newly formed northern state of Israel under Jeroboam I. Megiddo was later attacked by Shishak of Egypt in his Palestinian campaign (1 Kings 14:25-26; 2 Chron. 12:2-9) and came under Egyptian rule. The Bible only provides sporadic references to the city's numerous destructions, rulers, and frequent rebuilding. In 609 B.C., Necho of Egypt marched to the aid of Assyria at Carchemish; on his way he was opposed by Josiah, the good king of Judah. In the brief skirmish in the plain of Megiddo, Josiah was struck by an Egyptian arrow and soon died (2 Kings 23:30; 2 Chron. 35:20-27).[25] The Bible records, "His servants moved his body in a chariot from Megiddo, brought him to Jerusalem, and buried him in his own tomb" (2 Kings 23:30).

The last biblical reference to Megiddo is also the only reference in the Old Testament prophetic writings. Zechariah prophesied, after returning from exile, that the mourning for the false deities (Hadadrimmon) that took place in the valley of Megiddo would be matched by Israel's mourning for its smitten Lord (Zech. 12:11).[26] Van Beek thinks this may refer specifically to the mourning for Josiah who was killed at the battle of Megiddo (2 Chron. 35:22-23); or, in a general sense, a mourning for all who had lost their lives in the historic battles fought near the city.[27]

Like the plain of Megiddo, Jezreel (the eastern portion of the valley between Samaria and Galilee) was also the scene of many battles. It was here that Gideon with 300 men miraculously defeated the Midianites who

OLD
TESTAMENT

GIDEON'S
ARMY
DEFEATED THE
MIDIANITES
NEAR JEZREEL
IN THE
EASTERN
PORTION OF
THE VALLEY.

were encamped in the valley (Judg. 6:33-7:23). Also, from Jezreel was proclaimed the news of the death of Saul and Jonathan in the battle with the Philistines on neighboring Mount Gilboa (2 Sam. 1:4). The wicked Queen Jezebel (a fanatical worshipper of Astarte) and King Ahab also lived in the city of Jezreel. They were opposed by the ministry of the prophet Elijah (1 Kings 21). When Jehu defeated Ahab on the bloody battlefield of Jezreel and returned to the city, he had Jezebel thrown into the street from an upper window. As a result, she was trampled on by his chariot horses (2 Kings 9:30-37). Jehu later commanded "this cursed woman" to be buried "for she was a king's daughter" (2 Kings 9:34). But before they could bury her, she was eaten by dogs. This fulfilled the prophecy of Elijah the Tishbite (1 Kings 21:23). All that could be found of Jezebel was her "skull and the feet and the palms of her hands" (2 Kings 9:35). Once these two wicked enemies of God were disposed with, Jehu had Ahab's seventy sons killed and their heads sent to Jezreel in baskets (2 Kings 10:7).

MEGIDDO

Personal Reflections

FROM MAP INSIDE THE FRONT COVER: 8-9, B-C.

CHAPTER EIGHTEEN

Nazareth

Now in the sixth month the angel Gabriel was
sent by God to a city of Galilee named Nazareth,
to a virgin betrothed to a man whose name was Joseph,
of the house of David. The virgin's name was Mary.

LUKE 1:26-27

Nazareth is first mentioned in the New Testament as the home of Joseph and Mary at the time of the Annunciation (Luke 1:26). They journeyed to Bethlehem to be taxed, but returned to Nazareth after the birth of Jesus (Matt. 2:23). Even though Jesus was born in Bethlehem and made his home in Capernaum during the years of his ministry, He was called "Jesus of Nazareth." As a young boy He lived with His parents (Luke 2:39,51) and only finally left Nazareth when it was time to be baptized by John the Baptist (Mark 1:9). Only once does the New Testament specifically state that Jesus returned "where He had been brought up" (Luke 4:16). There are two other occurrences which speak of Jesus being from Nazareth:1) the account of the Triumphal Entry (Matt. 21:11), and 2) Peter's sermon before

WHERE JESUS
WALKED

AS A YOUNG BOY
JESUS LIVED WITH
HIS PARENTS AND
ONLY FINALLY
LEFT NAZARETH
WHEN IT WAS
TIME TO BE
BAPTIZED BY
JOHN THE
BAPTIST.

When Jesus preached at the synagogue in Capernaum, the people were "astonished" at His learning and the authority of His teaching. In Nazareth, the people were "astonished" but in an appalled manner; i.e., how dare He?!

Cornelius (Acts 10:38). Rivka Gonen records that Nazareth is considered one of the holiest towns in Christian understanding and is ranked near Jerusalem and Bethlehem in wealth of traditions, churches, monasteries, and other religious institutions.[1]

There is no scriptural explanation provided as to why Jesus left Nazareth to dwell in Capernaum (Matt. 4:13). He possibly could have relocated to Capernaum because of the negative response He received at Nazareth in the early moments of His ministry (Luke 4:16 ff.). When He preached at the synagogue in Capernaum, the people were "astonished" at His learning and the authority of His teaching (Mark 1:21-28). In Nazareth, the people were "astonished" but in an appalled manner; i.e., "How dare He?!" They murmured against Him and refused to acknowledge His teaching. As fellow Nazarenes, they thought they knew who He was and were convinced that He could not be anyone special. Therefore, Matthew 13:58 says, "He did not do many mighty works there because of their unbelief."

Charles Page II believes Jesus' move from Nazareth to Capernaum reflects a philosophical shift in belief and practice instead of a mere change in geographical location.[2] He describes Nazareth as "a small, inwardly focused, fundamentalist village" and Capernaum as "a more moderate village closely aligned with the theology of the House of Hillel."[3] At the time, there existed two schools of Pharisaic thought. Simply stated, the school of Hillel was more liberal and basically

WHERE JESUS
WALKED

NAZARETH
REACTED WITH
MUCH HOSTILITY
TO THE WORDS
OF JESUS.

maintained that people were more important than tradition. The school of Shammai was more conservative and maintained that tradition was more important than people. Many of the words of Jesus, and especially His perceived Sabbath-breaking actions, depict Hillelian overtones. The prevailing attitude among the inhabitants of Capernaum was seemingly Hillelian according to Page, because there was no hostile reaction, nor rejection, of His healing on the Sabbath (Mark 1:21-25; Luke 4:31-37).[4] So Jesus' move from Nazareth to Capernaum could have been a move away from His Hasidic roots, upbringing, and parental training. It was also a break with the Nazarene/Natzareen sect who expected Messiah to come from their people (Isa. 60:21-22).

Nazareth means "branch" or "shoot" *(netzer)*.[5] A marble fragment was found during the 1962 excavations of Caesarea Maritima with an inscription that spelled Nazareth with the Hebrew letter *tzade* (pronounced with a *tz* sound) or Natzareth.[6] Page believes "the village was so named (Natzareth) because the residents considered themselves the *netzer* ("shoot") from the clan of David, from whom the Messiah would come."[7] It is no wonder the crowd in the synagogue at Nazareth reacted with such hostility to the words of Jesus. He not only attributed the Messianic words of Isaiah to Himself, but He also exalted the faith of the Gentiles over their stiff-necked opposition to the will of God (Luke 4:16-30). The angry crowd rose up and attempted to throw Him over a cliff on which the city was built.

Nazareth lies to the north of the Plain of Jezreel (Esdraelon or Megiddo with its many battlefields) in a valley open to the south. The village is mainly on the western and northwestern slopes of the hills of Galilee facing the east (Luke 4:29).[8] It is 15 miles from the Sea of Galilee and 20 miles from the Mediterranean.[9] The altitude and protected position provide a moderate climate and ample rainfall which make conditions favorable to vegetation. The town, however, is handicapped by possessing only one spring which must be supplemented by cisterns.[10]

From its 1600-foot elevation, one can view a panorama of history. Nearby are many biblical sights: the city of Sepphoris (Roman administrative center for the entire province); Mount Tabor (location of the victory by Barak and Deborah, where the prophet Hosea attacked the pagan altars, and where Jesus was transfigured); Cana (the first miracle of turning "water into

NAZARETH

THE CHURCH OF THE ANNUNCIATION IN NAZARETH.

wine"); Mount Gilboa (where the tragic end of King Saul and Jonathan took place); the Spring of Herod (where Gideon separated his men by the ways they drank water); Endor (where Saul sought counsel from a witch); Nain (where Jesus raised a widow's son from the dead when encountering his funeral); and Megiddo (supposed plain of history's final battle—Armageddon).

SITE OF
INTEREST

THE CHURCH
OF THE
ANNUNCIATION

Nazareth is best remembered as the site of the Annunciation where the angel Gabriel appeared to Mary to proclaim the coming birth of Messiah. The Church of the Annunciation is thought to be the most highly decorated church in the Holy Land.[11] Tradition states that the original church was built over a cave believed to be the dwelling place of Mary and Joseph after returning from Egypt.[12] But Nazareth was not an important holy site until the Christian influence of Constantine (A.D. 324-37). It is recorded that Count Joseph of Tiberias appealed to the emperor to build a church in Nazareth, as he did on behalf of other cities.[13]

The pilgrim nun, Egeria (A.D. 384), told in her travels how she was shown the original Church of the Annunciation and a cave in which Mary lived.[14] She also reported a cave with an altar and a spring—known to many today simply as "Mary's well," which is an authentic locale that dates back to the time of Jesus. This one spring that has served the town for centuries remains its only source of water, and a visitor can still drink at this actual site in the Greek Orthodox Church of St. Gabriel.

SITE OF
INTEREST

THE CHURCH OF THE ST. GABRIEL.

> Now in the sixth month the angel Gabriel was sent by God to a city of Galilee named Nazareth, to a virgin betrothed to a man whose name was Joseph, of the house of David. The virgin's name was Mary. And having come in, the angel said to her, "Rejoice, highly favored one, the Lord is with you; blessed are you among women!" But when she saw him, she was troubled at his saying, and considered what manner of greeting this was. Then the angel said to her, "Do not be afraid, Mary, for you have found favor with God. And behold, you will conceive in your womb and bring forth a Son, and shall call His name JESUS. He will be great, and will be called the Son of the Highest; and the Lord God will give Him the throne of His father David. And He will reign over the house of Jacob forever, and of His kingdom there will be no end."
>
> LUKE 1:26-33

Following the Nativity at Bethlehem and the flight into Egypt, the family returned to Nazareth where "Jesus increased in wisdom and stature, and in favor with God and men" (Luke 2:52). He later preached His first sermon in the synagogue at Nazareth and received a very hostile reaction as noted earlier (Luke 4:29). An interesting arched hall of the Crusader Period, traditionally considered the synagogue, can be visited today. It is located about two hundred yards from the Church of the Annunciation in the heart of the local market.

SITE OF
INTEREST

AN INTERESTING ARCHED HALL OF THE CRUSADER PERIOD CAN BE VISITED TODAY IN NAZARETH.

> So He came to Nazareth, where He had been brought up. And as His custom was, He went into the synagogue on the Sabbath day, and stood up to read. And He was handed the book of the prophet Isaiah. And when He had opened the book, He found

233

the place where it was written: "The Spirit of the LORD is upon Me, because He has anointed Me to preach the gospel to the poor; He has sent Me to heal the brokenhearted, to proclaim liberty to the captives and recovery of sight to the blind, to set at liberty those who are oppressed; to proclaim the acceptable year of the LORD." Then He closed the book, and gave it back to the attendant and sat down. And the eyes of all who were in the synagogue were fixed on Him. And He began to say to them, "Today this Scripture is fulfilled in your hearing." So all bore witness to Him, and marveled at the gracious words which proceeded out of His mouth. And they said, "Is this not Joseph's son?" He said to them, "You will surely say this proverb to Me, 'Physician, heal yourself! Whatever we have heard done in Capernaum, do also here in Your country.'" Then He said, "Assuredly, I say to you, no prophet is accepted in his own country."

LUKE 4:16-24

Many New Testament passages refer to Jesus as "the Nazarene" (Mark 10:47 NASB; John 18:5,7 NASB; Acts 2:22, 3:6 NASB). Jesus' followers are also referred to as "the Nazarenes" (Acts 24:5), but only one time. While there is much theological debate as to the significance of this term, the most common and probable interpretation is that in the New Testament the word *Nazarene* means "of Nazareth"—as is specifically stated in Matthew 2:23.[15] The term should not be confused nor used synonymously with *Nazrite,* those who through vow consecrated themselves by abstinence to a life of holiness, separation, and special service (Judg. 13:5-7).

It was only the fact that Jesus spent the early years of His life in Nazareth that gives the town its status of interest. Aside from this, it is mentioned only once in Scripture. There is no mention of Nazareth in the Old Testament, the Talmud, the Midrash, the Apocrypha, the Intertestamental Jewish writings, or by the Jewish historian Josephus.[16] The one time it is addressed, aside from the fact that it served as Jesus' hometown, it is addressed with a noticeably sarcastic tone.

Philip found Nathanael and said to him, "We have found Him of whom Moses in the law, and also the prophets, wrote—Jesus of Nazareth, the son of Joseph." And Nathanael said to him, "Can anything good come out of Nazareth?" Philip said to him, "Come and see."

JOHN 1:45-46

The Bible provides no reason why Nazareth would be addressed so unfavorably by Nathanael (possibly it was local reputation or expressed indignation). Nathanael himself was a Galilean from Cana (John 21:2). The emphasis in the text by the form of a question implies that Nazareth was not highly regarded among other Galileans. Situated in lower Galilee, Nazareth remained outside Israelite life and held the position of a frontier town. It may have been this geographical independence that created the perceived scorn.[17] Jerry Batson suggests such lack of respect was due "to an unpolished dialect, a lack of culture, and quite possibly a measure of irreligion and moral laxity."[18] So the term "Nazarene" provided both a positive and negative application. Matthew interprets it as a fulfillment of Old Testament prophecy.

There shall come forth a Rod from the stem of Jesse, and a Branch shall grow out of his roots.

ISAIAH 11:1

And he came and dwelt in a city called Nazareth, that it might be fulfilled which was spoken by the prophets, "He shall be called a Nazarene."

MATTHEW 2:23

It is possible that Matthew intended to draw a parallel between the image of Messiah as stated in Isaiah 53 ("despised, rejected—we did not esteem Him") and the low estate in which Nazareth was held. A variant manuscript reads, "Can the Holy One proceed from Nazareth?" (John 1:46).

The name *Nazarene* was an honorable term when voiced on the lips of Jesus' friends and followers. Contrariwise, it also represented bitterness and hatred when used by His enemies. To those who rejected Christ, it was a title of scorn, derision, and doubt that compressed the attitude of Nathanael into a single statement. The term would accompany Him even in His death, as a vehicle of expressed hatred by the priests.

> Now Pilate wrote a title and put it on the cross. And the writing was: JESUS OF NAZARETH, THE KING OF THE JEWS. Then many of the Jews read this title, for the place where Jesus was crucified was near the city; and it was written in Hebrew, Greek, and Latin. Therefore the chief priests of the Jews said to Pilate, "Do not write, 'The King of the Jews,' but, 'He said, "I am the King of the Jews."'" Pilate answered, "What I have written, I have written."
>
> JOHN 19:19-22

WHERE JESUS
WALKED

"NAZARENE" WAS
A NAME THAT
CLUNG TO JESUS
THROUGHOUT HIS
ENTIRE LIFE.

Among the masses, *Nazarene* was a name that clung to Jesus throughout His entire life—"Jesus of Nazareth" (Mark 10:47; Luke 24:19). The evil spirits feared Him under this name (Mark 1:24), the angel of the resurrection called Him thus (Mark 16:6), and Jesus Himself applied the title (Acts 22:8). Hence, it was also a name used persistently by the early Church.

> Then Peter said, "Silver and gold I do not have, but what I do have I give you: In the name of Jesus Christ of Nazareth, rise up and walk."
>
> ACTS 3:6

> How God anointed Jesus of Nazareth with the Holy Spirit and with power, who went about doing good and healing all who were oppressed by the devil, for God was with Him.
>
> ACTS 10:38

Through the centuries of alternating control between Arabs and Crusaders, Nazareth has suffered much persecution and its churches much destruction. The Turks took control in 1517 and asked all Christians to leave.[19] In 1620, when the Christians returned, the

Franciscans were granted the title, as P. C. Pellett penned, "guardians of the holy places" of Nazareth.[20]

Personal Reflections

FROM MAP INSIDE THE FRONT COVER: 8-9, B-C.

CHAPTER NINETEEN

The Sea of Galilee

And when the disciples saw Him walking on the sea,
they were troubled, saying, "It is a ghost!"
And they cried out for fear.
But immediately Jesus spoke to them, saying,
"Be of good cheer! It is I; do not be afraid."

MATTHEW 14:26-27

There is no other body of water on the face of the earth that has witnessed more miracles than the Sea of Galilee. On these shores Jesus called His first disciples, four of whom were fishermen (Peter, Andrew, James and John), to become "fishers of men" (Matt. 4:18-19). The biblical writers portray this area as having a prosperous fishing industry with fleets of fishing vessels (Mark 1:16-20; Luke 5:2-10). Today only a few pleasure boats are seen on the lake. Some watercraft have been constructed out of wood and made to appear like ancient boats used in the days of the Bible. They are normally used to transport pilgrims on an inspiring excursion across the lake.

WHERE JESUS
WALKED

ON THESE
SHORES JESUS
CALLED HIS FIRST
DISCIPLES.

The Sea of Galilee is mentioned in both the Old and New Testaments. It has five distinct names which are all derived from places on the western shore.[1]

1) The Sea of Galilee (Matt. 4:13-25): the name means "ring or circle" and is probably a reference to the circle of Gentile nations which had infiltrated the region. This is the most familiar name, due to its association with the province of Galilee to the west (Matt. 4:18).

2) The Sea of Chinnereth (Num. 34:11; Deut. 3:17; Josh. 13:27): *Chinnereth* resembles a Hebrew term (*kinnor*) for "harp-shaped" designating the possible shape of the lake.[2] Chinnereth also refers to the district of the plain (Matt. 14:34; Mark 6:53). It is sometimes called the Sea of Kinneret.

3) The Sea of Chinneroth (Josh. 12:3; 1 Kings 15:20): named after a walled town on the western shore of the lake (Josh. 11:2; 19:35).

4) The Lake of Gennesaret (Luke 5:1-2; 8:22-23,33): referred to as such because of the fertile Plain of Gennesaret that lies to the northwest of the lake (Matt. 14:34). Only Luke uses the Greek term *Limnen Gennesaret* (lake); whereas, Matthew and Mark use the Greek term *Thalassantes Galilaias* (sea).[3]

5) And finally, the Galilee is also referred to in Scripture as the Sea of Tiberias (John 6:1; 21:1): Tiberias was the capital city on the southwestern shore built by Herod Antipas. The Jews would not populate Tiberias because it was supposedly built over an ancient cemetery, and thus became occupied by Gentile peoples. The gospel of John was written to Gentile readers who

The lake resides in the lower depression of the Jordan Valley and is the largest fresh-water lake in Israel. It is part of the Jordan Valley rift and part of the greater Syro-African geological fault line.

would understand the author's designation of the Sea as Tiberias. The name remains an Arabic form, *Tabariyeh*.[4] The modern Hebrew name is *Yam Kinneret* (Josh. 12:3). In both the Hebrew and Aramaic, *Yam* can mean "lake" and "sea" as well as in the Greek expression *Thalassa*.[5]

The Sea of Galilee is located approximately 90 miles north of Jerusalem. The lake resides in the lower depression of the Jordan Valley and is the largest fresh-water lake in Israel. It is part of the Jordan Valley rift and part of the greater Syro-African geological fault line in the crust of the earth.[6] The entire basin reflects a volcanic origin with cliffs of hard, porous basalt and hot springs (known for their medicinal value). The fresh water of the lake is sparkling sweet and abounds with fish. The water's surface lies about 700 feet below the level of the Mediterranean with depths that vary to a maximum of 150 feet.[7] The lake is almost completely surrounded by mountains of considerable height, but is open on both the north and south ends where the River Jordan enters and departs. The Jordan River descends from Mount Hermon (site of the Transfiguration), enters the Sea of Galilee on its northern end, then flows out some 14 miles later. The lake is 8 miles wide (the greatest width is noted at Magdala) and encompasses an area of 112 square miles.[8] The Mount of the Beatitudes lies to the north, the Golan Heights to the northeast, and the land of the Gadarenes—where the healing of the demoniac took place—lies to the southeast. The terrain is open on the south where the Jordan River exits through the desert and continues its course to the Dead Sea.

WHERE JESUS WALKED

JESUS HEALED A DEMONIAC IN THE LAND OF THE GADARENES ON THE SOUTHWEST-ERN SHORE OF THE SEA OF GALILEE.

THE SEA OF GALILEE

> Then they came to the other side of the sea, to the country of the Gadarenes. And when He had come out of the boat, immediately there met Him out of the tombs a man with an unclean spirit, who had his dwelling among the tombs; and no one could bind him, not even with chains, because he had often been bound with shackles and chains. And the chains had been pulled apart by him, and the shackles broken in pieces; neither could anyone tame him. And always, night and day, he was in the mountains and in the tombs, crying out and cutting himself with stones. When he saw Jesus from afar, he ran and worshiped Him. And he cried out with a loud voice and said,

A SUNSET ON THE SEA OF GALILEE.

"What have I to do with You, Jesus, Son of the Most High God? I implore You by God that You do not torment me." For He said to him, "Come out of the man, unclean spirit!" Then He asked him, "What is your name?" And he answered, saying, "My name is Legion; for we are many." Also he begged Him earnestly that He would not send them out of the country. Now a large herd of swine was feeding there near the mountains. So all the demons begged Him, saying, "Send us to the swine, that we may enter them." And at once Jesus gave them permission. Then the unclean spirits went out and entered the swine (there were about two thousand); and the herd ran violently down the steep place into the sea, and drowned in the sea. So those who fed the swine fled, and they told it in the city and in the country. And they went out to see what it was that had happened. Then they came to Jesus, and saw the one who had been demon-possessed and had the legion, sitting and clothed and in his right mind. And they were afraid. And those who saw it told them how it happened to him who had been demon-possessed, and about the swine. Then they began to plead with Him to depart from their region. And when He got into the boat, he who had been demon-possessed begged Him that he might be with Him. However, Jesus did not permit him, but said to him, "Go home to your friends, and tell them what great things the Lord has done for you, and how He has had compassion on you." And he departed and began to proclaim in Decapolis all that Jesus had done for him; and all marveled.

Now when Jesus had crossed over again by boat to the other side, a great multitude gathered to Him; and He was by the sea.
MARK 5:1-21

"The Sea of Galilee is noted for its sudden and violent storms caused by cold air sweeping down from the vast naked plateaus of Gaulanitis, the Hauran, and Mount Hermon," notes Arthur M. Ross.[9] The province of Gaulanitis northeast of the sea was ruled by Herod Antipas. The name *Gaulanitis* is derived from *Golan,* a city of Manasseh in Bashan—one of three cities of refuge east of Jordan (Deut. 4:43; Josh. 20:8; 21:27). The cold air in the region passes over the mountains and descends through the ravines and gorges before converging with the warm air over the lake.[10] Even the experienced fishermen would not venture too far from the shore unless the lake was in a very settled condition. Jesus and His disciples were caught several times in treacherous storms that quickly and unexpectedly arose on the lake.

It was in such a storm that Jesus rebuked the wind and waves with His famous proclamation, "Peace, be still" (Mark 4:39). Another time, the disciples were trying to reach Bethsaida but were hindered by bad weather (because "a great wind" prevented any headway) when Jesus appeared walking on the water (Mark 6:45-53; John 6:15-21):[11]

Immediately Jesus made His disciples get into the boat and go before Him to the other side, while He sent the multitudes away. And when He had sent the multitudes away, He went up

WHERE JESUS WALKED

THE DISCIPLES WERE TRYING TO REACH BETHSAIDA BY CROSSING THE SEA OF GALILEE WHEN JESUS CAME TO THEM WALKING ON THE WATER.

on the mountain by Himself to pray. Now when evening came, He was alone there. But the boat was now in the middle of the sea, tossed by the waves, for the wind was contrary. Now in the fourth watch of the night Jesus went to them, walking on the sea. And when the disciples saw Him walking on the sea, they were troubled, saying, "It is a ghost!" And they cried out for fear. But immediately Jesus spoke to them, saying, "Be of good cheer! It is I; do not be afraid." And Peter answered Him and said, "Lord, if it is You, command me to come to You on the water." So He said, "Come." And when Peter had come down out of the boat, he walked on the water to go to Jesus. But when he saw that the wind was boisterous, he was afraid; and beginning to sink he cried out, saying, "Lord, save me!" And immediately Jesus stretched out His hand and caught him, and said to him, "O you of little faith, why did you doubt?" And when they got into the boat, the wind ceased. Then those who were in the boat came and worshiped Him, saying, "Truly You are the Son of God."

When they had crossed over, they came to the land of Gennesaret. And when the men of that place recognized Him, they sent out into all that surrounding region, brought to Him all who were sick, and begged Him that they might only touch the hem of His garment. And as many as touched it were made perfectly well.

MATT 14:22-36

WHERE JESUS WALKED

THIS FAMOUS LAKE AND ITS SURROUNDING AREAS WERE THE PRIMARY LOCATIONS OF JESUS' MINISTRY.

Most notable of this famous lake and its surrounding areas is that it was a primary location of Jesus' ministry. Nine cities of 15,000 or more inhabitants surrounded its shores (Capernaum, Magdala, Tiberias, Bethsaida, Gergesa, Chorazin, and others). Magdala, home of Mary Magdalene (Luke 8:1-3), was called *Tarichaea* in Greek. The name means "preserving" and described the main export of the town—salted fish that were sent throughout the Roman world.[12] Pliny states that the Lake of Gennesaret was called Tarichaea by some.[13] St. Peter's fish is one of the most popular meals in Israel. Holy Land pilgrims often and commonly are afforded the opportunity to sample this local delicacy during a seaside luncheon on the

> *In 1986 a boat was discovered buried*
> *along the shoreline of the lake. . . .*
> *The craft has been called the "Jesus Boat"*
> *because it dates to the time of the Bible.*

beautiful shores after a boat ride across the lake. In Hebrew this fish is called *amnun,* which may find its root in the term for "mother." This unique, female fish hatches her little babies in her mouth. In order to get her mouth widely stretched, she collects stones and stores them in her cheeks. When the little ones are born, she spits out the stones and keeps the newborns in the newly formed, protective cavity. Galilee's St. Peter's fish also testifies to the miraculous event that occurred when Jesus instructed Peter to catch a fish which had a coin in its mouth that was the exact amount needed to pay the taxes (Matt. 17:27).

WHERE JESUS WALKED

Because so much of Jesus' ministry occurred within the boundaries of this tiny region, the Sea of Galilee has been called the Sea of Miracles.[14] Many of the signs, wonders, and preaching of Jesus transpired in this vicinity, mainly on the north end of the lake—including the miracle catch of fish after the Resurrection (John 21:5). It was the rejection of His ministry in this area that brought His pronouncement of judgment on these cities as recorded in the gospel of Matthew.

THE SEA OF GALILEE HAS ALSO BEEN CALLED THE SEA OF MIRACLES BECAUSE OF JESUS' ACTIVITIES IN THE AREA.

> Then He began to rebuke the cities in which most of His mighty works had been done, because they did not repent: "Woe to you, Chorazin! Woe to you, Bethsaida! For if the mighty works which were done in you had been done in Tyre and Sidon, they would have repented long ago in sackcloth and ashes. But I say to you, it will be more tolerable for Tyre and Sidon in the day of judgment than for you. And you, Capernaum, who are exalted to heaven, will be brought down

THE SEA OF GALILEE

to Hades; for if the mighty works which were done in you had been done in Sodom, it would have remained until this day. But I say to you that it shall be more tolerable for the land of Sodom in the day of judgment than for you."
MATT 11:20-24

Only a few of these towns survived that have any present-day activity. The exact archaeological location of many of them remains in question (their disappearance from time and history so indisputably complete).

In 1986 a boat was discovered buried along the shoreline of the lake. A severe drought caused the sea to recede exposing its outline that lay deep in the mud. The craft has been called the "Jesus Boat" because it dates to the time of the Bible. Archaeological examination showed that it was constructed with mortise and tenon joints. This was a boat-building technique used in the Mediterranean area from the second millennium B.C. to the end of the Roman period. Two pottery pieces discovered nearby also helped fix the time period in which the boat was used. Radiocarbon analysis has yielded a date which locates the construction of the ship between 120 B.C. and A.D. 40. To extract the vessel from its grave, it had to be kept wet at all times lest it would crumble. The craft was so fragile that it had to be encased carefully with polyurethane foam while still in its originally discovered position. It was then floated to its new home at the Kibbutz Ginosar where it has undergone conservation efforts. By pumping a synthetic wax into its timbers (a process that took ten years), the main structure of the craft has been preserved intact.[15] It sparks the imagination to think the recovered craft possibly could have sailed Galilee's waters when Jesus frequented the many inlets and coves of this famed locale.

The shoreline of the Sea of Galilee has changed dramatically through the years, especially with the influx of beaches and luxury hotels for the tourists. In ancient times (332 B.C.—A.D. 630), there existed some 16 different ports around the lake which provided a means of transportation and communication for the thousands of residents living in the area. Vessels could load and unload passengers as well as cargo onto the piers, which extended 100 feet out into the lake from the promenade.

Until the 1990s, the harbors remained undetected. The water level today is actually about four feet higher than it was during the time of Jesus. A natural change in the outflow of the lake occurred 1,000 years ago which caused the water level to rise and a new narrower outlet for the River Jordan to be created. Only when the region experiences a dramatic decrease in precipitation do the breakwaters, piers, and promenades appear. The shallow shoreline reveals the components were made of the local, black basalt boulders so plentifully prevalent on the surrounding hills. The harbors consisted of two basic elements: a short pier jutting into the water and a curved stone breakwater that protected moored boats from the common fierce storms that swept across the lake. Boats could slide through the narrow passageway between the pier and the breakwater and into the open waters.[16]

The breakwaters were originally about 10 feet tall, but through the years, the erosive action of the waves has demolished the structures, leaving only the foundations. To the trained eye, they are visible after a dry summer when the water level is at its lowest point.

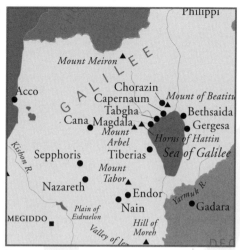

FROM MAP INSIDE THE FRONT COVER: 8-9, B-C.

CHAPTER TWENTY

Tiberias

However, other boats came from Tiberias, near the place where they ate bread after the Lord had given thanks.

JOHN 6:23

While it is not recorded that Jesus ever visited Tiberias, it had historical significance and played an influential part in biblical times. Tiberias was established upon the western shore of the Sea of Galilee. It was built over the old city *Rakkath,* or *Hammath* (Josh. 19:35), meaning "strip" or "coast." Jewish rumor said a cemetery was uncovered during excavation, therefore, the city was considered unclean (cf. Num. 19:11-13) and was boycotted by the Jews (*Antiq.* 18.2.3).[1] It is mentioned only once in the New Testament (John 6:23), although there are several biblical references to the Sea of Tiberias (John 6:1; 21:1). This famous body of water is more commonly known as the Sea of Galilee.[2] The apostle John, who was writing to non-Jewish readers, uses the Gentile designation, Tiberias. His readers would relate to the purposeful use of the local name.

Tiberias was a city built by the tetrarch, Herod Antipas, between the years A.D. 18-22. Herod Antipas was the Herod at the time of Christ

GREEK/
ROMAN

TIBERIAS WAS THE
CITY BUILT BY
THE TETRARCH,
HEROD ANTIPAS.

TIBERIAS

249

(Luke 3:1). Jesus called him "that fox" (Luke 13:32) which had reference to the Herodian cunningness that was characteristic of the family. However, the Bible does record a slight glimmer of hope concerning Herod's character when we read: "Herod feared John, knowing that he was a just and holy man, and he protected him. And when he heard him, he did many things, and heard him gladly" (Mark 6:20). Herod's downfall came at the celebration of his own birthday. After he incarcerated John the Baptist for denouncing his marital sins, he decapitated John at the request of Salome (Mark 6:17-29). It was a crime from which Herod Antipas never recovered, either personally or politically.

Tiberias was a new city and was to serve as the capital for the territories of Galilee and Perea. The town was conveniently located to serve both districts and was strategically placed on the well-travelled local and international roads.[3] The site offered two attractive features: 1) a defensive position that projected itself on a natural acropolis above the lake, and 2) close proximity to the already-famous hot springs to the south.[4] The city was named after the reigning Roman emperor, Tiberius Caesar (A.D. 14-37).[5] The name is still preserved in the modern town Tabariyeh. From Tiberias several important cities could be observed visually and readily reached by boat. Magdala (el-Mejdel), home of Mary Magdalene, was several miles to the north; Capernaum was less than five miles across the upper curve of the lake; and Bethsaida was very close by.[6] It is the site of modern-day Migdal.

The ruins of Tiberias indicate that Herod built ambitiously. The archaeological excavations reveal a palace, a forum, and a great synagogue that reflected the dual Herodian policy which sought to combine pro-Roman philosophy with effective patronage to the Jews.

The ruins of Tiberias indicate that Herod built ambitiously. The archaeological excavations reveal a palace, a forum, and a great synagogue that reflected the dual Herodian policy which sought to combine pro-Roman philosophy with effective patronage to the Jews.[7] The heartfelt nature of Tiberias is demonstrated on a coin displaying the emperor Trajan on one side and on the other, a figure of Hygeia (health) feeding a serpent (sign of Aesculapius, god of healing) as she sits on a rock over a spring.[8] According to the historian Josephus, since the Jews would not populate the site, the city attracted a heterogeneous population of "undesirables." It included both Galileans and foreigners of high and low social status, poor and newly freed, who settled here either by force or inducement of lands and houses (*Antiq.* 18.2.3).[9] So even though many of the residents held Jewish sympathies, the Tiberian population was completely Gentile and is probably why Jesus never ministered in the new city. When the revolt broke out against Rome in A.D. 65-66, the city wholly supported Josephus and the Jewish resistance. Then it fell to the Roman armies of Vespasian in A.D. 67.[10]

Tiberias has only one New Testament reference which follows the miracle of the feeding of the multitude somewhere on the east coast of the lake. After the disciples departed, some small boats from Tiberias embarked the next day to follow them to Capernaum. It was during this renowned voyage that Jesus appeared to the disciples while walking on the water:

> So when they had rowed about three or four miles, they saw Jesus walking on the sea and drawing near the boat; and they were afraid. But He said to them, "It is I; do not be afraid." Then they willingly received Him into the boat, and immediately the boat was at the land where they were going.
>
> On the following day, when the people who were standing on the other side of the sea saw that there was no other boat there, except that one which His disciples had entered, and that Jesus had not entered the boat with His disciples, but His disciples had gone away alone—however, other boats came from Tiberias, near the place where they ate bread after the Lord had given thanks—when the people therefore saw that Jesus was not there, nor His disciples, they also got into boats and came

WHERE JESUS WALKED

IT WAS DURING THE RENOWNED VOYAGE FROM TIBERIAS THAT THE DISCIPLES SAW JESUS WALKING ON THE WATER.

TIBERIAS

to Capernaum, seeking Jesus. And when they found Him on the other side of the sea, they said to Him, "Rabbi, when did You come here?" Jesus answered them and said, "Most assuredly, I say to you, you seek Me, not because you saw the signs, but because you ate of the loaves and were filled. Do not labor for the food which perishes, but for the food which endures to everlasting life, which the Son of Man will give you, because God the Father has set His seal on Him." Then they said to Him, "What shall we do, that we may work the works of God?" Jesus answered and said to them, "This is the work of God, that you believe in Him whom He sent." Therefore they said to Him, "What sign will You perform then, that we may see it and believe You? What work will You do? Our fathers ate the manna in the desert; as it is written, 'He gave them bread from heaven to eat.'" Then Jesus said to them, "Most assuredly, I say to you, Moses did not give you the bread from heaven, but My Father gives you the true bread from heaven. For the bread of God is He who comes down from heaven and gives life to the world." Then they said to Him, "Lord, give us this bread always." And Jesus said to them, "I am the bread of life. He who comes to Me shall never hunger, and he who believes in Me shall never thirst. JOHN 6:19-35

After the Second Jewish Revolt and fall of Jerusalem in A.D. 135, Tiberias became a strong Jewish center and was considered one of the four sacred cities of Israel.[11] The Sanhedrin moved from the city of Sepphoris to Tiberias in A.D. 150 and subsequently established their schools of rabbinic study there. The Jews would later refer to Tiberias as *Tabur* meaning "navel"—the center of the rabbinic world following the destruction of Jerusalem. The Talmud reported thirteen synagogues in Tiberias, affirming its flourishing growth as a Jewish metropolis.[12] The Talmud was developed at Tiberias, though it had two antecedents—the Midrash and Mishna. The Midrash was the earliest method of teaching the "oral" law by running commentary on the biblical text and was the method employed by Ezra and his associates in the public reading of Scripture.[13] The name *Midrash* is a rabbinic term for biblical exegesis. It means "to guide out, inquire,

ANCIENT RUINS AT TIBERIUS.

investigate, or interpret in an attempt to make a biblical text contemporary and relevant."[14]

> And Ezra opened the book in the sight of all the people, for he was standing above all the people; and when he opened it, all the people stood up. And Ezra blessed the Lord, the great God. Then all the people answered, "Amen, Amen!" while lifting up their hands. And they bowed their heads and worshiped the Lord with their faces to the ground . . . . So they read distinctly from the book, in the Law of God; and they gave the sense, and helped them to understand the reading.
> NEHEMIAH 8:5-6,8

The *Mishna* (meaning "repetition") was a later development and refers to a method of teaching the "oral" law without reference to the Holy Writ. It is distinct from *Mikra*—which denotes the Law transmitted by written

TIBERIAS

documents (scripture) and learned by reading.[15] The Mishna was completed sometime before A.D. 220 and contained the laws (civil and ritual), decrees, and customs held as binding obligation in Jewish society, though it had no Old Testament scriptural authenticity.[16] While this permitted flexibility of topical discussion (absent the restriction of the biblical text), it was biblically based (cf. Matt. 15:1-9). The teachers, or rabbinic sages and scriptural reciters, represented in the Mishna (first and second centuries) are referred to as the *Tannaim* ("to hand down orally").[17] The Mishna is the basis for the Gemara and the Talmud. The *Gemara* (meaning "acquired learning") is a summary of important points of rabbinic discussion on the Mishna.[18]

The *Talmud* (meaning "study" or "learning") is a collection of Jewish writings dated approximately 450 B.C. to 500 A.D.[19] The Law found in the Torah of Moses was the only written law which the Jews possessed after their return from the Babylonian exile. New ordinances became necessary because of the ever-changing conditions of life. What was added to the "Pentateuchal Torah" was, for a long time, handed down orally. The increase of such material eventually required the formal adjustment of order, arrangement, and recording. The Talmud was a repository of oral legal teachings (*halakah*) and ranks in Jewish eyes, second only to the Hebrew Scriptures, as being influential upon life as a Jew. The Talmud was the making of bylaws that covered the period of almost 1000 years (from the time of Ezra to the middle of the sixth century). Its chapters include laws concerning agriculture, feasts, marriage, civil disobedience, sacrificial rites, and levitical purity.

The Palestinian or Jerusalem Talmud was completed in 400 A.D. and is one of two Talmuds developed. Although termed the *Jerusalem Talmud,* it was not completed in Jerusalem (due to its destruction), but in Tiberias, Caesarea, and Sepphoris. The other Talmud was the Babylonian. It was considered the most authoritative due to its more sophisticated style and the political fortunes of the Jewish communities. It was also recognized to have been completed a century later, in the words of S. Humphries-Brooks, so as "to absorb or supersede the Jerusalem Talmud."[20]

The Tiberian vowel-pointing system was also developed in Tiberias (900 A.D.).[21] It was added to the Hebrew text of the Old Testament to develop that which has become known as the Masoretic text. It is from the

Masoretic text that the translators of the *King James Version* of the Bible rendered the Old Testament. Problems of proper punctuation have frequently influenced the tradition of biblical interpretation (Isa. 40:3). The Masoretic vowel points were therefore developed to contain accents and other signs endowed with phonetic meaning to help determine the punctuation of a passage. In many cases, the accents were used to indicate, by their position, the stressed syllable of a respective word.

Personal Reflections

FROM MAP INSIDE THE FRONT COVER: 5-10, A-I.

Mountains of Israel

As the mountains surround Jerusalem, so the Lord
surrounds His people from this time forth and forever.

PSALM 125:2

When compared to the mountains of Europe or America, the mountains of the Land of the Bible are not considered of any great height. What gives the mountains of Palestine their impressive appearance is their close proximity to the Mediterranean Sea in the west and the Dead Sea in the southeast, which is 1300 feet below sea level.[1] In the Bible, mountains are mentioned in varying ways and for unique purposes:

1) A designated locality for worship (Exod. 19:20; Deut. 12:2).

2) As part of God's creation (Ps. 104:8).

3) As geographical boundaries (Josh. 13:8).

4) A point of ambush (Judg. 9:25).

5) The scene of military combat (1 Sam. 23:26).

OLD
TESTAMENT

IN THE BIBLE,
MOUNTAINS WERE
OFTEN
MENTIONED FOR
UNIQUE
PURPOSES.

MOUNTAINS OF ISRAEL

257

6) A habitat for animals (Ps. 11:1, 104:10; 1 Sam. 26:20).

7) A place of refuge (Judg. 6:2).

8) For spiritual retreat (1 Kings 19:8).

9) A sign of God's power over nature (Ps. 97:5).

10) As figurative representations of stability (Ps. 30:7) or obstacles (Zech. 4:7; Matt. 17:20).[2]

The Land of Palestine can be divided into several distinct geographical regions. Actually, five narrow bands run north and south, each with their own unique characteristics: 1) the Coastal Plain—the narrow, rolling strip along the Mediterranean coast; 2) the Shephelah—a narrow band of foothills located between the coastal plains and the central hill country in southwest Palestine; 3) the Central Range (called the backbone of the land)—the highland and hilly area that runs throughout the length of the land west of the Jordan; 4) the Jordan Valley—a geographical rift in the earth's crust that reaches a depth of minus 1,295 feet; and 5) the Eastern Range or Transjordan—the highland plateau east of the Jordan Valley.[3]

The eastern and western part of the country is cut into two sections by the geographical fault known as el Ghor. It extends southward from Syria between the Lebanon Mountain Range (west of the Jordan River) and the Anti-Lebanon Mountain Range (east of the Jordan River).[4] The depression includes the entire Jordan Rift Valley incorporating Lake Huleh, the Sea of Galilee, and the Dead Sea. The fault line continues all the way into southern Africa. Consequently, the Mountains of Palestine fall into two distinct groups that are divided east and west by the Jordan River. All the mountains west of the Jordan River are part of the Central Range. They are, listed north to south: the Lebanon Range (the two highest peaks are Jebel Makmal and Kurnat es-Sauda rising to heights ca. 10,200 feet), Mount Meiron or Jebel Yarmuk in Upper Galilee, the Horns of Hattin (near the traditional Mount of Beatitudes), Mount Arbel, Mount Carmel, Mount Tabor, the Hill of Moreh or "Little Hermon," Mount Gilboa, Mount Ebal, Mount Gerizim, Mount Moriah, Mount Zion, and the Mount of Olives.[5]

The mountains on the east of the Jordan are higher and steeper than those on the west. Proceeding north to south they include: Mount Hermon, Mount Gilead, and Mount Nebo. The northern section, which

MOUNTAINS OF ISRAEL

extends from Damascus to the Yarmuk River, is known as Bashan. The area is known for its productivity in Old Testament times. Bashan was the former kingdom of Og during the time of the Exodus. It contained at least 60 cities (Num. 21:33; Deut. 29:7) and was assigned to the tribe of Manasseh. *Bashan* literally means "fertile plain."[6] It was a plateau of lush grazing land used for fattening cattle. These animals took a great deal of special care, water, and pasture. The term *Bashan* was used allegorically when the prophet Amos addressed the pleasure-seeking women of Samaria as the "cows of Bashan" (Amos 4:1).[7] The region of Bashan also included 350 square miles of petrified lava fields and was called by the Greek name Trachonitis in Luke 3:1.

Bashan encompassed the area east of the Sea of Galilee and the Jordan River. It was bordered on the north by Mount Hermon and on the east by Jebel Druse extending west of the slopes of the Sea of Galilee and upper Jordan. *Jebel* is Arabic for "Mount." It extends south about six miles beyond the Yarmuk River.[8] It had excellent wheat fields, pasture for cattle, and groves of oak trees (Mic. 7:14; Jer. 50:19). The prosperity of Bashan is also used scripturally as a representation of arrogant pride (Ps. 22:12). Metaphorically, God's judgment is on the haughty and proud who are like the "oaks of Bashan" (Isa. 2:13). The Phoenicians had their oars made from the "oaks of Bashan." As a point of interest, they were expert sailors. They were the first to sail at night using the stars and were instrumental in creating the modern concept of the lighthouse. But they were condemned for their arrogant ways (Ezek. 27:1-6).

Situated between the Yarmuk Valley and Moab, by the Dead Sea on the east side of the Jordan River, lies the land of Gilead. There is no single Mount Gilead as the *King James Version* of the Scriptures may imply (Gen. 31:21). The rendering "hill country" is more exact. Gilead is a general highland region crossed by the Jabbok River. It is well watered, making the region rich in vegetation and very fruitful. The expression "balm of Gilead" was proverbial of its bounty and the healing balsams that came from its forests (Jer. 8:22; 46:11).[9] It was settled by the Gadites and the Reubenites (Josh. 13:8-12). The famous Mount Nebo, from which Moses surveyed the Promised Land, is in Gilead. Continuing south, the next area is known as Moab. The River Arnon (which enters the Dead Sea at its

OLD
TESTAMENT

BASHAN WAS
ASSIGNED TO THE
TRIBE OF
MANASSEH.

OLD
TESTAMENT

MOSES
SURVEYED THE
PROMISED
LAND FROM
MOUNT NEBO
IN GILEAD.

MOUNTAINS OF ISRAEL

259

central point on the eastern shore) served as the northern border for Moab (Num. 21:13). The River Zered (*Wadi el-Hasa*) formed the southern boundary, separating Moab from Edom. The mountains of Moab run parallel to the eastern rim of the Dead Sea and stand erect like a wall 3,000 feet high.[10]

Because Israel's mountains are so often spoken of in Scripture and are such an integral part of God's Promised Land, we will discuss each one of them (alphabetically) in concluding our Holy Land tour.

Mount Arbel

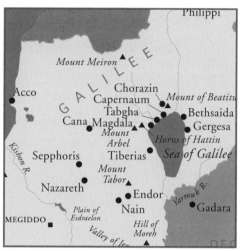

Mount Arbel is situated on the west side of the Sea of Galilee and offers a wonderful panoramic view of the basin below. The mountain is so named after the city Arbela of Galilee. Arbela is a village northwest of Tiberias and west of Magdala. Arbela is most likely the same place as Beth-Arbel spoken of by the prophet Hosea in chapter 10, verse 14 of his book. It has been associated with the unexcavated ruins found in the modern village of Irbid.[1] The village sits on the southeast side of the Wadi Haman. On the opposite side of the ravine is a row of caves in the face of the cliffs of the mountain.

Josephus notes that Bacchides, a Syrian general, was sent with a large army to crush the Maccabean revolt and protect the Hellenizers in this area. He defeated Judas Maccabeus in the plain of Arbel (1 Macc. 9:1 ff.). The place of battle was termed "Messaloth in Arbela." It is assumed that "Messaloth" was the name of the caves in the vicinity of Arbela to which the besieged Jews had fled.[2] To the Jews, Arbela is another Masada. Josephus mentions Arbela's caves as hideouts for Zealots who were extracted violently with hooks by the Roman soldiers (*Antiq.* 14.15.4).[3] Herod also had his men lowered over the cliffs by ropes where they pulled the people out of the caves to their deaths. After the destruction of the Second Temple, Arbela became the seat of the priestly family of Jeshua.[4]

OLD TESTAMENT

BETH-ARBEL WAS SPOKEN OF BY THE PROPHET HOSEA.

BETWEEN THE TESTAMENTS

BACCHIDES, A SYRIAN GENERAL, DEFEATED JUDAS MACCABEUS ON THE PLAIN OF ARBEL.

MOUNTAINS OF ISRAEL

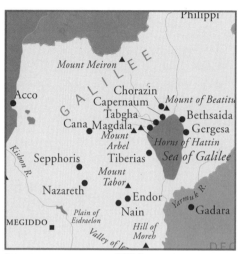

Philippi

Mount Meiron

Acco
Chorazin
Capernaum   Mount of Beatitu
Tabgha   Bethsaida
Cana Magdala   Gergesa
Mount
Arbel   Horns of Hattin
Sepphoris   Tiberias   Sea of Galilee
Mount
Tabor
Nazareth
Endor
Nain   Gadara
MEGIDDO
Plain of
Esdraelon   Hill of
Moreh

FROM MAP INSIDE THE FRONT COVER: 8-9, B-C.

WHERE JESUS
WALKED

JESUS DELIVERED
THE "SERMON ON
THE MOUNT" ON
THE MOUNT OF
BEATITUDES.

Mount of Beatitudes
(The Horns of Hattin)

The name, "Mount of Beatitudes" is ascribed to the area where Jesus delivered the "Sermon on the Mount." The exact location of the discourse is disputed and the biblical record is of little assistance in determining the actual spot. Only Matthew mentions in his gospel that Jesus was on a mountain during this discourse (Matt. 5:1; 8:1). Luke's account states the sermon took place in the plain, on a level area (Luke 6:17). Jesus went directly from there to Capernaum which must have been relatively close by (Matt. 8:1-5; Luke 7:1). The title "Sermon on the Mount" has long contributed to the belief that a specific mountain was intended—a mountain known to the readers of that time. However, others interpret "the mountain" to be more general, meaning "the tableland, the mountainous district."[1] Nevertheless, it seems a particular mount is noted upon which Jesus spent the night in prayer (Luke 6:12) and then descended to a level place to preach His sermon (Luke 6:17).

Mountains in the gospel of Matthew are places where many special events take place; i.e., the mountain of temptation (4:8); the mountain of prayer (14:23; 15:29); the mountain of transfiguration (17:1); and the mountain of the resurrection appearance where Jesus gave the Great Commission (28:16). Donald A. Hagner observes, "Since Matthew emphasizes mountains in special narratives usually having to do with revelation, 'the mountain,' here functions as a literary device."[2] Bearing Hagner's view in mind, Matthew, writing to a Jewish audience, may have taken the symbolism of a mount as an ideal. That is, the setting could have been meant to be analogous to that described in the Old Law (Ex. 29:18-22) to demonstrate another Sinai and a New Law; i.e., "You have heard that it was said to those of old . . . But I say to you . . . " (Matt. 5:21 ff.).[3]

MOUNTAINS OF ISRAEL

The Sermon on the Mount is best remembered for the Christian introduction to the Beatitudes. The word "beatitude" is not found in the English Bible. It is derived from the Latin word, *beautitudo* (Rom. 4:6; Ps. 32:1-2). In the Latin church, *beatitudo* meant the declaration of blessedness and has been attached specifically to the words of blessing which began Jesus' proclamation since the days of Ambrose (340-397 A.D.).[4] Ambrose was a church leader and a theologian who was trained in both Greek and Latin. He is noted for having tutorial influence on Augustine, who is considered one of the greatest theologians of the early Church. A beatitude, in the words of L. Mowry, constitutes "a declaration of praise for an individual regarded as an unusual example of moral rectitude and piety, who, as a consequence, might anticipate some appropriate reward from God."[5] Authors usually constructed a beatitude by using the adjective "blessed" or "happy" and a relational clause to designate the type of persons considered blessed. In the Psalms, David is said to pronounce the "beatitude" of the man whose transgressions are forgiven. Other beatitudes appearing in the Old Testament include Job 5:17; Ps. 41:1; 65:4; 84:5; 106:3; 112:1; 128:1; and Prov. 8:34; 16:20. Beatitudes in the New Testament include Matt. 5:1-12; Luke 6:20-26; John 20:29; Rom. 4:7-8; 14:22; and Rev. 1:3; 14:13; 16:15; 19:9; 20:6; 22:7, 14.

The New Testament beatitude differs from the Old Testament beatitude in one important aspect: The beatitudes of the New Testament stress the future joy of participating more in eternity rather than in the rewards for this earthly life.[6] So an element of paradox is evident. Those who appear to be unfortunate in this present earthly life; i.e., the poor, distressed, barren, and martyred, are those who are declared blessed because of their readiness for the eternal kingdom.

> And seeing the multitudes, He went up on a mountain, and when He was seated His disciples came to Him. Then He opened His mouth and taught them, saying: "Blessed are the poor in spirit, for theirs is the kingdom of heaven. Blessed are those who mourn, for they shall be comforted. Blessed are the meek, for they shall inherit the earth. Blessed are those who

A BEAUTIFUL CHURCH BUILT IN 1937 COMMEMORATES THE MOST POPULAR SITE FOR THE SERMON ON THE MOUNT.

hunger and thirst for righteousness, for they shall be filled. Blessed are the merciful, for they shall obtain mercy. Blessed are the pure in heart, for they shall see God. Blessed are the peacemakers, for they shall be called sons of God. Blessed are those who are persecuted for righteousness' sake, for theirs is the kingdom of heaven. Blessed are you when they revile and persecute you, and say all kinds of evil against you falsely for My sake. Rejoice and be exceedingly glad, for great is your reward in heaven, for so they persecuted the prophets who were before you."

MATTHEW 5:1-12

Two locations are typically suggested for the possible location of the Mount of Beatitudes, but the more popular site is up the slope of the hill on the north end of the Sea of Galilee. A beautiful church built in 1937 commemorates the spot. It was built of local basalt, using white Nazareth stone for its arches and Roman travertine for the columns.[7] The octagonal plan of the church offers a panoramic view of the area and the Sea of Galilee below. The eight sides of the church are dedicated to Matthew's eight recorded beatitudes. The dome of the church symbolizes the ninth beatitude which pronounces blessing on those who are persecuted for His sake—"for great is your reward in heaven."[8] The mountain, where Jesus possibly stayed time and again (Mark 6:45-46; John 6:14-15), rose above the springs of Ma-gadan. Verbal tests have been conducted that demonstrate a voice could be carried down the hill by the wind at certain times of the year and heard over a mile away. On the hill facing the lake is a grotto known as the Eremos cave or Magharat Ayub which is situated below a hanging cliff.[9] Here, Jesus could find shelter from the damp evening winds and solitude for prayer. On one particular night, a cold east wind (called *Sharkiyeh*) suddenly sprang up, endangering the disciples on the lake.

Immediately He made His disciples get into the boat and go before Him to the other side, to Bethsaida, while He sent the multitude away. And when He had sent them away, He departed to the mountain to pray. Now when evening came, the boat was in the middle of the sea; and He was alone on the land. Then He saw them straining at rowing, for the wind was against them. Now about the fourth watch of the night He came to them, walking on the sea, and would have passed them by. And when they saw Him walking on the sea, they supposed it was a ghost, and cried out; for they all saw Him and were troubled. But immediately He talked with them and said to them, "Be of good cheer! It is I; do not be afraid." Then He went up into the boat to them, and the wind ceased. And they were greatly amazed in themselves beyond measure, and marveled.

Mark 6:45-51

WHERE JESUS
WALKED

THIS HORNS
OF HATTIN
WERE LOCATED
AT THE CENTER
OF JESUS'
GALILEAN
MINISTRY.

The other proposed site for the Mount of Beatitudes is the *Kurun Hattin* or the "Horns of Hattin," which are stationed seven miles to the west of the lake. There are both positives and negatives which may or may not make

MOUNTAINS OF ISRAEL

this designation an acceptable location. The site meets all the requirements of biblical narrative; however, there are a number of hills to the west that appear equally as suitable. If these hills were in fact this designated area, it would not give proper force to *"the* mountain" which seems to designate the place as distinct from the hills of almost uniform height in the vicinity.[10] *Kurun Hattin* derives its name from the two cones, or horns, which crown its summit. This mountain was located at the center of Jesus' Galilean ministry. It was within close distance of Nazareth, Cana, and Mount Tabor to the southwest, the Sea of Galilee to the east, Capernaum, Magdala, and Bethsaida to the northeast.

The Horns of Hattin is the only height to the west that can be seen from the shores of the Sea of Galilee (ca. 1,816 feet).[11] Its topography consists of a low ridge extending east-west about a quarter of a mile long that rises to an extremity. The "horn" is about 60 feet above the ridge. Between the horns lies an uneven plateau which could accommodate the crowds that followed Jesus. Some believe the spot on which the discourse was given was lower down on the southern side of the mountain. Tradition says there was a village on the mountaintop, "a city that is set on a hill" (Matt. 5:14), and beautiful flowers in abundance, "lilies of the field" (Matt. 6:28). The Jews in the area point out that this is the location of the tomb of Jethro, the father-in-law of Moses.[12]

OLD TESTAMENT

THE JEWS IN THE AREA POINT OUT THAT THIS IS THE LOCATION OF THE TOMB OF JETHRO, FATHER-IN-LAW OF MOSES.

CRUSADERS

THE BATTLE OF HATTIN, JULY 4, 1187, DEALT THE WORST DEFEAT INFLICTED UPON THE UNITED CRUSADER FORCES.

During the Crusades, the Horns of Hattin were the scene of a major battle. The Crusades began in response to an appeal made in 1095 by Pope Urban II to rescue the Holy Land from Islam. The knights first arrived in Palestine in May of 1099. By 1153 the entire country was under Crusader rule.[13] It was the Crusaders who first called the country "the Holy Land." But the Crusader dominance was short-lived. The Battle of Hattin, July 4, 1187, dealt the worst defeat inflicted upon the united Crusader forces. The great Muslim general Saladin turned Egypt into an Ayubid power and trained an army to recapture the territory the Crusaders had taken. Of this army Saladin boasted in a letter, "that the widest plain was too narrow for such an army" and that "the dust it raised on the move would darken the eye of the sun."[14] It was an army consisting of at least 30,000 soldiers.

MOUNTAINS OF ISRAEL

Saladin would not risk his army on a direct assault or prolonged military campaign. So by attacking Tiberias, he drew out the Crusader forces and maneuvered them toward the Horns of Hattin. The Crusaders were forced to camp on the barren double hill without water and shelter. The Muslim forces surrounding them then set fire to the area's brushwood causing intense heat, thirst, and exhaustion. The entire Christian force, now weary and dehydrated, was slaughtered in a single day. Jerusalem later surrendered peaceably.[15]

FROM MAP INSIDE THE FRONT COVER: 7-8, C-D.

Mount Carmel

The city of Haifa lies on the northern slopes of Mount Carmel. Though it is not directly mentioned in the Bible, Haifa does have significant associations with biblical characters and miraculous events. Mark Twain called Haifa "just a dirty small village" when he traveled through the Holy Land. It is presently Israel's third largest city and chief seaport on the Mediterranean. And, nearly half the world's diamonds come through the city's markets. It has been said that "Jerusalem is the city of the past, Tel Aviv is the city of the present, and Haifa is the city of the future." Modern Haifa houses one of the largest concentration of Druze villagers—a religious offshoot that derived from Islam.

Mount Carmel itself stretches for 13 miles, reaching a maximum elevation of 1,742 feet and is a continuation of the hills of Samaria.[1] The northeast sides are steep, while the southwest gives way more gradually to the coasts. The excellent soil and luxuriant growth of plants, for which the mountain has always been known, still cover its topography.[2] Mount Carmel splits the Palestinian coastal plain into two geographical sections: 1) the plain of Acco and Esdraelon to the north, and 2) the plain of Sharon and Philistia to the south.[3] The area of Acco was assigned to the tribe of Asher during the possession of the land, but they failed to occupy it (Josh. 19:24-32; Judg. 1:31). The first historical mention of Mount Carmel is focused in the Egyptian writings of Ramses and suggests that it was an early holy place and sanctuary.[4] In the Old Testament, an altar to Baal was set on the mountain. In Hellenistic times, a temple of Zeus was erected.[5] Currently, Haifa is the center of the Bahai faith (site of the tomb of the Bahilla) and home of several other religious faiths. So Carmel has a history of extrabiblical faiths. It was here that Elijah challenged the prophets of Baal when God supported his ministry with supernatural fire.

OLD TESTAMENT

ELIJAH CHALLENGED THE PROPHETS OF BAAL ON MOUNT CARMEL.

"Now therefore, send and gather all Israel to me on Mount Carmel, the four hundred and fifty prophets of Baal, and the four hundred prophets of Asherah, who eat at Jezebel's table."

So Ahab sent for all the children of Israel, and gathered the prophets together on Mount Carmel. And Elijah came to all the people, and said, "How long will you falter between two opinions? If the LORD is God, follow Him; but if Baal, follow him." But the people answered him not a word. Then Elijah said to the people, "I alone am left a prophet of the LORD; but Baal's prophets are four hundred and fifty men. Therefore let them give us two bulls; and let them choose one bull for themselves, cut it in pieces, and lay it on the wood, but put no fire under it; and I will prepare the other bull, and lay it on the wood, but put no fire under it. Then you call on the name of your gods, and I will call on the name of the LORD; and the God who answers by fire, He is God." So all the people answered and said, "It is well spoken."

Now Elijah said to the prophets of Baal, "Choose one bull for yourselves and prepare it first, for you are many; and call on the name of your god, but put no fire under it." So they took the bull which was given them, and they prepared it, and called on the name of Baal from morning even till noon, saying, "O Baal, hear us!" But there was no voice; no one answered. Then they leaped about the altar which they had made. And so it was, at noon, that Elijah mocked them and said, "Cry aloud, for he is a god; either he is meditating, or he is busy, or he is on a journey, or perhaps he is sleeping and must be awakened." So they cried aloud, and cut themselves, as was their custom, with knives and lances, until the blood gushed out on them. And when midday was past, they prophesied until the time of the offering of the evening sacrifice. But there was no voice; no one answered, no one paid attention.

Then Elijah said to all the people, "Come near to me." So all the people came near to him. And he repaired the altar of the LORD that was broken down. And Elijah took twelve stones, according to the number of the tribes of the sons of Jacob, to

THIS DEPICTION OF ELIJAH AS HE CALLED DOWN FIRE FROM HEAVEN ON THE PROPHETS OF BAAL STANDS ON MOUNT CARMEL.

whom the word of the LORD had come, saying, "Israel shall be your name." Then with the stones he built an altar in the name of the LORD; and he made a trench around the altar large enough to hold two seahs of seed. And he put the wood in order, cut the bull in pieces, and laid it on the wood, and said, "Fill four waterpots with water, and pour it on the burnt sacrifice and on the wood." Then he said, "Do it a second time," and they did it a second time; and he said, "Do it a third time," and they did it a third time. So the water ran all around the altar; and he also filled the trench with water. And it came to pass, at the time of the offering of the evening sacrifice, that Elijah the prophet came near and said, "LORD God of Abraham, Isaac, and Israel, let it be known this day that You are God in Israel and I am Your servant, and that I have done all these things at Your word. Hear me, O LORD, hear me, that this people may know that You are the LORD God, and that You have turned their hearts back to You again." Then the fire of the LORD fell and consumed the burnt sacrifice, and the wood and the stones and the dust, and it licked up the water that was in the trench.

MOUNTAINS OF ISRAEL

Now when all the people saw it, they fell on their faces; and they said, "The Lord, He is God! The Lord, He is God!" And Elijah said to them, "Seize the prophets of Baal! Do not let one of them escape!" So they seized them; and Elijah brought them down to the Brook Kishon and executed them there.

1 Kings 18:19-40

Mount Carmel is often used paradoxically in Scripture as an illustration of a beautiful, fruitful place (Isa. 35:2; Jer. 50:19; Mic. 7:14)—and as a picture of decay, desolation, and God's judgment (Isa. 33:9; Amos 1:2; Nah. 1:4).[6] The word, *carmel* is a contraction of a Hebrew word that means "vineyard of God" (2 Chron. 26:10), fruitful garden, or orchard. The mountain's fertility served the writer as poetic inspiration in Song of Solomon 7:5.[7] It was also from this mountain that Elijah, after discrediting the gods of Jezebel and slaying the prophets of Baal, prayed for rain that ended the 3½ year drought.

Then Elijah said to Ahab, "Go up, eat and drink; for there is the sound of abundance of rain." So Ahab went up to eat and drink. And Elijah went up to the top of Carmel; then he bowed down on the ground, and put his face between his knees, and said to his servant, "Go up now, look toward the sea." So he went up and looked, and said, "There is nothing." And seven times he said, "Go again." Then it came to pass the seventh time, that he said, "There is a cloud, as small as a man's hand, rising out of the sea!" So he said, "Go up, say to Ahab, 'Prepare your chariot, and go down before the rain stops you.'" Now it happened in the meantime that the sky became black with clouds and wind, and there was a heavy rain. So Ahab rode away and went to Jezreel. Then the hand of the Lord came upon Elijah; and he girded up his loins and ran ahead of Ahab to the entrance of Jezreel.

1 Kings 18:41-46

SITE OF INTEREST

Caves on Mount Carmel

There are several caves on Mount Carmel that have historical signifi-cance. A small cave on the mountain (under the Carmelite Monastery) is held sacred by both Christians and Jews. In the Christian tradition it is

MOUNTAINS OF ISRAEL

The prophet Elisha, who received a double portion of Elijah's anointing, also lived on Mount Carmel. It was from this site that he was called to raise the Shunammite woman's son from the dead.

believed to be the place where the prophet Elijah lived. In the Jewish tradition the cave is connected to Elijah's pupil, Elisha, who is believed to have been buried there.[8] The Carmelites built a monastery in 1767 at the northwest edge of the ridge. (It was used by Napoleon as a hospital for his soldiers). The building suffered a fire, but was rebuilt in 1827.[9] It is believed that other caves on the northern slope of the mountain also served as shelter for the prophet Elijah. It is possible that he hid from the wicked queen Jezebel in a cave site traditionally known as the "Cave of Elijah." Rivka Gonen notes that "curative properties have been ascribed to the cave over the years and in particular its ability to cure mental ailments."[10] Those who suffer such illness (as well as barren women) have been left alone in the cave for three days with reports of wellness. South of Haifa, archeologists have also discovered human remains and artifacts that date to earliest human history. Evidently, in ancient times the caves were used as shelters and dwellings.[11]

OLD TESTAMENT

THE PROPHET ELISHA ALSO LIVED ON MOUNT CARMEL.

The prophet Elisha, who received a double portion of Elijah's anointing, also lived on Mount Carmel. It was from this site that he was called to raise the Shunammite woman's son from the dead. The Church has interpreted this miracle and the proclamation by the mother, "It is well," as one of the great lessons of faith in Scripture (2 Kings 4:17-37). Centuries later, its inspiration still serves as a foundation for enduring the trials of life. One of the great poems of the Christian faith applied this mother's words. It was written by Horatio Spafford, a wealthy Chicago lawyer (and friend of revivalist Dwight L. Moody), who lost much of his fortune in the 1871

MOUNTAINS OF ISRAEL

Chicago fire. What the fire didn't take, he lost in the 1873 financial panic that followed.

Adding to that the fact that his wife Annie's health was suffering, the Spafford family physician recommended an ocean trip away from the States for the entire family. Horatio agreed. But at the last minute, because of unexpected business demands, he was forced to send his wife and four daughters (ranging in ages from eighteen months to eighteen years) on ahead without him, promising to join them in a couple of weeks. Six days out and in mid-ocean, the steamer *Ville du Havre* collided with the English sailing vessel *Lochearn* and sank within fifteen minutes. From France Mr. Spafford received a wire from his wife which read: "Saved alone. Children lost. What shall I do?"

Spafford set sail immediately to be with his wife. After six days at sea, the captain notified him of their position when passing over the place where his four beautiful daughters were buried at the bottom of the sea. Standing speechless on the deck, he gazed at the spot where the ship was said to have gone down. Then he suddenly turned away and proceeded to his berth. There he sat and wrote the lyrics that would later be set to a lovely melody written by P. P. Bliss shortly before Bliss would die in a flaming train accident while trying to rescue his trapped wife. The song, "It Is Well With My Soul," became one of the most inspiring hymns to come out of the gospel-song movement, and it is one of the greatest hymns about faith ever written. Could Mr. Spafford have been thinking of the words of the Shunammite woman when contemplating the passing of his own children? He wrote:

When peace, like a river, attendeth my way,
When sorrows like sea billows roll;
Whatever my lot, Thou has taught me to say,
It is well, it is well with my soul.

Though Satan should buffet, though trials should come,
Let His blest assurance control,

MOUNTAINS OF ISRAEL

That Christ hath regarded my helpless estate,
And hath shed His own blood for my soul.

My sin, oh, the bliss of this glorious thought!
My sin, not in part but the whole,
Is nailed to the cross, and I bear it no more,
Praise the Lord, praise the Lord, O my soul.

And, Lord, haste the day when the faith shall be sight,
The clouds be rolled back as a scroll;
The trump shall resound, and the Lord shall descend,
Even so, it is well with my soul.

MOUNTAINS OF ISRAEL

FROM MAP INSIDE THE FRONT COVER: 8-9, D-E.

Mount Ebal

OLD TESTAMENT

IN ISRAEL'S COVENANT WITH JEHOVAH, THE BLESSINGS WERE TYPIFIED BY MOUNT GERIZIM AND THE CURSES BY MOUNT EBAL.

Upon entering the land of Canaan, the Hebrews were to confirm their covenant with Yahweh. The ceremony involved a dramatic illustration of the promises contained in the covenant. It meant blessing for obedience to the agreement typified by Mount Gerizim and cursing for disobedience to the agreement typified by Mount Ebal. A pronouncement of judgment was declared upon any persons who broke the commandments.

The covenantal ceremony is described in the Scriptures under the leadership of Joshua. Six tribes assembled in front of Mount Gerizim and the other six in front of Mount Ebal. The Ark of the Covenant rested between them (Josh. 8:30-33). The Law was to be written on stones coated with lime, and an altar was to be built to sacrifice to the Lord. Mount Ebal was selected as the mount of cursing in this historic event. Joshua later built an altar on this mount and sacrificed burnt offerings as directed by Moses (Deut. 27:1-8). Mount Ebal (modern Jebel Eslamiyeh) with its stark rock and barrenness of vegetation, provides the appearance of a curse. It stands in contrast to the fruitful Mount Gerizim (modern Jebel et-Tor).[1] Twelve curses were given to intentionally correspond with the number of Israel's tribes. Those tribes who were to live in the southern part of Canaan were to pronounce the blessings (Simeon, Levi, Judah, Issachar, Joseph, and Benjamin). Those who were to live in the north and to the east of the Jordan were to pronounce the curses (Reuben, Gad, Asher, Zebulun, Dan, and Naphtali). Evidently, six tribes were to make the proclamations and the other six would say "amen" to the pronouncement (Deut. 27:13-26). Moses spoke out the curses the people were to repeat, then in Deuteronomy 28, he spoke the blessings.

"Now it shall come to pass, if you diligently obey the voice of the Lord your God, to observe carefully all His commandments which I command you today, that the LORD your God will set you high above all nations of the earth. And all these blessings shall come upon you and overtake you, because you obey the voice of the LORD your God.

But it shall come to pass, if you do not obey the voice of the LORD your God, to observe carefully all His commandments and His statutes which I command you today, that all these curses will come upon you and overtake you."

DEUTERONOMY 28:1-2,15

After the defeat of Ai, when Israel was entering the land, Joshua copied upon the stones and read God's Law:

Now Joshua built an altar to the LORD God of Israel in Mount Ebal, as Moses the servant of the LORD had commanded the children of Israel, as it is written in the Book of the Law of Moses: "an altar of whole stones over which no man has wielded an iron tool." And they offered on it burnt offerings to the LORD, and sacrificed peace offerings. And there, in the presence of the children of Israel, he wrote on the stones a copy of the law of Moses, which he had written. Then all Israel, with their elders and officers and judges, stood on either side of the ark before the priests, the Levites, who bore the ark of the covenant of the LORD, the stranger as well as he who was born among them. Half of them were in front of Mount Gerizim and half of them in front of Mount Ebal, as Moses the servant of the LORD had commanded before, that they should bless the people of Israel. And afterward he read all the words of the law, the blessings and the cursings, according to all that is written in the Book of the Law. There was not a word of all that Moses had commanded which Joshua did not read before all the assembly of Israel, with the women, the little ones, and the strangers who were living among them.

JOSHUA 8:30-35

MOUNTAINS OF ISRAEL

In addition, Joshua's memorialized farewell address "but as for me and my house, we will serve the Lord" was spoken at this sacred site.

In ancient times there was confusion about the location of the hills of Gerizim and Ebal. In the biblical reference they are placed near Gilgal, beside the Plain of Moreh. The Samaritans claimed they were situated near ancient Shechem (Neapolis). The famous Madaba map marks them near Neapolis and is accepted by chroniclers.[2] The Roman name *Flavia Neapolis* means "new city." Titus founded the settlement (A.D. 72) just 1¼ miles from ancient Shechem after the destruction of Jerusalem. The town was later granted the status of *colonia*.[3] In time, it acquired a Christian community which produced the apologist Justin Martyr (ca. A.D. 100-165). The current name of the village is Nablus and is the Arabic pronunciation of the Roman name *Neapolis*.[4]

Shechem was one of the major religious and political centers in Israel, second only to Jerusalem during the united monarchy. LaMoine F. DeVries notes, "The Bible, extrabiblical sources, and archaeological discoveries confirm ancient Shechem of the Canaanite, Israelite, and Samaritan periods as a city of altars, sacred pillars and trees, temples, covenants, covenant renewals, and political confirmation ceremonies."[5] Shechem is mentioned a number of times in Scripture in reference to a host of situations and occurrences. Both Abraham (Gen. 12:6-7) and Jacob (Gen. 33:18-20) built altars at Shechem. It was also the gruesome site where the daughter of Jacob was molested which led to an attack on the city (Gen. 34). Under the oak at Shechem, Jacob buried the foreign gods (Gen. 35). And, it was in Shechem that Joseph went to search for his brothers (Gen. 37:12-14). Joseph's bones were eventually buried in the Shechem plot his father Jacob had purchased (Josh. 24:32).[6] In addition, Joshua's

GREEK/ROMAN

TITUS FOUNDED THE CITY OF FLAVIA NEAPOLIS NEAR SHECHEM, THE TRADITIONAL SAMARITAN SITE OF MOUNT EBAL.

OLD TESTAMENT

BOTH ABRAHAM AND JACOB BUILT ALTARS AT SHECHEM.

MOUNTAINS OF ISRAEL

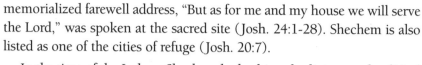

memorialized farewell address, "But as for me and my house we will serve the Lord," was spoken at the sacred site (Josh. 24:1-28). Shechem is also listed as one of the cities of refuge (Josh. 20:7).

OLD
TESTAMENT

AFTER
SOLOMON'S
DEATH, ISRAEL
BROKE AWAY
FROM JUDAH
AND ESTAB-
LISHED
SHECHEM AS
THEIR CAPITAL.

In the time of the Judges, Shechem had achieved religious and political status. Rehoboam sought confirmation of his kingship at the famed city following the death of Solomon (1 Kings 12:1-20), but he was rejected by the northern tribes. They chose Jeroboam I who then built the first capital of the northern kingdom at Shechem (1 Kings 12:25). In Hebrew *sekem* probably means "back" or "shoulder" and may have obtained the name from its geographical location on the shoulder of Mount Ebal.[7] Mount Gerizim (elevation ca. 2,900 feet), facing to the north-northwest, and Mount Ebal (elevation ca. 3,000 feet) which faces to the south-southwest, are the two highest peaks in central Palestine. The two mountains which also face one another form the sides of an important east-west pass.[8] The city of Shechem was positioned at the east end of the pass between the two historic mountains where several trade routes converged. The major highway which cut through the central hill country led to Megiddo in the north and Jerusalem in the south. Another major east-west highway moved west to the Via Maris—the coastal-plain road by the Mediterranean Sea.[9] Shechem is mentioned in the New Testament (Sychem) in the speech by Stephen where the martyr refers to the remains of Joseph (Acts 7).[10] Although the city had an excellent water supply, it was vulnerable to attack due to its position on the lower slopes of the mountain. Eventually, following the future development of the northern kingdom, its capital was moved from Schechem to the city of Samaria.

The Samaritans revered Mount Ebal as the mountain of God, as opposed to Mount Zion in Jerusalem.[11] They subsequently built a temple on the adjacent Mount Gerizim for worship. The Samaritan beliefs regarding the sacredness of the site are reflected in the comments by the Samaritan woman to Jesus at the well in John 4:7-26. Today the hundreds of Samaritans who still live in the area observe the rituals of the Day of Atonement much as they did in biblical times.[12] Tradition states that the head of John the Baptist is buried on Mount Ebal. In the Middle Ages, the Muslims erected a monument over the alleged site.[13]

MOUNTAINS OF ISRAEL

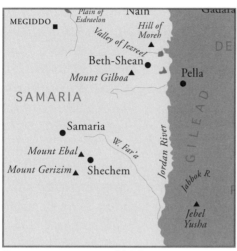

MEGIDDO ■
Plain of Esdraelon
Nain
Gadara
Hill of Moreh
Valley of Jezreel
Beth-Shean
Mount Gilboa
Pella
SAMARIA
Samaria
Mount Ebal
W. Far'a
Jordan River
GILEAD
Jabbok R.
Mount Gerizim ▲ Shechem
Jebel Yusha

FROM MAP INSIDE THE FRONT COVER: 8-9, D-E.

Mount Gerizim

OLD TESTAMENT

MOUNT GERIZIM TYPIFIED THE BLESSINGS OF ISRAEL'S COVENANT WITH JEHOVAH.

Mount Gerizim (modern Jebel et-Tor) was the mountain of blessing designated in the covenantal ceremony in which the people engaged upon entering the land of Canaan. It is directly across from Mount Ebal and is about 100-200 feet lower. Gerizim is made up of three summits which became the high places established for religious practices.[1] It stands about 2,900 feet above the Mediterranean Sea and about 700 feet above the narrow Valley of Nablus between Mount Ebal and itself. It is the only passage across to the hill country of Ephraim. Due to its Eocene limestone consistency, the mountain provides a somewhat grayish and forbidding appearance, especially on the upper slopes.[2] It is located almost exactly in the center of Palestine, west of the Jordan River. The book of Judges implies that Mount Gerizim is the "center of the land" (Judg. 9:37). The Septuagint calls it "the navel of the earth," giving great significance to the site. The mountain is understood to be a connection between heaven and earth and therefore consecrated as a sacred area for worship.[3] From Mount Gerizim, Jotham (the youngest of Gideon's sons) proclaimed to the citizens of Shechem his famous kingship fable regarding Abimelech (Judg. 9:7). A ledge halfway to the top is popularly called "Jotham's pulpit."[4] It was there that he took advantage of the sacred tradition of the area to reinforce the authority of his proclamation.[5]

SITE OF INTEREST

JOTHAM'S PULPIT

The mountain held a strategic position both militarily and commercially. Again, it was Gerizim (the mountain of blessing) and Ebal (the mountain of cursing) that formed an important east-west pass. In the words of W. L. Reed, "The mountains, standing like two sentinels, could be fortified and assured control of the roads in the vicinity."[6] Another highway from Jerusalem to the area of Galilee crossed close by near Shechem. These factors, plus a reliable water source (cf. Jacobs well: John 4:6) made the area attractive for habitation from a very early period.

MOUNTAINS OF ISRAEL

Gerizim and Ebal were the sight of Israel's declaration of the blessings and cursings in Deuteronomy 27. The Hebrew people were instructed by Moses, and later it was enacted by Joshua, to stand upon Mount Gerizim and pronounce the blessings for obeying God's Word. They also were to stand upon Mount Ebal to pronounce the cursings for not obeying God's Word. Six tribes were to stand on Gerizim: Simeon, Levi, Judah, Issachar, Joseph, and Benjamin (Deut. 27:12). The six others were to stand on Ebal: Reuben, Gad, Asher, Zebulun, Dan, and Naphtali (Deut. 27:13).

Initially, Abraham entered the Promised Land in the area of these mountains through Shechem at the "oak of Moreh." It is also the location of Abraham's first altar after arriving in Canaan from Mesopotamia (Gen. 12:6 ff.). Jacob later followed (Gen. 33:18-20), as did Joshua (Josh. 8:33). A religious ceremony was conducted in each instance, hence the location was subsequently revered as a site of liturgical importance. However, its presence as a religious center dissipated when David made Jerusalem the capital. Nevertheless, the Samaritans continued to celebrate the Passover on the summit of the mountain.

OLD
TESTAMENT

THE SAMARITANS
BUILT A RIVAL
TEMPLE TO
JERUSALEM ON
MOUNT GERIZIM
DURING THEIR
SCHISM WITH THE
JUDEANS.

The Samaritans built a rival temple to Jerusalem on Mount Gerizim during their schism with the Judeans. After the Assyrians captured the northern kingdom, the new mixed race intermingled the worship of Yahweh with the worship of false deities (2 Kings 17:24-33).[7] The Samaritans were thus rejected by the Judeans. The reforms by Ezra and Nehemiah insisted on Jewish ethnic purity. So the dating of the Samaritan temple may be either in the time of Nehemiah or during the rise of Hellenization with Alexander the Great. According to Josephus, the

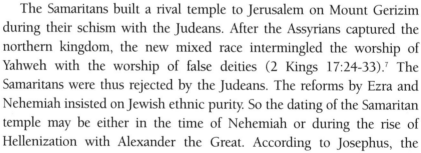

According to Josephus, the Samaritans built a temple on Mount Gerizim with the aid of Sanballat III, grandson of the earlier Sanballat who opposed Nehemiah's rebuilding of the Temple in Judea.

Samaritans built a temple on Mount Gerizim with the aid of Sanballat III, grandson of the earlier Sanballat who opposed Nehemiah's rebuilding of the Temple in Judea.[8] During the rise of Hellenization, it seems that Alexander himself gave permission to the Samaritans to build a house of worship on the esteemed site.

GREEK/
ROMAN

ALEXANDER THE GREAT GAVE PERMISSION FOR THE SAMARITANS TO BUILD A HOUSE OF WORSHIP HERE WHILE HE CONTROLLED ISRAEL.

The Samaritan Pentateuch replaces Ebal with Gerizim concerning the command to erect an altar (Deut. 27:4). Thereafter, say their writings, Gerizim became the visible, spiritual center for the Samaritans, and it has remained so since the return from Babylon until today. The division between the Jew and the Samaritan was made complete by the construction of their special place of worship. Samaritan tradition even places the sacrifice of Isaac on Mount Gerizim (Gen. 22:2) substituting Moreh for Moriah which is the sacred mount in Jerusalem.[9] The Samaritans also claimed national descent from the old tribes of Joseph of the north— Ephraim and Manasseh. They desired to worship God at Shechem as the true sanctuary in their understanding.[10] But Antiochus IV Epiphanes desecrated the Samaritan temple and dedicated it to Zeus Helios, "patron of strangers" (2 Macc. 6:2). It was also destroyed by the Hasmonean John Hycranus a few decades later (128 B.C.) according to Josephus (*Antiq.* 13.9.1). Nonetheless, the Samaritan woman's words to Jesus in John, chapter 4, share the sentiments of the people concerning the sacred site.

A woman of Samaria came to draw water. Jesus said to her, "Give Me a drink." For His disciples had gone away into the city to buy food. Then the woman of Samaria said to Him, "How is it that You, being a Jew, ask a drink from me, a Samaritan woman?" For Jews have no dealings with Samaritans.

Jesus answered and said to her, "If you knew the gift of God, and who it is who says to you, 'Give Me a drink,' you would have asked Him, and He would have given you living water." The woman said to Him, "Sir, You have nothing to draw with, and the well is deep. Where then do You get that living water? Are You greater than our father Jacob, who gave us the well, and drank from it himself, as well as his sons and his livestock?" Jesus answered and said to her, "Whoever drinks of this water will

thirst again, but whoever drinks of the water that I shall give him will never thirst. But the water that I shall give him will become in him a fountain of water springing up into everlasting life." The woman said to Him, "Sir, give me this water, that I may not thirst, nor come here to draw." Jesus said to her, "Go, call your husband, and come here." The woman answered and said, "I have no husband." Jesus said to her, "You have well said, 'I have no husband,' for you have had five husbands, and the one whom you now have is not your husband; in that you spoke truly." The woman said to Him, "Sir, I perceive that You are a prophet. Our fathers worshiped on this mountain, and you Jews say that in Jerusalem is the place where one ought to worship." Jesus said to her, "Woman, believe Me, the hour is coming when you will neither on this mountain, nor in Jerusalem, worship the Father. You worship what you do not know; we know what we worship, for salvation is of the Jews. But the hour is coming, and now is, when the true worshipers will worship the Father in spirit and truth; for the Father is seeking such to worship Him. God is Spirit, and those who worship Him must worship in spirit and truth." The woman said to Him, "I know that Messiah is coming" (who is called Christ). "When He comes, He will tell us all things." Jesus said to her, "I who speak to you am He."
JOHN 4:7-26

GREEK/
ROMAN

IN A.D. 70, THE ROMAN GENERAL CEREALIS UNDER VESPASIAN SLEW 11,600 SAMARITANS ON TOP OF MOUNT GERIZIM.

BYZANTINE

THE CHRISTIAN EMPEROR ZENO DROVE THE SAMARITANS FROM MOUNT GERIZIM IN A.D. 486 TO BUILD A CHURCH TO MARY, MOTHER OF GOD.

In A.D. 70, the Roman general Cerealis under Vespasian slew 11,600 Samaritans on top of the mount.[11] Later, the Emperor Hadrian rebuilt the temple of Zeus over the Samaritan ruins. Archaeologists believe they have found the temple and over 1500 marble steps that led to the pagan site.[12]

During the Byzantine period, there was continuous fighting between the Samaritans and the Christians. The Christian Emperor Zeno drove the Samaritans from Mount Gerizim in A.D. 486 and ordered a church to be built and dedicated to Mary, Mother of God (Maria Theotokos). The Samaritans destroyed it, but it was reconstructed by Justinian I in 530 A.D.[13] The structure was totally demolished again when the Arabs invaded. Near the site of the Samaritan, Roman, and Christian excavations is a flat rock the Samaritans call "The Rock of Foundation." They believe it was from this spot that the act of the world's creation began.[14] The Samaritans consider the flat rock holy. It lies near where the remnant of the Samaritan community still celebrates the Feast of Passover with the sacrifice of the Paschal Lamb. When you visit Israel you will find that Mount Gerizim is still considered special in the eyes of the Samaritans today.

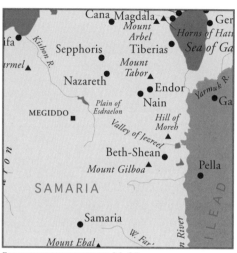

FROM MAP INSIDE THE FRONT COVER: 8-9, C-D.

EARLY KINGS

MOUNT GILBOA IS BEST KNOWN AS THE PLACE WHERE SAUL AND JONATHAN WERE SLAIN IN A BATTLE WITH THE PHILISTINES. DAVID SANG A LAMENT OVER THE TRAGEDY AND CURSED MOUNT GILBOA.

Mount Gilboa

Mount Gilboa stands at an elevation of ca. 1,630 feet and means either "hill country" or "bubbling fountain."[1] It is one of the two mountains that overlook the Jezreel Valley. The other is the Hill of Moreh, also known as "Little Hermon."[2] Mount Gilboa is best known as the place where Saul and Jonathan were slain in battle with the Philistines (1 Sam. 31:1-8). Saul chose to defend Gilboa and use the high ground of the mountain as an advantage over the superior weapons of the Philistines. On the eve of the fight, Saul had visited the witch of Endor, a woman with a "familiar spirit", and was warned of his approaching death by a supposed vision from the deceased prophet Samuel (1 Sam. 28). The next day he was killed in battle by the Philistines. After the battle his body was fastened to the wall of the Canaanite fortress city of Beth-Shean, located at the junction of two important valleys—the Jezreel Valley (north-south) and the Jordan Valley (east-west). But his body was retrieved by the warriors of Jabesh-gilead who remembered the deliverance of their city by Saul when it was attacked by the Ammonites.[3] David sang a lament over the tragedy and cursed Mount Gilboa (2 Sam. 1:17-27). Notwithstanding, it was Saul's death on this mountain that made possible David's rise to power and the golden age of Israel.

The Philistines were people of Aegean origin who occupied the southern coast of Palestine. The book of Exodus refers to the Mediterranean Sea as the Sea of Philistia (Ex. 23:31) which testifies to their power and importance. They are mentioned in literature outside the Bible as part of the sea peoples who invaded Egypt in 485 B.C., and are believed to have migrated from the Aegean area after being pushed out by the arrival of the Greeks.[4] The Bible acknowledges that they came from Crete (Gen. 10:14; 1 Chron. 1:12; Deut. 2:23; 1 Sam. 30:14; Eze. 25:16; Zeph. 2:5). The prophets Amos and Jeremiah state that they came from *Caphtor*—the biblical term for "Crete" (Amos 9:7; Jer. 47:4).

MOUNTAINS OF ISRAEL

The Philistines settled in Canaan after being resisted by the Egyptians. The term *Palestina* is derived from the name *Pelishtim* or *Philistines* and was first applied by the Greeks to the entire southeastern Mediterranean region.[5] So *Palestina* is an alternate name for *Philistia* (Ex. 15:14; Isa. 14:29, 31). The term was later adopted by the Roman ruler Hadrian to designate the entire country, particularly the land west of the Jordan River. The Philistines are some of the most heralded foes of Israel mentioned in the Old Testament. The Scriptures state they maintained a monopoly of iron weapons (1 Sam. 13:19-22). Their armies were well-armed troops containing foot soldiers, archers, and charioteers (1 Sam. 13:5; 29:2; 31:3).[6] When David moved the capital to Jerusalem, the Philistines recognized the threat to their southern towns and attacked. It was David's victory over the Philistines that led Israel to become a leading power in the land of Canaan.[7]

Mount Gilboa was frequently the scene of military conflict due to its position near one of two valleys which lead into the Plain of Jezreel (also known as the Valley of Armageddon). Although it is not directly mentioned by name, Mount Gilboa was more than likely the location of Gideon's camp. In this famous conflict recorded in the book of Judges, the Midianites were stationed on the north side of the valley (Judg. 7:1), probably on the Hill of Moreh, four miles northwest of the small Israelite army.[8]

OLD
TESTAMENT

MOUNT GILBOA
WAS MORE THAN
LIKELY THE
LOCATION OF
GIDEON'S CAMP
IN HIS DEFEAT OF
THE MIDIANITES.

The Midianites had joined forces with the Amalekite Bedouins in a series of invasions that devastated central Palestine. Raids were conducted during the harvest season which caused the Israelites to flee into the mountainous caves for refuge while the invaders stole the crops.[9] After Gideon was called by God to deliver the nation, he summoned his countrymen to Mount Gilboa and with just 300 men, won a great victory attacking at night. The Midianites retreated past Beth-Shean at the point where the Valley of Jezreel connects with the Jordan Valley. They then continued down through the Jordan Valley through Abel-meholah (midway between the Sea of Galilee and the Dead Sea) where they were confronted by the men of Ephraim at Beth-barah (Judg. 7:24). There, the two Midianite princes, Oreb and Zeeb, were slain. Gideon finally caught up with the remainder of the Midianite army and encountered them at Karkar, near the lower Jabbok River. It was there that he captured Zebah and Zalmunna, kings of the Midianites, and had them executed.[10]

MOUNTAINS OF ISRAEL

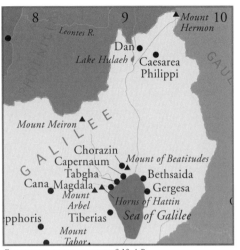

FROM MAP INSIDE THE FRONT COVER: 9-10, A-B.

Mount Hermon

Mount Hermon means "a consecrated place, a sanctuary." It stands about 9,230 feet above the Mediterranean.[1] It is the highest mountain in Syria and can be seen from as far away as the Dead Sea. The mountain provides a majestic view of the surrounding area rising above the land of Mizpah and the Valley of Lebanon (Josh. 11:3-8,17). Mizpah is where Joshua chased the kings of the Canaanites under the leadership of Jabin in the battle at the waters of Merom. The designation of the waters may be a reference to Lake Huleh or Meiron, a town southeast of Hazor.[2] The view from the top encompasses a large portion of northern Israel and Syria. To the south can be seen the Gilead Mountains, the Jordan Valley, Lake Huleh, and the Sea of Galilee. To the west can be seen Galilee, the Carmel Mountain Range, the Mediterranean Coast, Tyre, and the mountains of Lebanon. To the north, the Anti-Lebanon peaks are visible; to the northeast lies Damascus; and to the southeast lies the Golan and Bashan.[3]

The Sidonians (Phoenicians) called Mount Hermon *Sirion* and the Amorites called it *Shenir* (Deut. 3:9; Ps. 29:6).[4] Both names signify "breastplate," evidently because of the mountain's rounded, snow-covered top that glistened in the sunlight.[5] Its white crown can be seen from many places in Israel. Due to its snowy cap during most of the year, the Arabs call it "the gray-haired mountain" (*Jebel el-Sheikh*) or "mountain of the snow" (*Jebel el-Thalj*).[6] The River Jordan finds its bountiful source from the snows that cover the peak.

The mount forms the southern spur of the Anti-Lebanon chain of mountains which are 28 miles in length and at some points stretch 15 miles in width. The Anti-Lebanon Range (to the east of the Jordan River) runs parallel to the Lebanon Range (to the west of the Jordan River) and is separated by the Valley of Beqaa.[7] In the biblical text, Shenir may be a

MOUNTAINS OF ISRAEL

reference to the northern part of the Anti-Lebanon Range and Hermon a reference to the southern part. Regardless, its impressive view has memorialized the mountain as a sacred place. A. Haldar declares, "The Hebrew name may be interpreted as an allusion to this fact."[8] Mount Hermon's name literally means "devoted mountain" and has been used often over the centuries for cultic practices and sacred ordinances. The oldest historic record known is a treaty between the Hittites and the Amorites (1350 B.C.) consecrated at this revered spot. Moreover, the name Mount Baal-hermon indicates that Baal was worshiped on or near the mount (Judg. 3:3; 1 Chron. 5:23).[9] In the Bible, Mount Hermon is associated with "dew," which is a symbol for richness of life and vegetation (Ps.133:3). To many in the Christian faith, "dew" may reflect the promise of God and His manifest presence. Because ancient Near East beliefs associated mountains with the dwelling place of gods, a Greek inscription has been found describing the local god of the mountain.[10]

OLD
TESTAMENT
▬▬▬▬
MOUNT HERMON
MARKS THE
NORTHERN LIMIT
OF THE
CONQUEST OF
JOSHUA AND
ISRAELITE EXPAN-
SION.

Situated on the northern border of Palestine, Mount Hermon marks the limit of the conquest of Joshua and Israelite expansion on the east side of the Jordan (Deut. 3:8, 4:48; Josh 11:17). Prior to the conquest by the Hebrews, it was mentioned as the place where the Hivites lived (Judg. 3:3) under the reign of Og, king of Bashan. He was of the remnant of the giants (Josh. 12:1-5). The mountain's location is also mentioned as belonging to the Gebalites (Josh. 13:5) and the Amorites (Josh. 13:10-11).

Although Hermon is praised for its moisture that flowed over the mountains, it was also known for its animals (lions and leopards), its cypresses (Ezek. 27:5), and its flora.[11] Because of the rain, snow, and dew that sweep over the mountain, the terrain is dominated by lush vegetation and forests. Large orchards of apple trees thrive in certain mountain areas. At other various levels on the slopes can be found vines, oak trees, bushes, and fruit trees—including plums, cherries, pears, and almonds.[12]

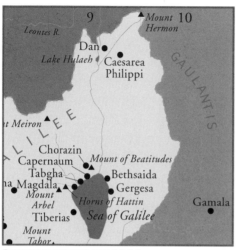

FROM MAP INSIDE THE FRONT COVER: 8-9, F-G.

SITE OF
INTEREST

HEROD'S
PALACE
FORTRESS OF
MOUNT
HERODIUM

Mount Herodium

The Herodium is a mountain palace-fortress built by Herod the Great. It is known in Arabic as *Jebel el-Fureidis* ("hill of paradise"), and is seven miles south of Jerusalem and several miles to the southeast of Bethlehem. It is positioned on the edge of the Judean desert, a three to four hour walk from the Holy City.[1] Herod built several fortresses in the wilderness to protect his kingdom (Masada, Herodium, Alexandrium, Hycrania, and Machaerus) and to serve as refuge for him and his family in the case of insurrection.[2] And the Herodium is one of them. Considered one of the most remarkable architectural structures in the western world, the mountain palace on Mount Herodium appears as a volcanic cone from a distance.[3] The distinctive conical shape was achieved by excavating the hill next to it and transferring the dirt to the top of the Herodium Mount. This unique building rises 195 feet above the summit of the natural hill.

The artificial conical shape gives it a striking appearance from many points in southern Judea. "Herod crowned the hill with a ring of three concentric walls with round towers standing at the four cardinal directions," notes R. W. Funk.[4] The king sloped the hill to meet the walls (one inside the other) and formed a hollow in which he built his villa-palace fortress.[5] The outside diameter of the fortress is 180 feet, while the inside it spans 150 feet.[6] Overall, there are seven stories of rooms. Within the mount are numerous hidden passages, underground chambers, cisterns and reservoirs, a garden courtyard, and luxurious living quarters at least two stories high. The floors were decorated with mosaics and the walls plastered with white moulded stucco.[7] Outside the structure, at the foot of the mountain, Herod erected other palaces, buildings, pools, terraces and gardens, a bathhouse, and villas providing all the appropriate features of a palace retreat. This area is known as the Lower Herodium Complex. A stairway of 200 white marble steps led up to the citadel. To supply the

MOUNTAINS OF ISRAEL

fortress with water, an expensive aqueduct was constructed to bring sufficient amounts down from the springs of Bethlehem.[8]

BETWEEN THE
TESTAMENTS

The Herodium commemorates the site where Herod won a decisive
victory. As he fled from the Parthians, in 40 B.C., he was attacked by hostile
Jews. Josephus writes that the crucial battle was between Herod, son of
Antipater, and the Hasmonean prince, Matthias Antigonus. Ehud Netzer
notes, "The event was a result of an agreement between Antigonus and the
Parthians . . . to displace John Hycranus II and the Romans, who had
dominated Judea since 63 B.C."[9] Herod inflicted on them a severe defeat
which allowed him to proceed to Rome and lay claim to his kingdom.

HEROD WON A
DECISIVE VICTORY
HERE OVER THE
HASMONEAN
PRINCE,
MATTHIAS
ANTIGONUS.

It is reported that Herod was entombed in the Herodium after his death
in Jericho (4 B.C.). Josephus records that Herod was carried to the
Herodium by a parade of his
kinsmen, a Thracian company,
Germans and Gauls in full battle
order, and 500 slaves and freed-
men carrying hundreds of
pounds of burial spices.[10] But his
burial chamber has never been
found. It is possible that his
servants kept his grave site a
secret to prevent its desecration
by the populace who had come
to detest his reign. Ehud Netzer
believes he located the Herodian
burial chamber on the Lower
Complex. The Israeli archaeologist discovered an impressive
building that might be the
mausoleum of Herod the Great.[11]

Jesus may have made reference to the Herodium mountain
as He was passing along from
Bethphage to the Mount of
Olives. After the cleansing of the

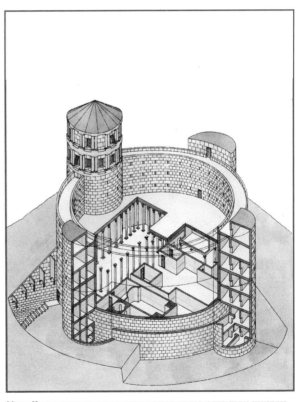

MOUNT HERODIUM IS CONSIDERED ONE OF THE MOST REMARKABLE ARCHITECTURAL STRUCTURES
IN THE WESTERN WORLD.

MOUNTAINS OF ISRAEL

WHERE JESUS
WALKED

HERODIUM MAY
HAVE BEEN THE
MOUNTAIN TO
"BE REMOVED"
TO WHICH JESUS
REFERRED IN
MARK 11.

Temple (Mark 11:15-19), Jesus departed the Holy City and returned to Bethany where He often stayed with Mary, Martha, and Lazarus. The next morning He and His disciples returned again to Jerusalem, passing a fig tree He had cursed the day before (Mark 11:12-14). When the disciples questioned Jesus regarding the miracle of the withered tree, some believe He could have been referring to Herod's mountain site.

> Now in the morning, as they passed by, they saw the fig tree dried up from the roots. And Peter, remembering, said to Him, "Rabbi, look! The fig tree which You cursed has withered away." So Jesus answered and said to them, "Have faith in God. For assuredly, I say to you, whoever says to this mountain, 'Be removed and be cast into the sea,' and does not doubt in his heart, but believes that those things he says will come to pass, he will have whatever he says."
> MARK 11:20-23

Looking south from the road that Jesus and the disciples traveled, one can see on the horizon Herod's imposing mountain palace-fortress.[12] The Herodium was a mountain that literally had been moved. So some believe it was Herodium to which Jesus referred in His teaching. During the First Jewish Revolt (A.D. 66-70), Jewish Zealots took control of the fortress, but the Romans won it back in A.D. 72. The Herodium was one of the last remaining strongholds of Jewish resistance including Masada and Machaerus. The citadel exchanged hands again in the Second Jewish Revolt, also known as the Bar Kochba Revolt (A.D. 132-135). The mountain was well used by Jewish rebels as a military and administrative center.[13]

BYZANTINE

A BYZANTINE
COMMUNITY
SETTLED IN
AND AROUND
HERODIUM IN
THE FIFTH AND
SIXTH
CENTURIES.

The site remained uninhabited until the fifth or sixth century when a Byzantine community settled both inside and outside the ruins. It was finally abandoned at the beginning of the Early Arabic Period.[14]

MOUNTAINS OF ISRAEL

Modern Walls of
Old City

*Mount
Moriah*

FROM INSERT IN THE MAP INSIDE THE FRONT COVER.

Mount Moriah

Mount Moriah is possibly the best-known mount in the vicinity of the Holy City due to its recognized position. *Moriah* in Hebrew, *Mora,* means "fear"—and that is appropriate, because the fear (or reverence) of God spread around the world from this hill. Today the mountain's location is considered to be the rocky hilltop of Jerusalem, north of

EARLY
KINGS

TODAY MOUNT
MORIAH'S
LOCATION IS
CONSIDERED TO
BE THE HILL
UPON WHICH
SOLOMON BUILT
THE TEMPLE.

the city, upon which Solomon built the Temple (2 Chron. 3:1). It is designated as the third of the five hills of Jerusalem and is called Temple Mount. The biblical text acknowledges that this was the sacred place chosen by David. He purchased the site from Araunah (or Ornan) the Jebusite (2 Sam. 24:18-25; 2 Chron. 21). The location was described as a threshing floor and implies "go up" since such activities were on high ground.[1]

The significance of the mount is its identification with the spot where Abraham prepared the sacrifice of his son. The connection with Temple Mount is noted in Josephus, in Islamic folklore, and in rabbinical literature.[2] The "land of Moriah" is mentioned in the Bible as a mountainous district, three-days' journey from Beer-Sheba (Gen. 22:1-4). Otherwise, the location is unspecified. The biblical reference in 2 Chronicles 3:1 is more than likely intended to associate the Temple Mount with the former appearances of the Lord (Gen. 22:14; 2 Sam. 24).

OLD
TESTAMENT

ABRAHAM WAS
DIRECTED BY
GOD TO OFFER
UP HIS ONLY SON,
ISAAC, IN SACRI-
FICE ON THIS
MOUNTAIN.

Abraham was directed by God to offer up his only son in sacrifice on this mountain. But he was prevented from his faithful act as the angel of the Lord intervened. The Bible informs us:

> Then Abraham lifted his eyes and looked, and there behind him was a ram caught in a thicket by its horns. So Abraham went and took the ram, and offered it up for a burnt offering

MOUNTAINS OF ISRAEL

291

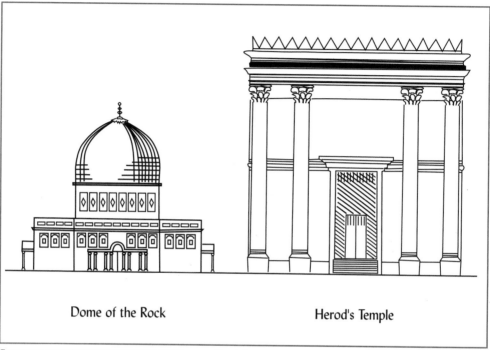

Dome of the Rock   Herod's Temple

THIS DRAWING COMPARES THE SIZE OF TODAY'S DOME OF THE ROCK WITH HEROD'S TEMPLE AS IT WAS DURING JESUS' MINISTRY.

instead of his son. And Abraham called the name of the place, THE-LORD-WILL-PROVIDE; as it is said to this day, "In the Mount of The Lord it shall be provided."
GENESIS 22:13-14

"THE-LORD-WILL-PROVIDE" stems from *Jehovah-jireh* (KJV) meaning "Jehovah shall see." The Latin Vulgate has interpreted the "land of Moriah" as the "land of the vision" *(in terran visionis)* in conformity with the Hebrew tradition.[3] Today, Mount Moriah is dominated by the Moslem mosque—The Dome of the Rock. It stands over the sacred rock of sacrifice and the possible location of the Holy of Holies. The "Wailing Wall" supports the western portion of Temple Mount.

There have been numerous speculations regarding the actual spot of the Holy of Holies where the Ark of the Covenant rested. According to Josephus and the Mishna, the Ark sat on a bedrock platform. Randall Price states, "In the Jewish tradition, this platform was called 'Even Ha-Shetiyah' ("the Foundation Stone"), and in Arabic *es-Sakhra* ("the Rock")."[4] The former chief architect of the Temple Mount excavations, Leen Ritmeyer, notes the huge rock within the Islamic Dome has to be the bedrock area stationed in the Holy of Holies.[5] The Crusaders quarried the Rock when they captured the city from the Muslims in 1099. They then converted the Holy Mount into a Christian church called "The Temple of the Lord" (*Templum Domini*). In the reconstruction process, they reshaped the Rock and built an altar on top of it covering it with marble slabs. They also enlarged the natural cave on top of the mount for use as a sanctuary and cut a hole in the ceiling for ventilation which allowed the burning of candles and incense. In addition, they dug a number of deep tunnels possibly looking for the hiding place of the Ark.[6]

The Caliph Saladin removed the Crusader marble slabs that covered the Rock when he recaptured the Holy Mount. Today, the Rock is visible, and tourists can enter the Dome (at most times) to view the sacred space. According to Ritmeyer's research, there is a depression in the Rock viewed from the northern scarp which served as a base to secure the Ark within the Holy Place.[7] The dimensions of this indented basin agree with the Ark of the Covenant's listed measurements in the Bible (2' 7" x 4' 4").

CRUSADERS

THE CRUSADERS CONVERTED THE TEMPLE MOUNT INTO A CHURCH CALLED "THE TEMPLE OF THE LORD."

SITE OF INTEREST

TODAY, MOUNT MORIAH IS DOMINATED BY THE MOSLEM MOSQUE—THE DOME OF THE ROCK.

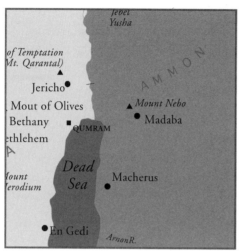

FROM MAP INSIDE THE FRONT COVER: 9-10, F-G.

Mount Nebo

Mount Nebo is a mountain of the Abarim Range in Jordan opposite the city of Jericho. It stands 12 miles east of the mouth of the Jordan River. According to the Scriptures (Num. 33:47), it was a stopping place for the Israelites on their journey to the Promised Land ("in the mountains of Abarim, before Nebo"). Moses was commanded to ascend the Mount, which is in the land of Moab, in order to view the land of Canaan. *Nebo* means "height" and commands a magnificent view north, west, and southwest. E. D. Grohman observes,

> "To the north and the northeast is the fertile plateau of Transjordan. Far to the north, under favorable conditions can be seen snow-capped Mount Hermon. As the eye moves south, there can be seen Mount Tabor, Ebal, and Gerizim, the heights of Judah and Benjamin, the ridge stretching to the south on which lie Bethlehem and Hebron, the Dead Sea as far as En-Gedi, and directly below is the Valley of the Jordan."[1]

CRUSADERS

IT WAS FROM MOUNT NEBO THAT MOSES VIEWED THE LAND OF CANAAN BEFORE HIS DEATH.

It was on Mount Nebo that Moses was to die after his final blessing of the people. From this vantage point, some 2,740 feet above the level of the Mediterranean and 4,030 feet above the Dead Sea, the Lord showed him all the Land of Promise.

> Then Moses went up from the plains of Moab to Mount Nebo, to the top of Pisgah, which is across from Jericho. And the LORD showed him all the land of Gilead as far as Dan, all Naphtali and the land of Ephraim and Manasseh, all the land of Judah as far as the Western Sea, the South, and the plain of the Valley of Jericho, the city of palm trees, as far as Zoar. Then the LORD said to him, "This is the land of which I swore to give Abraham, Isaac, and Jacob, saying, 'I will give it to your descendants.' I

MOUNTAINS OF ISRAEL

have caused you to see it with your eyes, but you shall not cross over there."

So Moses the servant of the LORD died there in the land of Moab, according to the word of the LORD. And He buried him in a valley in the land of Moab, opposite Beth Peor; but no one knows his grave to this day.

DEUTERONOMY 34:1-6

In the days of the Old Testament, ownership of Mount Nebo changed hands several times. It was to this area that Balak, king of Moab, brought Balaam to curse the Israelites (Num. 23:14,28). The territory was assigned to the tribes of Reuben and Gad during the conquest. However, in the time of the Judges, Eglon, the king of Moab, possessed Jericho and most likely Mount Nebo as well (Judg. 3:12-30). David once again subdued the Moabites, and Mount Nebo was, for a time, an Israelite possession (2 Sam. 8:2-12).

The Bible refers twice to Mount Nebo (Deut. 32:49; 34:1). In the first reference, the Mount is stated as being in the Abarim Mountains. In the second reference, Mount Nebo is identified with a headland that forms the western extremity of a ridge that is an extension of the plateau more to the east (about six miles northwest of Madaba in East Jordan).[2] There are several springs in the area that supply water to the fields to the west and the town of Madaba in the east. The springs have been named, *Ayun Musa,* "the springs of Moses." The great leader was buried in Moab Valley opposite Beth-Peor, but no one is certain of its location. However, the site of Ayun Musa does satisfiy the requirements of the biblical text and provides an approximate location.[3]

BYZANTINE

IN THE FOURTH CENTURY A.D., EGERIA (ETHERIA), THE PILGRIM NUN, WAS SHOWN A CHURCH ON TOP OF MOUNT NEBO.

In the fourth century A.D. during Byzantine times, Egeria (Etheria), the pilgrim nun, was shown a church on top of Mount Nebo. It is said the hermits of the area pointed out a monument denoting the tomb of Moses. The church was constructed over a cave in which he was supposedly buried. Archaeologists have confirmed the presence of a three-apsed monument that was constructed in the highest spot of Siaghah. Evidence signified that the mausoleum was later reconstructed into a church. It was this church that Egeria probably witnessed. The sanctuary later underwent another reconstruction in the first years of the seventh century.[4]

Jerusalem Today

FROM INSERT IN THE MAP INSIDE THE FRONT COVER.

Mount of Olives

The Mount of Olives has both Old Testament and New Testament distinction. It has been an eventful location in the history of Jerusalem. According to the Talmud, the burning of an unblemished red heifer was performed on the mount so that its cremated ashes could serve to purify the bodies of the priests before they entered the Temple (Num. 19:1-10). The mount also provided storehouses for the Temple.[1] A path and a bridge connected the Temple to the mount. Topographically, it consists of a flattened, rounded ridge with four identifiable summits. The Mount of Olives stands as the highest in the series of hills that lie to the east of Jerusalem. It belongs to the mountain range that traverses (north to south) the central and southern portions of Palestine. The western slope of the mount, which faces Jerusalem, still provides remnants of the ancient olive groves for which its name was derived. Tradition has it that the olive branch which was retrieved by the dove sent out from Noah's Ark came from the Mount of Olives (Gen. 8:11).

The western slope drops down to the Kidron Valley and offers a wonderful panoramic scene of the old city of Jerusalem. Mount Olivet, which comes from the Latin Vulgate (*Olivetum*),[2] is over a mile long and rises 250 feet above the Temple Mount. It maintained a supreme tactical vantage point and is the only place that looks down directly into the city with a plain view of the Temple below. When the Romans laid siege to Jerusalem in A.D. 70, they named the northern extension of the ridge "the lookout," or "Mount Scopus," for this very reason.

The eastern slope descends sharply to the Judean Desert. It provides a magnificent view of Jericho, the Jordan Valley, and the Dead Sea.[3] Beyond are the mountains of Moab. The Mount of Olives is not only the eastern boundary of Jerusalem, it also serves as a weather boundary that separates the wet Mediterranean climate region (west) from the arid desert climate

OLD
TESTAMENT

THE OLIVE BRANCH RETRIEVED BY THE DOVE SENT FROM NOAH'S ARK IS TRADITIONALLY BELIEVED TO HAVE COME FROM THE MOUNT OF OLIVES.

MOUNTAINS OF ISRAEL

A VIEW OF THE OLD CITY OF JERUSALEM FROM THE MOUNT OF OLIVES.

region (east).[4] It may have been related formerly to the Old Testament site of Nob (cf. Isa. 10:32; 1 Sam. 21:1; 22:9-11; Neh. 11:32), although there is no certain evidence of this.[5] One Old Testament passage recounts how "the glory of the LORD went up from the midst of the city and stood upon the mountain, *which is on the east side of the city*" (Ezek. 11:23, *Author's emphasis*).

EARLY
KINGS

SOLOMON MAY
HAVE BUILT
PLACES OF
WORSHIP FOR
HIS FOREIGN
WIVES NEAR
HERE.

One of the four summits, the Mount of Offense (which is above the old village of Siloam or modern Selwan), faces west along the Valley of the Sons of Hinnon, or Gehanna (hellfire). Its name *Offense* is derived from the tradition that Solomon had built altars there to Chemosh, "the abominations of Moab," and to Molech, "the abomination of the children of Ammon" (1 Kings 11:7-8). The western slopes were the site of Jebusite tombs, a probable location for the worship of pagan gods. Solomon built high places of worship for his foreign wives. It is inconceivable that Solomon would have desecrated the Holy City by bringing such false gods into the city proper.[6] The "offense" was purged by Josiah 4½ centuries later (2 Kings 23:13).[7] In this passage there is a possible play on words where the *mount of corruption*, i.e., "offense, scandal, or corruption," is

MOUNTAINS OF ISRAEL

similar to "anointing" or "ointment" and may allude to the Mount of Olives where anointing oil was produced.[8] The Jewish Talmud calls the Mount of Olives—"The Mount of Ointment."[9]

The Mishna states that Jews in Jerusalem announced the new moon (for the computation of the months) from the Mount of Olives to their exiled brethren in Babylonia. It was accomplished "by means of a chain of signal fires, the first of which began on Olivet" as noted by Warren J. Heard Jr.[10] These signals could be relayed from a second fire station on the Alexandrium, or Qarn Sartabeh, 27 miles to the north-northeast.[11] Hence, Jewish usage called Olivet "The Mountain of Lights."[12] W. S. Lasor concludes, "A similar fire was used for the time of the burning of leaven on the eve of Passover."[13] Many years before, the ridge, or ascent, was the route of David's flight into the wilderness from Absalom in the time of the palace rebellion. It also served as the highway into the city (2 Sam. 15:30; 16:1,13).[14]

EARLY KINGS

THIS ASCENT WAS THE ROUTE OF DAVID'S FLIGHT FROM ABSOLOM.

On the lower slopes of Olivet is the Garden of Gethsemane where Jesus often retreated and agonized in prayer the night before His crucifixion. Before Titus destroyed the area's timber during his A.D. 70 siege, the area outside the city walls in the vicinity of Gethsemane was heavily wooded and may have been a park used to get away from the crowded streets. It was to "the mountain" of this area that Nehemiah commanded the people to "Go out to the mountain, and bring olive branches . . . and branches of leafy trees, to make booths" to celebrate the Feast of Tabernacles in 445 B.C. (Neh. 8:15).[15] The palm branches waved by the people on the day of Jesus' acclaimed Triumphal Entry into Jerusalem were probably gathered here as well. Because the road over the Mount served as the route of Jesus' eastern approach to the Holy City, it was probably the place where He was met by the proclaiming multitudes (John 12:12-13). And, it was to the slopes of this area that Jesus Himself retreated to get away from the noise and stress, especially during feasts and festivals.

WHERE JESUS WALKED

GETHSEMANE, ON THE LOWER SLOPES OF THE MOUNT OF OLIVES, IS WHERE JESUS AGONIZED IN PRAYER THE NIGHT BEFORE HIS CRUCIFIXION.

> Now when they drew near Jerusalem, to Bethphage and Bethany, at the Mount of Olives, He sent two of His disciples; and He said to them, "Go into the village opposite you; and as soon as you have entered it you will find a colt tied, on which no one has sat. Loose it and bring it. And if anyone says to you, 'Why are you doing this?' say, 'The Lord has need of it,' and

immediately he will send it here." So they went their way, and found the colt tied by the door outside on the street, and they loosed it. But some of those who stood there said to them, "What are you doing, loosing the colt?" And they spoke to them just as Jesus had commanded. So they let them go. Then they brought the colt to Jesus and threw their clothes on it, and He sat on it. And many spread their clothes on the road, and others cut down leafy branches from the trees and spread them on the road. Then those who went before and those who followed cried out, saying: "Hosanna! 'Blessed is He who comes in the name of the Lord!' Blessed is the kingdom of our father David that comes in the name of the Lord! Hosanna in the highest!" And Jesus went into Jerusalem and into the temple. So when He had looked around at all things, as the hour was already late, He went out to Bethany with the twelve.

Mark 11:1-11

This cemetery on the Mount of Olives is one of the largest and oldest Jewish cemeteries in the world.

Rivka Gonen notes that "since the Canaanite period," the slopes of the Mount of Olives have been used for burial.[16] During the prominence of the Temple periods, the upper classes of Jerusalem built many tombs in the area. Many elaborate, free-standing structures, such as the Monument to Absalom, can be seen in the Valley of Jehoshaphat which makes up an adjacent portion of the Kidron Valley. The area is considered one of the most ancient and largest Jewish cemeteries in the world.[17] The slopes are still used for this purpose even today. The Mount of Olives has special significance to Jews who believe that Messiah will descend upon the mountain and proceed across the valley to the Eastern or "Golden Gate" of the Holy City. The prevailing belief is that anyone who is buried on the mount will be resurrected first and follow the Messiah into Jerusalem.[18] Because of this expectation, burial is always carried out with the feet toward Jerusalem. Upon resurrection, it is believed, the revived will stand up and walk down the hill into the city.

All four gospels agree that during the "Passion Week" preceding His arrest, Jesus returned in the evening to the Mount of Olives after visiting the Temple during the day (Luke 21:37). Exactly where Jesus spent His nights, however, is not clear. It is possible that He lodged in either Bethany at the house of Simon the leper, or at the home of Mary, Martha, and Lazarus (Matt. 26:6; Mark 14:3).[19] Besides, He could have stayed in the Garden of Gethsemane ("as he was accustomed" Luke 22:39), on the lower slopes of the Mount where He often met with His disciples (John 18:2). The last meeting with His followers after the resurrection was most likely in this vicinity (Luke 24:50). Luke states that "He led them out as far as Bethany." From the biblical reference (Acts 1:12), one may infer that the disciples were on their way back "from the mount called Olivet" immediately following the Ascension.

The first Christian sanctuary, the Church of Eleona, (recognizing where Jesus taught His disciples on the mount) was built by Constantine and dedicated to his mother, Helena, in 325 A.D. It was later destroyed by the Persians in the seventh century. The pilgrim Aetheria (or Egeria) mentions that on Palm Sunday, the people went to the Church of Golgath (Holy Sepulchre), then to *Eleona* (Greek for "olive grove"), and finally to *Inbumm* (translation of a Greek phrase "upon the height").[20] Between 1869 and 1875, the Church of the *Pater Noster* ("Our Father"), or the Eleona Church, was

BYZANTINE

THE FIRST CHRISTIAN SANCTUARY, THE CHURCH OF ELEONA, WAS BUILT HERE BY CONSTANTINE AND DEDICATED TO HIS MOTHER IN A.D. 325.

MOUNTAINS OF ISRAEL

THE PATER NOSTER CHURCH, ON THE SPOT WHERE JESUS TAUGHT THE LORD'S PRAYER, DISPLAYS THE PRAYER IN 60 DIFFERENT LANGUAGES.

rebuilt on the belief that the Lord's Prayer (Luke 11:1-4) was given there. When Jerusalem was occupied by the Crusaders (1102 A.D.), two marble slabs were found upon which were written the Lord's Prayer in Hebrew and Greek.[21] The church has the prayer written on its walls in nearly 60 different languages.

Nearby was the village of Bethany. As previously noted, it was the home of Mary, Martha, and Lazarus. Jesus' friendship with them must have frequently taken Him across the summit called Olivet (Luke 21:37). It was from here that Jesus first saw the unrepentant city and wept for His nation (Luke 19:41). Today pilgrims can visit a chapel on the mount known as *Dominus Flevit*—"the Lord wept." The chapel is dedicated to Jesus' weeping over Jerusalem. Stones shaped like tear bottles adorn its four corners. The cursing of the barren fig tree probably took place on the Mount of Olive's slopes as well, as a lesson on fruitless profession (Mark 11:12-26). This is probable because Jesus crossed this mountain many times going to and from the feasts in Jerusalem. The Jewish custom was to avoid passing through Samaria by detouring across Jordan to the north, then recrossing to the west bank near Jericho, and proceeding up to the city from there.[22] The mount was also the scene of

SITE OF
INTEREST

DOMINUS
FLEVIT
CHAPEL

MOUNTAINS OF ISRAEL

Jesus' apocalyptic proclamation of the passing of this world and a "doomed Jerusalem" that was most likely inspired by the view of the city from the mountainside (Matt. 24-25). The isolated episode of the woman taken in adultery who was forgiven by Jesus is formally localized on the mount (John 8:1-11). And, it was from one of the four summits, the *Viri Galilaei* (the Latin invocation of "ye men of Galilee"), that Jesus ascended (Acts 1:11). Nonetheless, the most famous description of the Mount of Olives comes from Zechariah's apocalyptic vision of the Day of the Lord (Zech. 14:1-5). It is to this hill, Zechariah prophesies, that the Lord will come again—splitting the mount in half—on the day of His earthly return.

A PANORAMIC VIEW OF THE OLD CITY OF JERUSALEM FROM *DOMINUS FLEVIT* CHAPEL.

> Behold, the day of the LORD is coming,
> And your spoil will be divided in your midst.
> For I will gather all the nations to battle against Jerusalem;
> The city shall be taken,
> The houses rifled,
> And the women ravished.

WHERE JESUS WALKED

THE MOUNT WAS ALSO THE SCENE OF JESUS' APOCALYPTIC PROCLAMATION OF THE PASSING OF THIS WORLD.

Half of the city shall go into captivity,
But the remnant of the people shall not be cut off from the city.
Then the LORD will go forth
And fight against those nations,
As He fights in the day of battle.
And in that day His feet will stand on the Mount of Olives,
Which faces Jerusalem on the east.
And the Mount of Olives shall be split in two,
From east to west,
Making a very large valley;
Half of the mountain shall move toward the north
And half of it toward the south.
ZECHARIAH 14:1-4

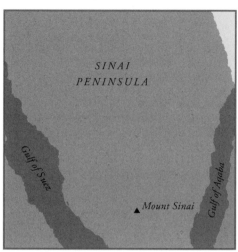

SINAI
PENINSULA

Gulf of Suez

Gulf of Aqaba

▲ Mount Sinai

FROM THE SINAI PENINSULA INSERT OF MAP INSIDE THE FRONT COVER.

Mount Sinai

OLD TESTAMENT

MOUNT SINAI IS THE PLACE WHERE YAHWEH MET WITH ISRAEL AND REVEALED BOTH HIS PRESENCE AND HIS WORD.

Mount Sinai is mentioned 15 times in the Bible as the place where Yahweh met with Israel and revealed both His presence and His Word. The name probably means "shining,"[1] although the term *Sinai* may find its root in the word "bush" from the plants that covered the mountain (Ex. 19:14).[2] In the narratives of the Pentateuch, Mount Sinai is the name of the sacred mountain the Israelites camped next to when entering into covenant with God (Ex. 19-24). The relationship between Israel and God would be governed by this agreement. It embraced every aspect of a Hebrew's life—religious, civil, and criminal. Moses publicly read the details of the document. The statutes were accepted by all and sealed with a ceremony (Ex. 24:4-8). After the celebration, Moses went back up into the mountain and remained there for 40 days and nights (Ex. 24:18). In his absence, Aaron, besieged by the demands of the people for a visible symbol of the continual presence of God, fashioned a golden calf. The idolatrous image aroused the anger of God and judgment fell upon those who chose to remain disobedient. The ongoing need for a concrete symbol was fulfilled in the construction of the Tabernacle, which remained thereafter the focus of the religious life of the Israelites (Ex. 25:1-31:11). Nevertheless, it was at Sinai that God first revealed Himself to the Hebrews.

Then it came to pass on the third day, in the morning, that there were thunderings and lightnings, and a thick cloud on the mountain; and the sound of the trumpet was very loud, so that all the people who were in the camp trembled. And Moses

MOUNTAINS OF ISRAEL

305

brought the people out of the camp to meet with God, and they stood at the foot of the mountain. Now Mount Sinai was completely in smoke, because the LORD descended upon it in fire. Its smoke ascended like the smoke of a furnace, and the whole mountain quaked greatly. And when the blast of the trumpet sounded long and became louder and louder, Moses spoke, and God answered him by voice. Then the LORD came down upon Mount Sinai, on the top of the mountain. And the LORD called Moses to the top of the mountain, and Moses went up.

EXODUS 19:16-20

In the poetic passages, Sinai generally refers to the place where Yahweh "dwells" or from which He comes (Deut. 33:2; Judg. 5:5; Ps. 68:8). In the book of Numbers, Sinai is called "the mountain of Yahweh," but elsewhere the mountain of Yahweh refers to Mount Zion in Jerusalem.[3] *Horeb,* which means "desolate region, desert, or wilderness," is another term for the sacred mount.[4] According to G. E. Wright, there is no geographical distinction between Horeb and Sinai so "the two must be reckoned as synonyms." (cf. Exod. 3:1; 18:5; Deut. 4:10; 5:2).[5] Mount Horeb is the adjacent peak to the northwest (Jebel Sufsaheh). The two mountain names possibly describe the general area and not just a specific location. The Sinai Peninsula lies between Egypt and Palestine. It is triangular in shape and bordered by the two arms of the Red Sea—the Gulf of Aqaba on the east— and the Gulf of Suez on the west. The northern part of the peninsula is a sandy plateau with low hills, while the southern area consists of granite mountains reaching heights of 8,600 feet. The tall, rifted mountains (known for their barrenness) show a variety of forms and colors that range from shades of red, brown, and gray.[6] Sinai is also the only land bridge that connects Egypt with Palestine, Syria, and Mesopotamia. Several important trade routes ran east-west across the northern part of the peninsula. In early times, the Patriarchs crossed the Sinai on their way to Egypt and back to the land of Canaan, as noted by Avraham Negev.[7]

The actual location of Mount Sinai is disputed. It is possible to reconstruct both a northern and southern position from the biblical descriptions. But the site remains in question. In modern times there have been at least a dozen different theories proposed that place the mountain in the north and west of the Sinai Peninsula, in southern Palestine, in Transjordan (Gal. 4:25), or in Saudi Arabia. Tradition has held since the fourth century A.D. that Mount Sinai is located in the high mountains at the apex of the Sinai Peninsula.[8] There, the site was marked by a monastic community. It is widely believed that Christian refugees fleeing from religious persecution in the latter half of the third century were the founders of the monastic center in Sinai.[9] But, not all withdrawals into the mountains or deserts were for religious solitude. Other political and social factors contributed to the retreat as well. Climate directed the monastic communities to locate themselves near water. Furthermore, the hostility of the Saracen tribes forced the people to cling together. So monks congregated in large centers and constructed fortified churches and towers for self-defense.[10]

Mount Sinai is also associated with the name Jebel Musa ("The Mount of Moses"). The name was given to the mount by the Arabs who also regard it with veneration. At first it was known as Tur-Sina, based on the Syriac-Aramaic Tur-Sinai. In time it came to be called at-Tur which is a term used to denote venerated mountains; i.e., "the mountain."[11] The pilgrim nun Egeria identified Mount Sinai, the "Holy Mount," with Jebel Musa. The Mount is approximately 7,500 feet high and one of three red granite peaks. Rivka Gonen observes, the entire mountain range is "bounded by geological faults, giving it its spectacular features of sheer slopes and deep valleys."[12] When Egeria visited Sinai and Palestine (381-384) she climbed the summit where she came upon a church and many monks.

On the northwest slope of Jebel Musa is The Monastery of St. Catherine. To the southeast is the mount known as Jebel Katerin, which rises another 1000 feet above Jebel Musa. The monastery is actually located between the two mountains.[13] The Emperor Justinian I (527-565 A.D.) established the religious center on the site where Constantine's mother Helena erected a small church two centuries earlier. On the summit is also an open mosque. According to Moslem tradition, the niche in the mosque is where Moses hid himself from God.[14]

St. Catherine's in the area is considered one of the oldest monasteries in the world and the most famous of Christian monuments. It is surrounded by gardens and cypress trees and has close fitting, granite stones for walls.

BYZANTINE

THE EMPEROR JUSTINIAN I ESTABLISHED THE MONASTERY OF ST. CATHERINE ON THE SITE CONSTANTINE'S MOTHER HAD ERECTED A CHURCH TWO CENTURIES EARLIER.

SITE OF INTEREST

THE MONASTERY OF ST. CATHERINE

MOUNTAINS OF ISRAEL

The height of the walls can vary from 40 to 200 feet and has permitted the structure to withstand numerous attacks. The walls were fortified with a watchtower and machicolations, i.e., a gallery with openings for pouring boiling oil on attackers.[15] Prior to the twentieth century, the only entrance into the monastery was a small door some 30 feet high up to which people and provisions were lifted with a system of pulleys. Food was also lowered to travelers and nomads below.[16] The original gates were blocked with stones in the fifteenth and sixteenth centuries after the Muslim conquest.

St. Catherine's is also a rare example of a Byzantine fortification. It was built to protect the alleged site of the Burning Bush. Monks point to a raspberry bush as the setting of the biblical account. The holy bush grew in a garden close to the bottom of the riverbed that ran through the area. The church was constructed precisely parallel to the stream, facing east. It is believed the bush withered in the Middle Ages and that The Chapel of the Burning Bush was built on the site where the bush once thrived.[17] The monastery has a library with ancient manuscripts and documents. And, it has a refectory room with a sixteenth-century mural of the Last Supper. The revered biblical manuscript *Codex Sinaiticus* was discovered in the mid-nineteenth century by the German Count Tischendorf in the monestary's library.[18] It was a fourth-century Greek copy of the Bible that contained most of the Old and New Testaments. It is estimated that the copy required 360 goats and/or sheep skins to produce. The monastery also includes a set of carved doors with both the names and weapons of certain knights of the Crusader period.[19]

CRUSADERS

THE MONASTERY INCLUDES A SET OF CARVED DOORS WITH BOTH THE NAMES AND WEAPONS OF CERTAIN KNIGHTS OF THE CRUSADER PERIOD.

St. Catherine was a young Christian woman and quite well educated. At the age of eighteen, she presented herself before the emperor Maxentius Daia. The Roman ruler was persecuting the Christians, and she pleaded that his unjust cruelty be halted. Astounded by her audacity and wisdom, Maxentius detained her and brought in scholars to either make her apostatize her Christian beliefs or commit heresy against the Roman religion—a sure death sentence. But her knowledge and eloquence of both religion and science led to the conversion of many of the scholars, who themselves were subsequently put to death. Catherine was scourged and imprisoned, although her conversions continued. Maxentius finally ordered Catherine to be broken on the wheel, that is, to be literally strapped to a contraption

MOUNTAINS OF ISRAEL

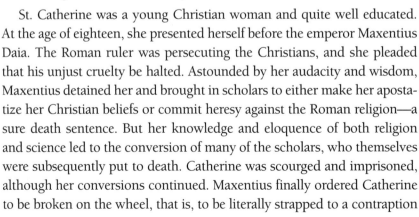

and rolled down a hill. However, the wheel was miraculously broken by her touch. Maxentius thus had her beheaded. According to tradition, Catherine's body was carried to Mount Sinai by angels.[20] It is said that a monk who dreamed about a treasure hidden on the peak discovered her body and that an edifice was built in her memory. In time, the tradition continues, her bones were brought down and buried in a golden box in the chancel of the church.[21] The place where Catherine's body is said to have been found is also believed to be the site of Moses' burning bush. Nevertheless, fifteen centuries separate the journey of the Israelites through the wilderness and the traditional location.[22]

The Hebrews' experience at Sinai involved what appears to be seismic phenomena—fire, smoke, and a quaking earth (Exod.19:16-18). But there is no volcanic activity detected in the Sinai Peninsula. It is therefore proclaimed in the Bible, and universally held by the Bible's believers that the entire Sinaitic encounter was supernatural, accompanied by sounds of a trumpet and the voice of God (Exod. 19:19).[23] Attempts were made in the nineteenth century to locate Mount Sinai in northwest Arabia, near the land known biblically as Midian. This is where Josephus notes that the mount stands—in Midian, to the east of the Red Sea. Other locations in the vicinity of Kadesh-Barnea (Deut. 33:2; Judg. 5:4-5) have been historically considered by many others.

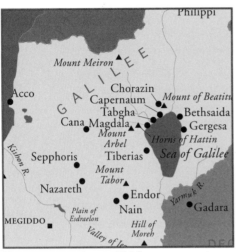

Philippi

Mount Meiron ▲

GALILEE

Acco
Chorazin
Capernaum ● Mount of Beatitu
Tabgha ●
Cana ● Magdala ● Bethsaida
Mount ● Gergesa
Arbel ▲ Horns of Hattin
Sepphoris ● Tiberias ● Sea of Galilee
Mount
Tabor ▲
Nazareth ●
● Endor Yarmuk R.
Plain of Nain ● Gadara
MEGIDDO ■ Esdraelon Hill of
Valley of Je Moreh ▲

Kishon R.

FROM MAP INSIDE THE FRONT COVER: 8-9, B-C.

Mount Tabor

Mount Tabor is an isolated mound in the northeast corner of the Valley of Jezreel. It is 6 miles straight east from Nazareth and 12 miles west from the southern end of the Sea of Galilee. It rises to an elevation of about 1,930 feet. The mountain holds an isolated position with steep sides that project a very unusual shape. It provides a striking appearance. The distinct configuration was a special landmark that could be seen from great distances.[1] Its inverted, bowl-like shape has attracted much attention through the centuries.[2] It also has many historic associations with both the Old Testament and the New Testament. It was originally covered with oak, olive, and fig trees.[3] During the Babylonian Exile, it was one of the high places on which signal fires were lit to announce the new moon to those in captivity.

The sides of the mount rise sharply from the Valley of Jezreel below and curve gently to form a dome-shaped summit.[4] The surface of the summit is fairly level and presents a rectangular plateau sloping steeply in all directions. It is connected to the hills in the northwest by a low saddle. The mountain commands a magnificent view of the entire valley—a feature symbolically reflected in Holy Scripture (Jer. 46:18; Ps. 89:12). K. G. Jung notes,

> Looking south from its summit, over Little Hermon with Endor and Nain at its base, one can glimpse Mount Gilboa. Scanning from this point . . . one sees the hills on the northern boundary of Samaria, Taanah and Megiddo, Carmel by the sea, and the oak forest north of Kishon gorge. Looking west from Mount Tabor . . . one can see the higher houses of Nazareth. Eastward lies the Jordan Valley, the mountains of Gilead, the great chasm of the Yarmuk, and the steep cliffs east of the Sea of Galilee. To the north, the mountains of Zebulun and Naphtali span to culminate in the shining mass of Great Hermon."[5]

MOUNTAINS OF ISRAEL

The mountain holds a strategic position and dominates two important routes: 1) the east-west road connecting the Valley of Jezreel and the Sea of Galilee, and 2) the north-south road between Beth-Shean and Damascus.

Mount Tabor is first mentioned in the Bible by name in association with the division of the land among the tribes after the conquest. It was the meeting place of the territories of Issachar, Naphtali, and Zebulun (Josh.19:12, 22, 34). It was also the base from which Deborah and Barak launched their attack against the confederation of Canaanite kings led by Sisera (Judg. 4:1-22; 5:19-31). Sisera was Jabin's general, the Canaanite leader who ruled the powerful city-state of Hazor. Deborah was the only woman judge to rule in Israel. When confronted by Sisera, she called upon Barak of Naphtali to assist in gathering an army from the northern tribes. It was at Mount Tabor that the army gathered as the Canaanites camped below. A storm caused the River Kishon to overflow its banks causing the chariots of Sisera to be unusable. So Sisera fled the battle on foot and took refuge in the tent of Jael the Kenite. He fell asleep and was then killed by a tent pin driven through his head. The victory made it possible for the Israelites to settle in the Plain of Jezreel without fear of Canaanite oppression.[6]

Mount Tabor has been considered one of the holiest Christian sites in Palestine since the fourth century. Pilgrims used to climb up the 4,300 steps cut into the difficult slopes of the mount.[7] The primary fame of Mount Tabor is its identification as the Mount of Transfiguration (though the actual site is not specifically named in the Gospels [Matt. 17:1-8; Mark 9:2-8; Luke 9:28-36] and is referred to only as "the holy mountain"). The tradition formed because of the mountain's noted appearance and sacred historical character. Helena, the mother of Emperor Constantine, built a church on the mount in A.D. 326. By the seventh century, three shrines existed on the summit dedicated to Jesus, Moses, and Elijah. Then, in 1099, the Crusader knight, Tancred, Prince of Galilee, constructed a fortress known as "The Gate of the Winds," on the summit. It was built on the same location occupied 1,000 years earlier by Josephus Flavius during the First Jewish Revolt against the Romans. The Benedictines later received the fortress as a gift.[8] But Saladin turned every one of these churches, shrines, and monasteries into ruins a century later when he destroyed them in 1187. His brother refortified the mountain and repelled a Crusader

OLD TESTAMENT

MOUNT TABOR IS THE BASE FROM WHICH DEBORAH AND BARAK LAUNCHED THEIR ATTACK ON THE CANAANITES.

BYZANTINE

HELENA, THE MOTHER OF EMPEROR CONSTANTINE, BUILT A CHURCH ON THE MOUNT IN A.D. 326.

CRUSADERS

IN 1099, THE CRUSADER KNIGHT, TANCRED, PRINCE OF GALILEE, CONSTRUCTED A FORTRESS HERE KNOWN AS "THE GATE OF THE WINDS."

SITE OF INTEREST

THE
FRANCISCAN
LATIN
BASILICA

attempt to retake it in 1217. Later, in the nineteenth century, the Greek Orthodox community built both a church and a monastery. Then in the twentieth century (1921-1924), a modern Latin Basilica was erected by the Franciscans.[9] Visitors will notice this Fransciscan edifice designed by the Italian architects, Antonio and Barlozzi, to be the most prominent structure on Mount Tabor's summit. Constructed to commemorate the Christ's Transfiguration (Matt. 17:3), it is considered one of the most beautiful churches in the Holy Land. It has two chapels, one of which is dedicated to Moses, the other to Elijah. The rock floor of the church is believed to be the very spot where Jesus stood during the mystical event.[10]

MOUNTAINS OF ISRAEL

Mount of Temptation

(Mount Qarantal)

Seven miles northwest of Jericho is a prominent hill known to the Arabs as Qarantal—The Mount of Temptation.[1] The name *Qarantal* is an Arabic mispronunciation of the Latin word *Quarantena*, which means "forty". According to tradition, Jesus fasted for 40 days and was tempted of the devil in the vicinity of this mount. To be tested could mean either in a good way (to prove the nature of a person) or with an evil intent (to incite a person to sin).[2] Jesus was tempted in every way, yet without sin (Heb. 4:15). Jewish thought promoted the concept that a man of God could prove his faith through trials. Near the Dead Sea is a stretch of terrible wilderness (15 x 35 miles) known as *Jeshimmon* which means "The Devastation." William Barclay notes,

> The hills were like desert heaps; the limestone looked blistered and peeling; the rocks were bare and jagged; the ground sounded hollow to the horses' hooves; it glowed with heat like a vast furnace and ran out to precipices, 1,200 feet high which swooped down to the Dead Sea. It was in that awesome devastation that Jesus was tempted.[3]

Then Jesus was led up by the Spirit into the wilderness to be tempted by the devil. And when He had fasted forty days and forty nights, afterward He was hungry. Now when the tempter came to Him, he said, "If You are the Son of God, command that these stones become bread." But He answered and said, "It is written, 'Man shall not live by bread alone, but by every word

WHERE JESUS WALKED

ACCORDING TO TRADITION, JESUS FASTED FOR 40 DAYS AND WAS TEMPTED BY THE DEVIL IN THE VICINITY OF THIS MOUNT.

MOUNTAINS OF ISRAEL

313

that proceeds from the mouth of God.'" Then the devil took Him up into the holy city, set Him on the pinnacle of the temple, and said to Him, "If You are the Son of God, throw Yourself down. For it is written: 'He shall give His angels charge over you,' and, 'In their hands they shall bear you up, lest you dash your foot against a stone.'" Jesus said to him, "It is written again, 'You shall not tempt the Lord your God.'" Again, the devil took Him up on an exceedingly high mountain, and showed Him all the kingdoms of the world and their glory. And he said to Him, "All these things I will give You if You will fall down and worship me." Then Jesus said to him, "Away with you, Satan! For it is written, 'You shall worship the Lord your God, and Him only you shall serve.'" Then the devil left Him, and behold, angels came and ministered to Him.

MATTHEW 4:1-11

Jesus was baptized by John at Bethabara, beyond the Jordan (John 1:28). John's preaching called people to repentance in preparation for the coming kingdom. And his baptism was something new. The Jewish people were accustomed to ritual baths that were believed to restore one to a state of ritual purity from uncleanness.[4] The bath used for ritual immersion was called a *miqvah*. They have been discovered in excavations throughout the Holy Land, many of which have been uncovered south of Temple Mount in Jerusalem.

There are two prominent locations that mark Jesus' temptation in the wilderness. The first is Mount Qarantal. The summit of this mountain overlooks the Jericho Valley, the Dead Sea, Moab, Gilead, the northern Judean Desert, and the Jerusalem mountains.[5] The site was first occupied by the Hasmonean-Herodian fortress, Dok-Dagon. It was one of a chain of fortresses that stood guard over the eastern flank of the country. The fortress held a strategic position and was naturally protected in the mountains. It was, however, later conquered by the Romans in A.D. 68.

In A.D. 340, St. Chariton built a chapel on the summit of Qarantal over the ruins of the old Hasmonean fortress. Chariton is considered the pioneer of the monastic movement in the Judean Desert. He was a native

BYZANTINE

IN A.D. 340, ST. CHARITON BUILT A CHAPEL ON THE SUMMIT OF QARANTAL OVER THE RUINS OF THE OLD HASMONEAN FORTRESS.

of the city Iconium in Asia Minor.[6] Another chapel was built near the cave where it is believed Jesus took shelter. In the fourth century, hermits initially lived in the caves on the side of the hill before the Byzantine monastery, Duka, was established. Monastic activity in the Judean Desert reached its zenith in the fifth to seventh centuries. There were approximately 70 monasteries in existence. Most of them were concentrated in two regions: 1) in the northwest along the desert's western margin, and 2) in the Jericho Valley on the plain between Jericho and the Jordan River.[7] In the seventh century, the Byzantine monastery was destroyed by Arabs. The Crusaders would later build a small castle on the former ruins. However, the Persian invasion halted the growth of the monastic movement leaving most of the monasteries in the Judean Desert abandoned after the Muslim Conquest in A.D. 638. Only the monasteries close to the road that ran from Jerusalem to the Jordan survived.[8] The Greek Orthodox Church built the Sanandenion Monastery halfway up the steep hill of Mount Qarantal in 1895. The structure appears to be literally growing out of the mountain. Geography was a major factor in shaping the architecture of the monasteries. A path runs from the monastery up to the summit and to the remains of St. Chariton's Chapel and the former Hasmonean fortress.[9]

SITE OF INTEREST

SANANDENION MONASTERY; THE REMAINS OF ST. CHARITON'S CHAPEL AND A HASMONEAN FORTRESS

The second location, noted by tradition for the testing of Jesus, is an area southwest of Jericho called the Wadi Qelt. It is a canyon-like valley that runs through the hills of Judea into the plain of Jericho.[10] A Jewish fast that does not prohibit the drinking of water and liquids would have been necessary for the sustained 40-day fast Jesus experienced according to Luke 4:1. The only water source in the Wilderness of Judea that is near the traditional site of Jesus' temptation is a spring formed at the western end of the Wadi Qelt.[11] Water flowed freely through the area. Herod had constructed an aqueduct to bring water from a spring (*Ein Qelt*) to his winter palace at Jericho. The aqueduct was repaired during the British Mandate and still carries water today.

The presence of water at this southern end of the Jordan where John baptized makes the Wadi Quelt an especially favored spot for Jesus' time of self-reflection. The landscape is barren, and stones in the area actually resemble loaves of fresh baked bread. The tempter explicitly said to Jesus,

THE GREEK ORTHODOX CHURCH BUILT ST. GEORGE'S MONASTERY ON THE BANK OF WADI QELT IN THE FIFTH CENTURY.

"command that these stones become bread" (Matt. 4:3). While standing on a high mountain overlooking the Wadi Qelt, Jesus could have looked down on the palatial Herodian complex. Thus, Jericho could have possibly represented "all the kingdoms of the world" (Matt. 4:8).

An impressive monastery named St. George's, or Choziba, was built by the Greek Orthodox Church on the bank of Wadi Qelt (*Nabal Prat*) in the fifth century. It is located about three miles from Jericho.[12] The monastery (ca. 480 A.D.) was dedicated to the Holy Virgin but was renamed after its founding father, John of Thebes in Egypt, upon his death. It was eventually renamed after the most famous monk who lived in the abbey, Georgias of Choziba. It was destroyed in 614 by the Persians but remained somewhat active until the end of the Crusader Period. The monastery's restoration was finally undertaken in 1878 by a Greek monk, Kalimikos, who settled in the Wadi Qelt.[13] The monastery has a chapel that honors the prophet Elijah. Though the site is disputed, the Medieval Period identified the Wadi Qelt with the Brook Cherith where Elijah was fed by ravens

(1 Kings 17:6). Other scholars believe the brook to be on the eastern side of the Jordan, in the highlands of northern Gilead. Elijah himself was a Gileadite (1 Kings 17:1), and there is a Wadi that empties into the Jordan River south of Pella.[14]

Monastic life was governed by fixed rules that controlled much of the daily life of a monk. There were two kinds of monasteries to which a monk could submit: the Laura and the Coenobium. The distinctions were dictated by the religious practices of the monks and the architecture of the priory. The physical layout of the Laura-type monastery was composed of dispersed cells that were connected to each other and to a central building by a single path. The designation Laura is derived from the Greek term and means "lane."[15] The distance between the cells varied according to the topography and number of monks in the community. In the Laura, each monk lived in solitude during the week and would only meet communally on weekends for prayer and a meal.

Conversely, in the Coenobium-type monastery, monks practiced communal life and met daily for church prayers and meals.[16] The physical layout of a Coenobium monastery followed a square plan that was surrounded by walls which gave it the appearance of a fortress (cf. St. Catherine's). The common ingredient of these monasteries was a covered passageway, or a connected architectural element, that led directly from the church to the refectory. The partaking of the common meal in the dining hall was a direct continuation of the prayer ceremony held in the church.[17]

Mount Zion

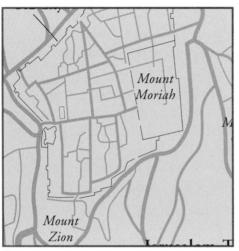

FROM INSERT IN THE MAP INSIDE THE FRONT COVER.

Finally along our Holy Land tour, we come, as all true believers will exuberantly one day—to Mount Zion, God's holy hill of habitation in His sacred city. Jerusalem is built on a cluster of five hills: the Western Hill (the Upper City), Zion (the Lower City), Mount Moriah, Bezetha (the hill just north of the city), and Ophel (the hill between the Lower City and Temple Mount). The Psalmist wrote eloquently concerning the hills around Jerusalem: "As the mountains surround Jerusalem, so the Lord surrounds his people from this time forth and forever" (Ps. 125:2). The city also has three principal ravines and several lateral valleys. Skirting the city on the west and south is the Hinnon Valley, or in Greek—*Gehenna* (used metaphorically for "hell fire", Matt. 5:22). Josiah turned the valley into a garbage dump where a perpetual fire burned (2 Kings 23:1-14; 2 Chron. 34:1-7). Solomon erected high places to Molech here (1 Kings 11:7), and Ahaz and Manasseh practiced human sacrifice in this valley (2 Kings 16:3; 23:10; 2 Chron. 28:3; 33:6; Jer. 7:31). Gehenna was described by Jesus as the place of eternal torment (Mark 9:43-44).

Hedging Jerusalem on the east, between the city and the Mount of Olives, is the Valley of Jehoshaphat. It was in this valley that Jehoshaphat overthrew the united armies of Israel (2 Chron. 20:26). The final judgment on God's enemies is stated to occur here by the Old Testament prophets (Joel 3:2,12; Zech. 14:1-9). The Kidron Valley is an extension of the Valley of Jehoshaphat. It is now known as the *Wadi Sitti Maryann,* or "Valley of Mary."[1] It was through this valley that Absalom fled from David (2 Sam. 15-23). The abominations of idol worship were also destroyed in this valley by King Josiah (2 Kings 23:4). The area of the Brook of Kidron became a cemetery during his reign (2 Kings 23:6). During the time of the Temple restoration by Zerubbabel, this cemetery stretched over three miles. The more well-known tombs are Absalom's Tomb and the Tomb of

MOUNTAINS OF ISRAEL

Zacharias. The names, however, do not signify accurate dating, and the actual location of the valley's royal tombs remain in dispute. The common people were also buried here (Jer. 26:23; 31:40). It was to the tombs in the Kidron Valley that Jesus made reference when He criticized the Pharisees for being like "whited sepulchers" (Matt. 23:27 KJV). He also crossed this valley after the Last Supper (John 18:1).

WHERE JESUS
WALKED

IT WAS TO THE
TOMBS IN THE
KIDRON VALLEY
THAT JESUS MADE
REFERENCE WHEN
HE CRITICIZED
THE PHARISEES
FOR BEING LIKE
"WHITED SEPUL-
CHERS."

There is also an interior north-south ravine in Jerusalem known as the Tyropoeon Valley or, translated by Josephus, as the "Valley of the Cheesemakers" (a corruption of the Hebrew name).[2] The valley is known today as *el-Wad*. It divides the Ophel Hill from the western ridge and runs along the base of the Western Wall. The Ophel Hill and the Temple Mount composed the Lower City (indicating its elevation) which is called the City of David as well as Zion in Scripture, near the Gihon Spring. It was the original site conquered by David that encompassed no more than eight to ten acres.[3] To the west of the Tyropoeon Valley is the Western Hill. Mare describes the hill as having two sections: 1) the southwestern hill, named the Upper City by Josephus which is usually mistakenly referred to as Zion, and 2) the northwest hill which has the Church of the Holy Sepulchre at its center.[4]

Zion, or Ophel, is one of the five hills upon which Jerusalem is erected, and because of this, is often interpreted as a synonym for Jerusalem. It is used 150 times in the Old Testament both topographically and metaphorically.[5] In biblical usage, the term *Zion* has at least four different applications. First, and possibly the earliest, the name *Zion* was used in reference to the ridge in the southeast section of Jerusalem which lies between the Kidron and the Tyropoeon valleys. Solomon built the Temple on what can be called Mount Zion (Ps. 78:68-69). Second, Zion was the name of the Jebusite fortress during the period just before David captured ancient Jerusalem. He changed the name from the "stronghold of Zion" (2 Sam. 5:7-9) to the "City of David." Third, Zion came to refer to Jerusalem itself. The book of Lamentations uses the names Zion and Jerusalem interchangeably (Lam. 2:6-8). In the same sense, Zion also came to refer to the people of Israel (Isa. 51:16; Zech. 2:11). Lastly, Zion today refers to the name of the western hill in Jerusalem upon which the tomb of David and

EARLY
KINGS

ZION WAS THE
NAME OF THE
JEBUSITE
FORTRESS
DURING THE
PERIOD JUST
BEFORE DAVID
CAPTURED
ANCIENT
JERUSALEM.

MOUNTAINS OF ISRAEL

SITE OF INTEREST

THE UPPER ROOM

the Upper Room reside. But this is an inaccurate post-biblical assertion that reflects a Byzantine understanding of the word.[6]

> Great is the LORD, and greatly to be praised
> In the city of our God,
> In His holy mountain.
> Beautiful in elevation,
> The joy of the whole earth,
> Is Mount Zion on the sides of the north,
> The city of the great King.
> PSALM 48:1-2

Personal Reflections

A Prayer for Jerusalem

Our Father and our God, our Creator, and our Redeemer,
You are merciful and gracious and full of lovingkindness forever.

We pray for the peace of Jerusalem, Your Holy City.
Remember her and Your people for Your name's sake.
Establish Your covenant of peace with her and Your people.
Cause Your people to live in peaceful habitation
and in secure dwellings.
You are peace, Oh Lord, and Your name is her peace.

Our Father and our King,
Return to Jerusalem and establish Your righteousness in her.
Make peace her administrator and righteousness her overseer.
Establish Jerusalem as a crown of praise in all the earth.
May Your peace flow from her like a river and encompass the
whole earth.

Friends of Faith

A Final Note ▪

It is my fervent hope that this guide to the Holy Land has served to enrich your special pilgrimage to Israel, and that you will refer to it as a resource again and again. Now that you have visited the land of the Bible, both in geography and in this print, you possess the vital perspective necessary to experience the exciting stories of Scripture. So please take the time to share what you've learned with others. Remind them that Jesus of Nazareth was born in Judea, ministered in Galilee, died in Jerusalem, and will return to the Mount of Olives from where He ascended.

To further your study of God and His land, I have include a series of historical tables on the following pages to help you refer quickly to certain people, places, and events. I deeply respect and appreciate your interest in the Bible and God's redemptive acts.

The Archaeological Periods of Palestine

Name	ca. Date	Historical Reference	Notable Events
Paleolithic (*Old Stone Age*)	700,000-15,000 B.C.	Gen. 1-11	
Epipaleolithic (*Middle Stone Age*)	15,000-8300	Gen. 1-11	
Neolithic (*New Stone Age*) Pre-pottery Pottery	8300-4500 8000-6000 6000-4500	Gen. 1-11	
Chalcolithic	4500-3100	Gen. 1-11	
Early Bronze Age I	3150-2850		Archaic Period (Egypt) Pyramids and Temples
Early Bronze Age II	2850-2650		
Early Bronze Age III	2650-2350		
Early Bronze Age IV	2350-2200		
Middle Bronze Age I	2200-2000	Gen. 11:10; 25:11	Abraham
Middle Bronze Age II	2000-1750	Gen. 25:12; 49:33	Jacob enters Egypt
Middle Bronze Age III	1750-1550		
Late Bronze Age I	1550-1400	Exodus, Leviticus Numbers, Deuteronomy	The Exodus and conquest of the Promised Land
Late Bronze Age II	1400-1300	Joshua	
Late Bronze Age III	1300-1200	Judges, Ruth	Period of the Judges
Iron Age IA	1200-1150	Judges 13-16	Invasion of the Sea Peoples
Iron Age IB	1150-1000	1 Samuel	David is crowned king
Iron Age IIA	1000-900		
Iron Age IIB	900-800	1 Kings	Divided Monarchy
Iron Age IIC	800-586	2 Kings 15-17 2 Kings 18-25	The Fall of Israel (722) and Judah (586)
Babylonian and Persian Periods	586-332	Psalm 137 Daniel	Babylonian captivity (586-539)
Hellenistic I	332-152		Alexander the Great
Hellenistic II (Hasmonean)	152-37	1 & 2 Maccabees	Maccabean Revolt

Early Roman	63 B.C.-A.D. 70	Matthew, Mark, Luke, John, Acts	Herod the Great - Jesus Christ
Middle Roman	60-180		Destruction of Jerusalem (70 A.D.) and Rebuilding (135 A.D.)
Late Roman	180-325		
Byzantine I	324-451		
Byzantine II	451-640		
Early Arab Period	640-1099		The Dome of the Rock
Crusader Period	1099-1291		

Kings of Judah and Israel

The United Monarchy

Name	ca. Date	Historical Reference	Notable Events
Saul	1020-1004 B.C.	1 Sam.; 1 Chron. 9-10	First king of Israel
David	1004-965	2 Sam. 5-6; 1 Chron. 11; 15-16	United the Twelve Tribes; Returns Ark to Jerusalem
Solomon	965-928	1 Kings 5-9; 2 Chron. 2-7	Construction of the Temple

The Divided Monarchy (Judah)

Name	ca. Date	Historical Reference	Notable Events
Rehoboam	928-911 B.C.	1 Kings 11-14; 2 Chron. 9-12	First King of Judah
Abijah (Abijam)	911-908	1 Kings 14-15:8; 2 Chron. 13-14:1	
Asa	908-867	1 Kings 15; 2 Chron. 14-16	Religious reforms
Jehoshaphat	867-846	I Kings 22; 2 Chron. 17-20	Made alliance with Ahab
Jehoram	846-843	2 Kings 8; 2 Chron. 21	Brought Baal worship to Judah
Ahaziah	843-842	2 Kings 8:25-9:29 2 Chron. 22	Assassinated by Jehu
Athaliah	842-836	2 Kings 11; 2 Chron. 22-23	Only woman to rule Judah; Assassinated by army
Joash (Jehoash)	836-798	2 Kings 11-12; 2 Chron. 22-24	Assassinated by servants
Amaziah	798-769	2 Kings 14; 2 Chron. 25	Conquered Edom; Assassinated

Name	ca. Date	Historical Reference	Notable Events
Uzziah (Azariah)	769-733	2 Kings 15:1-7; 2 Chron. 26	Conquered the Philistines and refortified walls of Jerusalem
Jotham	758-743	2 Kings 15:32-38; 2 Chron. 27	
Ahaz	733-727	2 Kings 16; 2 Chron. 28	Surrendered to Assyrian domination
Hezekiah	727-698	2 Kings 18-20; 2 Chron. 29-32	Religious reform— organized the Levites
Manasseh	698-642	2 Kings 20-21; 2 Chron. 33	Longest reign—blamed for ultimate destruction
Amon	641-640	2 Kings 21:19-24; 2 Chron. 33:21-25	Assassinated by servants
Josiah	640-609	2 Kings 21:24-23:30; 2 Chron. 34-35	Religious reform—tore down altars of Baal
Jehoahaz	609	2 Kings 23:31-34; 2 Chron. 36:1-4	Deported to Egypt
Jehoiakim	609-598	2 Kings 23:35-24:6; 2 Chron. 36:5-8	Died in siege
Jehoiachin	597	2 Kings 24:8-25:30; 2 Chron. 36:9-10	Taken into captivity by Nebuchadnezzar
Zedekiah	596-586	2 Kings 24:17-25:7; 2 Chron. 36:11-21	Last King of Judah - died captive in Babylon

The Divided Monarchy (Israel)

Name	ca. Date	Historical Reference	Notable Events
Jeroboam	928-907 B.C.	1 Kings 11-14:20; 2 Chron. 9:31-12:16	First king of Israel - replaced Jerusalem worship
Nadab	907-906	1 Kings 15:25-28	Idolatrous king - assassinated; Conquered Gibbethon
Baasha	906-883	1 Kings 15:16-16:7; 2 Chron. 16:1-6	Assassinated Nadab, built Ramah
Elah	883-882	1 Kings 16:6-14	Reigned two years - killed by Zimri
Zimri	882	1 Kings 16:9-20	Committed suicide - name means "King killers"- shortest reign - 7 days
Omri	882-871	1 Kings 16:8-28	Built new capital at Samaria and introduced Baal worship
Ahab	871-852	1 Kings 16:29-22:40; 2 Chron. 18	Married Jezebel, took up Baal worship; Died in battle
Ahaziah	852-851	1 Kings 22:48-53; 2 Chron. 20:35-37	Had peace with Judah

Jehoram (Joram)	851-842	2 Kings 3:1-9:26; 2 Chron. 22:5-7	Attacked Moab; Assassinated by Jehu
Jehu	842-814	2 Kings 9-10; 2 Chron. 22:7-9	Removed Baal out of Israel
Jehoahaz	814-800	2 Kings 13:1-13	Delivered from the Arameans through prayer
Jehoash (Joash)	800-784	2 Kings 13:10-13; 2 Chron. 25:17-24	Defeated Judah; plundered the Temple
Jeroboam II	784-748	2 Kings 14:23-29	Restored boundaries of Davidic Empire
Zechariah	748	2 Kings 14:29-15:12	Reigned for six months, murdered by Shallum
Shallum	748	2 Kings 15:10-15	Ruled one month, contemporary of Uzziah; Assassinated by Menahem
Menahem	747-737	2 Kings 15:10-22	Paid tribute to Tiglath-Pileser
Pekahiah	737-735	2 Kings 15:22-26	Assassinated by Pekah
Pekah	735-733	2 Kings 15:25-31; 2 Chron. 28:6	Held military command in Gilead and Samaria; Assassinated by Hoshea
Hoshea	733-724	2 Kings 15-17	End of the Northern Kingdom

Selected Kings of Assyria

Name	ca. Date	Historical Reference	Notable Events
Adad-Narari I	1307-1275 B.C		
Shalamaneser I	1274-1245		Defeated the Hittites, Arameans, and Mitannians
Tiglath-Pileser I	1115-1077		Greatest of the kings - expanded the empire
Ashurnasirpal I	1050-1032		
Shalmaneser II	1031-1020		
Tiglath-Pileser II	967-935		
Adad-Nirari II	911-891		
Ashurnasirpal II	883-859		Development of the capital city of Calah
Shalmaneser III	858-824		Added new territory to the Assyrian Empire
Adad-Nirari III	810-783		Capture of Damascus and Babylonia; influence of Babylonian gods

Shalmaneser IV	782-772		
Tiglath-Pileser III (Pul)	744-727	2 Kings 15:19-29; 16:7-10	Assisted Ahaz of Judah
Shalmaneser V	726-722	2 Kings 17:1-6	Conquered capital of Israel—the city of Samaria
Sargon II	721-705	Isaiah 20	Built new capital near Ninevah
Sennacherib	704-681	2 Kings 18-19; Isa. 36-37; 2 Chron. 32	Siege of Jerusalem; Hezekiah
Esarhaddon	680-669	Ezra 4:2	Conquest of Egypt
Ashurbanipal (Osnapper)	668-627	Ezra 4:10	The Fall of Assyria

Selected Kings of Babylon

Name	ca. Date	Historical Reference	Notable Events
Merodach-Baladan II (*Marduk-apal-iddin*)	721-689 B.C.	2 Kings 20:12; Isa. 39:1	
Nabopolassar	626-605		Conquered Babylon
Nebuchadnezzar II (*Nebuchadrezzar II*)	605-562	2 Kings 24-25; Jer. 29:1-18; Dan. 1-4	Laid siege to Jerusalem; Temple destroyed; Jews in exile
Evil-Merodach (*Amel-Marduk*)	562-560	2 Kings 25:27-30; Jer. 52:31-34	
Nergal-Sharezer (*Nergal-shar-usur, or Neriglissar*)	560-556	Jer. 39:3, 13	
Labashi-Marduk Nabonidus (Nabunaid)	556 556-539		
Belshazzar (*Bel-shar-usur*)	Co-regent with Nabonidus 556-539	Dan. 5; 7:1	

Selected Kings of Persia

Name	ca. Date	Historical Reference	Notable Events
Darius the Mede	539 B.C.	Dan. 5-6; 9:1; 11:1	Daniel in the Lions' Den
Cyrus	539-530	2 Chron. 36; Ezra 1; Isa. 44-45	Conquers the Babylonian Empire; decree to rebuild Jerusalem

Cambyses	530-522		Haggai and Zechariah
Darius I (*Hystaspes*)	522-486	Ezra 4-6; Neh. 12:22; Hag. 1:1; Zech. 1:1-7	
Xerxes (*Ahasuerus*)	486-464	Ezra 4:6; Esther	Esther became his wife
Artaxerxes I (*Longimanus*)	464-423	Ezra 4:7-23; 7; 8:1 Neh. 2:1-8	Authorized Ezra's mission to the Holy City—Jerusalem; Nehemiah recalled
Darius II (*Nothus*)	423-404		Assisted Sparta in Peloponnesim War
Artaxerxes II (*Mnemon*)	404-359		
Artaxerxes III (*Ochus*)	359-338		
Arses	338-335		
Darius III (*Codomanus*)	335-331	1 Macc. 1:1-8; Dan. 11:2	Defeated by Alexander

The Ministry of the Prophets

		Reigning Rulers				
Prophet	ca. Dates	Judah	Israel	Babylon/ Persia	Biblical Ref. to the times of their Ministry	Notable Events
Elijah	870 B.C.		Ahab, Ahaziah		1 Kings 17-21; 2 Kings 1:1-2:12	Divided Kingdom (922) Baal Worship in Israel
Elisha	850 B.C.		Ahab, Ahaziah, Jehoram, Jehu, Jehohaz, Jehoash		1 Kings 19:19-21; 2 Kings 2-10; 13:14-21	Baal Worship brought to Judah
Joel	837-800 B.C.	Joash (Jehoash) Amaziah, Uzziah (Azariah)	Jehu		2 Kings 11: 1-15:7 Joel	
Jonah	825-782 B.C.	Amaziah, Uzziah	Jeroboam II	Shalmaneser IV	2 Kings 13-14 Jonah	
Amos	810-745 B.C.	Uzziah (Azariah)	Jeroboam II		2 Kings 14:23; 15:7; Amos	
Hosea	782-720 B.C.	Uzziah, Jotham, Ahaz, Hezekiah	Jeroboam II, Zechariah, Shallum, Menahem, Pekahiah, Pekah, Hoshea		2 Kings 14:23-18:37 Hosea	

Micah	742-690 B.C.	Jotham, Ahaz, Hezekiah	Pekah Hoshea		2 Kings ; 15:32-20:21; ; 2 Chron. 27:1-32:33 Isa. 7:1-8:22; Jer. 26:17-19 Micah	Fall of Samaria (722)
Isaiah	758-685 B.C.	Uzziah (Azariah), Jotham, Ahaz, Hezekiah, Manasseh	Pekah Hoshea	Tiglath-pileger III Shalmaneser V Sargon II Sennecherib	2 Kings 15:1-20:21; 2 Chron. 26:1-32:33 Isaiah	Seige of Jerusalem (705)
Nahum	664-612 B.C.	Josiah Manasseh		Ashurbanipal	2 Kings 22:1-23:30; 2 Chron. 34:1-36:1; Zeph. 2:13-15 Nahum	Fall of the Assyrian Empire (610)
Zephaniah	640-610 B.C.	Josiah			2 Kings 22:1-23:34; 2 Ch. 34:1-36:4 Zephaniah	Rise of the Babylonians
Jeremiah	627-580 B.C.	Josiah, Jehoahaz, Jehoiakim, Jehoiachin, Zedekiah		Nebuchadnezzar	2 Kings 22:1-25:30; 2 Ch. 34:1-36:21; Jer. 37:4-10; 52:12-14	Fall of Jerusalem (597 B.C.) Babylonian Exile
Habakkuk	609-598 BC.	Jehoiakim		Nebuchadnezzar	2 Kings 23:31-24:7 Habbakkuk	
Daniel	605-530 B.C.	Jehoiakim, Jehoiachin, Zedekiah		Nebuchadnezzar Belshazzar Darius I Cyrus	2 Kings 23:35-25:30; 2 Chron. 36:5-23 Daniel	Destruction of Jerusalem (586 B.C.); End of the Kingdom of Judah
Ezekiel	593-570 B.C.	Zedekiah		Nebuchadnezzar	2 Kings 24:8-25:26; 2 Chron. 36:9-21 Ezekial	Exile in Babylon
Obadiah	586-583 B.C.	Zedekiah		Nebuchadnezzar	2 Kings 25; 2 Chron. 36:11-21 Obadiah	Fall of Babylon by Cyrus (539 B.C.)
Haggai	520 B.C.	Governor Zerubbabel		Darius I	Hag. 1:1-2:19; Ezr. 5:1-6:22; Ps. 137 Neh. 8:1-8	Rebuilding the Temple begins (537 B.C.)

Zechariah	520 B.C.	Governor Zerubbabel		Darius I	Ezra 5:1-6:22 Zechariah	Work resumed (520) Temple completed (516)
Malachi	433-425 B.C.	Governor Nehemiah		Artaxerxes I	Neh. 13 Malachi	

Selected Greek Kings of the Seleucid Empire (Syria)

Name	ca. Date	Historical Reference	Notable Events
Seleucus I Nicator	312-281 B.C.		
Antiochus I Soter	281-261		
Antiochus II Theos	261-246		
Seleucus II Callinicus	246-225		
Seleucus III Soter	225-223		
Antiochus III the Great	223-187		Seleucids take Palestine
Seleucus IV Philopator	187-175		
Antiochus IV Epiphanes	175-163	Dan. 11:21-35	Desecration of the Temple Worship halted
Antiochus V Eupator	163-162		Hasmonean Period begins
Demetrius I Soter	162-150		
Alexander Balas	150-145		
Demetrius II Nicator	145-139		
Antiochus VI Epiphanes	145-138		
Antiochus VII Sidetes	139-129		
Demetrius II Nicator	129-125		
Cleopatra Thea	126		
Cleopatra Thea and			
Antiochus VIII Grypus	125-121		
Seleucus V	125		
Antiochus VII Grypus	121-96		
Antiochus IX Cyzicenus	115-95		
Seleucus VI Epiphanes Nicator	96-95		
Demetrius III Philopator	95-88		
Antiochus X Eusebes	95-83		
Antiochus XI Philadelphus	94		

Philip I Philadelphus	94-83		
Antiochus XII Dionysus	87-84		
Antiochus XIII	69-64		
Philip II	67-65		

Selected Greek Kings of The Ptolemaic Empire (Egypt)

Name	ca. Date	Historical Reference	Notable Events
Ptolemy I Soter	322-282 B.C.		332 Jews fall under Greeks
Ptolemy II Philadelphus	282-246		Ptolemies in Palestine
Ptolemy III Euergetes I	246-222		
Ptolemy IV Philopator	222-204		
Ptolemy V Epiphanes	204-180		
Ptolemy VI Philometer	180-145		
Ptolemy VII Neos Philopator	145-144		
Ptolemy VIII Euergetes II	145-116		
Ptolemy IX Soter II	116-107		
Ptolemy X Alexander I	107-88		
Ptolemy IX Soter II (restored)	88-80		
Ptolemy XI Alexander II	80		
Ptolemy XII Neos Dionysos	80-58; 55-51		
Ptolemy XIII	51-47		
Cleopatra VII Philopator	51-30		
Ptolemy XIV	47-44		
Ptolemy XV	44-30		

Rulers of the Hasmonean Dynasty

Name	ca. Date	Historical Reference	Notable Events
Mattathias Asmoneus	165 B.C.		
Judas Maccabeus	165-160		
Jonathan Maccabeus	160-142		
Simon Maccabeus	142-135	1 Macc. 14:41-49	Led period of peace; Strengthened the prosperity of Judea

John Hycranus I	135-104	Josephus, *Antiq.* 13.10.5-6	Transfer of sympathies from the Pharisees to the Sadducees; Persecuted the Samaritans
Aristobulus I	104-103		Extended the boundaries northward into the Galilee of the Gentiles
Alexander Jannaus	103-76		Expanded the kingdom and disposed his political enemies by crucifixion; Persecuted the Pharisees
Salome Alexandra	76-67		Gave the Pharisees wider control over internal affairs
Aristobulus II	67-63		Captured by Pompey and taken to Rome; Judea under supervision of Rome, Hasmonean Dynasty ends
Hyrcanus II	63-43		High priest and ethnarch without the title king
Matthias Antigonus	40-37		Supported by the Parthians; became king of Judea but defeated by Herod

Rulers of the Herodian Dynasty

Name	ca. Date	Historical Reference	Notable Events
Antipater I		Josephus, *Antiq.* 14.10	Grandfather of Herod the Great; Governor of Idumea
Antipater II		Josephus, *Antiq.* 14.37	Supporter of Hycranus II and friend of the Romans bringing them to Palestine
Herod I (*the Great*)	37- 4 B.C.	Matt. 2:1-19; Luke 1:5	King over all of Palestine
Archelaus	4 B.C. - 6 A.D.	Matt. 2:22; Josephus, *War* 3.7.3	Banished to France
Herod Philip I	4 B.C. - 34 A.D.	Luke 3:1; Josephus, *Antiq.* 18.4.6	Married to Salome who danced before Antipas— renamed the city Paneas "Caesarea Philippi"
Herod Antipas (*The tetrach*)	4 B.C. - 39 A.D.	Luke 3:19-20; 13:31-33; 23:6-12	Death of John the Baptist; The Fox; Trial of Jesus; built Tiberias; First husband of Herodias, mother of Salome

Herod II		Mark 6:17	
Herod Agrippa I	37-44	Acts 12:1-23	Killed James and arrested Peter; Smitten by an Angel
Felix	52-60	Acts 23:24-24:27	Wife, Drusilla, was an Herodian
Agrippa II	50-100	Acts 25:13-27; 26:32-39	Trial of Paul, assisted Rome in the assault on Jerusalem

Roman Procurators of Judea

Name	ca. Date	Historical Reference	Notable Events
Coponius	6-10 A.D.		Jesus at the Temple age 12
M. Ambivius	10-13		
Amnius Rufus	13-15		
Valerius Gratus	15-26		Josephus Caiaphas high priest (18-37 A.D.)
Pontius Pilate	26-36	Matt. 27:2 Luke 3:1; 23:1	John the Baptist begins his ministry; The crucifixion of Jesus; Pentecost and the martyrdom of Stephen; conversion of Saul
Maryllus	38-41		First visit of Saul to Jersualem
Marcellus	36-38		
Herod Agrippa	41-44		James, the Son of Zebedee martyred (42 A.D.)
Cuspius Fadus	41-46		Famine; Paul's second visit to Jerusalem
Tiberius Alexander	46-48		Paul's first missionary journey (47-48 A.D.)
Ventidius Cumanus	48-52		Council of Jerusalem; Paul's third visit to Jerusalem (49 A.D.); Jews expelled from Rome (50 A.D.)
M. Antonius Felix	52-59	Acts 23-24	Paul's third missionary journey; Paul arrest in Jerusalem
Porcius Festus	52-62	Acts 25-26	The Trial of the Apostle Paul (57-58 A.D.); Paul taken to Rome
Albinus	61-65		Martyrdom of James, the brother of Jesus
Gessius Florus	65-66		Martyrdom of Peter and Paul
The Destruction of Jerusalem			

Vettulenus Cerials	72		
Lucilius Bassus	72-75		
M. Salvienus	75-86		
Flavius Silva	75-86	Josephus: War 7.8.1;7.8.2 - 9.2	Led the assault on Masada
Pompeius Lomginus	86		John exiled to Patmos

Selected Roman Emperors

Name	ca. Date	Historical Reference	Notable Events
Augustus "savior of mankind"	27 B.C.-14 A.D.	Luke 2:1-7	The birth of Jesus Christ and the beginning of the Imperial Cult and/or emperor worship
Tiberius	14-37	Luke 3:1	The ministry and death of Jesus
Caius Caligula "incarnation of Jupiter"	37-41		
Claudius "lord and savior of the world"	41-54	Acts 11:28 Acts 18:2	Famine; Expulsion of the Jews from Rome
Nero "master and god, Apollo"	54-68	Acts 25:10-12 2 Tim. 4:16-17	Trial of the Apostle Paul (56-68 A.D.); Persecution of the Christians at Rome; Martyrdom of James and Peter (62-68 A.D.)
Galba	68		
Otho	69		
Vitellius	69		
Vespasian "lord and savior"	69-79	Matthew 24	The destruction of Jerusalem; The fall of Masada; Josephus published "War"
Titus "savior of the world"	79-81		Burning of Rome; Dedication of Colosseum
Domitian "our lord and god"	81-96	Book of Revelation	Persecution of the church; Banishment of John to Patmos; Josephus published "Antiquites"
Nerva	96-98		
Trajan	98-117		Persecution of Christians

Hadrian *"olympious zeus"*	117-138	Mic. 3:12	Second Jewish Revolt (132 A.D.); Expulsion of the Jews from Jerusalem; Reconstruction of the Holy City (*Aelia Capitolina*)
Antoninus Pius *"Caesar is lord"*	138-161		
LuciusVerus	161-169		
Marcus Aurelius	161-180		
Commodus *"our lord commander the emperor"*	180-192		
Septimus Severus *"lord"*	193-211		
Pescennius Niger	193-194		
Geta	211-212		
Carcalla	211-217		
Macrinus	217-218		
Diadumenianus	218		
Elagabus	218-222		
Alexander Severus	222-235		
Maximian I	235-238		
Gardien III	238-244		
Phillip the Arab	244-249		
Decius	249-251		
Trebonianus Gallus	251-253		
Valerian	252-268		
Gallienus	253-268		
Aurelian	270-275		
Probus	276-282		
Diocletian *"lord and god"*	284-305		
Maximianus	286-305		
Constantius I	293-306		
Galerius	293-311		

Selected Byzantine Emperors

Name	ca. Date	Historical Reference	Notable Events
Constantine I	306-337 A.D.		Declares Christianity the state religion of the Roman Empire
Magnentius	337-353		
Constantine II	337-361		
Constance	353-362		
Julian the Apostate	361-363		
Valens	364-378		
Valentinian	364-375		
Theodosius I	379-383		
Arcadius	395-408		
Theodosius II	408-450		
Marcian	450-457		
Leo I	457-474		
Leo II	474		
Zeno	474-491		
Anastasius I	491-518		
Justin I	518-527		
Justinian I	527-565		
Justin II	565-578		
Tiberius II	578-582		
Mauricius	582-602		
Phocas	602-610		
Heraclius	610-641		
Constans II	641-668		
Constantine IV	668-685		
Justinian II	685-695		
Leontius	695-698		
Tiberius III	698-705		
Justinian III	705-711		

Islamic Dynasties

Name	ca. Date	Historical Reference	Notable Events
Umayyads	658-750 A.D.		
Abbasids	750-868		
Tulunids	868-905		
Ikhshidids	906-969		
Fatimids	969-1171		
Ayyubids	1171-1250		
Mamelukes	1250-1517		
Ottomans	1517-1798		

Selected Crusader Kings and Queens of Jerusalem

Name	ca. Date	Historical Reference	Notable Events
Baldwin I	1100-1118		
Baldwin II	1118-1131		
Fulk	1131-1143		
Melisande	1131-1152		
Baldwin III	1152-1163		
Amalric	1163-1174		
Baldwin IV	1174-1186		
Baldwin V	1185-1186		
Guy of Lusignan	1186-1192		
Sybilla	1186-1190		
Isabella I	1190-1205		
Aimery of Lusignan	1194-1205		
John of Brienne	1210-1225		
Maria	1210-1212		
Frederick II	1125-1243		
Yolande	1225-1228		
Conrad	1243-1254		
Conradin	1254-1268		

Hugh III	1269-1284		
John I	1284-1285		
Henry II	1286-1291		

Gods of the Ancient World

Greek	Roman	Description	Symbol
Aphrodite	Venus	The Greek goddess of love, beauty and sexual desire. Related to the fertility goddesses of the East—Isis, Ishtar (Asherah, Astartea). She is the daughter of Zeus and Dione.	Dove
Apollo	Phoebus *"The shining one"*	The Greek god of prophecy, the patron of poetry, music, and the healing arts. He is the son of Zeus and Leto.	Sun, bow, and/or lyre
Ares	Mars	The Greek god of tumult and war. He is the son of Zeus and Hera.	Spear and/or helmet
Artemis	Diana *"nature goddess"*	A Greek goddess associated as both protector and destroyer of earthly wild life, fertility, and desire. She is the daughter of Zeus and Lito and twin sister of Apollo.	Moon and/or a stag
Athena	Minerva	The Greek goddess of war, wisdom, and the arts. She is the daughter of Zeus and Metis.	Owl and/or the olive
Demeter	Ceres	The Greek earth goddess of fruits and grains. She is the daughter of Kronos and Rhea and sister of Zeus.	Sheaf and/or the sickle
Hades (Aides or Aidoneus	Pluto (Dis)	The Greek god alloted the rule of the nether world. He is the son of Kronos and brother of Zeus and Poseidon.	Scepter and/or the horse
Hephaestus	Vulcan	A Greek deity of craftsmanship, metal work, and worker with fire. He is associated with volcanic fire; i.e., *volcan*. He is the sonof Zeus and Hera.	Hammer and/or the anvil
Hera	Juno	The queen of the Olympian deities. She is the wife and sister of Zeus and the eldest daughter of Kronos and Rhea.	Peacock

Hermes	Mercury	The Greek god of trade, riches, and good fortune. He is considered the messenger of the gods and the patron deity of thieves and tricksters. He is the son of Zeus and Maia, the daughter of Atlas.	Caduceus (a staff with two entwined snakes and two wings at the top)
Hestia	Vesta	The Greek goddess of the hearth fire (home) and the altar fires in the temples. She is the daughter of Kronos and Rhea.	
Poseidon	Neptune	The Greek god of the sea and creator of waters. He is the son of Kronos and Rhea and brother of Zeus and Hades.	Trident (a three-pronged spear)
Zeus	Jupiter	The Greek god, head of the Olympian Pantheon in Greece. He is considered the king of gods and men. He is the youngest son of Kronos and Rhea and the brother to Poseidon, Hades, Hestia, Demeter, and Hera.	Scepter and/or thunder

A Brief History of Jerusalem and the Nation of Israel

[1] W. Harold Mare, *The Archaeology of the Jerusalem Area*, (Grand Rapids, MI: Baker Book House, 1987), 20.

[2] Walter A. Elwell et al., eds., *Baker Encyclopedia of Bible Places*, Vol. 2, J-Z, (Grand Rapids, MI: Baker Book House, 1988), 1123.

[3] John J. Bimson, ed., *Baker Encyclopedia of Bible Places*, (Grand Rapids, MI: Baker Book House Company, 1995), s.v. "Jerusalem" by D.F. Payne & J. Bimson, 170.

[4] Rivka Gonen, *Biblical Holy Places: An Illustrated Guide*, (Jerusalem, Israel: Palphot Ltd., 1994), 102.

[5] Mare, *Archaeology of the Jerusalem Area*, 20.

[6] David Noel Freedman et al., eds., *Anchor Bible Dictionary*, Vol. 3, H-J, (New York: Doubleday, 1992), s.v. "Jerusalem" by Philip J. King, 751.

[7] Trent C. Butler et al., eds., *Holman Bible Dictionary*, (Nashville, TN: Holman Bible Publishers, 1991), s.v. "Jerusalem" by Joe R. Baskin, 765.

[8] Benjamin Mazor quoted in Mare, *Archaeology of the Jerusalem Area*, 20.

[9] Elwell, *Baker Encyclopedia of Bible Places*, Vol. 2, J-Z, 1123.

[10] Mare, *Archaeology of the Jerusalem Area*, 59.

[11] Freedman, *Anchor Bible Dictionary*, Vol. 3, H-J, s.v. "Jerusalem" by Philip J. King, 754.

[12] Ibid., 751.

[13] Elwell, *Baker Encyclopedia of Bible Places*, Vol. 2, J-Z, 1125.

[14] Freedman, *Anchor Bible Dictionary*, Vol. 3, H-J, s.v. "Jerusalem" by Philip J. King, 754.

[15] Mare, *Archaeology of the Jerusalem Area*, 66.

[16] Ibid., 18.

[17] Ibid., 75.

[18] Ibid., 82.

[19] Ibid., 76.

[20] Ibid., 77.

The Rise and Fall of the Two Kingdoms

[1] Freedman, *Anchor Bible Dictionary*, Vol. 3, H-J, s.v. "Israel" by Leslie J. Hoppe, 562-563.

[2] Ibid.

[3] Ibid.

[4] Jack Finegan, *Light from the Ancient Past*, (Princeton, NJ: Princeton University Press, 1959), 310.

[5] J. D. Douglas et al., eds., *New Bible Dictionary*, (Wheaton, IL: Tyndale House Publishers, 1982), s.v. "Israel" by F. F. Bruce, 534.

[6] Allen C. Myers, ed., *The Eerdmans Bible Dictionary*, (Grand Rapids, MI: Eerdmans Publishing Co., 1987), 907.

[7] Trent C. Butler et al., eds., *Holman Bible Dictionary*, (Nashville, TN: Holman Bible Publishers, 1991), s.v. "Jerusalem" by Joe R. Baskin, 769.

The Rebuilding of the Temple

[1] Roland H. Bainton, *Christendom: A Short History of Christianity and Its Impact on Western Civilization*, Vol. 1, (New York, NY: Harper & Row Publishers, 1966), 13.

[2] John Bright, *The History of Israel*, Third Edition, (Philadelphia, PA: Westminster Press, 1981), 344.

[3] Charles R. Page, II and Carl A. Volz, *The Land and the Book: An Introduction to the World of the Bible*, (Nashville, TN: Abingdon Press, 1993), 43.

[4] Butler, *Holman Bible Dictionary*, s.v. "Jerusalem" by Joe R. Baskin, 769.

[5] Freedman, *Anchor Bible Dictionary*, Vol. 6, Si-Z, s.v. "Synagogue" by Eric M. Meyers, 252.

[6] Bright, *History of Israel*, 345.

[7] Freedman, *Anchor Bible Dictionary*, Vol. 6, Si-Z, s.v. "Synagogue" by Eric M. Meyers, 252.

[8] Page and Volz, *The Land and the Book*, 49.

[9] Freedman, *Anchor Bible Dictionary*, Vol. 3, H-J, s.v. "Jerusalem" by Philip J. King, 757.

[10] Finegan, *Light from The Ancient Past*, 310.

[11] Page and Volz, *The Land and the Book*, 47.

[12] Ibid.

[13] Bright, *History of Israel*, 370.

[14] Ibid., 367.

[15] Freedman, *Anchor Bible Dictionary*, Vol. 3, H-J, s.v. "Jerusalem" by Philip J. King, 756.

[16] Bright, *History of Israel*, 378.

[17] Freedman, *Anchor Bible Dictionary,* Vol. 3, H-J, s.v. "Jerusalem" by Philip J. King, 757.

[18] Bright, *History of Israel,* 377.

[19] Butler, *Holman Bible Dictionary,* s.v. "Jerusalem" by Joe R. Baskin, 772.

The Infiltration of Hellenism

[1] Freedman, *Anchor Bible Dictionary,* Vol. 3, H-J, s.v. "Jerusalem" by Philip J. King, 757.

[2] Elwell, *Baker Encyclopedia of Bible Places,* Vol. 2, J-Z, 1123.

[3] Myers, *Eerdmans Bible Dictionary,* 907.

[4] Ibid.

[5] Finegan, *Light from The Ancient Past,* 312.

[6] Myers, *Eerdmans Bible Dictionary,* 907.

[7] Page, *Jesus & the Land,* 23.

[8] George Arthur Buttrick et al., eds., *The Interpreter's Dictionary of the Bible,* Vol. 2, E-J, (Nashville: Abingdon Press, 1985), s.v. "Jerusalem" by M. Burrows, 856.

[9] Freedman, *Anchor Bible Dictionary,* Vol. 3, H-J, s.v. "Jerusalem" by Philip J. King, 758.

[10] Page, *Jesus & the Land,* 24.

[11] Mare, *Archaeology of the Jerusalem Area,* 131.

[12] Elwell, *Baker Encyclopedia of Bible Places,* Vol. 2, J-Z, 1133.

[13] Bright, *History of Israel,* 423.

The Maccabean Revolt

[1] Bright, *History of Israel,* 424.

[2] Hershel Shanks, *Jerusalem: An Archaeological Biography,* (New York, NY: Random House, Inc., 1995), 126.

[3] Page, *Jesus & the Land,* 25.

[4] Ibid.

[5] Freedman, *Anchor Bible Dictionary,* Vol. 3, H-J, s.v. "Jerusalem" by Philip J. King, 758.

[6] Freedman, *Anchor Bible Dictionary,* Vol. 3, H-J, s.v. "Hasmonean Dynasty" by Tessa Rajak, 68.

[7] Buttrick, *Interpreter's Dictionary,* Vol. 2, E-J, s.v. "Hasmonean" by N. Turner, 529.

[8] Bright, *History of Israel,* 426.

[9] Shanks, *Jerusalem: An Archeological Biography,* 126.

[10] Freedman, *Anchor Bible Dictionary,* Vol. 3, H-J, s.v. "Jerusalem" by Philip J. King, 758.

[11] Freedman, *Anchor Bible Dictionary,* Vol. 3, H-J, s.v. "Hasmonean Dynasty" by Tessa Rajak, 69.

[12] Page and Volz, *The Land and the Book,* 57.

[13] Buttrick, *Interpreter's Dictionary,* Vol. 2, E-J, s.v. "Jerusalem" by M. Burrows, 858.

[14] Elwell, *Baker Encyclopedia of Bible Places,* s.v. "Jerusalem" by D.F. Payne and J. Bimson, 175.

[15] Buttrick, *Interpreter's Dictionary,* Vol. 2, E-J, s.v. "Hasmoneans" by N. Turner, 530.

[16] Ibid., 531.

[17] Ibid.

[18] Ibid.

[19] Ibid., 529.

[20] Bainton, *Christendom,* Vol. I, 23.

[21] Merrill Tenney, *The Zondervan Pictorial Encyclopedia of the Bible,* Vol. 5, Q-Z, s.v. "Sanhedrin" by D. A. Hagner, 270.

[22] Buttrick, *Interpreter's Dictionary,* Vol. 2, E-J, s.v. "Hasmoneans" by N. Turner, 532.

[23] Buttrick, *Interpreter's Dictionary,* Vol. 2, E-J, s.v. "Jerusalem" by M. Burrows, 858.

[24] Buttrick, *Interpreter's Dictionary,* Vol. 2, E-J, s.v. "Hasmoneans" by N. Turner, 529.

[25] Ibid., 533.

[26] Shanks, *Jerusalem: An Archeological Biography,* 135.

[27] Buttrick, *Interpreter's Dictionary,* Vol. 2, E-J, s.v. "Hasmoneans" by N. Turner, 538.

The Imperial Rule of the Roman Empire

[1] Buttrick, *Interpreter's Dictionary,* Vol. 2, E-J, s.v. "Hasmoneans" by N. Turner, 538.

[2] Ibid.

[3] Freedman, *Anchor Bible Dictionary,* Vol. 3, H-J, s.v. "Hasmoneans" by Rajak, 76.

[4] Ibid.

[5] Buttrick, *Interpreter's Dictionary,* Vol. 2, E-J, s.v. "Hasmoneans" by N. Turner, 535.

[6] Shanks, *Jerusalem: An Archaeological Biography,* 138.

[7] Ibid., 156.

[8] Avraham Negev, ed., *The Archaeological Encyclopedia of the Holy Land,* (Nashville, TN: Thomas Nelson Publishers, 1986), 201.

[9] Ibid.

[10] Elwell, *Baker Encyclopedia of the Bible,* Vol. 2, J-Z, 1134.

[11] Freedman, *Anchor Bible Dictionary,* Vol. 3, H-J, s.v. "Jerusalem" by Philip J. King, 758.

[12] Page and Volz, *The Land and the Book,* 65.

[13] Ibid.

[14] Ibid., 145.

[15] Mare, *Archaeology of the Jerusalem Area,* 142.

[16] Shanks, *Jerusalem: An Archaeological Biography,* 60.

[17] Mare, *Archaeology of the Jerusalem Area,* 146-147.
[18] Ibid.
[19] Ibid.
[20] Shanks, *Jerusalem: An Archaeological Biography,* 61.
[21] Mare, *Archaeology of the Jerusalem Area,* 157.
[22] Shanks, *Jerusalem: An Archaeological Biography,* 61.
[23] Freedman, *Anchor Bible Dictionary,* Vol. 3, H-J, s.v. "Jerusalem" by Philip King, 758.
[24] Mare, *Archaeology of the Jerusalem Area,* 147.
[25] Ibid., 148.
[26] Ibid., 147.
[27] Shanks, *Jerusalem: An Archaeological Biography,* 144.

The Destruction of Jerusalem

[1] Mare, *Archaeology of the Jerusalem Area,* 191.
[2] Ibid.
[3] Ibid., 172.
[4] Ibid.
[5] Flavius Josephus, *The Works of Josephus,* Translated by William Whiston, A.M., (Mass: Hendrickson Publishers, 1987), 704.
[6] Mare, *Archaeology of the Jerusalem Area,* 204.
[7] Ibid., 205.
[8] Ibid., 201-202.
[9] Hillel Geva, "Searching for Roman Jerusalem," *Biblical Archaeology Review,* Vol. 23, No. 6 (November, December, 1997), 45.
[10] John McRay, *Archaeology and the New Testament,* (Grand Rapids, MI: Baker Book House, 1991), 39.
[11] Ibid.
[12] Mare, *Archaeology of the Jerusalem Area,* 268.
[13] Shanks, *Jerusalem: An Archaeological Biography,* 240.
[14] Ibid., 241.

Bethany

[1] Negev, *Archaeological Encyclopedia of the Holy Land,* s.v. "Bethany," 96.
[2] Tenney, *Zondervan Pictorial Encyclopedia of the Bible,* Vol. 1, A-C, s.v. "Bethany" by H. G. Andersen, 527.
[3] Buttrick, *Interpreter's Dictionary,* Vol. 1, A-D, s.v. "Bethany" by K. W. Clark, 387-388.
[4] Merrill C. Tenney et al., eds., *The Zondervan Pictorial Bible Dictionary,* (Grand Rapids, MI: Zondervan Publishing House, 1963), 107-108.
[5] Freedman, *Anchor Bible Dictionary,* Vol. 1, A-C, s.v. "Bethany" by L. J. Perkins, 702.
[6] Buttrick, *Interpreter's Dictionary,* Vol. 1, A-D, s.v. "Bethany" by K. W. Clark, 388.
[7] Elwell, *Baker Encyclopedia of the Bible,* Vol. 1, A-I, 284-285.
[8] Tenney, *Zondervan Pictorial Encyclopedia of the Bible,* Vol. 1, A-D, s.v. "Bethany" by H. G. Andersen, 529.
[9] Buttrick, *Interpreter's Dictionary,* Vol. 1, A-D, s.v. "Bethany" by K. W. Clark, 388.
[10] Pierson Parker quoted in G. W. Bromiley, ed., *The International Standard Bible Encyclopedia,* (Grand Rapids, MI: William B. Eerdmans Publishing Co., 1979), Vol. 1, A-D, s.v. "Bethabara" by R. Earle, 463.
[11] Freedman, *Anchor Bible Dictionary,* Vol. 1, A-C, s.v. "Bethany" by L. J. Perkins, 703.

Bethlehem

[1] Buttrick, *Interpreter's Dictionary,* Vol. 1, A-D, s.v. "Bethlehem" by G. W. Van Beck, 394.
[2] Gonen, *Biblical Holy Places,* 55.
[3] Tenney, *Zondervan Pictorial Bible Dictionary,* 111.
[4] Page and Volz, *The Land and the Book,* 70.
[5] Gonen, *Biblical Holy Places,* 60.
[6] Ephraim Stern et al., eds., *The New Encyclopedia of Archaeological Excavations in the Holy Land,* Vol. 2, (Jerusalem, Israel: The Israel Exploration Society & Carta, Jerusalem, 1993), s.v. "Bethlehem" by Michael Avi-Yonah, 204.
[7] Ibid.
[8] Buttrick, *Interpreter's Dictionary,* Vol. 1, A-D, s.v. "Bethlehem" by G. W. Van Beck, 394.
[9] Tenney, *Zondervan Pictorial Bible Dictionary,* 111.
[10] Buttrick, *Interpreter's Dictionary,* Vol. 1, A-D, s.v. "Bethlehem" by G. W. Van Beck, 395.
[11] Stern, *New Encyclopedia of Archaeological Excavations,* Vol. 2, s.v. "Bethlehem" by Michael Avi-Yonah, 204.
[12] Ibid.
[13] J. D. Douglas et al., eds., *New Bible Dictionary,* (Wheaton, IL: Tyndale House Publishers, 1982), s.v. "Nazareth" by J. W. Charley, 819.
[14] Gonen, *Biblical Holy Places,* 60.
[15] Ibid.
[16] Ibid.
[17] Sarah Kochav, *Israel: Splendors of the Holy Land,* (New York: Thames and Hudson, Inc., 1995), 262.
[18] Ibid.
[19] Stern, *New Encyclopedia of Archaeological Excavations in the Holy Land,* Vol. 2, s.v. "Bethlehem" by Vassilios Tzaferis, 208.

[20] Kochav, *Israel: Splendors of the Holy Land,* 78.

[21] Saint Jerome quoted in Gonen, *Biblical Holy Places,* 60.

[22] Ibid., 66.

[23] Tenney, *Zondervan Pictorial Bible Dictionary,* 112.

[24] Gonen, *Biblical Holy Places,* 59.

[25] Stern, *The New Encyclopedia of Archaeological Excavations,* Vol. 2, s.v. "Bethlehem" by Vassilios Tzaferis, 208.

Bethsaida

[1] Tenney, *Zondervan Pictorial Bible Dictionary,* 113.

[2] G. W. Bromiley, ed., *The International Standard Bible Encyclopedia,* Vol. 1, A-D, (Grand Rapids, MI: William B. Eerdmans Publishing Co., 1979), s.v. "Bethsaida" by R. H. Mounce, 475.

[3] Tenney, *Zondervan Pictorial Bible Dictionary,* 113.

[4] Ibid.

[5] Elizabeth McNamer quoted in Karen Laub, "Biblical Town Unearthed," *The Beacon Journal,* (Akron) 18 June 1995, 11A.

[6] Ibid.

Beth-Shan

[1] Freedman, *Anchor Bible Dictionary,* Vol. 1, A-C, s.v. "Beth-Shan" by Patrick McGowen, 693.

[2] Lamoine F. DeVries, *Cities of the Biblical World,* (Peabody, MA: Hendrickson Publishers, Inc., 1997), s.v. "Bethshan," 156.

[3] Tenney, *Zondervan Pictorial Encyclopedia of the Bible,* Vol. One, A-C, s.v. "Beth-Shean" by J. M. Houston, 543.

[4] DeVries, *Cities of the Biblical World,* s.v. "Bethshan," 158.

[5] Bromiley, *International Standard Bible Encyclopedia,* Vol. One, A-D, s.v. "Beth-Shean" by A. F. Rainey, 475.

[6] Trent G. Butler et al., eds., *Holman Bible Dictionary,* (Nashville: Holman Bible Publishers, 1991), s.v. "Beth-Shean" by Dennis Cole, 174.

[7] DeVries, *Cities of the Biblical World,* s.v. "Beth-shan," 156.

[8] Ibid.

[9] Bromiley, *International Standard Bible Encyclopedia,* Vol. One, A-D, s.v. "Beth-Shean" by R. H. Mounce, 475.

[10] Joseph P. Free and Howard F. Vos, *Archaeology and Bible History,* (Grand Rapids, MI: Zondervan Publishing House, 1992), s.v. "The Beginning of the Monarchy," 128.

[11] Ibid.

[12] Buttrick, *Interpreter's Dictionary,* s.v. "Beth-Shan" by R. W. Hamilton, 401.

[13] Butler, *Holman Bible Dictionary,* s.v. "Beth-Shean" by Dennis Cole, 175.

[14] Roberta L. Harris, *The World of the Bible,* (London, England: Thames and Hudson, Ltd., 1995), s.v. "Beth Shean, Byzantine City," 166.

[15] Ibid.

[16] Ibid.

[17] Bromiley, *International Standard Bible Encylopedia,* Vol. One, A-D, s.v. "Beth-Shean" by A. F. Rainey, 477.

[18] Freedman, *Anchor Bible Dictionary,* Vol. 1, A-C, s.v. "Beth-Shan" by Patrick McGowen, 693.

[19] The Ministry of Tourism, *The Tourist Development Authority - Bet She'an,* (Israel: Y.A.R. Publishers Ltd., n.d.) s.v. "Theater."

[20] The Ministry of Tourism, *The Tourist Development Authority - Bet She'an,* s.v. "Amphiteater."

[21] Tenney, *Zondervan Pictorial Encyclopedia of the Bible,* Vol. One, A-C, s.v. "Beth-Shean" by J. M. Houston, 543.

[22] Bromiley, *International Standard Bible Encylopedia,* Vol. One, A-D, s.v. "Beth-Shean" by A. F. Rainey, 478.

[23] Buttrick, *Interpreter's Dictionary,* s.v. "Beth-Shan" by R. W. Hamilton, 401.

[24] Bromiley, *International Standard Bible Encyclopedia,* Vol. One, A-D, s.v. "Beth-Shean" by A. F. Rainey, 478.

[25] The Ministry of Tourism, *The Tourist Development Authority - Bet She'an,* s.v. "Baths."

[26] Freedman, *Anchor Bible Dictionary,* Vol. 1, A-C, s.v. "Beth-Shan" by Patrick McGowen, 693.

Caesarea Maritima

[1] Buttrick, *Interpreter's Dictionary,* Vol. 1, A-D, s.v. "Caesarea" by D. C. Pellett, 479.

[2] Gonen, *Biblical Holy Places,* 71.

[3] Butler et, *Holman Bible Dictionary,* s.v. "Caesarea" by George W. Knight, 218.

[4] Tenney, *Zondervan Pictorial Bible Dictionary,* 135.

[5] Butler, *Holman Bible Dictionary,* 218.

[6] Freedman, *Anchor Bible Dictionary,* Volume 1, A-C, s.v. "Caesarea" by Robert L. Hohlfelder, 800.

[7] Ibid.

[8] Ibid., 799.

[9] Tenney, *Zondervan Pictorial Bible Dictionary,* 135.

[10] Bimson, *Baker Encyclopedia of Bible Places,* s.v. "Caesarea" R. K. Harrison, 74.

[11] Freedman, *Anchor Bible Dictionary,* Volume 1, A-C, s.v. "Caesarea" by Robert L. Hohlfelder, 798.

[12] James Orr et al., eds., *The International Standard Bible Encyclopedia,* Volume I, (Grand Rapids: Wm. B. Eerdmans Publishing Co., 1984), 536.

[13] Buttrick, *Interpreter's Dictionary,* s.v. "Caesarea" by D. C. Pellett, 480.

[14] Freedman, *Anchor Bible Dictionary,* Vol. 1, A-C, s.v. "Caesarea" by Robert L. Hohlfelder, 799.

[15] Ibid.

[16] Kochav, *Israel: Splendors of the Holy Land*, 244.

[17] Stern, *New Encyclopedia of Archeological Excavations in the Holy Land*, s.v. "Caesarea" by Avrer Raban, 289.

[18] Kochav, *Israel: Splendors of the Holy Land*, 244.

[19] Ibid.

[20] Page and Volz, *The Land and the Book*, 121.

[21] Elwell, *Baker Encyclopedia of the Bible*, Vol. 1, A-I, s.v. "Caesarea" by E. M. Blaiklock, 390.

[22] Kochav, *Israel: Splendors of the Holy Land*, 244.

[23] Bromiley, *International Standard Bible Encyclopedia*, Vol. 1, A-D, s.v. "Caesarea" by W. Ewing, 569.

[24] Kochav, *Israel: Splendors of the Holy Land*, 241.

[25] Stern, *New Encyclopedia of Archeological Excavations in the Holy Land*, s.v. "Caesarea" by Avraham Negev, 274.

[26] Buttrick, *Interpreter's Dictionary*, Vol. 1, A-D, s.v. "Caesarea" by D.C. Pellett, 480.

[27] Kochav, *Israel: Splendors of the Holy Land*, 244.

[28] Freedman, *Anchor Bible Dictionary*, Vol. 1, A-C, s.v. "Caesarea" by Robert L. Hohlfelder, 800.

[29] Elwell, *Baker Encyclopedia of Bible Places*, Vol. 1, A-I, (Grand Rapids: Baker Book House, 1988), 390.

[30] Stern, *The New Encyclopedia of Archeological Excavations in the Holy Land*, s.v. "Caesarea" by Antonio Frova, 270.

[31] Douglas, *New Bible Dictionary*, 155.

[32] Gonen, *Biblical Holy Places*, 73.

[33] Douglas, *New Bible Dictionary*, 156.

[34] Gonen, *Biblical Holy Places*, 72.

[35] Butler, *Holman Bible Dictionary*, s.v. "Caesarea" by George W. Knight, 219.

[36] Kochav, *Israel: Splendors of the Holy Land*, 66.

[37] Elwell, *Baker Encyclopedia of Bible Places*, Vol. 1, A-I, 390.

[38] Kochav, *Israel: Splendors of the Holy Land*, 66.

[39] Merrill C. Tenney, ed., *New Testament Survey Revised*, (Grand Rapids: W. B. Eerdmans Publishing Co., 1985), 43.

[40] Stern, *The New Encyclopedia of Archeological Excavations in the Holy Land*, s.v. "Caesarea" by Antonio Frova, 270-271.

[41] Freedman, *Anchor Bible Dictionary*, Volume 1, A-C, s.v. "Caesarea" by Robert L Hohlfelder, 800.

[42] Gonen, *Biblical Holy Places*, 75.

[43] Kochav, *Israel: Splendors of the Holy Land*, 241.

[44] Bromiley, *International Standard Bible Encyclopedia*, Vol.1, A-D, s.v. "Caesarea" by W. Ewing, 569.

[45] Orr, *International Standard Bible Encyclopedia*, Vol. I, s.v. "Caesarea" by W. Ewing, 536.

[46] Ibid.

[47] Page and Volz, *The Land and the Book*, 119.

[48] Elwell, *Baker Encyclopedia of Bible Places*, Vol. 1, A-I, 391.

Caesarea Philippi

[1] Bimson, *Baker Encyclopedia of Bible Places*, s.v. "Caesarea Philippi" D. F. Payne, 77.

[2] Buttrick, *Interpreter's Dictionary*, Vol. 1, A-D, s.v. "Caesarea Philippi" by P. C. Pellett, 480.

[3] Ibid.

[4] Gonen, *Biblical Holy Places*, 46.

[5] Tenney, *Zondervan Pictorial Bible Dictionary*, 136.

[6] Gonen, *Biblical Holy Places*, 46.

[7] Bargil Pixner, quoted in Page and Volz, *The Land and the Book*, 108.

[8] Gonen, *Biblical Holy Places*, 46.

[9] Freedman, *Anchor Bible Dictionary*, Vol. 1, A-C, s.v. "Caesarea Philippi" by John Kutsko, 803.

[10] Ibid.

[11] Elwell, *Baker Encyclopedia of the Bible*, Vol. 1, A-I, 391.

[12] Buttrick, *Interpreter's Dictionary*, Vol. 1, A-D, s.v. "Caesarea" Philippi by D. C. Pellett, 480.

[13] Gonen, *Biblical Holy Places*, 47.

Cana

[1] Tenney, *Zondervan Pictorial Bible Dictionary*, 143.

[2] Bimson, *Baker Encyclopedia of Bible Places*, s.v. "Cana" by J. D. Douglas, 80.

[3] Freedman, *Anchor Bible Dictionary*, Vol. 1, A-C, s.v. "Cana" by James F. Strange, 827.

[4] Elwell, *Baker Encyclopedia of the Bible*, Vol. 1, A-I, 406.

Capernaum

[1] Gonen, *Biblical Holy Places*, 76.

[2] Buttrick, *Interpreter's Dictionary*, Vol. 1, A-D, s.v. "Capernaum" by D. C. Pellet, 533.

[3] Bimson, *Baker Encyclopedia of Bible Places*, s.v. "Capernaum" by J. P. Kane, 83.

[4] Douglas, *New Bible Dictionary*, s.v. "Capernaum" by J.P. Kane, 177.

[5] Stern, *New Encyclopedia of Archaeological Excavations in the Holy Land*, Vol. 1, s.v. "Capernaum" by Stanislao Hoffredo, 292.

[6] Bimson, *Baker Encyclopedia of Bible Places*, s.v. "Capernaum" by J. P. Kane, 84.

[7] Gonen, *Biblical Holy Places*, 76-77.
[8] Trent C. Butler et al., eds., *Holman Bible Dictionary*, (Nashville: Holman Bible Publishers, 1991), s.v. "Capernaum" by George W. Knight, 232.
[9] Gonen, *Biblical Holy Places*, 77.
[10] Tenney, *Zondervan Pictorial Bible Dictionary*, s.v. "Capernaum" by Steven Barabas, 146.
[11] Bromiley, *International Standard Bible Encyclopedia*, Vol. 1, A-D, s.v. "Capernaum" by R. H. Mounce, 609.
[12] Buttrick, *Interpreter's Dictionary*, Vol. 1, A-D, s.v. "Capernaum" by D. C. Pellet, 533.
[13] Bimson, *Baker Encyclopedia of Bible Places*, s.v. "Capernaum" by J. P. Kane, 85.
[14] Buttrick, *Interpreter's Dictionary*, Vol. 1, A-D, s.v. "Capernaum" by D. C. Pellet, 533.
[15] Gonen, *Biblical Holy Places*, 78.
[16] Bromiley, *The International Standard Bible Encyclopedia*, Vol. 1, A-D, s.v. "Capernaum" by R.H. Mounce, 610.
[17] Freedman, *Anchor Bible Dictionary*, Vol. 1, A-C, s.v. "Capernaum" by Virgillio C. Corbo, 866.
[18] Ibid., 867.
[19] Ibid.
[20] Ibid.
[21] Stern, *New Encyclopedia of Archaeological Excavations in the Holy Land*, Vol. 1, s.v. "Capernaum" by Stanislao Hoffredo, 292.
[22] Bimson, *Baker Encyclopedia of Bible Places*, 84.
[23] Stern, *New Encyclopedia of Archaeological Excavations*, Vol. 1, s.v. "Capernaum, House of Saint Peter" by Stanislao Hoffredo, 295.
[24] Freedman, *Anchor Bible Dictionary*, Vol. 1, A-C, s.v. "Capernaum" by Virgillio C. Corbo, 867.
[25] Stern, *New Encyclopedia of Archaeological Excavations*, Vol. 1, s.v. "Capernaum, House of Saint Peter" by Stanislao Hoffredo, 295.
[26] Mendal Nun, "Ports of Galilee," *Biblical Archaeology Review*, Vol. 25, No. 4, (July/August 1999), 26.

Chorazin

[1] Tenney, *Zondervan Pictorial Encyclopedia of the Bible*, Vol. One, A-C, s.v. "Chorazin" by H. G. Anderson, 800.
[2] Bromiley, *International Standard Bible Encyclopedia*, Vol. One, A-D, s.v. "Chorazin" by R. H. Mounce, 652.
[3] Freedman, *Anchor Bible Dictionary*, Vol. 1, A-C, s.v. "Chorazin" by Robert W. Smith, 912.
[4] McRay, *Archaeology and the New Testament*, 66.
[5] Negev, *Archaeological Encyclopedia of the Holy Land*, 85-86.
[6] Freedman, *Anchor Bible Dictionary*, Vol 1, A-C, s.v. "Chorazin" by Robert W. Smith, 912.
[7] Negev, *Archaeology Encyclopedia of the Holy Land*, 86.

The Dead Sea

[1] Buttrick, *Interpreter's Dictionary*, Vol. 1, A-D, s.v. "Dead Sea" by W. H. Morton, 788.
[2] Ibid.
[3] Tenney, *Zondervan Pictorial Bible Dictionary*, s.v. "Dead Sea" by J. Barton Payne, 204.
[4] Buttrick, *Interpreter's Dictionary*, Vol. 1, A-D, s.v. "Dead Sea" by W. H. Morton, 789.
[5] Sami Awwad, *The Holy Land in Colour*, (Jerusalem: Golden Printing Press, 1994), s.v. "Dead Sea" by A. R. Millard, 99.
[6] Bimson, *Baker Encyclopedia of Bible Places*, s.v. "Dead Sea" by A. R. Millard, 99.
[7] Buttrick, *Interpreter's Dictionary*, Vol. 1, A-D, s.v. "Dead Sea" by W. H. Morton, 790.
[8] Bimson, *Baker Encyclopedia of Bible Places*, s.v. "Dead Sea" by A. R. Millard, 99.
[9] Sami Awwad, *The Holy Land in Colour*, New Edition, (Jerusalem, Israel: Golden Printing Press, 1994), s.v. "The Essenes", 140.
[10] Kochav, *Israel: Splendors of the Holy Land*, 270.
[11] Buttrick, *Interpreter's Dictionary*, Vol. 1, A-D, s.v. "The Dead Sea Scrolls" by O. Betz, 793.
[12] Ibid., 790.
[13] Bimson, *Baker Encyclopedia of Bible Places*, s.v. "En-Gedi" by G. G. Garner and J. Bimson, 126.
[14] Buttrick, *Interpreter's Dictionary*, Vol. 1, A-D, Vol. E-J, s.v. "En-Gedi" by V. R. Gold, 102.

Jericho

[1] Kochav, *Israel: Splendors of the Holy Land*, 36.
[2] Buttrick, *Interpreter's Dictionary*, Vol. 2, E-J, s.v. "Jericho" by J. L. Kelso, 836.
[3] Ibid., 835.
[4] Stern, *New Encyclopedia of Archaeological Excavations in the Holy Land*, Vol. 2, s.v. "Jericho" by Kathleen M. Kenyon, 674.
[5] Butler, *Holman Bible Dictionary*, s.v. "Jericho" by Karen Joines, 759.
[6] Tenney, *Zondervan Pictorial Bible Dictionary*, s.v. "Jericho" by John B. Grayhill, 415.
[7] Buttrick, *Interpreter's Dictionary*, Vol. 2, E-J, s.v. "Jericho" by J. L. Kelso, 836.
[8] Orr, *International Standard Bible Encyclopedia*, Vol. III, s.v. "Jericho" by George Frederick Wright, 1592.
[9] Ibid., 838.
[10] Bimson, *Baker Encyclopedia of Bible Places*, s.v. "Jericho" by K.A. Kitchen, 167.
[11] Buttrick, *Interpreter's Dictionary*, Vol. 2, E-J, s.v. "Jericho" by J. L. Kelso, 837.
[12] Kochav, *Israel: Splendors of the Holy Land*, 39.
[13] Freedman, *Anchor Bible Dictionary*, Vol. 3, H-J, s.v. "Jericho" by T. A. Holland, 737.
[14] Buttrick, *Interpreter's Dictionary*, Vol. 2, E-J, 838.

[15] Freedman, *Anchor Bible Dictionary,* Vol. 3, H-J, s.v. "Jericho" by Ehud Netzer, 738.

[16] Bromiley, *International Standard Bible Encyclopedia,* Vol. 2, E-J, Vol. 2, s.v. "Jericho" by R. A. Coughenoun, 996.

[17] Elwell, *Baker Encyclopedia of the Bible,* Vol. 2, J-Z, 1119.

[18] Gonen, *Biblical Holy Places,* 99.

[19] Buttrick, *Interpreter's Dictionary,* Vol. 2, E-J, s.v. "Jericho" by J. L. Kelso, 839.

[20] Freedman, *Anchor Bible Dictionary,* Vol. 3, H-J, s.v. "Jericho" by Ehud Netzer, 739.

[21] Elwell, *Baker Encyclopedia of the Bible,* Vol. 2, J-Z, 1118.

[22] Butler, *Holman Bible Dictionary,* s.v. "Jericho" by Karen Joines, 761.

[23] Freedman, *Anchor Bible Dictionary,* Vol. 3, H-J, s.v. "Jericho" by Ehud Netzer, 739.

[24] Ibid., 737.

[25] Buttrick, *Interpreter's Dictionary,* Vol. 2, E-J, s.v. "Jericho" by J. L. Kelso, 837.

[26] Elwell, *Baker Encyclopedia of the Bible,* Vol. 2, J-Z, 1119.

[27] Stern, *New Encyclopedia of Archaeological Excavations,* Vol. 2, s.v. "Jericho" by Kathleen M. Kenyon, 674.

[28] Buttrick, *Interpreter's Dictionary,* Vol. 2, E-J, s.v. "Jericho" by J. L. Kelso, 839.

Jerusalem

The Pool of Bethesda

[1] Gonen, *Biblical Holy Places,* s.v. "Pool of Bethesda," 159.

[2] Freedman, *Anchor Bible Dictionary,* Vol. 1, A-C, s.v. "Bethzatha" by James F. Strange, 700.

[3] Bimson, *Baker Encyclopedia of Bible Places,* s.v. "Bethesda, Bethzatha" by D.F. Payne, 68.

[4] Freedman, *Anchor Bible Dictionary,* Vol. 1, A-C, 701.

[5] Mare, *Archaeology of the Jerusalem Area,* 166.

[6] Buttrick, *Interpreter's Dictionary,* Vol. 1, A-D, 404.

[7] Freedman, *Anchor Bible Dictionary,* Vol. 1, A-C, 701.

[8] Bimson, *Baker Encyclopedia of Bible Places,* s.v. "Bethesda, Bethzatha" by D. F. Payne, 68.

[9] Freedman, *Anchor Bible Dictionary,* Vol. 1, A-C, 701.

[10] Gonen, *Biblical Holy Places,* 160.

[11] Ibid.

[12] Ibid.

[13] William Hendriksen, *New Testament Commentary: Exposition of the Gospel According to John,* (Grand Rapids, MI: Baker Book House, 1979), 190.

[14] Freedman, *Anchor Bible Dictionary,* Vol. 1, A-C, 701.

[15] Gonen, *Biblical Holy Places,* 160.

[16] Page, *Jesus & The Land,* 160-161.

[17] Page and Volz, *The Land and the Book,* 199.

[18] Gonen, *Biblical Holy Places,* 161.

The Garden of Gethsemane

[1] Douglas, *New Bible Dictionary,* s.v. "Gethsemane" by D. H. Tongue, 416.

[2] Tenney, *Zondervan Pictorial Encyclopedia of the Bible,* Vol. 2, D-G, s.v. "Gethsemane" by J. C. DeYoung, 706.

[3] Joan E. Taylor, "The Garden of Gethsemane," *Biblical Archaeology Review,* Vol. 21, No. 4, (July/August 1995), 26.

[4] Bromiley, *International Standard Bible Encyclopedia,* Vol. 2, E-J, s.v. "Gethsemane" by W. W. Gasque, 457.

[5] Elwell, *Baker Encyclopedia of the Bible,* Vol. 1, A-I, s.v. "Gethsemane" by James D. Price, 859.

[6] Orr, *The International Standard Bible Encyclopedia,* Vol. 2, E-J, s.v. "Gethsemane" by E.W.G. Masterman, 1221.

[7] Taylor, *Biblical Archaeology Review,* 29.

[8] Ibid., 30.

[9] Ibid., 31.

[10] Ibid., 35.

[11] Tenney, *Zondervan Pictorial Encyclopedia of the Bible,* Vol. 2, D-G, s.v. "Gethsemane" by J. C. DeYoung, 706.

[12] Ibid.

[13] Douglas, *New Bible Dictionary,* s.v. "Gethsemane" by D. H. Tongue, 416.

[14] Gonen, *Biblical Holy Places,* 121.

[15] Ibid., 136.

[16] Tenney, *Zondervan Pictorial Encyclopedia,* Vol. 4, M-P, s.v. "Mount of Olives" by R. L. Alden, 299.

[17] Page, *Jesus & the Land,* 159.

The Tower of Antonia

[1] Buttrick, *Interpreter's Dictionary,* Vol. 1, A-D, s.v. "Antonia, Tower of" by K. W. Clark, 153.

[2] Tenney, *Zondervan Pictorial Encyclopedia of the Bible,* Vol. 1, A-C, s.v. "Antonia, Tower of" by J. L. Kelso, 197.

[3] Freedman, *Anchor Bible Dictionary,* Vol. 1, A-C, s.v. "Antonia, Tower of" by John F. Hall, 274.

[4] Tenney, *Zondervan Pictorial Encyclopedia of the Bible,* Vol. 1, A-C, s.v. "Antonia, Tower of" by J. L. Kelso, 197.

[5] Buttrick, *Interpreter's Dictionary,* Vol. 1, A-D, s.v. "Antonia, Tower of" by K. W. Clark, 153.

[6] Freedman, *Anchor Bible Dictionary,* Vol. 1, A-C, s.v. "Antonia Fortress" John F. Hall, 274.

[7] Butler, *Holman Bible Dictionary,* 66.

[8] Freedman, *Anchor Bible Dictionary,* Vol. 1, A-C, 274.

[9] Awwad, *The Holy Land in Colour,* s.v. "Antonia Fortress," 54.

[10] Tenney, *Zondervan Pictorial Encyclopedia of the Bible,* Vol. 1, A-C, s.v. "Antonia, Tower of" by J. L. Kelso, 198.

[11] Page and Volz, *The Land and the Book,* 78.

[12] Shanks, *Jerusalem: An Archaeological Biography,* 193.

[13] Gonen, *Biblical Holy Places,* 147.

[14] Shanks, *Jerusalem: An Archaeological Biography,* 194.

[15] Tenney, *Zondervan Pictorial Encyclopedia of the Bible,* Vol. 1, A-C, s.v. "Antonia, Tower of" by J. L. Kelso, 197.

[16] Freedman, *Anchor Bible Dictionary,* Vol. I, A-C, 274.

The Via Dolorosa

[1] Tenney, *Zondervan Pictorial Bible Dictionary,* s.v. "Via Dolorosa" by Arthur B. Fowler, 880.

[2] Ibid.

[3] Gonen, *Biblical Holy Places,* 170.

[4] Tenney, *Zondervan Pictorial Encyclopedia of the Bible,* Vol. 4, S-Z, s.v. "Via Dolorosa" by B. Van Elderen, 880.

The Place of the Crucifixion: Golgotha

[1] Randall Price, *The Stones Cry Out,* (Eugene, OR: Harvest House Publishers, 1997), 308.

[2] McRay, *Archaeology and the New Testament,* 204.

[3] Price, *The Stones Cry Out,* 309.

[4] Harris, *World of the Bible,* 147.

[5] Mare, *Archaeology of the Jerusalem Area,* 199.

[6] Ibid., 198.

[7] Price, *The Stones Cry Out,* 305.

[8] Ibid.

[9] Freedman, *Anchor Bible Dictionary,* Vol. 2, D-G, s.v. "Golgotha" by Virgilio C. Corbo, 1071.

[10] Page and Volz, *The Land and Book,* 166.

[11] Price, *The Stones Cry Out,* 314.

[12] Ibid.

[13] Bromiley, *International Standard Bible Encyclopedia,* Vol. 2, E-J, s.v. "Golgotha" by D.F. Payne, 524.

[14] Mare, *Archaeology of the Jerusalem Area,* 188.

[15] Gonen, *Biblical Holy Places,* (Israel: Palphot Ltd., 1994), 131.

[16] Mare, *Archaeology of the Jerusalem Area,* 226.

[17] Ibid.

[18] Kochav, *Israel: Splendors of the Holy Land,* 172.

[19] Tenney, *Zondervan Pictorial Bible Dictionary,* s.v. "Golgotha" by Briggs P. Dingman, 317.

[20] Elwell, *Baker Encyclopedia of the Bible,* Vol. 1, A-I, s.v. "Golgotha" by Carl Wayne Hensley, 890.

[21] Bromiley, *International Standard Bible Encyclopedia,* Vol. 2, E-J, s.v. "Golgotha" by D. F. Payne, 523.

[22] Elwell, *Baker Encyclopedia,* Vol. 1, A-I, s.v. "Golgotha" by Carl Wayne Hensley, 890.

[23] Tenney, *Zondervan Pictorial Encyclopedia,* Vol. 2, D-G, s.v. "Golgotha" by R. L. Alden, 772.

[24] Bromiley, *International Standard Bible Dictionary,* Vol. 2, E-J, "Golgotha" by D. F. Payne, 524.

[25] Mare, *Archaeology of the Jerusalem Area,* 188.

[26] Ibid., 186.

[27] Freedman, *Anchor Bible Dictionary,* Vol. 1, A-C, s.v. "Burial Customs" by Rachel Itachlili, 789-790.

[28] Elwell, *Baker Encyclopedia of the Bible,* Vol. 1, A-I, s.v. "Golgotha" by Carl Wayne Hensley, 890.

[29] Bromiley, *International Standard Bible Dictionary,* Vol. 2, E-J, s.v. "Golgotha" by D. F. Payne, 524.

The Upper Room

[1] Tenney, *Zondervan Pictorial Bible Dictionary,* s.v. "Upper Chamber, Upper Room," 876.

[2] Bromiley, *International Standard Bible Encyclopedia,* Vol. 4, Q-Z, s.v. "Upper Chamber" by Nola J. Opperwall-Galluch, 949.

[3] Tenney, *Zondervan Pictorial Encyclopedia of the Bible,* Vol. 5, Q-Z, s.v. "Upper Room" by W. White Jr., 846.

[4] McRay, *Archaeology and the New Testament,* 79.

[5] Page, *Jesus and the Land,* 135.

[6] Ibid., 137.

[7] Buttrick, *Interpreter's Dictionary,* Vol. 4, R-Z, s.v. "Upper Room" by O.R. Sellers, 735.

[8] McRay, *Archaeology and The New Testament,* 203.

[9] Ibid.

[10] Ibid.

[11] Jacob Pinkerfield, quoted in *McRay, Archaeology and the New Testament,* 203.

[12] Bargil Pixner, quoted in *McRay, Archaeology and the New Testament,* 203.

[13] Gonen, *Biblical Holy Places,* 128.

[14] Ibid.

Joppa

[1] Butler, *Holman Bible Dictionary,* s.v. "Joppa" by Timothy Trammell, 811.

[2] Ibid.

[3] Butler, *Holman Bible Dictionary,* s.v. "Joppa" by Timothy Trammell, 812.

[4] Ibid., 813.

[5] Ibid.

[6] Bromiley, *International Standard Bible Encyclopedia,* Vol. 2, E-J, s.v. "Joppa" by A.F. Rainey, 1118.

[7] Bimson, *Baker Encyclopedia of Bible Places,* s.v. "Joppa" by D. F. Payne, 179.

[8] Buttrick, *Interpreter's Dictionary,* Vol. 2, E-J, s.v. "Joppa" by V. R. Gold, 971.

[9] Bromiley, *International Standard Bible Encyclopedia,* Vol. 2 E-J, s.v. "Joppa" by A.F. Rainey, 1119.

[10] Orr, *International Standard Bible Encyclopedia,* Vol. III, s.v. "Joppa" by W. Ewing, 1732.

[11] Elwell, *Baker Encyclopedia of the Bible,* Vol. 2, J-Z, 1209.

[12] Kochav, *Israel: Splendors of the Holy Land,* 84.

[13] Ibid., 86.

The Jordan River

[1] Butler, *Holman Bible Dictionary,* s.v. "Jordan" by Philip Lee, 813.

[2] Elwell, *Baker Encyclopedia of the Bible,* Vol. 2, J-Z, 1210.

[3] Ibid., 1211.

[4] Tenney, *Zondervan Pictorial Bible Dictionary,* s.v. "The Jordan River" by Wilber M. Smith, 446.

[5] Ibid.

[6] Buttrick, *Interpreter's Dictionary,* Vol. 2, E-J, s.v. "Jordan" by S. Cohen, 973.

[7] Ibid.

[8] Buttrick, *Interpreter's Dictionary,* Vol. 2, E-J, 977.

[9] Orr, *International Standard Bible Encyclopedia,* Vol. III, s.v. "Jordan" by George Frederick Wright, 1733.

[10] Buttrick, *Interpreter's Dictionary,* Vol. 2, E-J, s.v. "Jordan" by S. Cohen, 977.

[11] Bimson, *Baker Encyclopedia of Bible Places,* s.v. "Jordan, Valley and River" by J. M. Houston, 182.

[12] Gonen, *Biblical Holy Places,* 88.

[13] John Howard Yoder, *Body Politics,* (Nashville, TN: Discipleship Resources, 1994), s.v. "Baptism and the New Humanity," 28.

[14] Ibid., 32.

Masada

[1] Stern, *New Encyclopedia of Archaeological Excavations in the Holy Land,* Vol. 3, s.v. "Masada" by Ehud Netzer, 973.

[2] Freedman, *Anchor Bible Dictionary,* Vol. 4, K-N, s.v. "Masada" by Ehud Netzer, 586.

[3] McRay, *Archaeology and the New Testament,* 136.

[4] Bromiley, *International Standard Bible Encyclopedia,* Vol. 3, K-P, s.v. "Masada" by W.S. Lasor, 273.

[5] Ibid.

[6] Freedman, *Anchor Bible Dictionary,* Vol. 4, K-N, s.v. "Masada" by Ehud Netzer, 586.

[7] Elwell, *Baker Encyclopedia of the Bible,* Vol. 2, J-Z, s.v. "Masada," 1413.

[8] Stern, *New Encyclopedia of Archaeological Excavations in the Holy Land,* Vol. 3, s.v. "Masada" by Ehud Netzer, 973.

[9] Freedman, *Anchor Bible Dictionary,* Vol. 5, O-Sh, s.v. "Parthians" by Mark Olson, 170.

[10] G. B. Caird, ed., *A Commentary on the Revelation of St. John The Divine,* (Peabody, MA: Hendrickson Publishers, 1987), 122.

[11] Freedman, *Anchor Bible Dictionary,* Vol. 1, A-C, s.v. "Antonia, Tower of" by John F. Hall, 274.

[12] Buttrick, *Interpreter's Dictionary,* Vol. 3, K-Q, s.v. "Masada" by R.W. Funk, 294.

[13] Kochav, *Israel: Splendors of the Holy Land,* 275.

[14] Elwell, *Baker Encyclopedia of the Bible,* Vol. 2, J-Z, 1413.

[15] Ibid.

[16] Bromiley, *The International Standard Bible Encyclopedia,* Vol. 3, K-P, s.v. "Masada" by W. S. Lasor, 275.

[17] Kochav, *Israel: Splendors of the Holy Land,* 275.

[18] Ibid., 272.

[19] Bimson, *Baker Encyclopedia of Bible Places,* s.v. "Masada" by J. D. Douglas, 206.

[20] Elwell, *Baker Encyclopedia of the Bible,* Vol. 2, J-Z, 1413.

[21] Ibid.

[22] Bromiley, *International Standard Bible Encyclopedia,* Vol. 3, K-P, s.v. "Masada" by W. S. Lasor, 276.

[23] Kochav, *Israel: Splendors of the Holy Land,* 276.

[24] Elwell, *Baker Encyclopedia of the Bible,* Vol. 2, J-Z, 1414.

[25] Ibid.

[26] McRay, *Archaeology and the New Testament,* 136.

[27] Kochav, *Israel: Splendors of the Holy Land,* 275.

[28] Page and Volz, *The Land and the Book,* 155.

Megiddo

[1] Elwell, *Baker Encyclopedia of the Bible,* Vol. 2, J-Z, 1431.

[2] Freedman, *Anchor Bible Dictionary,* Vol. 3, H-J, s.v. "Jezreel" by Carolyn J. Pressler, 850.

[3] Freedman, *Anchor Bible Dictionary,* Vol. 3, H-J, s.v. "Jezreel" by Melvin Hunt, 850.

[4] Buttrick, *Interpreter's Dictionary,* Vol. 3, K-Q, s.v. "Megiddo" by G. W. Van Beek, 335.

[5] Awwad, *The Holy Land in Colour,* 212.

[6] Buttrick, *The Interpreter's Dictionary of the Bible,* Vol. 3, K-Q, Megiddo, by G.W. Van Beek, 336.

[7] Gonen, *Biblical Holy Places,* 186.

[8] Tenney, *Zondervan Pictorial Bible Dictionary,* s.v. "Megiddo" by Carl E. DeVries, 523.

[9] Ibid., 522.

[10] Butler, *Holman Bible Dictionary,* 941.

[11] Ibid.

[12] Elwell, *Baker Encyclopedia of the Bible,* Vol. 2, J-Z, 1431.

[13] James Strong, LL.D., S.T.D., *New Strong's Exhaustive Concordance of the Bible,* (Nashville, TN: Thomas Nelson Publishers, 1995), s.v. "Words in the Greek New Testament," 13.

[14] Frank E. Gaebelein, ed., *The Expositor's Bible Commentary,* Vol. 12, (Grand Rapids, MI: Zondervan Publishing House, 1981), 552.

[15] Ibid.

[16] Robert H. Mounce, *The New International Commentary on the New Testament: The Book of Revelation,* (Grand Rapids, MI: Wm. B. Eerdmans Publishing Co., 1977), 302.

[17] Ibid.

[18] Kochav, *Israel: Splendors of the Holy Land,* 230.

[19] Elwell, *Baker Encyclopedia of the Bible,* Vol. 2, J-Z, 1432.

[20] Freedman, *Anchor Bible Dictionary,* Vol. 4, K-N, s.v. "Megiddo" by David Ussishkin, 666.

[21] Bimson, ed., *Baker Encyclopedia of Bible Places,* s.v. "Megiddo" by T. C. Mitchell, 210.

[22] Butler, *Holman Bible Dictionary,* 941.

[23] Freedman, *Anchor Bible Dictionary,* Vol. 4, K-N, s.v. "Megiddo" by David Ussishkin, 677.

[24] Butler, *Holman Bible Dictionary,* 942.

[25] Orr, *International Standard Bible Encyclopedia,* Vol. III, s.v. "Megiddo" by W. Ewing, 2027.

[26] Butler, *Holman Bible Dictionary,* 943.

[27] Buttrick, *Interpreter's Dictionary,* Vol. 3, K-Q, s.v. "Megiddo" by G. W. Van Beek, 341.

Nazareth

[1] Gonen, *Biblical Holy Places,* 202.

[2] Page, *Jesus & the Land,* 63.

[3] Ibid.

[4] Ibid., 64.

[5] Butler, *Holman Bible Dictionary,* s.v. "Nazareth" by Jerry W. Batson, 1010.

[6] Page, *Jesus & the Land,* 34.

[7] Ibid.

[8] Orr, *International Standard Bible Encyclopedia,* Vol. III, s.v. "Nazareth" by W. Ewing, 2123.

[9] Buttrick, *Interpreter's Dictionary of the Bible,* Vol. 3, K-Q, s.v. "Nazareth" by D. C. Pellett, 525.

[10] Ibid.

[11] Gonen, *Biblical Holy Places,* 205.

[12] Ibid., 206.

[13] Freedman, *Anchor Bible Dictionary,* Vol. 4, K-N, s.v. "Nazareth" by James F. Strange, 1051.

[14] Kochav, *Israel: Splendors of the Holy Land,* 222.

[15] Buttrick, *Interpreter's Dictionary,* Vol. 3, K-Q, s.v. "Nazareth" by D. C. Pellett, 525.

[16] Elwell, *Baker Encyclopedia of the Bible,* Vol. 2, J-Z, 1531.

[17] Bimson, *Baker Encyclopedia of Bible Places,* s.v. "Nazareth" by J. W. Charley, 224.

[18] Butler, *Holman Bible Dictionary,* s.v. "Nazareth" by Jerry W. Batson, 1011.

[19] Elwell, *Baker Encyclopedia of the Bible,* Vol. 2, J-Z, 1531.

[20] Buttrick, *Interpreter's Dictionary,* Vol. 3, K-Q, s.v. "Nazareth" by D. C. Pellett, 525.

The Sea of Galilee

[1] Buttrick, *Interpreter's Dictionary of the Bible,* Vol. 2, E-J, s.v. "Galilee, Sea of" by K. W. Clark, 348.

[2] Gonen, *Biblical Holy Places,* 221.

[3] Freedman, *Anchor Bible Dictionary,* Vol. 2, D-G, s.v. "Sea of Galilee" by Sean Freyne, 900.

[4] Buttrick, *Interpreter's Dictionary,* Vol. 2, E-J, s.v. "Sea of Galilee" by K. W. Clark, 348.

[5] Bromiley, *International Standard Bible Encyclopedia,* Vol. 2, E-J, s.v. "Sea of Galilee" by W. W. Buchler, 391.

[6] Gonen, *Biblical Holy Places,* 221.

[7] Orr, *International Standard Bible Encyclopedia,* Vol. II, s.v. "Sea of Galilee" by W. Ewing, 1165.

[8] Buttrick, *Interpreter's Dictionary,* Vol. 2, E-J, s.v. "Sea of Galilee" by K. W. Clark, 348.

[9] Tenney, *Zondervan Pictorial Bible Dictionary,* s.v. "Sea of Galilee" by Arthur M. Ross, 297.

[10] Orr, *International Standard Bible Encyclopedia,* Vol. II, s.v. "Sea of Galilee" by W. Ewing, 1166.

[11] Tenney, *Zondervan Pictorial Bible Dictionary,* s.v. "Sea of Galilee" by Arthur M. Ross, 297.

[12] Buttrick, *Interpreter's Dictionary,* Vol. 2, E-J, s.v. "Galilee" by Clark, 349.

[13] Ibid., 348.

[14] Ibid., 349.

[15] Harris, *World of the Bible,* 145.

[16] Mendal Nun, "Ports of Galilee." *Biblical Archaeology Review,* Vol. 25, No. 4 (July/August 1999): 18-31.

Tiberias

[1] Bimson, *Baker Encyclopedia of Bible Places,* 298.

[2] Butler, *Holman Bible Dictionary,* s.v. "Tiberias" by John McRay, 1345.

[3] Buttrick, *Interpreter's Dictionary of the Bible,* Vol. 4, R-Z, s.v. "Tiberias" by K.W. Clark, 639.

[4] Bimson, *Baker Encyclopedia of the Bible,* 298.

[5] Gonen, *Biblical Holy Places,* 229.

[6] Buttrick, *Interpreter's Dictionary,* Vol. 3, K-Q, s.v. "Tiberias" by K.W. Clark, 639.

[7] Tenney, *Zondervan Pictorial Encyclopedia of the Bible,* Vol. 5, Q-Z, s.v. "Tiberias" by E. M. Blacklock, 745.

[8] Ibid., 746.

[9] Elwell, *Baker Encyclopedia of the Bible,* Vol. 2, J-Z, s.v. "Tiberias", 2060.

[10] Buttrick, *Interpreter's Dictionary,* Vol. 4, R-Z, s.v. "Tiberias" by K.W. Clark, 640.

[11] Ibid.

[12] Kochav, *Israel: Splendors of the Holy Land,* 217.

[13] Buttrick, *Interpreter's Dictionary,* Vol. 4, R-Z, s.v. "Talmud" by I. Epstein, 512.

[14] Freedman, *Anchor Bible Dictionary,* Vol. 4, K-N, s.v. "Midrash" by Gary Porton, 818.

[15] Buttrick, *Interpreter's Dictionary,* Vol. 3, K-Q, s.v. "Mishna" by I. Epstein, 404.

[16] Bromiley, *International Standard Bible Encyclopedia,* Vol. 4, Q-Z, s.v. "Talmud" by J. Neusner, 717.

[17] Freedman, *Anchor Bible Dictionary,* Vol. 6, Si-Z, s.v. "Tanna, Tannaim" by David Kraemer, 319.

[18] Elwell, *Baker Encyclopedia of the Bible,* Vol. 1, A-I, s.v. "Gemara," 844.

[19] Butler, *Holman Bible Dictionary,* s.v. "Talmud" by Stephen Humphries Brooks, 1320.

[20] Ibid., 1321.

[21] Buttrick, *Interpreter's Dictionary,* Vol. 4, Q-Z, s.v. "Tiberias" by K. W. Clark, 640.

The Mountains of Israel

[1] Buttrick, *Interpreter's Dictionary,* Vol. 3, K-Q, s.v. "Mount, Mountain" by W. L. Reed, 452.

[2] Ibid.

[3] De Vries, *Cities of the Biblical World,* 244.

[4] Charles F. Pfeiffer, ed., *Baker's Bible Atlas,* (Grand Rapids, MI: Baker Book House, 1997), 31.

[5] Ibid.

[6] Lloyd J. Ogilvie, ed., *The Communicator's Commentary: Hosea-Jonah,* (Dallas, TX: Word Books Publishers, 1990), 302.

[7] Charles F. Pfeiffer, Howard F. Vos, and John Rea, eds., *Wycliffe Bible Encyclopedia,* Vol. 1, A-J, (Chicago, IL: Moody Press, 1975), s.v. "Bashan" by Charles F. Pfeiffer, 206.

[8] Ibid.

[9] Buttrick, *Interpreter's Dictionary,* Vol. 2, E-J, s.v. "Gilead" by S. Cohen, 397.

[10] Pfeiffer, *Baker's Bible Atlas,* 28.

Mount Arbel

[1] Freedman, Vol. 1, A-C, *Anchor Bible Dictionary,* s.v. "Arbel, Mount" by D. G. Schley, 354.

[2] Ibid.

[3] Negev, *Archaeological Encyclopedia of the Holy Land,* 35.

[4] Ibid.

Mount of Beatitudes

[1] Andrews, *The Life of Our Lord* (New York, 1901); Tholuck, Die Bergrede, tr. "The Sermon on the Mount" (Philadelphia, 1860); VOTAW in HAST., Dict. of the Bible, Extra Volume, s.v. "Sermon on the Mount;" LE CAMUS The Life of Christ (tr. New York); MAAS, "The Gospel according to St. Matthew" (St. Louis, 1896), 57, 58; available from http://www.etf.cuni.cz/mirrors/www.knight.org/advent/cathen/02369a.htm.iso-8859-1; Internet; accessed 24 June 1998.

[2] Donald Hagner, ed., *Word Biblical Commentary,* Vol. 33a, Matthew 1-13, (Dallas, TX: Word Books, 1993), 86.

[3] Andrews, *The Life of Our Lord.*

[4] Orr, *International Standard Bible Encyclopedia,* Vol. I, s.v. "Mount of Beatitudes" by J. C. Lambert, 419.

[5] Buttrick, *Interpreter's Dictionary,* Vol. 1, A-D, s.v. "Mount of Beatitudes" by L. Mowry, 369.

[6] Ibid., 370.

[7] Stuggart Baedeker, *Israel,* 3d English ed., (New York: Macmillan Travel, 1995), 299.

[8] Ibid.

[9] Bargil Pixner, O.S.B., *Bargil Pixner with Jesus in Galilee According to the Fifth Gospel,* (Jerusalem, Israel: Corazin Publishing, 1992), s.v. "Galilee", 73.

[10] Andrews, *The Life of Our Lord.*

[11] Ibid.

[12] Ibid.

[13] Kochav, *Israel: Splendors of the Holy Land,* 84-86.

[14] "The Horns of Hattin"; available from http://www.web-site.co.uk/knights_templar/templar4_7.html; Internet; accessed 24 June 1998.

[15] Ibid.

Mount Carmel

[1] Orr, *International Standard Bible Encyclopedia,* Vol. I, s.v. "Carmel" by W. Ewing, 579.

[2] Buttrick, *Interpreter's Dictionary,* Vol. 1, A-D, s.v., "Carmel, Mount" by George W. Van Beek, 538.

[3] Butler, *Holman Bible Dictionary,* 236.

[4] Buttrick, *Interpreter's Dictionary,* Vol. 1, A-D, by George W. Van Beek, 538.

[5] Gonen, *Biblical Holy Places,* 193.

[6] Buttrick, *Interpreter's Dictionary,* Vol. 1, A-D, 538.

[7] Bimson, *Baker Encyclopedia of Bible Places,* 87.

[8] Gonen, *Biblical Holy Places,* 193.

[9] Elwell, *Baker Encyclopedia of the Bible,* Vol. 1, A-I, 418.
[10] Gonen, *Biblical Holy Places,* 194.
[11] Elwell, *Baker Encyclopedia of the Bible,* Vol. 1, A-I, 41.

Mount Ebal

[1] Butler, *Holman Bible Dictionary,* 386.
[2] Negev, *Archaeological Encyclopedia of the Holy Land,* 122.
[3] Baedeker, *Israel,* s.v. "Nablus," 304.
[4] Gonen, *Biblical Holy Places,* s.v. "Shechem-Nablus," 224.
[5] DeVries, *Cities of the Biblical World,* 231.
[6] Ibid., 232.
[7] Freedman, *Anchor Bible Dictionary,* Vol. 5, O-Sh, s.v. "Shechem" by Lawrence E. Toombs, 1175.
[8] Buttrick, *Interpreter's Dictionary,* Vol. 2, E-J, s.v. "Ebal, Mount" by W. L. Reed, 4.
[9] DeVries, *Cities of the Biblical World,* 232.
[10] Freedman, *Anchor Bible Dictionary,* Vol. 5, O-Sh, s.v. "Shechem" by Lawrence E. Toombs, 1175.
[11] DeVries, *Cities of the Biblical World,* 232.
[12] Ibid.
[13] Bomiley, *International Standard Bible Encyclopedia,* Vol. 2, E-J, s.v. "Ebal, Mount" by Gary A. Lee, 8.

Mount Gerizim

[1] Freedman, *Anchor Bible Dictionary,* Vol. 1, A-C, s.v. "Gerizim, Mount" by Jeffrey K. Lott, 993.
[2] Buttrick, *Interpreter's Dictionary,* Vol. 2, E-J, s.v. "Gerizim, Mount" by W. L. Reed, 384-385.
[3] Freedman, *Anchor Bible Dictionary,* Vol. 1, A-C, s.v. "Gerizim, Mount" by Jeffrey K. Lott, 993.
[4] Marshall, *New Bible Dictionary,* s.v. "Gerizim" by G. T. Manley and F. F. Bruce, 406.
[5] Butler, *Holman Bible Dictionary,* s.v. "Gerizim and Ebal" by Jimmy Albright, 544.
[6] Buttrick, *Interpreter's Dictionary,* Vol. 2, E-J, s.v. "Gerizim, Mount" by W. L. Reed, 385.
[7] Butler, *Holman Bible Dictionary,* s.v. "Gerizim and Ebal" by Jimmy Albright, 544.
[8] Shanks, *Ancient Israel,* s.v. "Exile and Return" by James D. Purvis, 174.
[9] Negev, *Archaeological Encyclopedia of the Holy Land,* 153-154.
[10] Shanks, *Ancient Israel,* s.v. "Gerizim, Mount" by James D. Purvis, 174.
[11] Negev, *Archaeological Encyclopedia of the Holy Land,* s.v. "Gerizim, Mount," 154.
[12] Butler, *Holman Bible Dictionary,* s.v. "Gerizim and Ebal" by Jimmy Albright, 544.
[13] Negev, *Archaeological Encyclopedia of the Holy Land,* s.v. "Gerizim, Mount," 154.
[14] Gonen, *Biblical Holy Places,* s.v. "Mount Gerizim," 196-197.

Mount Gilboa

[1] Butler, *Holman Bible Dictionary,* s.v. "Gilboa," 553.
[2] Freedman, *Anchor Bible Dictionary,* Vol. 2, D-G, s.v. "Gilboa, Mount" by Jeffries M. Hamilton, 1019.
[3] Pfeiffer, *Baker's Bible Atlas,* s.v. "The Kingdom of Saul," 128.
[4] Shanks, *Ancient Israel,* s.v. "Israel in Egypt" by Nahum M. Sarna, 43.
[5] Butler, *Holman Bible Dictionary,* s.v. "Palestine" by Timothy Trammer, 1063.
[6] Buttrick, *Interpreter's Dictionary,* Vol. 3, K-Q, s.v. "Philistines" by J. C. Greenfield, 792.
[7] Ibid.
[8] Buttrick, *Interpreter's Dictionary,* Vol. 2, E-J, s.v. "Gilboa, Mount" by W. L. Reed, 396.
[9] Charles F. Pfeiffer, ed., *Baker's Bible Atlas,* (Grand Rapids, MI: Baker Book House, 1997), 102-103.
[10] Ibid.

Mount Hermon

[1] Buttrick, *Interpreter's Dictionary,* Vol. 2, E-J, s.v. "Hermon, Mount" by A. Haldar, 585.
[2] Pfeiffer, *Baker's Bible Atlas,* 29.
[3] Freedman, *Anchor Bible Dictionary,* Vol. 3, E-J, "Hermon, Mount" by Rami Arav, 159.
[4] Negev, *Archaeological Encyclopedia of the Holy Land,* 172.
[5] Butler., *Holman Bible Dictionary,* s.v. "Hermon, Mount" by Gary Baldwin, 639.
[6] Buttrick, *Interpreter's Dictionary,* Vol. 2, E-J, s.v. "Hermon, Mount" by A. Haldar, 585.
[7] Butler, *Holman Bible Dictionary,* s.v. "Hermon, Mount" by Gary Baldwin, 639.
[8] Buttrick, *Interpreter's Dictionary,* Vol. 2, E-J, s.v. "Hermon, Mount" by A. Haldar, 585.
[9] Ibid.
[10] Freedman, *Anchor Bible Dictionary,* Vol. 3, E-J, "Hermon, Mount" by Rami Arav, 158.
[11] Ibid.
[12] Ibid.

Mount Herodium

[1] Freedman, *Anchor Bible Dictionary*, Vol. 3, H-J, s.v. "Herodium" by Ehud Netzer, 176.
[2] Shanks, *Ancient Israel*, s.v. "Roman Domination" by Shye J.D. Cohen, 208.
[3] Kochav, *Israel: Splendors of the Holy Land*, 264.
[4] Buttrick, *Interpreter's Dictionary of the Bible*, Vol. 2, E-J, s.v. "Herodium" by R. W. Funk, 595-596.
[5] Price, *The Stones Cry Out*, 300.
[6] Negev, *Archaeological Encyclopedia of the Holy Land*, 174.
[7] Kochav, *Israel: Splendors of the Holy Land*, 264.
[8] Buttrick, *Interpreter's Dictionary*, Vol. 2, E-J, s.v. "Herodium" by R. W. Funk, 595-596.
[9] Ibid.
[10] Price, *The Stones Cry Out*, 300.
[11] Ibid., 300-301.
[12] Page, *Jesus & The Land*, 126.
[13] Page and Volz, *The Land and the Book*, 140.
[14] Freedman, *Anchor Bible Dictionary*, Vol. 3, H-J, s.v. "Herodium" by Ehud Netzer, 180.

Mount Moriah

[1] Bromiley, *International Standard Bible Encyclopedia*, Vol. 3, K-P, s.v. "Moriah" by P. L. Garber, 413.
[2] Ibid.
[3] Buttrick, *Interpreter's Dictionary*, Vol.3, E-Q, s.v. "Moriah" by G. A. Barrios, 438.
[4] Price, *The Stones Cry Out*, 211.
[5] Ibid.
[6] Ibid., 212.
[7] Ibid., 215.

Mount Nebo

[1] Buttrick, *Interpreter's Dictionary*, Vol. 3, K-Q, s.v. "Nebo, Mount" by E.D. Grohman, 529.
[2] Bromiley, *International Standard Bible Encyclopedia*, Vol. 3, K-P, s.v. "Nebo, Mount" by S. J. Saller and M. Piccirillo, 504.
[3] Ibid.
[4] Ibid., 505.

Mount of Olives

[1] Bromiley, *International Standard Bible Encyclopedia*, Vol. 3, K-P, s.v. "Mount of Olives" by W. S. Lasor, 590.
[2] Orr, *International Standard Bible Encyclopedia*, Vol. III, s.v. "Olives, Mount of" by E. W. G. Masterman, 2186.
[3] Freedman, *Anchor Bible Dictionary*, Vol. 5, O-Sh, s.v. "Mount of Olives" by Warren J. Heard, Jr., 13.
[4] Gonen, *Biblical Holy Places*, 157.
[5] Orr, *International Standard Bible Encyclopedia*, Vol. III, 2187.
[6] Mare, *Archaeology of the Jerusalem Area*, 113.
[7] Douglas, *New Bible Dictionary*, s.v. "Mount of Olives" by R. A. Stewart, 856.
[8] Tenney, *Zondervan Pictorial Bible Dictionary*, Vol. 4, s.v. "Mount of Olives" by R. L. Alden, 300.
[9] Buttrick, *Interpreter's Dictionary*, Vol. 3, K-Q, s.v. "Mount of Olive" by G. A. Barrios, 597.
[10] Freedman, *Anchor Bible*, Vol. 5, O-Sh, s.v. "Mount of Olives" by Warren J. Heard, 13.
[11] Buttrick, *Interpreter's Dictionary*, Vol. 3, K-Q, s.v. "Mount of Olives" by G. A. Barrios, 597.
[12] Bromiley, *International Standard Bible Encyclopedia*, Vol. 3, K-P, s.v. "Mount of Olives" by W. S. Lasor, 589.
[13] Ibid., 590.
[14] Elwell, *Baker Encyclopedia of the Bible*, Vol. 2, 1587.
[15] Orr, *International Standard Bible Encyclopedia*, Vol. III, s.v. "Mount of Olives" by R. A. Stewart, 2187.
[16] Gonen, *Biblical Holy Places*, 157
[17] Bromiley, *International Standard Bible Encyclopedia*, Vol. 3, K-P, s.v. "Mount of Olives" by W. S. Lasor, 590.
[18] Gonen, *Biblical Holy Places*, 157.
[19] Freedman, *Anchor Bible*, Vol. 5, O-Sh, 14.
[20] Mare, *Archaeology of the Jerusalem Area*, 256.
[21] Page and Volz, *The Land and the Book*, 182.
[22] Tenney, *Zondervan Pictorial Encyclopedia*, Vol. 4, M-P, s.v. "Mount of Olives" by R. L. Alden, 300.

Mount Sinai

[1] Butler, *Holman Bible Dictionary*, s.v. "Mount Sinai" by J. Travis, 991.
[2] Bromiley, *International Standard Bible Encyclopedia*, Vol. 4, Q-Z, s.v. "Sinai, Mount" by Rick Harrison and J. K. Hoffmeier, 526.
[3] Freedman, *Anchor Bible Dictionary*, Vol. 6, Si-Z, s.v. "Sinai, Mount" by G. I. Davies, 47.
[4] Bromiley, *International Standard Bible Encyclopedia*, Vol.4, Q-Z, s.v. "Sinai, Mount" by Rick Harrison and J. K. Hoffmeier, 526.
[5] Buttrick, *Interpreter's Dictionary*, Vol. 4, R-Z, s.v. "Sinai, Mount" by Wright, 376.
[6] Yoram Tsafrir, ed., *Ancient Churches Revealed*, (Jerusalem, Israel: Israel Exploration Society, 1993), s.v. "Monks and Monasteries in Southern Sinai," 316.
[7] Negev, *Archaeological Encyclopedia of the Holy Land*, s.v. "Sinai, Mount," 350.

[8] Buttrick, *Interpreter's Dictionary,* Vol. 4, R-Z, s.v. "Sinai, Mount," 376.

[9] Tsafrir, *Ancient Churches Revealed,* s.v. "Monks and Monasteries in Southern Sinai," 320.

[10] Ibid., 321-322.

[11] Ibid., 327.

[12] Gonen, *Biblical Holy Places,* s.v. "Mount Sinai," 19.

[13] Bromiley, *International Standard Bible Encyclopedia,* Vol. 4, Q-Z, s.v. "Sinai, Mount" by Rick Harrison and J. K. Hoffmeier, 526.

[14] Gonen, *Biblical Holy Places,* s.v. "Mount Sinai," 20.

[15] Tsafrir, *Ancient Churches Revealed,* 328-331.

[16] Egypt, Travel - Sinai, Saint Catherine's Monastery; available from http://touregypt.net/ Catherines.htm; Internet; accessed 22 June 1998.

[17] Tsafrir, *Ancient Churches Revealed,* 328-331.

[18] Ibid., 325.

[19] Gonen, *Biblical Holy Places,* s.v. "Saint Catherine's Monastery," 25.

[20] A History of Christianity in Egypt - The Saints; available from http://touregypt.net/chiste.3.htm; Internet; accessed 22 June 1998.

[21] Tsafrir, *Ancient Churches Revealed,* 332.

[22] Shanks, *Ancient Israel,* s.v. "Israel in Egypt" by Nahum M. Sarna, 44.

[23] Butler, *Holman Bible Dictionary,* s.v. "Mount Sinai" by J. Travis, 992.

Mount Tabor

[1] Freedman, *Anchor Bible Dictionary,* Vol. 6, Si-Z, s.v. "Tabor, Mount" by Rafael Frankel, 304.

[2] Bromiley, *International Standard Bible Encyclopedia,* Vol. 4, Q-Z, s.v. "Tabor, Mount" by K. G. Jung, 713.

[3] Ibid.

[4] Buttrick, *Interpreter's Dictionary,* Vol. 4, R-Z, s.v. "Tabor, Mount" by G. W. Van Beek, 508.

[5] Bromiley, *International Standard Bible Encyclopedia,* 713, Vol. 4, Q-Z, s.v. "Tabor, Mount" by K.G. Jung, 713.

[6] Pfeiffer, *Baker's Bible Atlas,* 102.

[7] Gonen, *Biblical Holy Places,* s.v. "Mount Tabor," 200.

[8] Ibid.

[9] Bromiley, *International Standard Bible Encyclopedia,* Vol. 4, Q-Z, 714.

[10] Gonen, *Biblical Holy Places,* s.v. "Mount Tabor," 200.

Mount of Temptation

[1] Baedeker, *Israel,* s.v. "Jericho," 206- 207.

[2] Buttrick, *Interpreter's Dictionary,* Vol. 4, R-Z s.v. "Temptation of Jesus" by D. M. Beck, 568.

[3] William Barclay, *The Gospel of Luke,* (Philadelphia: The Westminster Press, 1975), 43.

[4] Page, *Jesus & the Land,* 59.

[5] Gonen, *Biblical Holy Places,* 197.

[6] Tsafrif, *Ancient Churches Revealed,* s.v. "Monasteries and Churches in the Judean Desert in the Byzantine Period" by Yizhar Hirschfeld, 149.

[7] Ibid.

[8] Ibid., 152.

[9] Baedeker, *Israel,* s.v. "Jericho," 206-207.

[10] Baedeker, *Israel,* s.v. "Wadi Qilt," 373.

[11] Page, *Jesus & the Land,* 62.

[12] Gonen, *Biblical Holy Places,* s.v. "Monastery of St. George," 188.

[13] Ibid., 189.

[14] Freedman, *Anchor Bible Dictionary,* Vol. 1, A-C, s.v. "Cherith, Brook of" by Randall W. Younker, 899.

[15] Tsafrif, *Ancient Churches Revealed,* s.v. "Monasteries and Churches in the Judean Desert in the Byzantine Period" by Yizhar Hirschfeld, 153.

[16] Stern, *New Encyclopedia of Archaeological Excavations in the Holy Land,* Vol. 3, s.v. "Monasteries" by Joseph Patrick, 1064.

[17] Tsafrif, *Ancient Churches Revealed,* s.v. "Monasteries and Churches in the Judean Desert in the Byzantine Period" by Yizhar Hirschfeld, 153.

Mount Zion

[1] McRay, *Archaeology and the New Testament,* 2.

[2] Freedman, *Anchor Bible Dictionary,* Vol. 3, H-J, s.v. "Jerusalem" by Philip J. King, 758.

[3] Elwell, *Baker Encyclopedia of the Bible,* Vol. 2, J-Z, 1124.

[4] Mare, *The Archaeology of the Jerusalem Area,* 22.

[5] Freedman, *Anchor Bible Dictionary,* Vol. 3, H-J, s.v. "Jerusalem" by Philip J. King, 751.

[6] Freedman, *Anchor Bible Dictionary,* Vol. 6, Si-Z, s.v. "Zion Traditions" by Jon D. Levenson, 1098.

A History of Christianity in Egypt - The Saints; available from http://touregypt.net/chiste3.htm; Internet; accessed 22 June, 1998.

Andrews, The Life of Our Lord (New York, 1901); Tholuck, Die Bergrede, trs. The Sermon on the Mount (Philadelphia, 1860); VOTAW in HAST., Dict. of the Bible, Extra Volume, s.v. Sermon on the Mount; LE CAMUS the Life of Christ (tr. Ne York); MAAS, The Gospel according to St. Matthew (St. Louis, 1896), 57, 58; available from http://www.etf.cuni.cz/mirrors/www.knight.org/advent/cathen/02369a.htm.iso-8859-1; Internet; accessed 24 June 1998.

Awwad, Sami. The Holy Land In Colour. New Edition 1994. Jerusalem, Israel: Golden Printing Press, 1994.

Baedeker, Stuggart. Israel. 3d English ed. New York: Macmillan Travel, 1995.

Bainton, Roland H. Christendom. A Short History of Christianity and Its Impact on Western Civilization. New York, NY: Harper & Row Publishers, 1966.

Barclay, William. The Gospel of Luke. Revised Edition. Philadelphia, PA: The Westminster Press, 1975.

Bimson, John J. Baker Encyclopedia of Bible Places. Grand Rapids, MI: Baker Book House Company, 1995.

Bright, John. The History of Israel. Third Edition. Philadelphia: Westminster Press, 1981.

Bromiley, G. W. ed. The International Standard Bible Encyclopedia. Grand Rapids, MI: William B. Eerdmans Publishing Co., 1979.

Bruce, F. F. Abraham and David: Places They Knew. Nashville, TN: Thomas Nelson Publishers, 1984.

Buksbazen, Victor. The Gospel in The Feasts of Israel. Fort Washington, PA.: Christian Literature Crusade, 1954.

Butler, Trent C. et al., eds. Holman Bible Dictionary. Nashville, TN: Holman Bible Publishers, 1991.

Buttrick, George Arthur et al., eds. The Interpreter's Dictionary of the Bible. Nashville, TN: Abingdon Press, 1985.

Caird, G. B., ed. A Commentary on the Revelation of St. John the Divine. Peabody, MA: Hendrickson Publishers, Inc., 1987.

DeVries, Lamoine F. Cities of the Biblical World. Peabody, MA: Hendrickson Publishers, Inc., 1997.

Douglas, J. D. et al., eds. New Bible Dictionary. Wheaton, IL: Tyndale House Publishers, 1982.

Elwell, Walter A. et al., eds. Baker Encyclopedia of the Bible. Grand Rapids, MI: Baker Book House, 1988.

Egypt, Travel - Sinai, St. Catherine's Monastery; available from http://touregypt.net/Catherines.htm; Internet; accessed 22 June 1998.

Finegan, Jack. Light from the Ancient Past. Princeton, NJ: Princeton University Press, 1959.

Free, Joseph P. and Howard F. Vos. Archaeology and Bible History. Grand Rapids, MI: Zondervan Publishing House, 1992.

Freedman, David Noel et al., eds. Anchor Bible Dictionary. New York: Doubleday, 1992.

Gaebelein, Frank E., ed. The Expositor's Bible Commentary. Grand Rapids, MI: Zondervan Publishing House, 1981.

Galbiati, Mgr. Enrico. The Old Testament. Vicenza, Italy: Istituto San Gaetano, 1977.

Galbiati, Mgr. Enrico. Acts of the Apostles. Vicenza, Italy: Istituto San Gaetano, 1977.

Galbiati, Mgr. Enrico. The Gospel of Jesus. Vicenza, Italy: Istituto San Gaetano, 1977.

Geva, Hillel, ed. Ancient Jerusalem Revealed. Jerusalem, Israel: Israel Exploration Society, 1994.

Geva, Hillel. "Searching for Roman Jerusalem," Biblical Archaeology Review. Vol. 23, No. 6, (November, December, 1997): 45.

Gonen, Rivka. Biblical Holy Places: An Illustrated Guide. Jerusalem, Israel: Palphot Ltd., 1994.

Hagner, Donald A., ed. Word Biblical Commentary. 33a, Matthew 1-13. Dallas, TX: Word Books, 1993.

Harris, Roberta L. The World of the Bible. London, England: Thames and Hudson, Ltd., 1995.

Hendriksen, William. New Testament Commentary: Exposition of the Gospel According to John. Grand Rapids, MI: Baker Book House, 1979.

The Horns of Hattin; available from http://www.web-site.co.uk/knights_templar/templar4_7.html; Internet; accessed 24 June, 1998.

Horsley, Richard A. *Galilee: History, Politics, People.* Valley Forge, PA: Trinity Press International, 1995.

Josephus, Flavius. *The Works of Josephus.* Translated by William Whiston, A.M. Peabody, MA: Hendrickson Publishers, Inc., 1987.

Kenyon, Kathleen M. *Archaeology in the Holy Land.* Nashville, TN: Thomas Nelson Publishers, 1979.

Kochav, Sarah. *Israel: Splendors of the Holy Land.* New York: Thames and Hudson, Inc., 1995.

Mare, W. Harold. *The Archaeology of The Jerusalem Area.* Grand Rapids, MI: Baker Book House, 1987.

Marshall, I. H. et al., eds. *New Bible Dictionary.* 3d ed. Downers Grove, IL: Intervarsity Press, 1996.

McRay, John. *Archaeology and the New Testament.* Grand Rapids, MI: Baker Book House, 1991.

The Ministry of Tourism. *The Tourist Development Authority - Bet She'an.* Israel: Y.A.R. Publishers Ltd.

Mounce, Robert H. *The New International Commentary of the New Testament: The Book of Revelation.* Grand Rapids, MI: Wm. B. Eerdmans Publishing Co., 1977.

Myers, Allen C. *The Eerdmans Bible Dictionary.* Grand Rapids, MI: Wm. B. Eerdmans Publishing Co., 1977.

Negev, Avraham. *The Archaeological Encyclopedia of the Holy Land.* Nashville, TN: Thomas Nelson Publishers, 1986.

Ogilvie, Lloyd J., ed. *The Communicator Commentary: Hosea-Jonah.* Dallas, TX: Word Books Publishers, 1990.

O'Neill, Amanda. *Historical Facts, Biblical Times.* Grange Yard, London, England: Grange Books, 1993.

Orr, James et al., eds., *The International Standard Bible Encyclopedia.* Grand Rapids, MI: William B. Eerdmans Publishing Co., 1939.

Page, Charles R., II. *Jesus & the Land.* Nashville, TN: Abingdon Press, 1995.

Page, Charles R., II, and Carl A. Volz. *The Land and the Book: An Introduction to the World of the Bible.* Nashville, TN: Abingdon Press, 1993.

Pfeiffer, Charles F., ed. *Baker's Bible Atlas.* Grand Rapids, MI: Baker Book House, 1997.

Pixner, Bargil. *Bargil Pixner with Jesus in Jerusalem-His First and Last Days in Judea.* Jerusalem, Israel: Corazin Publishing, 1996.

Pixner, Bargil. *Bargil Pixner with Jesus through Galilee according to the Fifth Gospel.* Jerusalem, Israel: Corazin Publishing, 1992.

Price, Randall. *The Stones Cry Out.* Eugene, OR: Harvest House Publishers, 1997.

Pritchard, James B. *The Harper Concise Atlas of the Bible.* New York: Harper Collins Publishers, 1991.

Schoville, Keith N. *Biblical Archaeology in Focus.* Grand Rapids, MI: Baker Book House, 1978.

Severance, W. Murray. *Pronouncing Bible Names.* Expanded Edition. Nashville, TN: Broadman & Holman Publishers, 1994.

Shanks, Hershel, ed. *Ancient Israel: A Short History from Abraham to the Roman Destruction of the Temple.* Washington, D.C.: Biblical Archaeology Society, 1988.

Shanks, Hershel. *Jerusalem an Archaeological Biography.* New York: Random House, Inc., 1995.

Smith, March A. Ellis. *Holman Book of Biblical Charts, Maps, and Reconstructions.* Nashville, TN: Broadman & Holman Publishers, 1993.

Stern, Ephraim, Ayelet Lewinson-Gilboa, and Joseph Aviram, eds. *The New Encyclopedia of Archaeological Excavations in the Holy Land.* Jerusalem, Israel: The Israel Exploration Society & Carta, Jerusalem, 1993.

Taylor, Joan E. "The Garden of Gethsemane: Not the Place of Jesus' Arrest," *Biblical Archaeology Review.* Vol. 21, No. 4, (July/August 1995): 26.

Tenney, Merrill C. et al., eds. *The Zondervan Pictorial Bible Dictionary.* Grand Rapids, MI: Zondervan Publishing House, 1963.

Tenney, Merrill C. et al., eds. *The Zondervan Pictorial Encyclopedia of the Bible.* Grand Rapids, MI: Zondervan Corp., 1975.

Tsafrir, Yoram, ed. *Ancient Churches Revealed.* Jerusalem, Israel: Israel Exploration Society, 1993.

365

Neal W. May is Senior Pastor and Founder of Faith Fellowship Church in Macedonia, Ohio. He attended Kent State University during the turbulent sixties and earned a Bachelor of Fine Arts degree with a minor in education. He also holds a Doctor of Ministry degree from Ashland Theological Seminary and is a 1977 graduate of Rhema Bible Training Center. He was ordained by Kenneth Hagin Ministries.

Pastor May is President and Founder of Hosanna Bible Training Center and instructor of Biblical Interpretation and Contemporary Preaching. In his diversity of education, he has experienced the balance of both Spirit and the Word, illumination and reason.

Currently, Pastor May is United States Mid-Region Representative and Chairman of the Education Committee for Faith Christian Fellowship International based in Tulsa, Oklahoma. In addition, he has served as an adjunct professor for Ashland Theological Seminary, where he has taught Small Group Ministry and Archaeology of the New Testament.

Pastor May frequently leads pilgrimages to the Holy Land. For more information regarding these tours, you may contact him at:

Faith Fellowship Church

10277 Valley View Road

Macedonia, Ohio 44056

330-467-1234

Or contact him through his church's website:

www.faithfellowship.org

Additional copies of this book and other book titles
from ALBURY PUBLISHING are
available at your local bookstore.

ALBURY PUBLISHING
P. O. Box 470406
Tulsa, Oklahoma 74147-0406

For a complete list of our titles,
visit us at our web site:

www.alburypublishing.com

For international and Canadian orders,
please contact:

Access Sales International
2448 East 81st Street
Suite 4900
Tulsa, Oklahoma 74137
Phone 918-523-5590 Fax 918-496-2822